seeing culture everywhere

from genocide to consumer habits

seeing culture everywhere

from genocide to consumer habits

JOANA BREIDENBACH

and

PÁL NYÍRI

A Samuel and Althea Stroum Book

UNIVERSITY OF WASHINGTON PRESS

Seattle and London

*This book is published with the assistance of a grant
from the Samuel and Althea Stroum Endowed Book Fund*

© 2009 by the University of Washington Press
Printed in the United States of America
13 12 11 10 09   5 4 3 2 1

University of Washington Press
PO Box 50096, Seattle, WA 98145, USA
www.washington.edu/uwpress

Library of Congress Cataloging-in-Publication Data
Breidenbach, Joana.
Breaking the culture myth : how ethnic stereotyping leads
to conflict / Joana Breidenbach, Pál Nyíri.
p. cm.
Includes bibliographical references and index.
ISBN 978-0-295-98950-1 (pbk. : alk. paper)
1. Ethnic conflict. 2. Ethnic conflic—Prevention. 3. Stereotypes
(Social psychology) 4. Violence—Prevention. I. Title.
HM1121.B74 2009   305.8—dc22   2009033451

In the light of her son's comments she reconsidered the scene at the mosque, to see whose impression was correct. Yes, it could be worked into quite an unpleasant scene. The doctor had begun by bullying her, . . . he had alternately whined over his grievances and patronized her, had run a dozen ways in a single sentence, had been unreliable, inquisitive, vain.

Yes, it was all true, but how false as a summary of the man; the essential life of him had been slain.

MRS. MOORE REFLECTS ON MAGISTRATE HEASLOP'S OPINION
OF DR. AZIZ IN E. M. FORSTER'S *A PASSAGE TO INDIA*

Contents

Preface and Acknowledgments

In 2001 we published an article in the German management journal *Organisationsentwicklung* (Organization development), criticizing the "intercultural communication" profession for perpetuating reductive views of cultural difference that, we argued, were often based on false premises and did not help reduce cultural misunderstandings and mistrust. Yehuda Elkana, rector of Central European University, where Pál worked at the time, read the article and said: "Fine. You convinced me that their approach is counterproductive. But then what do you propose? Government officials, too, are told these days that culture matters—but they have no clue in what way, and they have no place to find out." Stephan Breidenbach, Joana's husband, long involved with German government policy making, made the same point: "How are they supposed to know better if nobody offers them an alternative?"

In his book *Foreign News*, anthropologist Ulf Hannerz lamented the inability of anthropologists—the professional students of human cultures—to respond adequately to "one-big-thing" books such as Samuel Huntington's *Clash of Civilizations* by presenting alternative visions that were clear and accessible. "Leaving an intellectual vacuum behind is not much of a public service," Hannerz wrote.[1] In fact, his view may have been charitable. Alas, anthropologists rarely make as much as a dent in the armor of grand simplifiers like Huntington, much less leave behind a vacuum. A growing number of scholars recognize this as an urgent problem. In a recent debate on the subject, anthropologists Catherine Besteman and Hugh Gusterson wrote that "we need vigorous translation work" from the language of anthropology into a publicly accessible one "to explain that Islam is malleable and diverse, that Egyptian peasants are part of a globalized economy, and that ethnicity is always in historical flux."[2]

We felt that the bandying about of the word "culture" by well-meaning but clueless officials and corporate executives was an opportunity to do just that. After decades during which decision makers listened to political scientists and psychologists, wasn't this a chance for anthropologists to talk about the subject they knew best? As a first step, we began working on a course entitled "How Does Culture Matter?" intended to help government and corporate managers without a background in anthropology to make critical judgments in debates involving cultural claims. The course became a core unit of the applied anthropology curriculum at Macquarie University in Sydney and spun off a popular blog, Culture Matters.[3] Discussions with colleagues in both Sydney and Berlin (notably, Katherine Biber, Stephan Breidenbach, Alex Edmonds, Nicole Graham, Stephanie Lawson, Chris Lyttleton, Chris Houston, Bob Norton, and Paul Cohen),with students (such as Stephen Cox, María José Cruz-Guerrero de la Concha, Katrien Gedopt, Lindy McDougall, Atsushi Murata, Siham Ouazzif, Carlos Palacios Obregon, and Anupom Roy), with seminar guests (such as Bibiana Chan, Marc Rerceretnam, and Noelene Rudolph), and with blog readers helped raise new questions. We are grateful to them all. We also presented our ideas to Macquarie's Department of Law, which gave us some valuable exposure to the reactions of nonanthropologists. Farther afield, we are grateful to Alan Smart at the University of Calgary for his insights on the "cultural turn" in the competition between cities.

We began this book on a plane from Barnaul, Southern Siberia, to Moscow on an autumn day in 2004. We continued writing the manuscript in various settings: in Joana's houses in Berlin and on the Côte d'Azur; at Macquarie University and at Kawa and Dov, two cafés in Sydney; at the Satri House in Luang Prabang, Laos; and in Pál's Budapest flat. The Department of Anthropology at Macquarie University provided a stimulating and collegial home to Pál throughout this process. Our editor at the University of Washington Press, Lorri Hagman, helped and encouraged us along the way. Two anonymous readers for the University of Washington Press offered a great deal of helpful comments. Our thanks to them.

seeing culture everywhere

from genocide to consumer habits

Introduction

Muhamad Sadr-Azam's cell phone beeped: he had a new text message. Muhamad glanced at it as he pulled the Toyota over to the parking lot of his daughter's school. "Order your lamb for a joyful Eid now!" the message read. "If they have to pester everyone with this niche marketing, they should at least know their customers," Muhamad muttered. "Persians don't have a big Eid celebration the way Arabs do."

As his daughter got out of the car, Muhamad saw her greet a friend wearing a school uniform headscarf. At school Melissa was classified as a Muslim: this label was necessary so she would not be served pork at the lunchroom. It also meant that when her class took part in sport events or went on school trips, teachers always approached Melissa to ask whether she was going to participate. This annoyed Muhamad: *Why wouldn't she go like all the others?* But what really worried him was that since the summer holidays, his daughter had taken to hanging out with a bunch of headscarf-wearing Pakistani girls. His wife had once caught her trying one on in front of the mirror. And teachers at the school seemed to take this as a given: Muslim girls wore headscarves, after all.

Jack Straw, leader of the House of Commons, had been right to ask women visiting his office to remove the veil from their faces, Muhamad reflected. It did, as Straw had said, make communication difficult. But on this morning's radio news, there had been a big debate on his comments, with the head of the Racial Equality Commission warning of possible riots over these remarks. Next on the news had been a report about Liverpool's preparation for being the European Capital of Culture in 2008. The writer Kiran Desai had just received the esteemed Man Booker Prize for her novel about immigrants living between cultures, and twenty-five people had died in Iraq during one day's clashes between Sunnis and Shiites.

"The news used to be very different twenty-six years ago," Muhamad had said to his wife that morning as she pushed a bowl of Weetabix over the breakfast table toward him. In 1980, when he had arrived in London from Tehran after the Shah was deposed by Islamic revolutionaries, the world was also undergoing violent upheavals. But the way people talked about them was different. They said the Brixton riots were the result of social exclusion and economic deprivation. The formation of Solidarity in Poland was a struggle against Communist oppression, and the violent clashes during the British miners' strike were a class issue. Now, wherever one turned, people talked about culture as being at the root of things.

As Muhamad passed Brick Lane, his thoughts came back to Muslims in Britain. Some of them, perhaps from this neighborhood, were now planting bombs in the Tube, but others didn't think twice of putting Ganeshas in their restaurant windows to attract the tourists who came for "Indian food." Stepping out of the car in front of his Hampstead dental practice, Muhamad was greeted by the owner of the fish-and-chips shop next door. Mr. Xiang was pouring a bucket of fishy water into the gutter. *Why do the Chinese have to do this? Can't they behave like us?*, he thought, turning his head to avoid the pungent smell. A look at the full waiting room slightly improved his mood. Muhamad had been getting paranoid lately, with all the suspicious looks people gave him nowadays, especially on public transportation and when boarding a plane. When some of his old patients hadn't shown up for their regular checkups, it had been easy to imagine that they were afraid of handing themselves over to a Muslim dentist.

In his small back office Muhamad quickly checked the Web site of the local council. It was Black History Month: Hampstead was "celebrating the achievements and history of Black African and

Caribbean communities who live and work in the Borough." He went through the program and ordered two tickets for a poetry reading the coming Friday. Then he buzzed in his first patient.

Tarabuco, May 2007

It is market day in the Bolivian town of Tarabuco. Pilar Fernandez sits in front of her stall watching a group of tourists walk down the aisle. They could be Italians, by the way of their looks. Or Spaniards? No, their quilt-like coats clearly identify them as Italian. They have come here to the Altiplano to see "the famous handcrafts market, one of the most authentic on the continent. The inhabitants still wear traditional dress, and their lifestyle has not changed since the arrival of the conquistadores." Pilar has read this on a travel Web site in the local Internet café.

When the tourists pass her stall, Pilar draws their attention to a beautiful *manta,* a cape-like blanket. "These are a very important part of our traditional culture," she explains. "If you go to the textile museum in Sucre, you can see them displayed there too." Although this is a sales pitch Pilar often uses, it still fills her with immense pride to think about textiles like her own artfully displayed in the museum. It was good that Doña Cristina Bubba Zamora had fought for the museum and that she relentlessly tried to recover ancient Bolivian textiles that had been stolen by Spanish colonists and American art dealers. Doña Cristina was also the one to get Pilar and a group of other women weavers small credits for looms and workshops to revive their textile culture. Thinking of this, Pilar reminds herself of the appointment later this afternoon with the Fulbright researcher who has come to town to complete a cultural impact analysis of the microfinance project.

When the Italian tourists move on after having bought a colorful handwoven coca-leaf pouch, Pilar tells her neighbor in the market to look after the stall while she picks up little Juanita from school. Earlier this year, the school announced that it would switch from Spanish-language instruction to a bilingual program in Spanish and the local Quechua. Also, the Catholic religious lessons were to be replaced by instructions in Cosmovisión, the traditional religion.

Evo, the new president of Bolivia, had really delivered on some of the promises he had made in the campaign. And that wasn't the end of it. Hasn't she just heard that the justice minister, a former maid, wanted to strengthen the traditional justice system and have offenders brought before the *ayllu*, the indigenous kinship organization, which was already responsible for the water distribution?

As Pilar makes her way down the main street toward the primary school, the intense light of the midday sun reflected by the whitewashed walls causes her to squint. In a week's time her husband, Juan, would come back from Europe. As a member of Evo's Movimiento al Socialismo and leader of the local union of coca cultivators, he had received an invitation to the Enlazando Alternativas II, the second Alternative Development Summit in Vienna. The trip had been paid for by a German NGO, and Juan was to speak on the legalization of coca for medicinal and cosmetic purposes. Coca is their livelihood, and Juan had sent Pilar a newspaper clipping of himself and other Andean activists in front of a castle holding a banner announcing "Coca Is Part of Our Culture."

Waiting at the school gate, Pilar gets out the local paper, *Diario El Potosí*. On the front page is a report about five silver objects that have been stolen from the famous pre-Incan site of Tiwanaku. A spokesperson from the Directorate-General of Cultural Heritage is offering a reward for information leading to the recovery of the objects. In another article a representative of UNESCO—whose World Cultural Heritage list includes Tiwanaku—has asked whether the country has taken enough security precautions to safeguard its heritage. In the "Cultura" section of the paper Pilar reads about a Turkish writer, Orhan Pamuk, who has won the Nobel Prize. The prize committee praised him especially for "discovering new symbols for the clash and interlacing of cultures." Then the bell rings and hundreds of schoolchildren in uniforms burst out of their classrooms.

Shanghai, October 2008

Jason Carter was on his way out of the office. Tomorrow he would confront Mr. Li directly about the results. He was fed up with waiting, being put off day after day, week after week. This was simply costing too much money. The shampoos should already be in the third test phase by now, and he was still waiting for the results of the first round. Nobody in Cincinnati would give a damn about the reasons for the delay. The CEO couldn't care less if in Chinese culture people didn't talk straight. All the CEO wanted was a share of the booming Chinese cosmetics market.

The people at the TouchFeelCulture Lab—the company's recently created ethnographic research department—had done a good job. Chinese hair culture, they had found, was very different from its American counterpart. Not only did Chinese women wash their hair in summer much more often than in winter, depending on the season, they used different products too. And many used a water bowl instead of running water, which often was interrupted or not available. So when Jason had arrived in Shanghai six months ago, his first task had been to come up with a formula for easy-to-rinse shampoos. He had handed various options over to Mr. Li, the head of the local company laboratory, and has been waiting for the results ever since.

Leaving the building through the sliding brass doors and disappearing into the gray smog that covered the high-rises across the street, Jason felt drained. Where had he gone wrong? Why couldn't he communicate as efficiently as at home? The company had paid for a predeparture training to prepare him for this job. During those three days he had thought he learned a lot about Chinese culture. How the Chinese were collectivistic, and how he, an American, was individualistic. An important part of Chinese culture, the trainer had stressed, was acceptance of authority. Accordingly, Jason had tried to establish strong leadership over his department, even though this went against the egalitarian company culture. Yet what were the results? Maybe none of his formulas had worked and Li didn't want to make him, the boss, lose face by saying so? Or maybe Li was having problems getting them made and was afraid of losing face himself? This face business seemed to be an important part of the culture. Went all the way back to Confucius, or something like that. He would look it up in this book that had been lying on his bedside table for the last few months, *Doing Business with the Chinese*. Problem was, he always fell asleep after the first page.

In the back of his chauffeur-driven Mercedes, Jason began to relax. At least Mrs. Zhou had presented him with the list of ingredients used for hair treatment in Traditional Chinese Medicine (TCM). That was good: now he could push ahead with new products based on local raw materials. With the TCM fad in the West, this could prove to be a global marketing success. As the car inched forward toward the tunnel linking Pudong with the Bund in the usual evening queue, Jason turned his attention to the TV screen in front of him. Lovely-looking women were performing some kind of a courtship dance. Yes, despite all the skyscrapers around him, China was still full of exotic cultures. During the spring break he would take his family to Yunnan or some of these other places where the minorities lived. Before it was too late. His wife was right when she said that China was quickly losing its culture with all these Western shopping malls, McDonald's restaurants, and Starbucks at every corner. The government seemed to feel the same way. Hadn't this guy at the American Chamber of Commerce meeting last week spoken about a new Cultural Heritage Day, designed to boost the preservation and popularity of China's old folk customs and festivals?

Finally Jason arrived at his compound. Upon entering the flat on the eighth floor, he quickly changed into jeans and a T-shirt before joining his wife for the eight o'clock news in the living room. A study published in the medical journal *The Lancet* had come up with an estimate of 654,956 casualties since the start of the U.S.-led invasion in Iraq. President George W. Bush rejected the estimate, saying that he didn't consider the report credible. The Darfur crisis was next on the news. Minority Rights Group International blamed the world community for ignoring early warning signs of ethnic tension for the ensuing genocide in Sudan, which so far has killed more than two hundred thousand people and displaced a third of the population. "Can't they talk about anything else but killings?" Jason moaned, getting up to fetch a beer from the fridge. "Chris has a math test tomorrow," his wife shouted after him. "You better do some exercises with him. His scores are still way below the class average! It's really scary how good all the Asian kids are in math."

Culture Consciousness

For many in the West today's world is one shaped by clashing cultures. The work of Samuel Huntington, who predicted a "clash of civilizations" back in the early 1990s, enjoys unprecedented influence: for an academic book to have a sales rank around 2,000 on Amazon.com is indeed exceptional. News headlines use Huntington's terminology to make sense of American-Chinese relations, of "honor killings" of Muslim women in Germany, and of problems with the Daimler-Chrysler merger. A group convened by the secretary-general of the United Nations in 2006 to propose ways to bridge the gap between Western and Muslim societies called itself the Alliance of Civilizations, and in its report the group explicitly stated its aim to rebut the "clash of civilizations" theory. Wanting to emphasize the uniqueness of his nation, Toomas Hendrik Ilves, the president of Estonia, has called his country "a Huntingtonian subcivilization different from both its southern and eastern neighbors."[1] There is even a computer game called "The Clash of Civilizations."[2]

As Ilves's comment shows, however, the fear of clashing cultures is only one facet of the culturalist phase the world has gradually entered in the 2000s. Better put, today's world is a world shaped by a consciousness of culture that penetrates everyday life as well as matters of state in an unprecedented way. Culture—or rather, cultural difference—is now held to be the main explanation for the way the human world functions. Its allure is in the promise to explain a broader scope of phenomena than the previous grand narratives have. If the ideological alternatives posed by capitalism and communism worked to explain international dynamics, they said little about what was happening inside a society. For much of the second half of the twentieth century, people would invoke ideas of social class, colonial history, and scientific and technological development to make sense of their current situation and to imagine their futures. These ideas would be different in different places—Sheffield, Novosibirsk, or Dakar. By contrast, the logic of culture consciousness is deceptively universal, and thanks to today's media, the spread of standard models of economic and social policy and so on—a bundle of phenomena often called globalization—it is affecting people worldwide.

Muhamad Sadr-Azam, Pilar Fernandez, and Jason Carter are on the receiving end of ideas and stories produced by such institutions as governments, advertising companies, schools, and of course the media. The specter of culture is haunting public institutions and the private sector the world over. University degrees in "intercultural communication" and "intercultural management" are experiencing record enrollments. Doctors and police officers are sent to trainings in "cultural competence." Ministers of religion, eager to expand their markets to migrant and non-Western populations, take degrees in anthropology. Policy reports analyze the "cultural factors" and "cultural impact" of armed conflicts (in which the forms of warfare are also said to be cultural), international negotiations, and development projects. In an apparent shift of emphasis from searching for the causes of human behavior in the individual psyche to group cultural traits, banks, advertising agencies, defense lawyers, municipal administrations, and international organizations hire "culture experts." Makers of cultural policy, funders of art, and planners of cities want to be told about the impact of their decisions on cultural traditions and diversity. Minority groups worldwide—from the Ainu in Japan to the Yanomami in Brazil—enlist the help of NGOs and the global media in their fight for cultural survival. Debates on the cultural destiny of Russia fill bookshelves and airwaves. The Chinese government promotes the construction of "advanced culture" as a matter of national policy.

Why the Culturalist Phase?

It would be easy to tie the rise of culture as the paramount explanation to the end of the Cold War, when the ideological opposition between the two "worldviews" (and the political one between the two superpowers) came to an end, creating a vacuum of paradigms for global change. Yet in fact, the ascent of culturalism is the outcome of a number of social, political, and intellectual trends that have shaped the world since the 1960s, and by the turn of the millennium had acquired a force that suddenly swept "culture" into every living room. Only some of these changes have been related to tangible events—such as the collapse of the Soviet Union or the transformation of capitalist corporations—while others are rooted in the internal dynamics of the institutions and cultural elites that shape public opinion.

From cold war to ethnic conflict. Changes in global politics brought about by the end of the Cold War certainly formed the backdrop to much of the story this book tells. The Soviet bloc and the capitalist West both operated under versions of a rationalist, universalist development ideology, where economic growth necessarily led to a particular kind of more advanced society—liberal democracy or Communism—regardless of ethnicity or cultural context. The reach of these ideologies becomes obvious in places like today's Afghanistan, where the only voices rejecting ethno-tribal or religious politics—which have formed the basis of government since the U.S. intervention—in favor of a liberal modernization tend to be the voices of elites who studied in the Soviet Union in the 1980s. The collapse of the Soviet Union brought to the surface ethnic conflicts, many of which had been created by the state—for example, by the deportation of a range of peoples, including the Chechens, from the Caucasus to Central Asia—but had previously been contained by it.

In the absence of political explanations—all of the new states seemed, after all, to be marching toward market democracy—these conflicts were explained in terms of long-standing cultural and religious differences that had persisted despite having been swept under the carpet by the totalitarian regime. The same explanation was then applied to the bloody dismemberment of Yugoslavia and to the rest of the world. Indeed, cross-cultural handbooks on ethnic conflict for diplomats promised to "sort out ethnic identities and calculat[e] their strength."[3] While this explanation has often been false—sometimes tragically so—the withdrawal of the great powers from their respective backyards made room for the emergence of sundry political forces, some of which have pinned local or indigenous cultural purity on their banners. In other words the end of the bipolar world boosted the currency of both ethnic identities and ethnic explanations.

A more mobile world. The reach of nationalistic movements was greatly enhanced by the political, economic, and technological changes that revolutionized communications and facilitated human mobility in the decade following the changes of 1989 through 1991. Freedom of travel, previously restricted as a measure of both political control and currency protection (for example, South Korean citizens were not fully free to travel abroad until the 1990s, many years after the democratic transition!), was suddenly a reality. In the early 1990s in particular, with the memory of the Iron Curtain still fresh, both Western and Eastern European countries opened their borders. Although they began closing them again a few years later, this window initiated new flows of migrants and refugees, including those fleeing faraway conflicts, that turned out to be impossible to stop despite later attempts to do so.

According to the United Nations, 190 million people lived outside their countries of birth in 2005—compared with 76 million in 1960. Especially in societies that were used to homogeneity—or have forgotten their multiethnic histories, as did the successor states of the Austro-Hungarian and Ottoman empires—the appearance of more foreign-born individuals unable or unwilling to conform to traditional expectations of assimilation led to renewed discussions about the nature of national cultures. Even in societies that have always portrayed themselves as constituted by immigrants—such as the United States and Australia—more migration from non-European countries has triggered similar debates. This new movement of people was helped by dropping costs of travel (for example, a plane ticket from Lagos to London costs a tenth of what it did in 1960) and spurred by images of riches transmitted through satellite television to newly liberalized media markets. Indian villagers in 1985, if they were lucky enough to have access to a TV, saw educational dramas produced by the national broadcaster, Doordarshan. Ten years later, soap operas, celebrity shows, and advertising on eleven new satellite channels in India projected the glamour of global lifestyles to villages that were yet to build a latrine.[4]

Media liberalization. Television, videos, and the new medium, the Internet, far from imposing on the world the uniformity of Americanization as feared by early critics, also facilitated the creation and maintenance of what the anthropologist Benedict Anderson has called "imagined communities" within and across borders. According to him, the commodification of printed text in Europe in the seventeenth century and after made possible the wide circulation of narratives of the nation, thus creating the sense of a common belonging with people beyond one's immediate reach.[5] The spread of "visual capitalism" in the 1990s has created a fresh, powerful tool to strengthen that sense. In China the state's continuing hold on the media throughout the 1990s, when television ownership became nearly universal, created a national canon of cultural imagery—from the Great Wall to imperial-era costume dramas—that has informed a new generation's sense of being Chinese.

The same technologies have made it possible for migrants to maintain, enhance, or even create nationalist movements despite geographic dispersal and prolonged absence from their countries of origin. Soap operas and dance videos shot in Laos and China have helped Hmong Americans resettled in rural California in the 1970s codify a cultural identity that links them to the land they left but also to their close ethnic relatives, the Miao of Southern China. For the Miao the international ties witnessed by the same videos have reinforced a sense of cultural pride and strengthened their hand in negotiations with the Chinese government.[6]

Corporate globalization. The worldwide embrace of the free market has played an important role in stimulating both migration and the globalization of media. It has also had far-reaching consequences for companies and work environments. Corporations now want to sell the same product to people around the world, but often, both the products themselves and the marketing strategies need to be localized, as consumers have different needs and respond to different messages. The need to "know your consumer" has generated jobs in "global consumer research" and forced advertising agencies to develop locally sensitive campaigns. In Sri Lanka, for example, advertisements for beer and soft drinks developed in the United States and featuring close physical encounters between men and women are not well received, and embarrassment at the purchase of condoms and sanitary pads can be overcome by reframing them as medicines.[7]

The rationality of the free market brought people of diverse origins together on factory floors, in corporate boardrooms, and on housing estates. This diversification is driven by both corporations and localities competing for investment in a theoretically global market. The most basic form of that competition is lowering production costs. This "race to the bottom" between localities has favored the employment of migrant populations—either internal, as rural women working in China's clothing factories, or foreign, as Filipina maids in the Gulf or Romanian strawberry pickers in Spain—deprived of the economic and social rights enjoyed by locals. For their part, corporations are compelled to join this race to the bottom by moving production to China and outsourcing technical services to India or Eastern Europe. Moving production and services abroad has necessitated the hiring of local managerial, human resources, and public relations personnel, resulting in a fundamental change of their ethnic makeup and operating environment.

A culturally diverse workforce is seen to complicate communication processes within the company, as different work-related habits and values come into contact with one another—hence the avalanche of intercultural communication trainings and cross-cultural management workshops. But "successfully managed" diversity has come to be seen as an asset, not only mirroring and therefore anticipating the needs of the diverse customer base of companies but also enlarging the pool of ideas and releasing creativity in general. According to the new ideal championed by such hip business magazines as *Red Herring* and *Fast Company*, successful companies in the global market are those that not only embrace diversity but actively encourage "cultural hybridity." A feature in *Fast Company* enthused in 2000:

> Diversity defines the health and wealth of nations—as well as of companies and the people inside them. . . . Mixing . . . spawns creativity, nourishes the human spirit, spurs economic growth, empowers nations. . . . And those who wish to profit from changing economic conditions must view hybridity as their first and best option. . . .
>
> The best corporations set the pace in diversity. . . . Employers don't want hollow harmony. They want a cosmopolitan corporation. Hybrid teams are the new corporate ideal. . . . An unprecedented number of foreign-born CEOs run major companies in the United States, Britain, and several other countries, according to a study by Denis Lyons, an executive recruiter in New York City. . . . At the best companies, building diverse teams has become a routine part of business and a central piece of strategy. McKinsey & Co., the global consultancy, illustrates this trend. In the 1970s, most of its consultants were American, and its foreign contingent came from about 20 countries. . . . By 1999, McKinsey's chief partner was a foreign national (he hails from India); only 40% of its 4,800 consultants were American; and its foreign-born consultants came from more than 40 countries.[8]

Culture as capital. Contrary to *Fast Company*'s admonition, however, no nation-state has yet wholeheartedly embraced diversity. But "global cities," the ones whose growth strategies are based on the provision of services to the global market, have indeed recognized diversity as capital. This is because, although low cost is decisive in attracting production, banks and consultancies tend to set up their headquarters where they see the presence of a "creative environment." Since the financial crisis of the late 1990s, the government of Singapore, for example, has made great efforts to market Singapore as the global "Renaissance City" of the twenty-first century[9] and has forced its major regional competitor, Hong Kong, to follow suit. The Hong Kong chief executive, Tung Chee-hwa, said in his 2001 policy address: "An important

competitive edge in the knowledge-based economy is the possession of creative ideas, and the speed at which these ideas can be
transformed into products or services. World economic development is changing from a quest for resources to a quest for human
talents."[10]

Fostering the "creative industries"—from fine art to fashion—
as a vehicle of economic growth is a strategy that is now spreading from Singapore and Hong Kong to Shanghai and Beijing. But
the origin of this approach is in the United States, where since the
early 2000s an increasing number of city planners have followed
the advice of urban guru Richard Florida that "cultural diversity"—including a mix of ethnicities and a gay scene—is necessary
for creating the right environment. Emphasizing diversity is now
de rigueur for every city hoping to compete in the global market,
from Austin, Texas, to Singapore, where the in-flight menu cards
of the national airline feature work by expatriate artists. Consequently, states are selectively liberalizing their immigration regimes
to allow in a flow of highly skilled foreigners, even as they restrict
the entry of other migrants and refugees.

The race for "creative cities" is one sign that economic planners
of the 2000s treat culture as a form of capital, just as French sociologist Pierre Bourdieu suggested in 1986.[11] He defined it as the
set of knowledge, attitudes, and skills that give a person higher
status in society. As desires and opportunities of social advancement, employment, capital accumulation, and consumption diver-
sify and expand beyond national borders—and as the goal of
education shifts from abstract knowledge to universally marketable packages of habits and skills—cultural capital gains in importance. As a toolkit for global living, cultural capital is no longer
understood merely as a largely inherited set of class-related savoir
vivre, as in Bourdieu's work. The explicit or implicit assumption
behind both the Australian backpacker ethos of "discovering different cultures" and the Chinese government's exhortations to
improve peasants' "cultural quality" is that doing so increases
the individual's value in the "market of talent."[12] Increasingly, the
goal of education—especially higher education—is seen as acquiring globally marketable skills rather than universally applicable

knowledge. Part of this is a basic familiarity with "other cultures," whose spokespeople do their best to emphasize their distinctiveness as a way to draw tourists, whether to a remote country or to an urban neighborhood.

Becoming cosmopolitan globetrotters is no longer the Kantian promise of aesthetic pleasure in appreciating the foreign; parents and children now see "cross-cultural experiences" as linked to a good future life as a manager or consultant. So universities compete in providing programs with names like "Semester at Sea" or "Global Leadership Program." According to the Institute of International Education, almost two hundred thousand Americans were studying abroad in 2003 and 2004, up from seventy-six thousand ten years earlier. In particular, the number of those studying in China grew by 90 percent.[13] Yet the number of American students abroad is far below that of their Chinese peers. In the same academic year, fifty thousand new students from China went to Australia alone.[14] If twenty years earlier, Chinese students in the West had tended to be doing PhDs in science and engineering, now many of them were going abroad while in high school—and the quality of the school is often considered less important than the "intercultural experience." Proficiency in English is of course very important, but so is the ability to navigate among "whities."

The rush for Chinese nannies for the children of New York executives is about mastering interaction with the future's superpower—not just linguistically but also "culturally." Riding on the wave of this mutual obsession, such international schools as Yew Chung—which has campuses in four mainland Chinese cities as well as in Hong Kong and the Silicon Valley—advertises itself with the slogan "Educating the Global Child" and promises to deliver an "education that leads our students to an inner transformation whereby they are both Eastern and Western."[15]

The rise of "symbol analysts" and the cultural turn. The ascent of the economy of culture is part of a broader process: the rise of the group that the former U.S. secretary of labor Robert Reich has called "symbol analysts": people engaged in the manipulation— the creation, explanation, and distribution—of data, words, and visual representations.[16] These people, the ones "creative cities" compete for—consultants, lawyers, artists, software engineers, investment bankers, advertising executives, political analysts— produce goods and services that account for an increasing share of global consumption and wealth. They also wield tremendous influence in the interpretation of the world and in political and economic decision making as institutions of power devolve an increasing amount of responsibility for their decisions to such "experts." Situations range from court rulings involving expertise on cultural norms of a defendant's ethnic group to congressional hearings on foreign affairs to reviews of proposals by research funding bodies to reports prepared for the European Union. Thus the market increasingly encroaches on domains of policy that used to be limited to political elites or corporate boards as well as domains of knowledge production that used to be the sanctuary of scientists. This is related to an erosion of the authority of science as such and of natural science in particular, and to the democratization of the relation between scientists and the lay public.

Traditionally, policy makers—and the broader public—have seen science as a representation of objective reality, free from value components and expressed in a particular kind of formalized, structured language. Decision makers wishing to grasp social processes would likely turn to the kinds of work in social science that corresponded to these norms—modeled on the natural sciences— and that showed society as operating within a framework of structured mechanisms that one could understand and even predict, if only one put sufficient good research into it. But the growing anti-elitism of liberal democracies, the general distrust of state authority that intensified throughout the 1960s, the perceived complicity of the natural sciences in the arms race, and the growing influence of environmentalist movements all contributed to challenging the privileging of science over other forms of knowledge. Demand for democratic oversight over this class of experts was seconded by growing number of social researchers who called into question the value-free nature of scientific advice by claiming that scientific knowledge is itself powerfully shaped by cultural forces.

The declining influence of the sciences as ultimate arbiter of human dilemmas was inseparable from the rise of such cultural critique, resulting by the 1990s in a shift away from privileging "hard," quantitative, economic explanations and toward foregrounding "soft," cultural ones. This "cultural turn" was visible in public debate but had an even more powerful effect within such academic disciplines as history, sociology, and geography as well as economics, medicine, and even business studies. In 2006 and 2007, for example, the University of Leipzig in Germany offered a course called "The Cultural Turn and Its Consequences for Physical Education" to its physical education students.

In a review of the "cultural turn" in the humanities, historian Peter N. Stearns has pointed to how the inclusion of culture in research assumptions has enriched our understanding of the sense of smell, the history of emotions, the nature of illness, and gender roles in society among other benefits.[17] As before, cultural explanations have to contend with biological ones; in fact, they have to do so in more areas than before, as advances in genetics, claiming to have discovered genes responsible for obesity or human cooperation, continue to reshape the boundary between biological determination and cultural learning.[18] Nonetheless, it is safe to say that in the general public, cultural explanations are now much more readily invoked to challenge the authority of "hard" science than twenty years ago, while, surprising as it is, "culture experts" are less likely to be challenged, say, on the customs of Iraq than physicists on the safety of nuclear reactors. "The punditocracy," as anthropologist Bill Maurer has written, "are our modern day mythmakers."[19]

Civil rights. The "cultural turn," and indeed many of the processes we have outlined, would not have occurred without the emergence of the civil rights movement. From its inception in the United States during the 1950s and early 1960s, this movement developed from a struggle for "racial" equality based on ideals of universal rights and responsibilities into an ideology of asserting and celebrating cultural distinctiveness in the 1980s and 1990s, when the "politics of recognition" caused school curricula to be rewritten and museums established to showcase "Black history" as well as its Chicano, Asian American, and Native American equivalents. The rigid bounding of ethnoracial categories, a unique heritage of nineteenth- and twentieth-century America institutionalized in the U.S. Census, was now further solidified by turning it into a "heritage" to be cherished. This resulted in greater identification with what previously were stigmatized ethnic labels. Thus between 1970 and 1980, the population of American Indians in the United States grew from eight hundred thousand in 1970 to 2.5 million in 2000, a rate that can only be explained by more people identifying themselves as Indians. The anthropologist Marshall Sahlins has pointed to the civil rights movement as being at the root of "the formation of . . . a culture of cultures," as more and more groups, from American Indian "First Nations" to sexual subcultures, developed a new level of self-consciousness about their own way of life, discovering (and reinforcing and inventing) their own specificity relative to other groups in society.[20]

Although what public policy professor Dvora Yanow has called the "lumpy hyphen"—the creation of large, bounded ethnic categories like "Latino-American"—is unique to the United States, the effects of the politics of ethnic representation have been felt very widely.[21] First Canada and Australia, and then some European states, adopted ideologies of "multiculturalism," which stressed the right to cultural difference alongside the right to equal citizenship. In the international arena organizations fighting against racism, for minority rights, and for the recognition of indigenous peoples have adopted the language of cultural distinctiveness in advancing their causes. Support for such groups—whether Gypsies in Romania or Dayaks in Borneo—often comes from North America, Western Europe, or from activists of the "global South," and to be heard, their grievances must be articulated in the stylized language of cultural rights. Thus the Ainu, the indigenous people of officially ethnically homogenous Japan, have successfully managed to revitalize their cultural identity since the 1970s by establishing tourist villages, in which Ainu food and crafts are produced and sold, and children are taught the Ainu language and traditions. In 1997 a Japanese court for the first time officially accorded the Ainu minority status, potentially opening the way for land claims and representation in central or local government.[22]

How important a role culture plays for minority movements can also be seen from the story of a folklorist who was recently abducted by Khasi separatist rebels in the Indian state of Meghalaya and taken to a clandestine camp. According to an article in *Indian Folklife*, "They asked him to stay there for two weeks to talk about folklore of the Khasis in order to inspire some sort of unity among the cadres."[23]

Desecularization. The last great trend contributing to the culturalist phase is the desecularization of the world. Since the burning of novelist Salman Rushdie's *Satanic Verses* in 1989, religion has been steadily reclaiming the place in public and political spaces that it had lost during the rationalist era of the Cold War on both sides of the Iron Curtain. Evangelical Christianity and Islam in particular, but also other old and new religions, have been spreading rapidly and waging political claims in new arenas—from anti-abortion politics in Africa to Hindu mobilization in the diaspora and the Falungong's global war against the Chinese government. Although the relationship of religion to cultural representation is a complicated one—many religious movements want to transcend cultural divisions, while others, like the Christian Right in the United States, argue against them for political reasons—in a number of cases religious authority has reasserted itself as cultural authority. In Europe, states dissatisfied with the politics of liberal multiculturalism are seeking religious figures able to speak for and exert power over "Muslim" constituencies. In Iraq, based on a similar logic, religious divisions are taken for a synonym of ethnic groups, and religious leaders are endowed with a self-fulfilling clout of influence.

The Meanings of Culture

The fact that "culture" is increasingly frequently invoked does not mean that all people mean the same thing by it. Until the 1980s the term "culture" in everyday parlance referred mainly to the arts. Since the "cultural turn," however, people have started

Table 1. "Culture" as a group attribute

Cultural level	Scope	Number of groups
1	Languages, ethnolinguistic groups	Thousands
2	Ethnic groups with a declared cultural identity	Thousands
3	States	Hundreds
4	"Civilizations"	Eight, according to Samuel Huntington

Source: Schönhuth 2005, 45.

talking about "gay culture," "company culture," or "culture of poverty." Western businessmen have written bestsellers about "Confucian culture" in China, while Chinese newspapers have berated the "clique culture" of officials as they write about "residential culture" in articles promoting upmarket apartments. In other words, although the word "culture" is still in use in its first sense as art (and science), it is now increasingly used to encompass all human behavior that is not biologically determined. Although in principle such usage could refer to all of humankind, in practice it mostly constructs "culture as difference," as a set of attributes that distinguishes one group of people from another. As the political philosopher Seyla Benhabib has written: "Much contemporary cultural politics . . . is an odd mixture of the anthropological view of the democratic equality of all cultural forms of expression and the Romantic, Herderian emphasis on each form's irreducible uniqueness."[24]

Even when used in this most common sense, "culture" refers to different entities for different people. Michael Schönhuth, following the work of Christoph Antweiler, identifies four different levels at which "culture" is applied to human groups, which vary highly in terms of scope and range (see table 1).[25] At all of these levels, culture is roughly linked to ethnicity—although based on highly conflicting and contested claims.

The Purpose of This Book

Cultural differences are often an important factor in what happens in the world. For many in the West and beyond, however, this simple truth takes a distorted form: the view of a world shaped by clashing cultures. The story of clashing cultures is compelling because it is based on easily comprehensible categories, but it is wrong and even dangerous. To write a story that is equally compelling is difficult when you—as anthropologists tend to—believe that simple categories never capture reality. As the anthropologist Thomas Eriksen has written: "Our job partly consists in . . . making easy answers to complex questions slightly more difficult to defend."[26] Here we attempt to understand the world as a rapidly changing product of global trends shaping our perception, rather than as a sum of historically continuous civilizations. We are interested in the mechanisms that make us see the world in terms of "cultures."

We offer more than a criticism of a pervasive view we consider dangerous. We believe that a systematic examination of the rise of "culture" as an explanatory paradigm in human institutions can in itself be a compelling explanation of why we are where we are today: in the middle of a devastating war in Iraq; stuck between Islamophobia and anti-Americanism; and at a crossroads where liberal politics are retreating in the face of a seeming failure to maintain their traditional commitment to both individual freedoms and cultural openness, whether in Palestine after the democratic election of an Islamist group to power, or in Europe, where public debates on Islamic head covering recall the times of Peter the Great (who had men cut off their beards) and Mustafa Kemal (who forced his people into European clothes).

In today's institutions, from foreign ministries to advertising agencies, "culture" is the talk of the day. Yet it is more often than not a black box. Many people talk about culture, yet most are not able to describe and define it, let alone point to its actual impact and importance in their institutions and areas of work. The clash-of-civilizations view of the world is seemingly good for breaking complicated issues down into simple cultural categories, each of which has its practical list of dos and don'ts. But apart from the flawed assumptions on which this view is based, it inevitably creates a practical problem: claims about culture, coming from different spokespeople, are bound to contradict each other, leaving the decision maker with the task to adjudicate. A process-centered view that provides information not about "cultures" but about the forces that stand behind cultural claims is not only better for understanding the world, it is also practically useful. In some situations cultural claims do have explanatory power and must be taken into account; in others, however, they mislead. In a world where "culture matters," decision makers, from public hospitals to antiterrorism operations, must be knowledgeable about and sensitive to cultural differences; but rather than an atlas of folk customs, they need tools to critically evaluate the claims they encounter.

This book first looks at the uses of culture at the state-to-state level, then proceeds to examine how individual states deal with cultural diversity, and finally zooms in on the consequences of the "culture fever" for the functioning of institutions and for the lives of individuals. In exploring these diverse realms, we draw on a large body of existing scholarship as well as documents produced by political and business consultancies, mainstream media, and our own ethnographies. Chapter 1 describes a world trying to rationalize and contain the international "threats" to its "security" by a conceptual apparatus in which universalist paradigms increasingly serve as a mere fig leaf for deeply held assumptions of cultural difference. This is a trend occurring across the political spectrum—defense strategists planning the occupation of Iraq and antiglobalist demonstrators protesting it take cultural differences between "West" and "East" or "South" for granted.

While the so-called clash of civilizations has never been as close to being a self-fulfilling prophesy as in the United States' "war on terror," the logic of cultural relativism has also reshaped post–Cold War relations between the great powers of America, Russia, and China. We discuss a range of instances where it has led to a reworking of international dialogue and public discourse on subjects like human rights and democracy, such as the rise of the

"Asian values" discourse in the 1990s. In Europe, initial enthusiasm about the expansion of the European Union based on the principles of liberal democracy has been succeeded by overt statements about Europe's cultural limits, which seem to block Turkey's accession. In each of these cases we trace the mechanisms whereby essentialist assumptions and the "container view" of culture have risen to dominance through both misunderstandings and strategic instrumentalization of culture by particular interests—from politicians wishing to preserve their power to business consultants and the media.

If international security is about containment, then international development and aid is about engagement. Chapter 2 maps the rise of culture in development institutions and discourse. After some forty years of development strategies based on universal economic and technological indicators, which did not deliver the promised results, institutions like the World Bank have adopted an approach that focuses on local participation and cultural specificity. Those at one extreme of the debate see particular kinds of cultures as the main obstacle to development, while those at the other discard the notion of development as an instrument of continued Western hegemony. In the middle, however, there are approaches inspired by the well-known work of Amartya Sen, which maintain the possibility of useful intervention premised on recognizing culturally diverse views of the "good life." This chapter documents cases in which an infusion of local knowledge has led to positive results, but also those instances in which misrepresented or conflicting cultural claims—by local elites or global intermediaries—have resulted in waste, inaction, and even disaster. In addition to the problems of an essentialized view of cultures highlighted in chapter 1, these cases reveal the necessity of asking who has the right to speak for a group or community.

Chapter 3 moves from the international to the national level. Samuel Huntington's framework of clashing civilizations, while deployed mainly at the level of international conflicts, has also strongly influenced international interpretations of and interventions into local—interpreted as ethnocultural—conflicts, such as the wars in Bosnia (by the West) and in Chechnya (by Russia).

In other cases international discourse naturalized local conflicts into inevitable conflicts of historic ethnocultural difference, such as between the Tutsi and Hutu in Rwanda or the Shi'a and Sunni Arabs in Iraq. Exploring how these interpretations came to dominate over equally plausible ones based, for example, on conflicts between elites over economic resources and political power, sheds light on the limited explanatory power of culturalist explanations, the global conditions that make a conflict in Africa immediately perceived in ethnic terms, and the potentially disastrous consequences of interventions based on unexamined cultural assumptions.

In the nation-states that came to dominate the West in the early twentieth century, the view of ethnic diversity was not very different from that which prevails today in discussions of remote conflicts: it was a potentially dangerous thing that was either to melt into a national culture by itself (as in the United States) or had to be coerced into it by means of education or even violence. After World War II, and increasingly since the 1960s, cultural diversity began to be acknowledged and even celebrated in a number of Western societies. In the 2000s, however, concerns about the proper management of cultural diversity—particularly with regard to immigrant populations—have again begun to prevail over its affirmation. Chapter 4 reviews the range of public realms in which nation-states are engaged in culture management, from regulating immigration to urban planning, from education to the courts. We summarize some of the hallmark debates that continue to rage across Western (formerly?) liberal democracies, such as those on the Islamic headscarf, female circumcision, and citizenship tests. These cases, while foregrounding tensions between the cultural rights of groups and individual freedoms and pushing discussions of culture into both legislation and courts of law, have at the same time reignited public debates about national culture and its limits. Can a true Dutchwoman refuse to swim? Is street violence by Algerian youth in Paris culturally conditioned? Is a schoolteacher's insistence on having her face covered a cultural right, an offense against culture, or both? These debates are bringing a new guard of cultural (and religious) spokespeople to prominence, but, as this book shows, the difficulty is in establishing where cultural explanations are useful and where they are misplaced and self-serving.

Chapter 5 is an excursion into the world of cultural—and culturally justified—property. In a growing number of cases, "indigenous" groups have contested modern-era land titles granted by colonial powers or nation-states, asserted their right to control, or benefit from, cultural or intellectual property (such as the medical uses of particular plants) being commercially exploited by individuals or businesses, and challenged international environmental conventions. The cases reviewed—from contesting rights to the ownership of American Indian dances to Aboriginal land titles in Australia and the special permission to hunt whales granted the Makah Indians of Canada—illustrate conflicts arising from differences in the cultural construction of property. Recently, "indigenous" groups or mediators acting (or claiming to act) on their behalf have challenged medical patent rights and copyrights pertaining to texts and images. While a growing number of legal scholars argues that customary law should be recognized in legal proceedings, others advocate the lifting of existing cultural property rights in the name of free access. By analyzing existing conflicts and developing hypothetical scenarios for regulating the protection of cultural property, we point both to the usual problems with group representation (the problematic nature of the authority to identify group boundaries and to determine the content of cultural tradition) and to the importance of a case-by-case approach in attributing rights and revenues to develop a natural or cultural resource.

The last two chapters deal with the consequences of the "rise of culture" for institutions and individuals. Chapter 6 describes the "intercultural communication" (IC) industry that has developed on the fringes of business and government since the late 1980s, originating in the United States but by now spread globally. Corporate employees and government officials are trained in "intercultural competence" before they are posted abroad in order to sensitize them to working with a culturally diverse population. Unlike in the realms discussed in previous chapters, (inter-)cultural expertise here constitutes a fully formalized, practice-oriented field with its own conferences and journals, which claims to be indispensable to the effective operation of any institution.

We offer a critical look at the evolution of IC and its origins—mainly in social psychology and 1950s anthropology—as well as its dominant paradigms as exemplified in the highly influential but deeply flawed works of management gurus Geert Hofstede, Charles Hampden-Turner, and Fons Trompenaars. We then describe the way IC has been applied in various corporate and public fields, showing its effects on management training, health care, and education. IC classifies nations along a finite number of cultural variables and provides practical instructions depending on which two "cultures" are meeting in the situation at hand (for example, two-day trainings for German managers on "how to do business with Chinese"). Yet, while practical information on the Chinese etiquette can be useful, real-life experience calls the bluff of IC's claim that culture is "a language to be learned." The actual behavior of one's business partners, the preferences of one's students or patients, cannot be reduced to cultural characteristics putatively derived from the national tradition. We provide examples of more useful approaches to IC, ones that take into account not only group culture but social, economic, and individual variation as well as the context of the situation.

For businesses, however, the "culture fever" has meant more than diversity management and IC trainings. Businesses have also become increasingly attentive to local consumer needs and preferences. Although the basis of "ethnic marketing" has had the usual effect of accentuating differences across predefined groups, this time with the purpose of selling kosher food and hair-care products for black hair, the shift from traditional surveys to qualitative studies has had a rather different result. "Ethnography" became a corporate buzzword. In the 2000s anthropologists have begun working in consumer research positions at companies ranging from Intel to Procter & Gamble, as well as founding hip design and architecture consultancies. Their job is to identify consumer needs by spending weeks in a Brazilian slum, an Osaka bakery, or in an online chat group. In a number of examples, chapter 7 demonstrates that, while the words "culture," "values," and "community" are remarkably rare in corporate ethnographers' reports, they provide snapshots of constantly shifting practices and meanings—what do a pair of faded jeans mean to an inner-city black youth in Detroit, or a particular ringtone to a Jamaican schoolchild?—that go a long way in understanding cultural influences on individual behavior. If this works for Microsoft, couldn't it work for the Pentagon?

The conclusion returns to the picture of a world not so much "Riding the Waves of Culture"—the title of a best-selling intercultural management manual—as adrift on the waves of culturalism. The dilemma this book raises is how to retain sensitivity to the cultural impacts on and of policies and corporate decisions without falling into the trap of determinism, essentialization, and misrepresentation—a trap that, as we are currently witnessing, can have the dangerous consequences of a self-fulfilling prophesy. We suggest that it is more important to understand the motives of processes in which cultural claims arise than to study the supposed essence of a finite number of "cultures," and that this need not be a fantasy of the ivory tower. Corporate ethnographers, and some development practitioners who have begun applying similar approaches, have shown just that. We conclude by offering readers a series of questions designed to help anyone who needs to evaluate the impact of decisions potentially involving cultural difference to decide whether, in a particular case, culture matters.

chapter 1

Clashing Civilizations

In 2005, during a meeting with Russian president Vladimir Putin, U.S. president George W. Bush made a conciliatory gesture to his Russian counterpart, criticized for taking an authoritarian turn in Russian politics: Bush said that "democracies always reflect a country's culture and customs."[1] This idea must have been on Bush's mind that year. In another speech in Kyoto, he said that exporting democracy did not mean exporting American democracy; rather, it meant exporting such values as freedom of expression, property rights, the rule of law, and the like—and then letting individual cultures sort out the details.[2] The president of the United States telling the president of Russia that the form of democracy depends on culture? This incident, unimaginable fifteen years earlier, shows the degree to which "culture talk" has entered the mainstream of international politics since the end of the Cold War.

This has been a disconcerting time for nations. After the "long twentieth century"—when the fronts between colonizers and freedom fighters, right and left, America and the Soviet Union largely defined international relations—states suddenly found themselves with a bewildering array of choices.[3] Where does a new head of state make his or her first visit at the beginning of the twenty-first century? King Abdullah of Saudi Arabia, America's foremost Arab ally, chose China in 2006. The world is becoming more multipolar, and the historical rights of the West are suddenly being challenged. Who can have a nuclear bomb? Who may hold on to trade barriers? Who must liberalize? Who is allowed to pollute?

Universalism versus Relativism:
Francis Fukuyama and Samuel Huntington

The first attempts to provide direction in this new world suggested that history was over and that Western liberal democracy had triumphed. In 1992, when Francis Fukuyama's *The End of History and the Last Man* was published, this still seemed plausible. The violence surrounding the breakup of the Soviet Union and Yugoslavia and the suppression of the Chinese democracy movement in Tiananmen Square may have been the last bloody death throes of the old, divided world. Fukuyama recognized cultural differences between nations (he was not particularly interested in their internal cultural diversity). He believed, however, that the spread of liberal democratic institutions and the free market ultimately corresponded to the desires of individuals across these cultural barriers and represented, as it were, a final liberation of humankind from inherited shackles, a liberation that was now on the horizon.

But only a few years later, Fukuyama seemed naïve and the world a lot more confusing. China had begun a sustained period of phenomenal economic growth without inching any closer to liberal democracy. Autocrats consolidated their power in much of the former Soviet Union, violence in the Balkans continued, the Soviet withdrawal from Afghanistan left a civil war in its wake, and Islamist terrorism (previously associated with the Iran of Ayatollah Khomeini) was spreading. A year after *The End of History* was published—the year when terrorists attacked the World Trade Center in New York for the first time, and when historian Paul Kennedy mused that "the most important influence on a nation's responsiveness to change probably is its social attitudes, religious beliefs and culture"[4]—Samuel Huntington published "The Clash of Civilizations?" in *Foreign Affairs*. Three years later, he expanded his argument into a book, dropping the question mark from the title. Over the course of a decade, "the clash of civilizations" has become a household term for the Western middle classes but also a paradigm that nearly every practitioner or theoretician of international relations has to deal with—whether to embrace or to refute it. At Macquarie University in Sydney, for example, "The Clash of Civilizations" is assigned reading for nine courses across the social sciences, and at the time of this book's printing, Huntington's work still occupies the almost incredible (for an academic text) sales rank of around two thousand on Amazon.com.

Huntington—himself a former universalist who just two years earlier had pointedly argued against the thesis of culture being an obstacle to democratization—became the paradigmatic figure for all who were disillusioned with Fukuyama's universalistic promise and, seeking to understand why international conflicts endured despite the spread of free-market capitalism, were ready to accept cultural differences as their root cause.[5] "It is far more meaningful now," wrote Huntington, "to group countries not in terms of their political or economic systems or in terms of their economic development but rather in terms of their culture and civilization."[6] Indeed, the 1990s witnessed a fundamental shift in international politics, where differences in opinion between states came to be routinely placed in cultural rather than ideological or structural contexts. Whether it is human rights in China, Turkey's place in Europe, or terrorism, the dominant voices in these debates are those that talk about cultural difference, not about the power struggles of governments or factions like in old-fashioned Sovietology.

Fukuyama and Huntington represent the latest editions of two strands of Western political philosophy growing out of the European Enlightenment and nineteenth-century nationalism. For early European nationalists, the nation-state linked culture to ethnicity and territory as part of a national essence. In 1781, Justus Möser, a friend of Goethe's, called for the writing of a true German history, whose task he saw in examining "the origin and development" of "the national character" under changing historical circumstances.[7] Johann Gottlieb Fichte, one of the fathers of the German romantic nationalist movement known as Sturm und Drang, wrote in his *Addresses to the German Nation* in 1807–08 of "the . . . truly natural borders of the state. . . . That which speaks the same language is tied together with many invisible strings through nature itself, before all human artifice."[8]

Raymond Williams has noted that it may have been Johann

Gottfried von Herder, one of the founders of the German romantic movement, who first spoke of "cultures" in the plural. He used the term to describe differences both across nations and across distinct groups within them, but his followers, like Fichte, stressed the link between nation and culture and neglected the idea of internal differences.[9] At about the same time, Montesquieu wrote about the "spirit" of a nation, formed on the basis of natural conditions as well as laws, customs, and moral. This marked the beginning of a long line of studies of "national character." These were popular in international relations—such as the work of Hans Morgenthau—and with the broader public up to the 1960s, when they were picked up by such social psychologists as Alex Inkeles and eventually absorbed into the corpus of "intercultural communication theory" (see chapter 6).[10] In the first half of the twentieth century, some influential historians—notably Oswald Spengler, Arnold Toynbee, and Fernand Braudel—developed an alternative view, which focused on large civilizational units rather than nations as the broadest, and most important, units of cultural commonality. In their view the actors of world history were civilizations.

The national view of culture and the idea of civilizations was globally exported and appropriated during the colonial period. For example, the current words for "culture" (*wenhua*) and "civilization" (*wenming*) entered the Chinese language from the Japanese in the 1920s, where the terms *bunka* and *bunmei* had in turn been recently coined to translate the Western concept.[11] In a similar process the peoples of many Pacific islands have come to use the word *kastam* to refer to their traditional way of life. Of course, in some instances these ideas echoed parts of local traditions. Indeed, the common literary and ritual tradition had long been understood by Chinese scholars to differentiate them from the outside world.

At the same time, while postulating culture as a national-ethnic group trait, Enlightenment thinkers—beginning with Immanuel Kant—also held that the free will of the rational individual can transcend and transform the confines imposed by the group. This tension between the ethical imperative of individual self-determination and the imperative, in Fichte's words, to "realize the authentic national will—in a state of one's own" has continued in debates between universalist and relativist approaches to human rights and international relations.[12] The writings of Fukuyama and Huntington represent the popular version of this debate, whose significance for a broader public has suddenly expanded as people try to make sense of globalization.

After the brief moment of post–Cold War euphoria in the early 1990s, Huntington's following overtook Fukuyama's, and the New York terror attacks of 11 September 2001 appeared to discredit altogether the idea of a world converging toward a shared democratic modernity. Suddenly, the world looked like a battleground in which the West was fighting fanatical enemies that were trying to destroy its way of life. Every successful or foiled terrorist plot, every protest by Muslims against a perceived insult—such as the cartoons of Mohammed in the Danish newspaper *Jyllands-Posten* or Pope Benedict's belittling of the Prophet as unoriginal in 2006—and every court case about the wearing of the headscarf in schools looked like a new battle in this war, not between fundamentalism and secularism, but among cultures. Huntington's label fitted this new view perfectly. Cultural difference from the West was no longer, as Fukuyama saw it, a temporary impediment to progress; it was here to stay. Even the highly popular computer game "Civilization," where players relive history from 4000 B.C.E. to 2020 C.E., introduced culture as a fresh element in its new version launched in 2002. In this new version, players competed with other "civilizations" through the strength of one's "culture," not just their military, economic, and technological power.[13]

Fukuyama and Huntington are both heirs of the Fichtean view of culture as glue that bonds a large group of individuals together. But while Fukuyama stresses the individual's desire to rid himself of the cultural flypaper, Huntington takes the view that such efforts are doomed and are not even necessarily desirable. Both authors share the view, popular in the early 1990s, that the nation-state is weakening, but they make different predictions on this basis. For Fukuyama, globalization creates non-national forms of voluntary association that give rise to a thriving civil society in which cultural traditions fade. Huntington, however, predicts that the new bonds of the postnational world order—both across and within borders—will not be based on individual choice but on shared "civilization," on "cultural kinship." He wrote: "The world will be ordered on the basis of civilizations or not at all."[14] Civilizations are like tribes, and the clash of civilizations therefore is tribal conflict on a global scale. In short, Fukuyama is a prophet of convergence; Huntington, of divergence.

Civilization Talk

In *The Clash of Civilizations*, Huntington identifies seven or eight civilizations (he is hesitant about whether Africa constitutes one). The seven are the Sinic (Chinese), Japanese, Hindu, Islamic, Orthodox, Western, and Latin American civilizations. "The fault lines between civilizations," he argues, "will be the battle lines of the future."[15] This is once again the case in Europe, where the "Velvet Curtain of culture has replaced the Iron Curtain of ideology as the most significant dividing line" and "the great historic fault lines between civilizations are once more aflame."[16] He warns that "the dangerous clashes of the future are likely to arise from the interaction of Western arrogance, Islamic intolerance, and Sinitic assertiveness."[17]

For Huntington, "in order for the world to be relatively peaceful and stable, international relations should be governed by the recognition of these fault lines and respect for cultural difference across them. Underestimating such differences—for example, by trying to spread democracy—results in bloodshed. Migration, which mixes up people from different civilizations, is another recipe for trouble. Some states, such as the former Yugoslavia, have the misfortune of sitting atop fault lines; such 'torn countries' are 'candidates for dismemberment.'"[18] States that abandon their civilization and try to belong to another (Russia, Turkey, Mexico, or Australia in the 1990s), or where the mixing of ethnic groups belonging to different civilizations reaches a certain threshold (the United States), are "torn countries" of a different kind: they suffer from "cultural schizophrenia." Like American multiculturalists, political leaders outside the West who "infect" their countries with "the Western virus" therefore do so at their own peril.[19]

Huntington devotes much space to documenting the "bloody borders" of the Islamic civilization.[20] But his misgivings about a conflict between the Western and Asian civilizations are equally grave. In his view Asian states (he is not clear whether this includes just the Sinic and Japanese ones or also the Hindu) are united by an emphasis on "the value of authority, hierarchy, the subordination of individual rights and interests [and] the importance of consensus"; that is, they have "little room for social and political pluralism and the division of power."[21] In many Asian countries, Huntington is a well-known figure—although, as in the West, academics are mostly critical of him. In Bangladesh his work is required reading for university students in the social sciences. In Japan his *Clash of Civilizations*, originally published in 1998, was sold in bestseller corners and provoked vivid media discussions.

Many Japanese commentaries focused on Huntington's characterization of Japan and China as core states of two distinct civilizations. Coming at the time of the collapse of the bubble economy, this view coalesced with fears of China's economic and political ascent. Some commentators used Huntington's ideas to argue for an increase in military budgets, a return to "the samurai spirit" of a more assertive Japan, and greater pride in Japanese tradition. The Japanese government eventually adopted this rhetoric in the 2000s under the Koizumi and Abe administrations. Many universities have used *The Clash of Civilizations* as a textbook, with the international relations department at Takushoku University even designing an entire course around it.[22] A sequel produced exclusively for the Japanese market, *The Clash of Civilizations and Japan in the Twenty-first Century*, was published in 2001.

After the terror attacks of 9/11 in New York, several posts on Chinese Internet discussion forums— in both the mainland and Hong Kong—referred to *The Clash of Civilizations* in ways such as this: "While one participant believed that the U.S.-led Western civilization must fall before the Chinese civilization would be able to rebuild itself, another post admonished the sympathizers of Arab victims of the ill feelings that Islamic civilization has against

'Buddhist and Confucian civilization.'"[23] Talk about civilizations is rife in China. The 2006 Beijing Forum—China's answer to the Davos World Economic Forum, which pointedly emphasizes humanities and the social sciences over economics—had the theme "The Harmony of Civilizations and Prosperity for All: Reflections on the Civilization Modes of Humankind." Although, in line with the current rhetoric of the Chinese government, the forum stressed the "harmony" rather than conflict of "civilizations," its newsletter featured an article about elder philosopher Tang Yijie. Tang stated that "the conflict of civilizations is becoming increasingly fierce in the world today. . . . [T]he world is witnessing . . . oriental societies swept under the cultural wind from Europe and the United States, which is wearing away and disintegrating the Eastern culture. . . . An independent country needs a sole identity, which is the quintessence of its traditional culture."[24]

Some Chinese nationalists see the revolutionary years between 1911 and 1978 in the same way as their Russian counterparts see the Soviet years, or as some Eastern Europeans see the era of Soviet domination: as years when the nation deviated from its "natural" historical path. These views are of course contradictory. For Chinese and Russian nationalists Marxism is a Western import, but for Eastern Europeans it is a Russian imposition. For well-known Hungarian political commentator Debreczeni József, Nazism was an "awful derailment" of the European "system," but Bolshevism was an "organic product" of "the Asian model."[25] But all see the current moment as one in which the time has come for the nation to recover its "true self."[26] Consequently, in China, Huntington has been criticized not for his idea of "civilizations" but for his predictions of a clash and his warning of the danger coming from the Sinic civilization, which some commentators saw as a foil for strengthening U.S. hegemony in the world.[27]

That such a civilization exists does not seem controversial. Many commentators stress that China is able to aim for "harmony" precisely because of its unique civilization. However, some see Chinese civilization as a constantly changing one that has always owed its success to mixing, while others believe it has preserved more of the moral precepts that were originally common to human civilization. For example, Sheng Banghe, a professor at the Shanghai University of Finance, has written: "The reason we call for a dialogue of civilizations is precisely the reality of clashing civilizations."[28] Moreover, he and other commentators have suggested that even if Huntington is wrong in his predictions, his view that the Islamic and Sinic civilizations present the greatest danger to the West is "probably representative of a widespread belief in Western society: Huntington was just the first one to 'dare to eat the crab.'" Sheng and his coauthor believe that Huntington's theory should have concrete ramifications for China's foreign policy. As the rising core country of the Sinic civilization, it should exercise a "mediating" role within it, gain the support of other countries belonging to this civilization, and act as their spokesperson in negotiations with other "core countries."[29] (Ironically, although many Chinese political analysts do not raise objections to the concept of "civilizations," they tend to be the most hardcore of "realists" in seeing foreign affairs as very much a zero-sum game of national interests and alliances—not at all fitting the sort of contextual, not black-and-white, non-zero-sum thinking that theorists of "Asian values" such as Fons Trompenaars attribute to them.)

In most of these discussions the West figures as a homogeneous entity, often really a proxy for the characteristics attributed to the United States. In the words of Singapore's former prime minister, Lee Kuan Yew, these characteristics include "guns, drugs, violent crime, vagrancy, unbecoming behavior in public" as well as individualism, disrespect for tradition, and a decaying social fabric, but also modernity, democracy, wealth, and creativity. An article posted on the *People's Daily* online *Qiangguo* (Strengthen the country) forum dismisses Huntington's views as a foil for U.S. hegemony and a trick to gather other Western countries under America's wing. Nonetheless it asserts that the "moral decay and limitless hedonism" of "Western civilization" has reached a point where, "from a cultural studies point of view . . . it is no longer a cultural civilization but merely a lifestyle."[30] This view of the West was once contrasted to that of the Soviet bloc, but it has now expanded to a broad cultural category that can include Russia as well as Australia. Senior Minister Lee accordingly contrasts the "West's" decadence to "Asian values," a notion based on an equally homogenizing view of Asia with a history that precedes Huntington's conversion.[31]

The "re-enchantment with culture" in Asia, as the anthropologist Aihwa Ong has called it, goes back to the anticolonial modernizing project. For anticolonial elites, who were forced to adopt the Western trappings of the modernizing nation-state, the claim of cultural authenticity was an important tool to distinguish themselves from their colonial predecessors.[32] But the current infatuation with "Asianness" started with Western academics and business schools producing cultural explanations for the "economic miracles," first of the "Asian tiger economies" and then of China. For economists, of course, there was a set of measurable parameters that constituted the "Asian model": high savings rates, low overhead costs, low social spending, and so on. Nobel laureate Joseph Stiglitz, for example, has untiringly pointed out that savings rates in Asia before World War II were not very high, and that the reason for today's high savings rate in Malaysia and Singapore is that employees are required by law to pay higher percentages of their salaries into a compulsory savings fund than is required anywhere else.

Despite such simple explanations for economic facts, many commentators in the late 1980s and early 1990s were more interested in discovering the values that supposedly stood behind them— for example, thrift behind high savings rates, a family-oriented society behind low social spending. So they came up with "Asian values" such as—to present a typical set—education, teamwork, sacrificing the present for the future, planning for the long term, stability of society, acceptance of inequality, and moral behavior. The empirical justification for selecting these values was furnished by experimental psychological studies such as those by Michael Harris Bond and Kuo-shu Yang.[33] Although described as "Asian," these values were specifically linked to Confucian or Chinese ethics, since, as the writers pointed out, the economies of Southeast Asia were driven by overseas Chinese entrepreneurship. Max Weber had famously argued that Confucian ethics were to blame for a lack of capitalist development in modern China.[34] Now they were seen as singularly suited to what was at the time referred to as "Confucian capitalism" or "*guanxi* capitalism," a capitalism based on personal connections (*guanxi*) and the values of solidarity, hierarchy, discipline, and the like, rather than on the proverbial "level playing field."

The "Asian values" discourse was pioneered by Westerners and, to a lesser extent, ethnic Chinese academics in the United States, Hong Kong, and Taiwan.[35] This was one of the earliest examples of the now common trend of area-studies academics acting as business and political consultants. As it happened, they served as bridges between Western business and Asian politicians. The discourse was quickly picked up by other Asian leaders: Lee Kuan Yew of Singapore, whose interview with Fareed Zakaria, editor in chief of *Foreign Affairs*, was entitled "Culture Is Destiny"; Prime Minister Mahathir Mohamad and his deputy, Anwar Ibrahim, in Malaysia; to a lesser extent President Suharto of Indonesia; and later the leadership of the People's Republic of China (where it is usually referred to as "traditional Chinese virtues") and the Beijing-appointed chief executive of Hong Kong, Tung Chee Hwa.[36] In their politics, upholding Asian (or Chinese) values meant emphasis on traditional values and ethnic cohesion, the denial of universally applicable values such as human rights, the condemnation of Western "social evils," and an emphasis on virtuous, clean leadership and a loyal public service working in the best interest of the people, as opposed to the spontaneous preference of the people who do not have the qualifications to know what is best for society. Western individualism had done its positive job in the past but now has led to economic stagnations, cultural decline, and social disintegration.

The early 1990s, the time of the fastest economic growth in Southeast Asia, were also the heyday of "Asian values" in international politics. At the Asian Human Rights Conference in Bangkok in 1993, for example, China, Singapore, Malaysia, Indonesia, and Burma were the main articulators of a particularly Asian human rights concept (with lukewarm support from Thailand and the Philippines). They took a similar stand at the World Conference on Human Rights in Vienna that same year, where the Chinese foreign minister put forward a proposition that "individuals must put the states' rights before their own."[37]

The Asian values offensive came at a time when Western governments were attempting to find their way out of a breakdown of relations with China following the 1989 Tiananmen massacre. The cultural relativist argument put forward by Asian values proponents helped justify the choice of "constructive engagement" with China over sanctions; multilateral over bilateral (if any) human rights talks with China, Indonesia, and Burma; unlinking human and labor rights questions from trade; and stopping the sponsorship of UN resolutions condemning rights abuses. Apart from academics, lawyers and politicians advocating the cultural relativist concepts of "Asian democracy" or "Asian values" emerged in many Western countries. Discussions of cultural difference became a vehicle through which issues such as democracy, civil society, and human rights could be addressed or skirted. For example, as the political scientist Michael Drake has documented, the Asia-Europe Summit Meetings (ASEM), a standing consultation between the European Union and the Association of Southeast Asian Nations (ASEAN) in 1996, defers dialogue on the "respect for civil, political, social, economic, and cultural rights" until a "better understanding between the regions" is reached. Culture in this process is understood as the "heritage" of two regions that comprise "some of the oldest civilizations in the world," a formulation so vague as to exclude any debate on its content.[38]

At the same time, as is discussed in more detail in chapter 6, it has become commonplace to refer to the supposed cultural specificities of Asia—"face" or *guanxi*—in the context of international business negotiations. As Pascal Lamy, the director-general of the World Trade Organization, commented in 2006: "You can't deal with the Chinese by banging on the table. . . . You have to understand the notion of face-saving."[39] Smaller European states in particular are using cultural relativist discourse in their diplomacy, trying to outbid each other in accessing the Chinese market by repeating phrases China's government wants to hear. Alexandra Dobolyi, a Hungarian Socialist member of the European Parliament (EP) and a self-confessed lover of China who aspired for the chairmanship of the EP's foreign affairs committee, has cited classical aphorisms while praising the Chinese Communist Party's protection of private property.[40] Yet, since references to culture are devoid of attempts to introduce the complexities of contemporary China to European publics, the effect on these publics, rather than a greater understanding of China, is further alienation, compounded by an impression of cynical jockeying for the markets of an inscrutable but menacing country.

The financial crisis that hit Southeast Asia in 1997 and 1998 dampened Western interest in "Asian values," but the term has entered the language of mainstream media, and Asian political leaders and Western business school fans continue to employ it here and there. Jusuf Kalla, Indonesia's vice president and chairman of former dictator Suharto's Golkar Party, suggested that East Asian countries should "adopt Asian values," which he described as an ethic that prioritized cooperation over competition, to overcome gaps between their levels of development.[41] The champion of Asian values these days is China—as reflected in the tenor of the 2006 Beijing Forum and the broader ideology of a "harmonious society" and "community building" that the Communist Party has embraced since 2004.

The Asian values discourse appears to have been created and sustained by academics, outside observers, and ruling elites: nongovernmental organizations (NGOs), where they exist, have shown little interest for reasons that are discussed below. The case of Eurasianism, an ideology that similarly links the makeup of political institutions and choices of lifestyle to a deeply rooted Russian cultural essence that is contrasted with the West's, is somewhat different. The *Altai Messenger*, a bilingual publication of the Fund for a 21st Century Altai, an NGO in Southern Siberia, is, like the fund itself, financed by environmental foundations in the United States. The magazine's editors are passionate believers in Eurasianism, a philosophy that sees the Russian "civilization" as a bridge between "Oriental spirituality" and Western rationality. Editor Mikhail Shishin has stressed that "Russians are neither European nor Asian, but combine both heritages and are therefore ideally suited to holistic and organic thinking, ideally suited to solve global problems."[42]

An article by a local scholar in *The Altai Messenger* couches this thought in specifically Huntingtonian terminology: "Russia is the core of a special Eurasian civilization . . . which exists currently as a unity of the Slavic, Turko-Mongolic, and Arctic subcivilizations."[43]

Eurasianism as a philosophy is originally linked to the writings of the painter and theosophist Nikolai Roerich (1874–1947), who left Russia for India after the Bolshevik revolution, and geologist Vladimir Vernadskii's (1863–1945) theory of the "noosphere," composed of all the interacting minds on Earth. These ideas gained new popularity after the collapse of the Soviet Union. In the 1996 presidential decree on the transition of Russia to sustainable development, that goal is linked with the notion of the noosphere: "The advancement of humanity to sustainable development ultimately would lead to the emergence of the sphere of wisdom (the noosphere) . . . when the spiritual values and knowledge of humankind, existing in harmony with the environment, will become the criterion of national and individual wealth."[44] The decree states that "the idea of sustainable development is extremely consonant with the customs, spirit and mentality of Russia."[45]

A prime advocate of both sustainable development and the concept of the noosphere, academician Nikolai Moiseev is also a nationalistic theorist of "civilisational faultlines" who uses the term "ecological imperative" to denote the need for "restrictions on the activities of humankind."[46] But he represents only one strand in the motley Eurasianist movement, whose influence in Russia has expanded as it moved from the political and academic fringe to challenge "Atlanticism"—the view, dominant during the Yeltsin presidency, that Russia's natural allies were Europe and North America—near the centers of power.[47] While the Eurasianism of environmental NGOs emphasizes spirituality and ecology, other strands subscribe to an explicitly nationalistic, anti-Western political "theory" associated with such figures as the philosopher Alexandr Dugin, founder of the Eurasia Party, a former associate of the anti-Semitic and racist National Bolshevik Party, and later an adviser to leading Russian politicians, supposedly close to former Russian president Vladimir Putin. Like the Asian values discourse, this political Eurasianism has been invoked as a rationale not only for the rejection of Western demands for upholding regional autonomy and freedoms of association and the press during Putin's second presidency, but also for foreign policy choices.[48] This is in line with statements by Mikhail Titarenko, an influential China scholar and the head of the Institute for Far Eastern Studies of the Russian Academy of Sciences. Titarenko has written that "the Eurasian character of Russian civilization opens the possibility of new intercivilizational and international relations founded on the principles of co-development and mutual influence, allowing to solve the problems of . . . preserving civilization diversity."[49]

Discourses of regional cultural essence have also sprung up in other places, including the "Pacific Way," which emphasizes tradition, stability, and by implication "traditional" chiefly rule, in the South Pacific, and various attempts to define a pan-African political tradition.[50] Because of the relative weight of these regions in international politics, these discourses have not attracted the same attention as "Asian values" or Eurasianism. But the range of contexts in which the term "civilization" is now employed is even broader—from the chief brand manager of *The Times of India* rejoicing over the global expansion of Indian businesses to Maciej Giertych, the Polish professor and member of the European Parliament for the xenophobic League of Polish Families, whose report "Civilisations at War in Europe" caused an uproar in early 2007.[51]

Indeed, if "civilizational fault lines" are the cause of international conflicts, then "dialogue between civilizations" is the way to solve them. The concept was introduced to the UN by former Iranian president Mohammad Khatami and served as the basis for the United Nations' decision to make 2001 "the Year of Dialogue among Civilizations."[52] In 2005, Spanish prime minister José Luis Rodriguez Zapatero, supported by UN secretary general Kofi Annan and Turkish prime minister Recep Tayyip

Erdoğan, launched an initiative called Alliance of Civilizations, again intended to foster "mutual respect between civilizations and cultures."[53] As noted earlier, the Asia-Europe Summit Meetings also deploy the language of "cultural dialogue," and the European Union declared 2008 "the Year of Intercultural Dialogue." The German government has been actively promoting a "dialogue between cultures": the minister of defense, Franz Josef Jung, even declared that German soldiers in Afghanistan are "part of the dialogue of cultures."[54] The Chinese prime minister, Wen Jiabao, similarly called for a "wide-ranging dialogue of civilizations" in a speech at Harvard University on 10 December 2003. Institutes and centers for "civilizational dialogue" have sprung up from Kuala Lumpur to Buenos Aires. The International Progress Organiza-tion, a Vienna-based NGO that prides itself on being "among the first . . . worldwide to promote the idea of inter-civilizational dialogue," has contributed to twelve international conferences on the subject since the terror attacks of 9/11, covering terrain from Baku to Seoul and from Tehran to Copenhagen.[55]

Why Huntington Is Wrong

Huntington's civilizations, "Asian values," Eurasianism, and the other discourses of cultural specificities all share very similar flaws that render them useless as analytical categories but make them politically useful. Next we examine these flaws, the impact they have had on U.S. strategy in the "war on terror," and the service they have done to authoritarian leaders in Asia.

First, Huntington's grouping of countries into civilizations is arbitrary. In Western Europe he treats majority-Catholic and majority-Protestant countries as part of the same civilization (but, counterintuitively to many, he excludes its "cradle," Greece). Yet Huntington separates Latin America from Western civiliza-tion—an argument that becomes important in his later work on the "Hispanic Challenge" to the United States (see chapter 4)— mainly on the basis of its Catholic majority. Japan is singled out as a separate civilization, even though it, like Korea and Vietnam, was firmly in the orbit of Chinese cultural influence until the nineteenth century, when its government moved to adopt a nativist ideology and downplay shared traditions. The Islamic "civilization" includes Arabs, Bosnians, Iranians, Malays, Sudanese, and Turks, privileging a shared majority religion over extraordinarily different life-worlds that are, locally, shared with large numbers of Christians and adherents of other religions, or no religion. Huntington has not quite worked out Southeast Asia; his book ends with a scenario for a third world war that begins when the United States rushes to aid Vietnam (a Sinic nation if there ever was one!), which is being attacked by China.

For Huntington, of course, such shared life-worlds are part of the problem. They mark the frayed, conflict-prone edges of "civilizations." Huntingtonians' most important argument in support of their master is that, as he predicted, most conflicts take place across civilizational "fault lines." For a while the count appeared to be in his favor. Didn't Bosnia fall apart along the "fault lines" between the Western, Orthodox, and Islamic civilizations? Didn't the fighting in the Sudan pitch the Muslim rulers of the north against the Christian tribes of the south? But in Kosovo the "West" came to the rescue of "Islam" against the "Orthodox." And in the last Balkans battleground, Macedonia, a "Muslim" Albanian insurgency received remarkably little support from ethnoreligious kin in Albania or Kosovo.[56] The north-south conflict in the Sudan has come to an (at least provisional) end, while the fighting in the western province of Darfur, called a genocide by U.S. officials, involves Muslim militias killing Muslim villagers. Of course, there is no "fault line" anywhere near the bloodiest of civil wars: in Sri Lanka, Rwanda, and now Iraq.

Huntington ignores internal diversity. For him the East German neo-Nazi who spends his free time desecrating Jewish tombs shares his fundamental values with the charitable baroness from Frankfurt. In Huntington's view the Germans of today, preoccupied with shutting down nuclear power stations, are essentially the same as the Germans of the 1930s, preoccupied with locking up Jews. He does not deny internal diversity or cultural change over time. His views do not preclude friendship between individuals from different civilizations or enmity between those from the same one. Rather, Huntington's argument is that individual diversity is ultimately not what determines relations between societies, because it is relatively superficial compared with the deep-seated differences between civilizations. "A civilization," in this definition, is "the highest cultural grouping of people and the broadest level of cultural identity people have short of that which distinguishes humans from other species. It is defined both by common objective elements, such as language, history, religion, customs, institutions, and by the subjective self-identification of people."[57]

Huntington adds that the values that define a civilization are those "to which successive generations in a given society have attached primary importance."[58] A fundamental similarity of deeply held values prevents intracivilizational differences from spilling over into violent conflict. You may think that the average European dislikes the United States and is indifferent toward Japan, but according to Huntington: "The economic issues between the United States and Europe are no less serious than those between the United States and Japan, but they do not have the same political salience and emotional intensity because the differences between American culture and European culture are so much less than those between American civilization and Japanese civilization."[59] Conversely, even the most cordial understanding between two nations that belong to different civilizations is ultimately an illusion. Trade with China and Japan may be the foundation of Australia's prosperity, but don't be fooled. Huntington continues: "Asians generally pursue their goals with others in ways which are subtle, indirect, modulated, devious, non-judgemental, non-moralistic, and non-confrontational. Australians, in contrast, are the most direct, blunt, outspoken, some would say insensitive, people in the English-speaking world."[60]

Huntington does not acknowledge this, but when he posits the existence of shared values to which "successive generations in a given society have attached primary importance," he relies on the great nation-building projects of the nineteenth and twentieth centuries. A sixteenth-century Hungarian may have felt a bond to his fellow Catholics, but his sense of difference from a Protestant Saxon may not have been any less intense than when he faced a

Muslim Turk. Huntington's account of history considers the Cold War a glitch in the natural history of civilizations, but he makes no attempt to account for earlier wars such as the Hundred Years' War between France and England or the Thirty Years' War, which pitted Protestant and Catholic powers in Europe against each other. There is, as Benedict Anderson wrote, a paradox between "the objective modernity of nations to the historian's eye versus their subjective antiquity in the eyes of nationalists."[61]

The idea of a common Western civilization is similarly an "invented tradition," as Eric Hobsbawm and Terence Ranger have written: a product of the European Enlightenment that replaced the earlier, tentative notion of Christendom (from which those of a dissenting branch—Orthodox, Protestants, or Catholics—had often been excluded, not to mention such exotic varieties as Syrians or Ethiopians).[62] Similarly, "Hindu" as a cultural category covering the diverse inhabitants of the Indian subcontinent emerged from the interaction between colonial officials, missionaries, and local intellectual elites. The term "Japanese civilization" is an even more recent creation. Although it was the Meiji Restoration in 1868 that ushered in an era of modern Japanese nationalism and nation-building as a reaction to Western military power, it was not until the late 1920s that a self-conscious formulation of Japanese cultural distinctiveness, with "harmony" (wa) at its core, took a coherent shape, to a large extent as a reaction to the Japanese view of the West. After the war the idea of Japanese uniqueness lost much of its currency and returned to the mainstream only in the 1970s, at the very time when Western authors were beginning to explore the "values" behind the Japanese economic "miracle."[63]

What of Confucianism, often portrayed as the basis of "Asian values"? In his 1993 article, Huntington identifies "Confucian" as one of the civilizations (he later changed it to "Sinic"). It is considered commonplace among political scientists and journalists that in Chinese-majority societies, as well as in China's former vassals Korea and Vietnam, Confucian thought exercises a dominant influence on the norms of society and government. Essentially an ethical and political philosophy, Confucianism was first canonized in China in the twelfth century and then modified several times as it was adopted as the official teaching of successive imperial dynasties. But one of us remembers the embarrassment of a fellow American student who, making a presentation to a Chinese language class about the position of women in China, back-translated the term "Confucianism" into *Kongzizhuyi*, combining Confucius's Chinese name (Kongzi) with the usual Chinese term for "-ism." The Chinese students in the classroom burst out giggling. For in Chinese, there is no such thing as "Confucianism": the term was invented by Jesuits missionaries, seeking to encapsulate an essence of the Chinese worldview to match the West's Christianity, in the sixteenth through the eighteenth centuries.[64]

A decidedly secular philosophy, Confucianism has often been included in Western comparative writings on "world religions." In China itself, Chinese tradition is most often summarized as the "Three Teachings": Confucianism, Taoism, and Buddhism. Confucianism may have been favored by the late imperial state, which set up shrines of Confucius and conducted official worship ceremonies, but both popular religion and the writings of most literati reflected (and still reflect) syncretism. After the fall of the empire in 1911, the figure of Confucius faded, then fell victim to the "anti–Lin Biao, anti-Confucius" campaign during the Cultural Revolution and was not returned to its official pedestal as "Teacher of Generations" until the 1990s (the first time, incidentally, for a mainland Chinese government to introduce the English term "Confucianism" in its language).

The Confucian tradition does not constitute a hegemonic worldview. Rather, it consists of a large body of writings that lend themselves to different interpretations. For example, the Confucian hierarchy of the classes has the gentleman (the scholar-official) on top, followed by the farmer, the craftsman, and at the bottom the merchant. Adherents of the "Asian values" correspondingly stress the Confucian respect for learning and authority but also manage to credit the Confucian ethic with favoring trade. (This is not new; the *bourgeois gentilhommes* of imperial times who purchased official titles and educated their children in the classics attempted to elevate their status by using the term "Confucian merchant" [*rushang*].) One man who enriched himself through shady real-estate deals and served two years in administrative detention has recently opened a small Confucian "academy," actually a house on a hill near Beijing, where he and his guests talk about "national learning."

Proponents of "Asian values" stress such aspects of Confucian ethics as obedience to the authority of rulers and parents. No doubt, *The Analects of Confucius* and the works of nearly all of his followers lay great worth by the proper ordering of relationships and the fulfilment of obligations on both sides (ruler and subject, father and son, and so on). But for everyone who has actually read *The Analects*, it is also clear that the moral obligation of the subject to follow his ruler only exists when the ruler is just; in fact, when he is not, the subject is obliged to protest and refuse to serve him, as Confucius himself did. (In Book 12 of *The Analects*, he commented: "The term 'great minister' refers to those who serve their lord according to the Way and who, when this is no longer possible, relinquish office."[65]) Qu Yuan, an official who committed suicide after remonstrating with the prince he served, has been remembered in an annual festival for two millennia.

So while Confucianism is hardly a philosophy of democratic rights, neither is it an underpinning of uncritical obedience. It was precisely for this reason that Confucians were subjected to purges during the reigns of the Qin Emperor in the third century B.C.E. and Mao Zedong two thousand years later. Since the twentieth century, the leaders of the "new neo-Confucian" school—such as the Harvard professor Tu Wei-ming—have focused not so much on hierarchy and tradition as on the importance of virtuous leadership, meritorious advancement in life and work, and social solidarity, along with the defense of the doctrine (shared, of course, with Plato and Nietzsche) that the majority of people is unfit, insufficiently moral, and not cultured enough to decide what society to choose. Some philosophers—most recently joined by the venerable Daniel Bell—have actually tried to develop a Confucian theory of democracy and human rights.[66]

In any case, using "Confucianism" to explain the values of 1.4 billion Chinese is surely as absurd as trying to derive the behavior of contemporary Europeans from the Bible or from Plato's *Republic*.

It is even more absurd to extend the reasoning to an unknown number of "Asians" who can reach back to an even greater diversity of philosophical traditions that they can interpret in any way they please. For example, the Nobel Prize–winning economist Amartya Sen recently devoted an entire book to Indian traditions of egalitarianism and universal tolerance, particularly the writings of Emperor Ashoka in the third century B.C.E., and their similarities and differences compared with Chinese traditions.[67] Needless to say, the concept of Asia itself is a Western-invented category that meant different things at different times (even today, "Asian" means one thing in London and another in New York), and any common sense of "Asianness"—unclear though its reach may be—is a recent product of satellite television, karaoke, economic growth, and "Pacific Century" hype. It is hardly more than, in Aihwa Ong's term, "a momentary glow of fraternity."[68]

At first sight, such ahistoricity does not invalidate Huntington's argument. What he implies, after all, is that the cultural identity created in the process of nation-building—even if it is relatively recent—must be defended. When he writes that "when Americans look for their cultural roots, they find them in Europe," he is seemingly making a factually false statement (by ignoring all of those who do not).[69] But in fact, Huntington argues that the particular cultural identity that the United States gave itself at the time of its foundation, based on its European roots, should not be altered, and those Americans who hail from other parts of the world must also embrace it. In other words, he is taking a normative position rather than committing an analytical mistake. A much more serious problem with this argument is that it ignores all the changes cultural identities have already undergone since the creation of national ideologies. He argues, of course, that earlier migrants to the United States have embraced its "values," either because they (coming from Northern Europe) were culturally closer to them or because they were numerically insignificant. It is only today, with massive Latin American immigration, combined with the flawed policy of multiculturalism, that these values are in danger.

But what would Huntington say to Guy Verhofstadt and

Maciej Giertych, both Brussels-based politicians at pains to defend European values? Giertych, an extreme social conservative from strongly Catholic Poland, a Huntington adept, and an opponent of mixing, has written: "Our civilisation has to be actively defended. Even at the risk of poverty, we must insist on having control over our children. . . . We must demand that TV programs promote noble causes. . . . We must also demand that behaviour proper for our civilisation be lauded and improper scorned. We must insist that immoral music be banned. . . . Otherwise, our civilisation will lose."[70] Giertych's values are very close to the "Asian values" of filial piety, obedience, and propriety taught in Chinese schools, or to the "Islamic values" taught in Pakistani madrassas. (Among others, his party is trying to make possession of pornography a crime punishable by a year in prison.) In his criticism of British multiculturalism under Margaret Thatcher, the sociologist Andrew Jakubowicz charged that it "allowed the myths of 'Victorian Values'" such as family cohesion, hard work, and obedience to authority "to have contemporary currency . . . albeit culturally foreign."[71] Yet Giertych insists that these values are unique and fundamental to "Latin civilisation" and as such must be defended today against external influences. A hundred years ago his view would have been commonplace in Europe; today, these ideas are represented by the Vatican. Indeed, as the sociologist José Casanova has pointed out, the same accusations of being hostile to modernization that Huntington makes against Islam could not long ago have been made against Catholicism.[72]

The values emphasized by Giertych are also close to the values of family and religion often voiced in the United States. But a global Gallup opinion poll in 2007 found that "in terms of their spiritual values and the emphasis on the future, Americans have more in common with Muslims [i.e., people living in Muslim-majority Middle Eastern countries] than they do with their Western counterparts in Europe." What Muslims "admired" in "Western culture," the survey found, was "liberty, the democratic system, technology and freedom of speech." At the same time, they condemned "promiscuity and a sense of moral decay." That seems like the trademark of British and American conservatives.[73] Meanwhile,

Giertych's values are light years away from those of the former Belgian prime minister Guy Verhofstadt, another aspiring theorist of European values, as afraid as he is for their integrity. Verhofstadt's "Fourth Citizens Manifesto" bears the subtitle "A Plea for a Free and Open Society." According to this manifesto, in the face of the strengthening of fundamentalist religion and attacks on our freedoms, Europeans must resist defensive impulses of closure and defend their central values, "in which it is not tribal group think but each individual that occupies central position," from "the fear, the souring, the cramping-up that many of today's politicians preach."[74]

Both Giertych and Verhofstadt do what Huntington says responsible politicians should—but, though referring to the same corpus of European civilization, they could not disagree more about its contents. This is not mere sophistry or electioneering: European governments are making what seem to be earnest attempts to formulate the shared values of their societies—often with surprising results. During its brief reign in Rotterdam, the anti-immigrant party Leefbaar Nederland (Livable Netherlands) enacted a citizens' code that included such clauses as "We treat homosexuals in the same way as heterosexuals and with respect; We treat those of (other) faiths and those of no faith in the same way and with respect."[75] The center-right government produced a video to test the compatibility of would-be migrants with the Dutch lifestyle. It included a topless woman and two men kissing. Who would have thought, even thirty years ago, that a European conservative party would include such images in the essence of its national culture? And if such diversity of traditions and speed of change are realities in Europe, can they not exist in Asian countries as well?

Postulating cultural essences obscures not only historical change and internal diversity within a "civilization," it also conveniently hides the way particular traditions are used by political and business elites to serve their own interests. After the end of the Cold War (and after the Tiananmen massacre in China), a number of governments were keen to find justification for authoritarianism in imported views of their region. Singapore's leadership, headed by Lee Kuan Yew, was perhaps the first to actively promote "Confucian values" (renamed "Asian values" in 1991 to include the country's non-Chinese population). Lee's embrace of Confucian values occurred at a time when support for his People's Action Party (PAP) was waning. Earlier, in his struggle for independence from Britain, Lee—a Cambridge-educated socialist—had insisted on the right to peaceful protests in the colonial Legislative Assembly, commenting in 1956 that "repression is a habit that grows."[76]

In the early postindependence period—the 1960s—traditional cultural values had been seen as inhibiting modernization, and the government praised individualism as necessary for survival.[77] It was in the late 1970s, when the PAP vote started to decline with the erosion of the industrial proletariat, while the workers' movement was threatening to drive away investors, that Lee began talking about the corrosive effects of Western influence and exhorting Singapore's Chinese not to forget their traditions and cultural identity. Consequently, the government introduced measures to promote Mandarin, began teaching Confucianism at school (in 1982), suppressed the use of Chinese dialects and "Singlish" on television as inconsistent with the aim of cultivating cultural purity, promoted the revival of traditional Chinese clan and native-place associations, and created a Chinese Heritage Center. The *White Paper on Asian values* (1991) served to guide educational and cultural policies.[78] It was at this time that Samuel Huntington, yet to enter his clash-of-civilizations period, commented that "if he had wanted to, a political leader far less skilled than Lee Kwan Yew could have produced democracy in Singapore."[79]

Simultaneously, the government increased the intimidation of opposition leaders—Wah-Piow Tan was sentenced to a year in prison in 1976 and then exiled, along with Lee's former fellow socialists—and created the strict regulations of public and private life that Singapore is now famous for. In an article entitled "Ten Asian Values That Help East Asia's Economic Progress, Prosperity," Tommy Koh, Singapore's ambassador to the United States, listed collectivism, industry, and frugality ("in contrast to the Western addiction to consumption"), love of education, and importance of the family (low divorce rates and caring for one's parents) before moving on to "national team work. Unions and employers view each other as partners, not class enemies. Together, government, business and employees work cooperatively, for the good of the nation."[80]

For good measure, though, the observance of these values is assured through a compulsory savings fund (the Central Provident Fund, created by the British colonial authorities!) to which all employees contribute a fixed percentage of their incomes. Singles under thirty-five are not eligible for public housing, which accounts for 90 percent of all housing, and so they are forced to live with their parents. Medical expenses of a nonworking individual are paid for from the compulsory medical savings of his or her working spouse and children. Children are obligated by law to support their aged parents financially. Yet divorce is on the increase, and many young people choose to dodge their obligations by moving abroad. The Maintenance of Parents Tribunal heard 773 lawsuits by parents against delinquent children between 1996 and 2001.[81]

In the People's Republic of China the discourse on "the traditional virtues of the Chinese race"—solidarity, frugality, diligence, and patriotism—first showed up in the 1980s in publications for overseas Chinese as a strategy to rekindle their affiliation with China after a period of estrangement. In the 1960s and 1970s overseas Chinese property in China had been confiscated and relatives of overseas Chinese persecuted. Domestically, the government deployed this rhetoric after the Tiananmen Square crackdown, shifting the content of such projects as "building socialist spiritual civilization" and the "virtue education" curriculum in favor of an emphasis on the unique continuity of the "five-thousand-year-old Chinese civilization" and introducing the separate subject of "patriotic education." The China scholar Michael Lackner has written about this neotraditionalism: "From pieces put together eclectically and hardly ever interrogated for their origin and development arose a picture of an immutable culture in which Confucius stands peacefully next to the first emperor, mortal enemy of the Confucians; Mao Zedong next to his mortal enemy Chiang Kai-shek (at whose birthplace there is a memorial); the Communist Party with its mortal enemies the exiled intellectuals of the 1950s and 1960s; the man who launched the Taiping Rebellion (1851–1864), Hong Xiuquan, next to his mortal enemy Zeng Guofan, the man who annihilated the Taiping army, in a panorama of the officially proclaimed 'glorious five-thousand-year history of Chinese culture.'"[82]

The media researchers Song Xianlin and Gary Sigley have cited the following as a typical example of 1990s "civilizationism": "China is . . . a land . . . with an ancient history and glorious culture. She has nurtured generations of diligent, hardworking, intelligent and courageous sons and daughters. . . . She is without rival in this world. Ancient Babylon, Greece, Rome and India have all disintegrated, weakened and disappeared, only that known as the 'middle kingdom' refuses to sink. China has always strengthened itself in the fight against destiny and maintained her unity and civilisational luster."[83] The government also renewed its support for the promotion of traditional arts, kung fu, Confucianism, and religions deemed traditionally Chinese (as long as it is carried out by state-controlled, "patriotic" organizations) and of "scientific research" to prove that "Western democracy" is not suitable for Chinese conditions. The first international cultural conference to take place in China after Tiananmen was on Confucian thought.[84] A Confucius Association and a Yellow Emperor Association were established, headed respectively by a vice premier and a retired general. At the government-organized celebration of Confucius's 2545th birthday, Chairman Jiang Zemin personally delivered a two-hour speech on his Confucian upbringing.[85]

In the 2000s the promotion of a "harmonious society" (hexie shehui) and "community building" (shequ jianshe)—following, according to some, the model of Singapore—has produced slogans on apartment blocks such as "Everyone for the community, the community for everyone." "Harmony" (he), central for Japan's self-image since the 1920s, is an "Asian value" now ubiquitous in China too. Even in articles on real estate development, one finds passages like "the spirit of Chinese culture can be summarized in one character: he."[86] The concept of social harmony serves the purposes of state disciplining; it is invoked whenever protesters—

for example, against land confiscation—are subjected to arrest and moral condemnation.

In the run-up to the 2008 Beijing Olympics, campaigns to improve the manners of big-city residents as well as tourists traveling abroad refer to China in Confucian terms as "the land of propriety" (*li yi zhi bang*) and call on citizens to live up to that tradition. The discourse of "traditional values" continues to be routinely invoked in reports on Chinese migrants abroad—many of whom are entrepreneurs—and has established itself firmly in the vocabulary of ordinary citizens. Although, as in Singapore, few of them have ever read Confucius and most would have a hard time naming these values beyond, perhaps, solidarity and hard work, a popular Confucius industry is emerging (again, imitating Singapore a decade or two earlier). Yu Dan, a professor at Beijing Normal University, gained instant fame in 2006 with a series of televised lectures on Confucius, followed by a book that sold three million copies in three months. Universities are advertising programs in Confucianism aimed at business executives. Even street slogans produced by the Party's propaganda departments have begun quoting Confucius to buttress their messages, as in: "[The character] 'humaneness' is composed of 'man' and 'two': unity is strength!"

There are also explicit opponents of the Asian values discourse among Asia's prominent politicians. Not surprisingly, these tend to be those who have fought against autocratic regimes in their own countries. Apart from Lee Kuan Yew of the 1950s, these have included South Korean president Kim Dae Jung—who, as an ex-dissident and presidential candidate, challenged Lee's views in a rejoinder entitled "Is Culture Destiny? The Myth of Asia's Anti-democratic Values" in *Foreign Affairs*; the Philippine president Cory Aquino; and several leading Thai politicians.[87] These days, however, Asian culturalism seems on the rise—not only in China but also in Korea and Japan, where prime minister Abe Shinzō has presided over the introduction of a "patriotic education" curriculum in schools.

Yet another question is to what extent officially proclaimed values reflect the everyday behavior of average Chinese—or Singaporean, or Japanese—citizens. This is addressed in greater detail in chapter 6, were we contrast ethnographically documented behavior of Chinese migrants not only with the official discourse, but also the voluminous body of "intercultural expertise" that has emerged over the past decade to help (mostly) Western business-men deal with their Chinese counterparts. We conclude that, not really surprisingly, "Asian values" do correctly describe behavior in some situations but not in others. For example, experience bears out the idea of paternalistic employer-employee relations when managers of garment factories rely on kin and hometown networks of female workers to reduce fluctuation and discontent (counting on younger relatives not wanting to embarrass their older kin). But other factory managers—often fellow "Confu-cian" Taiwanese and Koreans—attempt to increase efficiency and reduce attrition using physical coercion, including locking dormi-tories and windows at night, not allowing toilet breaks, and using corporal punishment—even as they hang slogans saying "Take the Factory as Your Home" on the factory floor. Both systems have been widely documented in the Pearl River Delta.[88]

It is true that many fatal mining accidents are settled by com-pensation voluntarily paid by the mine to the worker's family, but the number of compensation cases reaching the courts is nonethe-less increasing rapidly. There were more than a hundred thousand court decisions on labor disputes in 2001, up from twenty-eight thousand in 1995.[89] Strikes and demonstrations by laid-off workers, many involving clashes with the police, are ubiquitous in Northeast China. And although, according to the idea of "*guanxi* capitalism," China and the other "Confucian economies" should be running on (to borrow the title of a book by Mayfair Yang) "gifts, favours and banquets," anger over corruption draws thou-sands of protesters to the streets every month.[90]

The perceived particularity of "Confucian capitalism" came in handy for governments when they wanted to convince foreign investors of the pliability of their workforce. Cultural arguments effectively worked in deflecting attention from dismal workplace conditions (even though no Western agency openly admitted having such multiple standards) and continue to be invoked by govern-

ments wanting to resist the push for Western labor and environmental standards that would raise the cost of their exports. The
investors are so convinced that by now they are leading the resistance against the adoption of these standards, slow and partial
though it may be. Thus Wal-Mart—which has used its buying
power to press its suppliers into paying even lower wages—is
spearheading an effort to derail a decision by the Chinese government to require the unionization of workers in foreign-owned
and joint-venture companies.[91] At the same time the company
boasts on its Web site of assuming corporate social responsibility in China, citing dozens of community projects from caring for
"senior citizens" to financing cleft palate surgeries for children.[92]

These corporations' insistence on keeping labor relations
informal is certainly reinforced by those business consultants
who have been exhorting Western companies to question their
"antagonistic" model of employer-employee relations and learn
from the "harmonious" practices of their Asian counterparts.
Fons Trompenaars, who calls himself "the world's greatest culture
guru," embraces this thesis, calling on his readers to face up "to
the Singaporean view that the West is, in some respects, decadent,
that its values belong to a retreating phase of Capitalism."[93] This
view earned him kudos from Singapore's ambassador-at-large,
Tommy Koh, who called the book "an impressive intellectual
achievement," and the personal encouragement by Lee Kuan Yew,
which Trompenaars proudly acknowledges in a later book, no
doubt facilitated the licensing of his consultancy in the country.

The "War on Terror": The West against Islam?

In 1993, Huntington singled out "the Confucian-Islamic connection" as the major threat "that has emerged to challenge Western
interests, values and power."[94] He devotes much space to documenting the "bloody borders" of the Islamic civilization, which,
according to him, has been at conflict with the West for the past
thirteen hundred years.[95] Many saw the attack on the World Trade
Center on 11 September 2001 as the ultimate confirmation of his
view as far as Islam was concerned (although reportedly Hunt-

ington himself did not share that view). Huntington-inspired Web sites, such as the Bloody Borders Project, were set up to monitor terrorist attacks by Islamists.[96] Suddenly, the clash of civilizations was also seen as a domestic concern. Europe—more than North America or Australia—saw a surge of books and articles asserting that it had been nurturing an enemy within. Ignoring Muslims who were unwilling to accept "Western values" and were in fact sharpening their claws in preparation for a showdown, Europe had turned its back on its civilizational ally, the United States. To name but a few of these books: *Londonistan* by Melanie Phillips, *America Alone* by Mark Steyn, *The Force of Reason* by Oriana Fallaci, and *While Europe Slept* by Bruce Bawer.

The Bush administration—since the early, infamous speech by the president in which he used the word "crusade"—has strenuously denied that its war was against Islam. Yet rather than turning to researchers of Muslim youth in the West (and it was Muslim youth who turned out to be the main perpetrators of the 9/11 attacks) the makers of American policy decided to enlist the expertise of Bernard Lewis and consult the work of Raphael Patai, scholars whose work describes Islam or "the Arab mind" from a classicist perspective, as a homogeneous whole. Previously, Palestinian, Lebanese, Libyan, and Iranian terrorism, and even the Taliban had been seen as growing out of more or less specific local conflicts, although with a potential to be united in a militant Islam—a possibility perhaps first discussed in 1989, when Ayatollah Khomeini issued the fatwa demanding the novelist Salman Rushdie's execution. But after 9/11, Islamic terrorism was seen as a product of Islam *tout court*, as reflecting the state of what Huntington labeled the "Islamic crescent" from Morocco to Indonesia.

Bernard Lewis is a British-born historian of the Ottoman Empire and a professor at Princeton University. Best known in academic circles for his early work on the modernization of Turkey, he has long been active as a public commentator on Middle Eastern affairs. In 1990, Lewis was the first to coin the term "clash of civilizations" to refer to the relationship between Islam and the West.[97] Hungarian-born Raphael Patai, who died in 1996, was a relatively obscure anthropologist who endeavored to uncover "the

Arab mentality" much in the way of "national character" studies. Media personality Lewis and quaint Orientalist Patai make an odd pair, yet the two have arguably had the greatest impact of all academic specialists on the Middle East on post-9/11 U.S. policy making. While Lewis received invitations to White House dinners, Patai's books were suddenly being unearthed, reissued, and ordered for the U.S. Army. The administration's interest in both scholars was, no doubt, aroused by their promise to describe the essential characteristics of "the Islamic/Arab world." Yet this promise was based on flimsy evidence.

Among other quotations from Patai's *The Arab Mind*, these few were culled by the Middle East editor of *The Guardian*, Brian Whittaker, who wrote an article on Patai's influence on the United States military establishment:

- "Why are most Arabs, unless forced by dire necessity to earn their livelihood with 'the sweat of their brow,' so loath to undertake any work that dirties the hands?"
- "The all-encompassing preoccupation with sex in the Arab mind emerges clearly in two manifestations."
- "Once aroused, Arab hostility will vent itself indiscriminately on all outsiders."[98]

Patai's book devotes twenty-five pages to "Arab sexuality," concluding that "the segregation of the sexes, the veiling of the women . . . and all the other minute rules that govern and restrict contact between men and women, have the effect of making sex a prime mental preoccupation in the Arab world."[99] He continued: "The Arab view is that masturbation is far more shameful than visiting prostitutes."[100] As for homosexuality in the Arab world, Patai describes it as hidden from the public eye, but it "is the rule, and practised completely in the open" in "outlying areas" such as the Siwa oasis in Egypt.[101]

A recent article in a popular Swiss weekly, *Die Weltwoche*, relies on Patai (plus quotations from the Koran) in its discussion of "Islam's problem with sex."[102] (We ask, What about Christianity's?) Yet it does not take a specialist to suspect that attitudes toward sex will differ between the Casablanca of the 1960s, where young women tended to go around in miniskirts rather than veils, and the Saudi Arabia of today. In the corporate boardrooms of Egypt, a secular state with vestiges of 1960s socialism, one sees more women than in those of Morocco, but they are also more likely to cover their heads. At university campuses in both countries, one sees lively interaction between the sexes, but with noticeably different dynamics. In Saddam Hussein's Iraq in the 1970s, women were allowed to join the army and made up nearly half of that country's teachers and dentists.[103] In today's Saudi Arabia, however, women are still prohibited to drive cars. Without going into a debate on the doctrinal differences between and within Shi'a, Sunni, and Sufi Islam, the variations of sex-related attitudes and practices even within the twenty-two Middle Eastern countries are easy to observe. The medical anthropologist Marcia Inhorn, for example, has noted the highly divergent policies on artificial insemination; it is banned in many Sunni countries, but couples often travel to Lebanon or Iran for the procedure.[104]

Patai's writing, a brand of cultural psychology, reflects the anthropological thinking of the so-called culture and personality school, popular in the mid-twentieth century (see chapter 6 for more on this topic). This school treats entire cultures as if they had personalities and makes broad generalizations based on coincidental evidence, not on any prolonged personal contact. Patai's insights on masturbation, for example, are based on a 1954 survey of Arab and U.S. students, in which Americans admitted to masturbating twice as often as Arabs, while Arabs declared to have visited more prostitutes. His views on homosexuality in "outlying areas" are drawn from 1935, 1936, and 1950 accounts, which, Patai admits, "need to be checked out by an anthropologically trained observer."[105] Elsewhere, ignoring substantial differences in marriage law and mistaking history for the present, he describes Arab men as being allowed to have four wives plus "slave girls" for concubines.

Pertinently for the current context, Patai states that Arabs "hate the West." He bases this on two quotations from 1950s books, one by Bernard Lewis. Here it is worthwhile to pause and think about both terms of the equation—not just "Arabs" but also "the West." A Gallup poll in 2007 found that although unfavorable views of the United States in Arab countries were more prevalent than ever, there was a wide variation in their dominance: 79 percent of Saudis held such views compared with 49 percent of Moroccans.[106] This latter statistic is similar to that of several European countries (in Germany and Spain it is 49 percent; in France, 47 percent).[107] Obviously, attitudes toward individuals depend on many factors. For example, a French tourist in French-speaking Morocco is likely to be viewed differently from an Oklahoman marine in Iraq. Finally, views have changed and fluctuated dramatically since Humphrey Bogart's visit to the opium den in Casablanca. In her research on Saudi tourists in Egypt, Lisa Wynn has found that local attitudes toward them were often far more negative than toward Western tourists, and that this is sometimes justified in terms of their "strange cultural habits."[108] Yet in Patai's account ways of life and attitudes to the West between Tangiers and Baghdad were more or less established by the fourteenth century and have changed little since.

The view of Islam as a fossilized civilization in fundamental opposition to the West is also the underlying theme of much of Bernard Lewis's scholarship. Lewis has long advanced the idea of a fundamental opposition between Islam and Christianity. He wrote in 1990: "The struggle between [Islam and Christianity] has now lasted for some 14 centuries. . . . For the first thousand years Islam was advancing, Christendom in retreat and under threat. . . . For the past 300 years, since the failure of the second Turkish siege of Vienna in 1683 and the rise of the European colonial empires in Asia and Africa, Islam has been on the defensive. . . . It should by now be clear that we are facing a . . . clash of civilizations—the perhaps irrational but surely historic reaction of an ancient rival against our Judeo-Christian heritage, our secular present, and the worldwide expansion of both."[109]

This rivalry, evolving in a straight line from the crusades to the Treaty of Carlowitz of 1699 (which marked the defeat of the Turkish army by the Hapsburg forces) right to the attack on the Twin Towers, is accompanied on the Muslim side by a "downward spiral of hatred and rage" against the West.[110] "I have no doubt that September 11 was the opening salvo of the final battle," commented Lewis in a *Newsweek* interview.[111] This conflated Osama bin Laden's religious mission with Saddam Hussein's recalcitrance toward the West and mainstream expression of frustration in a number of Muslim countries into a single force. In *What Went Wrong? Western Impact and Middle Eastern Response*, published a few months after 9/11, Lewis intends to analyze why the Middle East failed to modernize by itself—or to produce a positive response to Western modernization, a pattern that created the "downward spiral" and "in some measure produced" the terror attacks.[112]

In Lewis's reading, Muslim-Christian relations are symmetrical only in that they are described as one of "jihad and crusade, conquest and reconquest."[113] In most other aspects—such as in their curiosity about one another, their treatment of women, their sense of time, as well as the compatibility of Islam and Christianity with religious tolerance and democracy—they differ fundamentally.[114] In Lewis's writing, one can't miss a thinly concealed contempt for his subject matter, as when he contrasts the willingness to study Arabic, Persian, and Turkish and be curious about other civilizations in Christian countries with "the total lack of interest in Christian civilization" in the Islamic world.[115] He goes on to say: "The Renaissance, the Reformation and the technological revolution passed virtually unnoticed in the lands of Islam, where they were still inclined to dismiss the denizens of the lands beyond the western frontier as . . . barbarians."[116]

Many historians, including Columbia scholar Richard Bulliet, who recently completed a book entitled *The Case for Islamo-Christian Civilization*, disagree with Lewis's assessment.[117] Ottoman travelers, like Evliya Çelebi, whom Lewis repeatedly quotes, were the West's main sources of geographical knowledge on Eastern Europe and Western Asia. According to historian Shahid Alam, the most accurate map of the Americas, from 1513, was prepared by a Turkish admiral and cartographer. Unlike their British counterparts until 1882, married Muslim women in some regions could own property and enjoyed exclusive rights to their income.[118] Whether the main thrust of Lewis's historical argument is right or wrong—factoids can be found to support both sides—the fundamental problem with his method is that he wants to read the present through a lens of the relatively remote past, to the point of ignoring the twentieth century. This era, of course, brought the carving up and colonization of Arabic-speaking countries by the British and French, the subsequent European and U.S. support for corrupt and authoritarian regimes in Saudi Arabia, Egypt, Iraq, or Syria to secure oil and strategic positions in the Cold War, and the establishment and expansion of Israel and the continuing support it received from the West.

Bafflingly, Lewis treats these events not as history but as a "blame game" played by failed states. His chapters run rapidly through history from the Middle Ages till the last days of the Ottomans—or, rarely, the mid-twentieth century—and then extrapolate broadly to the present time. He also extrapolates across space. Lewis, whose reputation as a distinguished historian mainly rests on his early work on Ottoman and Turkish history and who has neither traveled extensively nor done fieldwork in Muslim countries, projects his view of that region onto the whole of the Middle East and beyond, to the "Islamic world." For him, what went wrong is Islam itself, becoming a closed-in, backward-looking religion in need of reformation, as Catholicism did before Luther.[119]

For a secularist who admires the antireligious legislation of the modern Turkish state founded by Atatürk, it is odd to expect so much from religion. It is also odd to put the 145 million Indian Muslims in the same basket with Iran's semi-theo-semi-democracy (based on radical reform!), Egypt's secular antidemocratism, and Saudi Arabia's absolute monarchy—a diversity that testifies to the region's highly divergent history since the Ottoman Empire was disbanded and Atatürk destroyed the caliphate, the central religious authority of the Muslim faith. In principle, Lewis's view of Islam as being stuck at an earlier developmental stage than Christianity is different from Patai's timeless Arabs. While Patai was a complete cultural determinist, Lewis is a universalist at the bottom of his heart. But in practice, Lewis's unwarranted temporal and spatial generalization reads much like Patai's. As Edward Said, a prominent critic of both Lewis and Patai, has pointed out: "The core of Lewis's ideology about Islam is that it never changes . . . and that any political, historical, and scholarly account of Muslims must begin and end with the fact that Muslims are Muslims."[120]

For many commentators, Lewis is the "intellectual godfather" of the Iraq invasion.[121] In the months following the 9/11 attacks, Lewis became a valued adviser to the U.S. administration. He attended a meeting of the Defense Advisory Board a week after the attacks.[122] Vice president Dick Cheney, at a later dinner in Lewis's honor, remarked that "in this new century, his wisdom is sought daily by policymakers, diplomats, fellow academics, and the news media."[123] In a similar vein, deputy secretary of defense Paul Wolfowitz paid tribute in 2002, saying that Lewis had "brilliantly placed the relationships and the issues of the Middle East into their larger context, with truly objective, original and always independent, thought. Bernard has taught us how to understand the complex and important history of the Middle East and use it to guide us where to go to build a better world for generations."[124]

Lewis's recipe for a "better world for generations" consisted in convincing the Bush administration to help history along, for "in that part of the world, nothing matters more than resolute will and force."[125] One official who sat in on some of the discussions between Cheney and Lewis remembers: "His view was: 'Get on with it. Don't dither.'"[126] Despite seeing "that part of the world" as long mired in immobility, Lewis was convinced that its ordinary residents would cheer a force that intervenes to get them moving, as they either "hold us responsible for the oppression and depredations" of their U.S.-friendly governments or else "look to us for help and liberation" from governments hostile to the United States.[127]

While Lewis's controversial expertise worked in the White House, Patai's *The Arab Mind* made it into the core of the U.S. Army's training curriculum and advanced, according to journalist Seymour Hersh, to the status of "the bible of the neocons on Arab behaviour . . . [convincing them] one, that Arabs understand only force and, two, that the biggest weakness of Arabs is shame and humiliation."[128] From *Fear Up Harsh*, an account by Todd Lagouranis, an ex-U.S. Army interrogator in Iraq, we know that Patai's portrait of sexually insecure and hung-up Arab men did play a role in designing culture-specific means of torture and lead to the sexual humiliation of prisoners at Abu Ghraib, where inmates were forced to masturbate in front of cameras. Lagouranis wrote that *The Arab Mind* was used by his colleagues as a "definitive guide" and "practical advice," enabling them to draw such conclusions as "Arabs, apparently, can't create a timeline. They don't think linearly or rationally. They have a different relationship with truth than we do—they think through association, not logic or reason. . . . Lying is not taboo or dishonourable to Arabs."[129] Commenting on an anthropology blog, Lagouranis adds: "I assure you that we used that book in order to develop methods to torture detainees. At Abu Ghraib and elsewhere. Interrogators were desperate for any information into the culture of the people."[130] Historian Alfred McCoy, in a study on the evolution of interrogation techniques employed by the CIA and its proxies, has described how U.S. interrogators at Guantánamo Bay used Behavioral Research Consultation Teams to exploit "cultural sensitivity, particularly Arab male sensitivity to issues of gender and sexual identity."[131]

The 2002 edition of *The Arab Mind* is prefaced with an enthusiastic introduction by Norvell B. De Atkine, head of Middle East Studies at the John F. Kennedy Special Warfare School at Fort Bragg, who claimed to have used it during the previous twelve years as essential reading and the basis of his cultural instruction.[132] After admitting to the same "incurable romanticism" regarding Arabs as the book's author, he follows Patai in his disdain for them, glossed over as "intellectual honesty and a true-to-life depiction of a people [during which] some less-than-appealing traits . . . surface."[133] Among these less appealing traits are the Arabs' inability to accept criticism, an idealization of their own history, the use of hyperbole, fatalism, their burning hatred for the West, as well as a lack of independent thinking and innovation. This missing dynamism is also the reason that, although written more than thirty years ago, Patai's book "has not aged at all. The analysis is just as prescient and on-the-mark now as on the day it was written."[134]

De Atkine adds his own cultural expertise when he supports Patai's view that fatalism is a prominent Arab cultural feature. He points out that the infrequent use of safety belts in cars in the Middle East reflects the Koranic saying that "death will overtake you even if you be inside a fortress."[135] According to this logic, Germany in 1976 must have been a strictly Muslim country, as a new law requiring the use of safety belts in cars provoked vivid protests. How can a work whose best use—in the words of one academic—"is as a doorstop" and which a course at Georgetown University had assigned as "an example of bad, biased social science" be used not only to inform hundreds of military teams but also in the past routinely be sent to officials before they were posted to U.S. embassies in the Middle East?[136] Partly the answer lies in the fact that to mainstream army professionals, it must seem progressive in itself to include cultural know-how in a military school curriculum. "Simply observing a culture through the prism of our own beliefs and cultural worldview leads to many misconceptions," writes De Atkine, and hails the culturally informed military officer as the new, nonethnocentric ideal.[137] Another reason for its appeal lies in its jargon-free style, which De Atkine contrasts positively with the "jargon- and agenda-laden" more recent scholarship, whose "fixation on race, class, and gender [has had] a destructive effect on Middle East scholarship."[138] Patai and Lewis give the military agenda of the Bush administration a veneer of academic respectability.

Area Studies

The stardom of Bernard Lewis, and even more the resurrection of Raphael Patai, is symptomatic of policy makers' thirst for a kind of regional-local cultural expertise that is suddenly perceived to be lacking. As Francis Fukuyama has written: "U.S. forces intervened in Iraq without basic cultural literacy." He links the "utter failure of the American academy to train adequate numbers of people with deep knowledge about the world outside the United States . . . and who are able to see the United States from the viewpoint of non-Americans" to two factors: (1) the decline of regional studies after the end of the Cold War, when foundations ceased to fund area study programs, language training, and fieldwork; and (2) the ascendancy of economics as a discipline, whose quantitative approach became the model for political science.[139]

Heir to a Western tradition of studying non-Western societies that became systematized as a by-product of colonialism, area studies in the way we know them are a Cold War artifact. Symbolically, their birth can be dated to the 1958 National Defense Education Act that provided funding for university teaching and research producing knowledge on areas of the world important to U.S. security: the Soviet Union, Asia (largely meaning China and Southeast Asia), Latin America, and the Middle East. These programs included language training, an expectation of personal contact with the area of research, and usually some measure of interdisciplinary exposure in the curriculum, although different area studies were dominated by different disciplines. Although anthropology—and the ethnographic approach in general—was central, for example, in the study of Southeast Asia, it has remained marginal in the Middle East. Legal anthropologist Lawrence Rosen describes how at a recent gathering of scholars of Islamic law he could not find one who had ever visited a present-day Muslim court.[140] (Many scholars of Western law are similarly content with studying texts, but they are inherently familiar with the cultural context they have emerged from.) The dearth of studies on contemporary Middle Eastern societies—and indeed the fact that so few Westerners have personal experiences there—might to a large part account for the fact that the conflation of religion and geography has raised so few objections in the debate on the "clash" between "the Islamic world" and the West (unlike, for example, in the "Asian values" debate).

An article underpinned by numerous biblical references, arguing that Christianity repressed sexual desire and oppressed women, would be read—by a narrow educated readership—as a comment on particular periods of European or Middle Eastern history rather than as a diagnostic of contemporary Western "civilization." Yet articles using the Koran in a similar way are often printed in the mass media as insights into the lives of today's

Arabs or Muslims. The discussion about Islamist terrorism continues to hover at the scriptural level, citing the Koran over and over again to decide whether Islam is a religion of peace or of war (or how to distinguish between "good" Islam that preaches peace and "bad" Islam that preaches hate). In 2004 a German scholar of Islam—writing under the pseudonym Christoph Luxenberg—claimed that the Koran's promise that martyrs for the faith would be greeted in paradise by "72 dark, wide-eyed maidens" is based on a mistranslation of an Aramaic term (instead, they would encounter white grapes). Published by an obscure German academic press, his book aroused such interest that it made it to the pages of the *New York Times*.[141]

Although it is probably right to heed the advice of scholars who point to the special place of scripture in Islam, this is surely no stand-in for the complexities of human lives. Worse, it often distracts attention from the historical and political roots of militant Islamism. As anthropologist Lila Abu-Lughod has noted about post-9/11 news programs, it is "striking . . . that there was a consistent resort to the cultural, as if knowing something about . . . the meaning of a religious ritual would help one understand the tragic attack . . . or how Afghanistan had come to be ruled by the Taliban . . . or why the caves and bunkers out of which Bin Laden was to be smoked . . . were paid for and built by the CIA. . . . In other words, the question is why knowing about the 'culture' of the region . . . was more urgent than exploring the history of the development of repressive regimes. . . . Such cultural framing . . . prevented the serious exploration of the roots . . . of human suffering in this part of the world. Instead of political and historical explanations, experts were being asked to give religio-cultural ones."[142]

In the 1980s the legitimacy and usefulness of area studies became the subject of questioning from various quarters. Especially with the crumbling of the Soviet bloc, when globalization became the talk of the day, academic interest shifted toward interconnectedness rather than regional specificity. Researchers were encouraged to uncover the laws of social and cultural change, of "time-space compression," that transcended national and regional borders.

The bits of local information could be supplied cheaply by collaborators in the countries that were now open to visits and communication; the idea of training cultural translators seemed outdated. Not least, it now also seemed condescending and hardly defensible to speak for others when they could speak for themselves. The feminist and postcolonialist critiques of the 1980s, in particular Edward Said's *Orientalism* (1978), as well as the so-called reflexive turn in anthropology, showed the complicity of Western knowledge production with the colonial and imperialist projects. Conflating postwar area studies with the earlier, European tradition of historical and philological Sinology, Indology, Arabistics, and so on (of which Lewis and Patai are examples) tarred them all with the same brush. In 1996 the Social Science Research Council (SSRC), one of America's main research funding bodies, disbanded its area studies committees after twenty-four years. SSRC president Kenneth Prewitt explained the decision in this way: "Now free from the bi-polar perspective of the cold war and increasingly aware of the multiple migrations and intersections of people, ideas, institutions, technologies and commodities, scholars are confronting the inadequacy of world 'areas' as bounded systems of social relations and cultural categories."[143]

After 9/11, Fukuyama was not alone in thinking that the West had dropped its guard too early by abandoning investment in area studies. The U.S. Army as well as the CIA began scrambling for anthropologists and culture experts—although not until the mid-2000s. The United Kingdom established a new area studies funding scheme in 2004, covering China, Japan, Russia, and the Middle East. But just as accusations of complicity with the colonial project stigmatized area studies in general, so today's criticism of Said's dismissal of "Orientalism" as nothing more than a reflection of Western desire for domination—exemplified by Robert Irwin's *Dangerous Knowledge: Orientalism and Its Discontents* (2006)—risks throwing the baby out with the bath water. The danger is that of rehabilitating the cavalier, decontextualized but ready-to-wear approach of the likes of Lewis and Patai instead of paying more attention to field-based studies.

Leaving politics aside, the intellectual and institutional debate about area studies has been taking place along two fault lines: (1) problem-oriented versus space-oriented organization of knowledge; and (2) locally specific explanations versus global theories of social change. There have been proposals to obviate the first question by redefining spatial categories of area studies based on observed social processes and allow them to shift correspondingly, instead of using permanent boundaries defined by presumed cultural traits. Most prominently, such a call has been made by anthropologist Arjun Appadurai, who wrote: "Traditional thinking about 'areas' has been driven by conceptions . . . that rely on some sort of trait list—of values, languages, material practices, ecological adaptations, marriage patterns, and the like. . . . They all tend to see 'areas' as relatively immobile aggregates of traits, with . . . durable historical boundaries and . . . more or less enduring properties. . . . In contrast, we need an . . . area studies that . . . sees significant areas of human organization as precipitates of various kinds of action, interaction, and motion."[144]

Such a process-oriented approach to area studies would produce insights like those by Mahmood Mamdani, who—like *Washington Post* editor Steve Coll—showed how, after the Soviet invasion of Afghanistan, the CIA under William Casey recruited radical Muslims throughout the world to come and train in Pakistan to fight the Soviets alongside the Afghan mujahideen. Under Pakistani and American supervision, madrassas were turned into political schools for training cadres. Their numbers soared; if there had been only nine hundred madrassas in the whole of Pakistan in 1971, then by 1988 there were eight thousand registered and another estimated twenty-five thousand unregistered ones.[145]

Writing in *Foreign Affairs*, Ahmad Rashid estimated that around thirty-five thousand Muslim radicals from forty countries joined Afghanistan's fight between 1982 and 1992.[146] Secular-minded royalist Afghans from the country's exiled tribal leadership and commercial classes had long warned both the Americans and the Saudis. As one put it, "For God's sake, you're financing your own assassins!"[147] But CIA officials regarded the Westernized Afghan rebels as weak and ineffective and were convinced that the religious fervor exhibited by Islamic fundamentalist warriors coming out of the Muslim Brotherhood and bin Laden's camp were just right to force the atheist, communist enemy to his knees. Consequently they commissioned an Uzbek exile living in Germany to produce translations of the Koran in the Uzbek language to stir unrest in this Soviet republic, printed thousands of copies of the Koran to be distributed to the mujahideen,[148] and annually fed millions of dollars into the coffers of jihadis and Pakistani officials, thereby reinforcing the Islamization of the Pakistani state under President Zia ul-Haq. The Afghan jihad was the largest covert operation in the history of the CIA, which transferred $600 million to the mujahideen in a single year, 1988, alone.[149]

Mamdani's and Coll's research shows that rather than being the product of a fossilized Islamic past, contemporary Islamist terrorism developed in such highly globalized places as Peshawar at the Afghan-Pakistani border, a city full of United Nations agencies, European charities, proselytizing Christian missionaries, and government relief agencies like U.S. AID, where a new generation of terrorists was being bred and supplied with electronic bomb detonators, stinger missiles, Lee Enfields, and sabotage training manuals. A decade later, these people were manning rebellions and terrorist attacks around the world, from Algeria and Yemen to Indonesia and London. This type of research, like the work of Olivier Roy on young Muslims in France and the Netherlands, makes use of an intimate knowledge of the terrain and the language but is sensitive to the global connections that shape developments on the ground. It demonstrates the advantage of area studies that, unlike most international relations scholarship, do not confine themselves to the ruling elites but extend to nonstate actors. The importance of such an approach is amply clear from Iraq—and indeed from the phenomenon of terrorism.

As Ulf Hannerz has written: "Bringing people back in will often show that culture tends not to be a long-durable consensus but a shifting, sometimes distracted debate. That there are many different ways of being more or less Christian, more or less Confucian, more or less Hindu, or more or less Muslim and that people can at the same time be a number of other things, outside religion, with which they might likewise identify more or less strongly."[150] For instance, the idea that Chinese are Confucian has helped little in understanding why they view the question of Tibet in a way so radically different from Westerners. It would be much more useful to consider that, for most ordinary Chinese, economic development is an unquestioned goal, and the central aspect of Tibetan history since its "peaceful liberation" in 1959 has been development. This view is deeply "cultural," but it has to do with the series of influences, socialist and capitalist, received and adopted by China in the twentieth century, as much as with the Confucian tradition of "self-development." In other words, it speaks to the fact that—*pace* Fukuyama—not all nations in the world are pursuing the same sort of modernity. Contrary to what Huntington believed, this divergence cannot be reduced to differing "civilizational" traditions. Culture *sometimes* matters, but in a far more complex way.

The "Re-Enchantment of Culture" in International Relations

Although 11 September 2001 seemed to vindicate Huntington's view of the world, the invasion and the early stages of U.S. occupation in Iraq were in fact motivated by the universalist agenda advocated by Francis Fukuyama and based on the belief that secular democracy is the destiny of people worldwide. Fukuyama, who had served on the policy planning staff of the U.S. State Department under presidents Ronald Reagan and George H. W. Bush, was a cofounder of the Project for the New American Century, perhaps the most important intellectual hub of American neoconservatives. Back in 1998, members of the project, including Fukuyama, called on president Bill Clinton to make "removing Saddam Hussein and his regime from power . . . the aim of American foreign policy."[151] Earlier, some of the signatories, along with others, such as George Soros, who later left the group, had made a similar appeal to Clinton to intervene in Bosnia.

During the presidency of George W. Bush, members of the project acquired unprecedented influence. They included vice president Dick Cheney, secretary of defense Donald Rumsfeld, his deputy Paul Wolfowitz, ambassador to the United Nations John Bolton, and trade representative Robert Zoellick. After 9/11, President Bush largely appropriated the assertive universalism of the neoconservatives in arguing that the United States had the obligation of spreading the values of freedom and democracy, which were—in secretary of state Condoleezza Rice's words—"not our values, they're not Western, they are universal."[152] Championed by Wolfowitz and his circle—supported by Bernard Lewis and seconded by Cheney and Rumsfeld—the plan of Iraq's occupation foresaw the installation of a secular, Westernized state, modeled on Kemal's Turkey and supported by enthusiastic, liberated citizens. Fukuyama denied that America's enemy was Islam; rather, it was Islamo-Fascism, which had appeared due to Saudi Arabia's export of its Wahhabi brand of Islam into a region abandoned by the United States after the Cold War and suffering from poverty, economic stagnation, and oppressive and corrupt regimes.

Yet the failure of the occupation and the increase in terrorism led to an unprecedented reinforcement of the rival Huntingtonian school of thought, which had cautioned against the export of democracy. In the face of endless debates about Islam, especially its relations to democracy and violence in U.S. and European policy circles and in the media, it seems fair to argue that the belief in a largely monolithic and ahistorical "Islamic civilization" sneaked right through the back door of the "war on terror." This was not so difficult, for in the end, the Fukuyamist view of culture is quite similar to the Huntingtonian one. Although Fukuyama argued that in modern societies cultural differences "tend to be put in a box, separated from politics, and relegated to the realm of private life"—in other words, that the obstacle of cultural difference would eventually be overcome—he had no fundamental disagreements with the view of culture as a set of inherited, collective values, which "societies are loath to give up."[153] Cultures will eventually converge; but for now the cultural dynamic that Fukuyama sees is an export of McDonald's and Hollywood on one side and a backlash to it on the other.

A third influential political scientist, Benjamin Barber, although opposed to the war and speaking from a Marxist perspective, has a similar view, in which the worldwide advance of "McWorld"—product of a misguided American cultural imperialism—is met with rising forces of religious fundamentalism (not only Islamic).[154] All three theoreticians (and, one might add, much of the "global Left" as well as various East Asian governments) share, then, a cultural reductionism that fails to acknowledge either local diversity or the variety of ways in which globalized ideas, practices, and goods are appropriated on the ground. So while McDonald's has been met with resistance in such places as Paris and Bangalore, empirical studies have shown that the fast-food chain is far more often incorporated into local worlds—used by different people for highly specific reasons, invested with local meanings. Take discotheques in Calcutta: Every Saturday afternoon in the center of the city, young professionals flock to day discos, which open at four and close at nine—in time for girls of good families to get home for dinner. The music is Bollywood, and everyone sings along; not much alcohol is consumed, but the DJs look as they do in New York. Similar discos in London cater to the South Asian population of Southall. But India also has its scene of late-night discos and house parties, where alcohol flows and girls stay out all night. Gurgaon, Delhi's upper-class suburb, abounds with these.

The idea of culture as a straitjacket of values that make people act in a certain way—as opposed to viewing it as a changing system of meaning, which individuals deploy selectively to make sense of the world and justify their choices—persists, despite obvious evidence to the contrary. In fact, the global proliferation of cultural revival movements as a tool for the empowerment of marginalized populations has added to the appeal of this discourse. While in the context of great-power antagonisms, cultural relativism's allies are generally on the conservative side—such as supporters of Huntington in the United States or of Eurasianism in Russia—its use to defend the weak has been associated with the global left. In some cases—such as the debate about unlinking China's trade benefits from its human rights record in the early 1990s—leftist opposition to imposing American standards on other countries meets with pragmatic conservatism that favors letting "the natives" sort out their own affairs, as long as they leave us alone. With overwhelming skepticism worldwide regarding America's recent interventions abroad, with the rise of Chinese power, and with governments in Russia and Japan emphasizing national values, the universalist agenda appears to have lost much of its appeal. To an increasing number of local leaders struggling for legitimacy, culturalist discourse seems a safer bet.

The political scientist Stephanie Lawson has shown how the Tongan aristocracy has defended its monopoly on power by arguing that it embodied tradition, and how coup leaders in Fiji in 1987 and 2000 attempted to rally support from "indigenous" Fijians (as opposed to Fijian Indians, whose rights are limited under the constitution) by claiming to defend native tradition from the Western form of representative democracy. After the 1987 coup, the Council of Advisors issued a statement that "democracy and its ideas of liberty and equality are . . . contrary to the Fijian way of life where liberty exists only within one's own social rank and equality is constrained by a fully developed social hierarchy."[155] Yet tradition, as Lawson has written, is deployed in a very selective way. Where the Fijian chiefs, whose Great Council had in fact been institutionalized by the British in the nineteenth century, considered representative democracy as alien, they had no such problems with Christianity (which is the majority religion of non-Indian Fijians). In fact, as the linguistic anthropologist Roger Keesing has written, "in the name of 'Fijian custom' Indians are being forced to observe Sabbath laws."[156]

In Melanesia, chiefdom is an even more recent institution and is directly related to the power struggles of decolonization and the postcolonial period. Postindependence leaders of Vanuatu and the Solomon Islands had great difficulties in formulating just what it was that *kastom*, the set of customary law and institutions that informed the postcolonial ideology of this diverse island nation, consisted of.[157] Evo Morales, a former coca farmer who became Bolivia's president in 2006 on a ticket of indigenous tradition, uses it in a similarly selective way. His minister of justice, a former maid, advocates a break with the "Western" judicial system and a "return" to customary law and social sanctions. But critics point out that fewer than half of the population still lives in rural communities in which such sanctions would make sense and accuse the minister of deflecting attention from the much-needed reform of the court and prison system.[158] The Chinese government insisted that it was acting to preserve tradition—which mandated that the Panchen Lama's successor be selected by drawing a name from a "golden urn" sent from Beijing—when it rejected the Dalai Lama's choice for the post in 1995, but Western public opinion allied itself overwhelmingly with the Dalai Lama's argument for greater cultural autonomy.[159]

Despite the proliferation of culture talk, it should by now be clear that the world we live in is not one of clashing civilizations—even though this view has the potential of becoming a self-fulfilling prophecy, with the view of the West as a homogeneously hostile cultural entity reinforced in the Middle East by the suspicion that any traveller from that region attracts at Western airports, and not only there. On a recent trip to Shanghai, when booking a hotel room by telephone, one of us was asked what his nationality was, as the hotel had a policy of not accepting guests from the Middle East. Presumably, the local police, unburdened by politically correct niceties, decided to secure a nearby American or British installation by this means. The spread of the "clashing civilizations" view is boosted by the fact that the way cultural differences are packaged in mundane, everyday settings such as companies and hospitals—as differences between stable national sets of values—appears to reinforce its validity. In fact, as we will see in chapter 6, cross-cultural psychologist Harry Triandis—who gave the world the gift of dividing it into "collectivist" and "individualist" societies and found that "the values that are the most important in the West are least important worldwide"—is approvingly quoted by both Huntington and the central figure of intercultural management, Geert Hofstede.[160]

If the clash of civilizations is not the dynamic that defines the interaction between nations, then international relations should not be governed by the idea of cultural differences between regions of the world. Differences should be taken into account, but in the specific contexts in which they arise rather than as a priori assumptions.

Cultural arguments in international relations belong to two categories: (1) "We can't do this to them because they are different," and (2) "Don't do this to us because we are different." Let us look at these categories in turn.

Huntington's advice against imposing democracy and other "Western values" on different civilizations belongs to the first category. This view presupposes the existence of distinct, geographically anchored sets of values and norms, or what Lawson has called the "fallacy of origin." Lawson continues: "Where an artefact, invention, practice, custom, law or idea comes from does not determine by whom it may be owned. Ideas and practices are never the exclusive preserve of those with whom they may have originated. The printing press is not distinctively Chinese by virtue of having originated in China. . . . Nor is the idea of democracy exclusively British or French or American, as distinct from, say, Spanish, Indian, or Japanese, merely because it caught on earlier in the first set of countries rather than in the second."[161]

To develop Lawson's argument along a tangent, positing a direct line of descent from the polis of ancient Athens to the latest elections in Belgium, is no more valid than drawing a line from Athens to Saddam. It is only to emphasize different elements of the political system and different strands of historical diffusion. There are very few ruling elites in the world who, like the Fijian chiefs in 1987, do not wish to call their countries "democratic" (see, for example, the Democratic People's Republic of Korea) or who deny that they are concerned about the "human rights" of their citizens (China, for example, has a Human Rights Commission and a seat on the UN's Human Rights Council, and the *People's Daily* ran a series of articles entitled "Answers to a Hundred Questions on Human Rights"). It is not the origins of these concepts, then, that we should be concerned about, but their local meanings. And those meanings, just as the meanings of "traditional" values, are more often than not contested. We should not expect, then, like Fukuyama, that once the people of Basra are free to articulate their aspirations, they will turn out to be the same as those of the people of Kansas. By the same token, we should not anticipate, with Huntington, that they will be the same as those in Istanbul and Jakarta.

The effect of new ideas and practices on societies is strongly influenced by preexisting cultural norms but is never quite predictable. Who would have thought that Germany, after its twentieth-century history and all the treatises on the "authoritarian personality," would become the way it is today? This is why, while we do not believe that "Asian values" determine a distinct sociopolitical model, we also do not consider the current form of Western liberal democracy the last word of history. In fact, it is precisely the unpredictable nature of interaction between globally circulating ideas and local ways of meaning-making that creates the exciting possibility of something radically new in places like China.

What to do with claims of the "don't do this to us" type? Typically, these arise in negotiated situations, as more and more global conventions and international treaties come into effect, regulating issues from the standards of pig farming to the protection of workers or simply attempting to establish common ground in matters like the protection of cultural heritage, the rights of children, or downloading music from the Internet. Inevitably, each treaty is accompanied by prolonged haggling. Typically, states do not want to be left out, but they also detest limiting their sovereignty. Undoubtedly, culturally constructed categories are at the core of these treaties. What is a life appropriate to a child: learning responsibility as early as possible to enhance their chances in society, or having a carefree time that lets his or her personality develop unimpeded? What is the right way of enjoying nature: hiking in the wilderness, cruising in your car on a good road, or having a feast at a restaurant on the top of the hill? What does it mean to maintain your cultural heritage: carefully preserving crumbling ruins or rebuilding them in new splendor?

The approach we suggest here is not to accept blanket claims of "this is how we do it" but to look at the context and the intended outcomes. If the intention is to increase the well-being of children in Bangladesh, it is appropriate to consider whether it is best served by preventing them from work until they are fourteen, or by carefully circumscribing their working conditions, considering not just the nature of work but also nurturing contact with the family and others and providing access to schooling and recreation. (In fact, the children of a Vietnamese couple in Berlin who run an Asia Snack from seven in the morning to midnight may be better off helping out at the shop after school than hanging out at the video arcade—a question we come back to in chapter 4.)

The global campaign against "human trafficking" rallies both conservative Christians and liberal green types, and is one of the few issues that elicits no cultural contestation, but it should be much more context-sensitive than it is. Surely the woman who is kidnapped from her home in Laos and sold to a brothel in Thailand should be seen differently from the one who marries a farmer across the border in China with the help of a middleman who pays her family. Antitrafficking campaigners would want to "rescue" both women, because borders are crossed, money changes hands, and the woman ends up (by their standards) exploited. But it is likely that the woman in the second case does not want to be rescued, because marrying a local farmer would not necessarily mean fewer hours in the rice paddy, or, indeed, more love.

It follows that "dialogue of civilizations," if it means annual congresses at which government delegates exchange formulaic statements on their national values, exchange assurances of good intentions, and skirt debate on substantive issues—as it happens at the cultural fora of the Asia-Europe Summit Meetings—is useless and sometimes worse. But this is not to say that in a world where culture is such a major export, there is no room for it to be harnessed for genuine bridge-building between countries. The first step is to acknowledge, as Germany's foreign minister Frank-Walter Steinmeier did in a speech at the 2006 Frankfurt Book Fair, that "culture means constantly confronting the big questions of life and humanity." He continued: "In this discussion between self and the other we continue to develop ourselves, our culture and our society."[162] As he explained in another speech on the tasks of Germany's foreign cultural and educational policy, such policy "therefore cannot work with culture as a homogeneous, fixed block or canon of works, values or cultural goods limited by the nation-state. . . . He who understands culture or identity in a static way cuts short cultural possibilities, particularly the possibilities to choose and to identify, that one's society offers its citizens."[163]

Steinmeier is putting this view to practical use in the highly sensitive negotiations about Turkey's accession to the European Union. Huntington sees Turkey as a "torn country," unable to decide between its Islamic roots and its twentieth-century reincarnation at the hands of Atatürk as a Western state. The debate in Europe about whether accession negotiations with Turkey—which has enacted a series of economic, political, and legal reforms to bring the country in line with European standards, including the criminalization of marital rape and allowing the use of the Kurdish language in private (but not public) schools—now focuses on human rights issues, such as the status of women and ethnic minorities, as well as the EU's capability to absorb a nation of eighty million with high population growth. Critics see this last argument as a transparent foil for European cultural fears of being overrun by a Muslim nation. Indeed, 69 percent of Germans are against Turkey's membership even if it fulfills all accession criteria, and 43 percent—as many as those who mention human rights—attribute this to cultural and religious differences.[164] This opposition mixes contradictory views of European values—secularism versus Christianity—in an uneasy and unarticulated fashion. Turkey as a state is, after all, considerably more secular than Ireland or Malta, both of which prohibited divorce at the time of their admission (Malta still does), while Turkish women not only had that right as early as the 1930s but were also able to gain custody of their children. As José Casanova has suggested, the debate on Turkey's accession may reflect that it is, in fact, Europe that is "torn" in its cultural identity.[165]

In this context, Steinmeier—in a particularly difficult position as his government was itself divided on Turkey's accession along party lines—launched a cultural exchange that departs from the conventional idea of showcasing mainstream German high culture by holding exhibitions of romantic painters or discussions between political philosophers, but also from the standard "dialogue of cultures" that involves, for example, inviting women from Germany to discuss child-rearing practices with their Turkish counterparts. Instead, the ministry organized a show on a Turkish television channel that involved young local Turks and their coethnics from Germany, including, among the latter, footballer Malek Fatih, rapper Mohabet, and actor Adnan Maral (star of the German soap opera "Turkish for Beginners"). Steinmeier's advisers hope that exchanges showing the actual diversity of lifestyles and opinions in both societies will do more to foster mutual trust than polite roundtables at which participants express their respect for each other's irreconcilable views, treated as representative of their respective nations. The same approach might do good for Europe's relationship with China.

chapter 2

Culture

One summer day in 1999, "a pair of students climbed up the face of the [World] Bank's headquarters, in Washington, D.C."— just two blocks away from the White House—"and unfurled a banner proclaiming, 'World Bank Approves China's Genocide in Tibet.'"[1] The protest—echoed by two Republican senators, who also accused the Bank of "cultural genocide"—was triggered by the approval of a loan to support a project in China's northwestern Qinghai Province. The project involved the relocation of fifty-eight thousand rural residents from an arid part of the province to another, which was irrigated by a newly built dam. At the time the students climbed up the building, though, the project was already before the Bank's Inspection Panel, a relatively autonomous in-house watchdog for controversial cases, headed at the time by a Canadian environmentalist.

A few months later the panel delivered a report that uncovered irregularities with the approval process: the project should have been placed in the highest environmental risk category (Category A) and should therefore have gone through a more stringent environmental assessment. In addition, more attention should have been paid to the impact on the lives of Mongolian and Tibetan nomads. Although they had been interviewed, the process had not been confidential.[2] The Bank's management agreed to more detailed studies, but the board rejected the plan, and NGOs continued to press for the project's cancellation. Finally, in July 2000 the Chinese government withdrew its request for financing.

Chapter 1 mentioned that cultural relativism—the idea that standards for democratic participation and rights protection differ from one society to another—has united political actors of different persuasions in a number of instances, including support from part of the American Left for delinking economic relations with China from its human rights record. Here we are witnessing cultural mobilization that succeeded in uniting Left and Right to the opposite end. Admittedly, the story had unique potential for such mobilization, as it involved Tibetans, dams, and accusations of ethnic cleansing. Dams are red cloth in the eyes of environmentalists, while the fate of Tibetan culture is the one that arguably rallies the most sympathy across the globe. The "Tibetan cause" also has a uniquely well-organized global advocacy network, which sprung into action immediately after news of the resettlement project's approval had reached the London headquarters of the Tibet Information Network (TIN).

Within a few weeks fifty-nine NGOs from Mexico to Thailand had dispatched a letter to World Bank president James Wolfensohn "protesting the transfer of 'Chinese farmers into a traditionally Tibetan area.'" Soon protesters were chanting outside the Bank's headquarters and a coalition of celebrities—including Richard Gere, sixty members of Congress ranging from liberal Democrat Nancy Pelosi to conservative Republican Jesse Helms, and a Beastie Boy—had been alerted to the cause. Activist Jonathan Fox later proudly concluded that this was "the first-ever *mass* protest that directly targeted a bank's loan decision process, and the protesters won"—the model of successful global advocacy in general, and in particular, of successful pressure for World Bank accountability.[3]

The advocates claimed to have prevented an act of cultural destruction. TIN's newsletter claimed the project would "dramatically affect the demography" of Qinghai; a press release issued for a protest event featuring Representative Nancy Pelosi (later to become Speaker of the House) with a Tibetan musician declared that it would destroy Tibetan culture because "60 thousand ethnic Chinese will move to Qinghai."[4] In fact, though, the project brief foresaw resettlement only within the province and claimed that only 40 percent of those would be Han; the majority would be Mongols, and the resettlers would also include thirty-five hundred

Tibetans. Furthermore, the protesters conflated the issue with that of China's occupation of Tibet, when, in fact, Qinghai had been under direct Chinese control, rather than that of the Dalai Lama, since imperial times. The actual outcome of the intervention seems to be far from success. As anyone who has worked in China would know, the thought that its government would meekly stop a project because it gained no support from the World Bank is naïve. A short while after the bank withdrew its loan application, Tibetan activists arrived back at Wolfensohn's door, saying that the Chinese government was now going ahead with the project on its own. This would leave it free to ignore the Bank's environmental standards and move more people into the area. They asked for Wolfensohn's help in finding out more details. Wolfensohn supposedly replied, "How the fuck do I know what they're doing? You just got us out of there!"[5]

This case illuminates many of the practical pitfalls that development projects face, but it also points to some central conceptual dilemmas regarding the role of "culture" in development. Although accusations of cultural destruction are particularly potent when it comes to the Tibetan cause—because they are linked to political and religious oppression and to the charismatic figure of the Dalai Lama—they also go to the heart of the debate of what constitutes "development." It is beyond dispute that China's rule in Tibet has produced significant cultural change, involving the disappearance or commodification (for tourists or for political purposes) of certain traditions. It has also resulted in demographic change, with ethnic Chinese moving into Tibet—as well as other Tibetan-inhabited areas—and occupying leading political and economic positions. But the same is true of all other less-developed regions of China.

As China modernizes—and there seems little dispute within the country that this is a good thing—and gets more deeply imbricated in the webs of global trade and tourism, villages around Beijing lose their traditional character just as rapidly as the stockades of the Akha people along the Lao border. Well-heeled entrepreneurs from China's eastern seaboard, small merchants from the overcrowded center, and laborers from impoverished regions flock to wherever there is economic opportunity, whether it is the Chinese heartland of Anhui Province or the Tibetan or Uyghur periphery. The latter attracts more attention because it is more exotic (for Chinese as well as for Westerners); because its ethnic distinctiveness has been officially institutionalized in a canon of dress, dance, song, and food; because its political status is contested; and because modernization comes to it later, at a time when sensitivity to "cultural survival"—the title of a popular activist journal—is at an all-time high. When ethnic difference is politicized, it is easy to point to Chinese invaders—and beyond them, the sinister hand of the Communist Party—as those responsible for cultural destruction.

No doubt, locals everywhere resent the profits of change going to the pockets of outsiders. But what if it goes into their own pockets? Western activists want to save "the Tibetans" from the cultural destruction wrought by "the Chinese," but their support for an oppressed people mingles with the assumption that Tibetans want to stay just the way they were fifty years ago. The anthropologist Ralph Litzinger's study of a road project in another Tibetan area in the northwest of Yunnan Province suggested that the efforts of The Nature Conservancy, concerned with the conservation of biological diversity but also pointing to the need to protect Tibetan religious practices, were at variance with the mood of local villagers. The villagers were "tired of isolation, eager for development, ready for change." They wanted the new road because "it would ease the burden of transporting goods into the village, provide faster access to the middle school . . . and . . . easier access to the hospital."[6] When villagers purchased a tractor, it took seventeen men and three days to carry it up the current bridleway.[7] Across the border in Yunnan, Lao villagers are eagerly embracing the planting of rubber, brought to them largely by Chinese investors who receive international development subsidies from the Chinese government. This is much to the horror of such Western donor organizations as the German development agency GTZ (the Society for Technical Cooperation), which has been teaching villagers "sustainable livelihoods" and "participatory development" for many years.[8]

In his study of tourism development in southwestern Guizhou Province in the 1990s, anthropologist Tim Oakes has documented that village elders from the Miao ethnic group flocked to the provincial tourism bureau with portfolios, pleading for their official recognition as tourism destinations.[9] Although in some cases it is the tourism authorities that order the tearing down of old houses they deem unworthy of a tourist attraction, in other cases—and with the same rationale—they restrain villagers from rebuilding their traditional wooden or brick dwellings in concrete and shiny tile. Nowadays, in many places local authorities attempt to recreate tradition by forcing residents to remove the tiles and paint their houses with "traditional" patterns. In the Danxia Mountains Scenic Area in Guangdong Province, they permit villagers to purchase only a single type of "traditional-looking" house.[10] It is therefore not unreasonable to think that many Chinese villagers would agree with tourism researcher Wei Xiaoan: "In a way, rich people and foreigners want to see places as Nature-made zoos: don't touch your environment, don't touch your culture; let us go and look at leisure. If so, are we still to have local development?"[11]

The Three Gorges Dam on the Yangtze River, the largest and perhaps the most controversial dam project in history—which resulted in the resettlement of more than a million people—was widely opposed outside China and even by many Chinese intellectuals from its inception to its completion in 2006. The project flooded one of the most celebrated scenic areas in China and erased the traditional way of life of a region regarded as highly important for the country's ancient history. The project was carried out in the name of securing Western China's energy supply for a period of accelerated development, not for the sake of improving local people's lives. Even so, many of the locals were happy to move to more economically advanced, less isolated parts of China, where they hoped to make more money. But those who were eking out a precarious existence in the first place and lacked the means, connections, and ability to defend their interests and lobby for more compensation were unlikely to recover from the disruption of their familiar way of life and build a new livelihood (for example, because they were unable to find a job in a nonagricultural environment). Even where some aspects of a household's material conditions improved, its well-being may have suffered other setbacks, such as the schooling of children, which became more expensive in the place of resettlement. As Bettina Gransow, a specialist of resettlement in China and a consultant to the Asian Development Bank, has written, the most obvious indicator of the negative consequences of resettlement is the government decision that households that had been resettled before 30 June 2006—an estimated twenty-two million people—will receive ongoing (though very small) compensation for twenty years.[12]

There are other places where development has meant subsistence farmers being kicked off their lands to make room for a road or a dam and being resettled in an unfamiliar environment, where they cannot employ the agricultural techniques they know and the compensation they receive is insufficient to build a new house. These people often end up in city slums, with high rates of alcoholism, drug abuse, and illness. This type of "development," for its victims, means both economic deprivation and cultural loss. The first large loan the World Bank ever gave for the construction of a dam turned out to be just such a case. The Kariba dam on the Zambezi River in Zambia was to supply the cities of Africa's "Copperbelt" as well as the capitals of British-ruled North and South Rhodesia with electricity. In the project, forty thousand Tonga villagers were resettled, some forcibly. They lost most of their possessions and ended up on inferior land that allowed only for one annual harvest instead of the usual two.

In 1959, at the time of the Kariba dam construction, developmental institutions and local governments showed a nearly total disregard for the fate of the victims, and it was left to two anthropologists, Elizabeth Colson and Thayer Scudder, to document the ensuing social catastrophe right into the 2000s. During this period material conditions in the resettled villages steadily worsened while the mortality rate rose; the social fabric broke apart with rituals and work ethic declining; famines, alcoholism, and HIV became widespread; and witchcraft accusations and trials became rampant. By the end of the 1990s the situation in the Tonga villages was so bad that the World Bank, alarmed by Scudder's findings, started a new rehabilitation plan, aimed at finally delivering some of the promises made fifty years earlier, such as supplying the villages with electricity, safe water, and roads. At the time of this writing, however, none of these promises has been fulfilled.[13]

While the Kariba development project clearly had a detrimental impact on the afflicted Tonga villages, in many other cases the evaluation of the socioeconomic and cultural changes triggered by development projects, from new divisions of labor to challenged authority patterns, is less clear-cut. In the case of the San Bushmen in Botswana, for example, both scholars and development workers are bitterly divided over the government's policy to relocate them from the Central Kalahari Game Reserve. The NGO Survival International accuses the government of cultural "genocide." The government argues that continued herding and hunting in the park is incompatible with wildlife conservation; that most San have long stopped relying on hunting and gathering, so it can no longer be seen as central to their lifestyle; and finally that San children and adults should have access to the same opportunities in Botswana—one of Africa's most successful economies—as other citizens. Others maintain that the struggle over the Kalahari has diverted attention from the problems of other, less politicized San groups, and that although these problems are real, they are complex. Some Sans have resisted the erosion of their hunting-gathering livelihoods and access to land, while others have allowed and even invited settlers to their land because of the benefits it brought. Still other San groups have "seized upon the symbolic and other resources NGOs offer in order to internationalize their struggles." Finally, some Sans "have actively resisted the paternalism that NGOs have often displayed."[14]

Whose culture are we, in the end, supposed to protect? That of the village, the ethnic group, the province, or the nation? How much change can occur before tradition ends? What is the price of maintaining tradition to locals, prevented from having flushing toilets, and outsiders, if they are hindered in their freedom to move where they can make a better living? But can higher incomes, better health, and more education be achieved in situations where a traditional lifestyle with the social networks that sustain it is suddenly disrupted?

The Development Agenda

Questions such as these have been asked since the international agenda of "development" first arose in the immediate aftermath of World War II. With decolonization looming large and Cold War rivalry beginning, the United States was concerned with setting up an international framework to ensure that the societies and economies of the newly independent "Third World" (itself a concept produced by the Cold War) take a direction that was both stable and aligned with its own principles and strategic aims. In his inaugural address in 1949, U.S. president Harry Truman called upon the UN and industrialized nations to join the United States in "a bold new program for making the benefits of our scientific advances and industrial progress available for the improvement and growth of underdeveloped areas," "a program of development based on the concept of democratic fair dealing."[15] The Marshall Plan for rebuilding Europe served as a blueprint for a global development agenda, focused on international economic stability and growth.

This agenda was based on modernization theory, which postulated that transition to a "modern" society—that is, a liberal, secular participatory democracy premised on the separation of powers and respect for individual rights—would follow a single, linear track throughout the world. This movement would occur with economic growth, which would thus also safeguard societies from the "Communist threat"; indeed, a key text of the era, Walter Rostow's *The Stages of Economic Growth* (1960), was subtitled "a non-Communist manifesto."[16] Economic growth was thus taken as the single measure of development. "Development aid" took the form of direct project funding, loans, technical assistance, and incentives for corporations to invest in or transfer technology to "underdeveloped" countries. For its part, the Soviet Union (and later, China) provided similar assistance to its non-European socialist satellites as well as other countries, nominally subscribing to the theory that the development of the material base will hasten the transition to socialism and then communism—but, in effect, competing with the United States for political influence.

The World Bank and the International Monetary Fund, established at the Bretton Woods conference in 1944 to help rebuild Europe, and their more recent offshoots, such as the European Bank for Reconstruction and Development and the Asian Development Bank, were given key roles in "developing" the rest of the world by providing loans. National agencies for international development aid were formed, often linked to arrangements between former colonial powers and their ex-colonies (most notably within the framework of the British Commonwealth). Since then, the economic goals and linear view of development ideology have become extremely influential globally. Despite obvious disagreements as to the link of economic development to the growth of civil society, state intervention into markets, and frequent criticism of the World Bank, there are few places today where the basic tenets of developmentalism are rejected.

Arguments linking economic development and the capacity to modernize to the cultural traits of a society go back at least to Max Weber's *The Protestant Ethic and the Spirit of Capitalism* (1930), which held that the advantage of northern frugality and a theological endorsement of wealth honestly gained had enabled the development of capitalism in Northwestern Europe and North America. The postwar development agenda at first ignored this tradition. Yet by the 1960s and the 1970s, the optimism of decolonization gave way to disappointment with lagging economic growth, lack of democratic reforms, corruption, and inefficiency. Marxist thinkers from Immanuel Wallerstein to Andre Gunder Frank pointed to the structural impossibility of overcoming economic and political dependency in a "world system" that carried on colonial inequalities of production and access to markets.

For its part, the World Bank began, in the 1980s, to insist on macroeconomic reforms (cutting back government expenditures, especially social spending, and privatization of core industries) as a condition for continued loans. Eastern European reform socialism and then the collapse of state socialist systems created new faith in the power of economic development to replicate liberal democracy worldwide and a new market for economic reformers such as Jeffrey Sachs and World Bank officials as development gurus. But the macroeconomic interventions of the World Bank remained highly unpopular and often unsuccessful. The United Nations Development Program (UNDP) estimated that the global wealth gap doubled between 1960 and 1989.[17] Critics focused on a whole range of reasons for this failure, such as the development agencies' lack of accountability toward the poor.[18] The more radical critics, notably the anthropologist Arturo Escobar, accused development institutions of perpetuating a neocolonial system of domination of poor countries by the rich, while a growing number of actors within and outside of the development scene pointed to the global development and aid regimes' refusal to consider wider sociopolitical factors as a source of their ineffectiveness.[19]

In his *Anti-Politics Machine* (published in 1990), anthropologist James Ferguson looked at the reasons behind the failure of a Livestock Improvement Project in Lesotho. The small African kingdom, encircled by South Africa and with a population of a mere 1.2 million, received an enormous amount of development assistance. Between 1975 and 1984 seventy-two organizations from twenty-seven countries gave aid to Lesotho, which amounted to $64 million in 1979 alone. Yet, most observers have agreed, the aid failed spectacularly. To understand why it did, and why donors kept distributing money despite achieving none of their objectives, Ferguson contrasts the World Bank's portrayal of Lesotho with a wider anthropological approach. The World Bank's 1975 country report on Lesotho described the country as a suitable target for interventions. It stated that at the time of independence, Lesotho "was virtually untouched by modern economic development" and "still is, basically, a traditional subsistence peasant society."[20]

This image was in stark contrast to reality, however. Since the beginning of the twentieth century, Lesotho had produced cash crops for the South African market; 60 percent of its adult men worked in South African farms, mines, and factories, and their remittances formed a crucial part of Lesotho's income. Based on such erroneous assumptions, the country report presented Lesotho's problems in such a way that they seemed solvable by economic intervention—the only kind of intervention the World Bank saw itself as capable of launching. As moving money around was the organizing principle of development agencies, the World Bank ignored the facts that made Lesotho a less than optimal recipient for its loans, from the corrupt leadership to its dependence on the powerful South African apartheid regime. As Ferguson wrote, "An analysis which suggests that the causes of poverty in Lesotho are political and structural (not technical and geographical), that the national government is part of the problem (not a neutral instrument for its solution), and that meaningful change can only come through revolutionary social transformation in South Africa has no place in 'development' discourse simply because 'development' agencies are not in the business of promoting political realignments or supporting revolutionary struggles."[21]

With its focus unrealistically narrowed, the World Bank in cooperation with the Canadian International Development Agency started a project to improve and commercialize livestock production in the rural areas by allowing farmers with better quality animals to use good grazing land and further increase their stock with the help of modern management practices. Their success, so the planners assumed, would demonstrate to all other farmers the superiority of commercialization and make them follow the new practices. But instead, farmers resisted having parts of their communal grazing lands fenced off. The fence was knocked down, the gates stolen, and the area freely grazed by all cattle. The office of the project manager was burned down, and the Canadian officer in charge of the program was said to fear for his life.[22] Ferguson's analysis suggests that, besides ignoring important sociopolitical factors, development agencies also failed to take the local cultural context into account (in this case the meaning of livestock for the rural population). Although many households had sheep, goats, and cattle, these were not considered an entrepreneurial asset but a sign and investment of wealth. Rather than parting with animals, even dying ones, they preferred to rely for a living on the remittances of relatives working as migrant workers in South Africa.

Similar criticism has been made of humanitarian interventions. To cite one example of many, the failure of the international aid effort in the 1998 famine in southern Sudan has been linked to an ignorance of local structures of ownership, kinship, and redistribution channels on the part of the aid agencies. Anthropologist and development consultant Simon Harragin has described how aid was seen by the local Dinka population as belonging to the same category as grazing land, which is to be equally distributed between the members of the large kinship groups headed since colonial times by so-called chiefs. The local understanding, whereby everybody should receive the same amount of aid, regardless of wealth and need, clashed with the explicit aims of the aid agency, Operation Lifeline Sudan, which wanted to feed the weakest members of the population first and foremost. When the agency ignored the local redistribution channels, a number of recipients secretly handed back their rations to the chiefs to distribute them through traditional channels. When this was disclosed, aid workers accused the chiefs of "elite capture" and made attempts to bypass local leadership structures. As a result, aid organizations like Doctors Without Borders (Médecins Sans Frontières) and the local authorities accused each other of withholding desperately needed aid.

Ignorance of the traditional practice of distributing food evenly also led to a misjudgment regarding the spread and severity of the approaching famine. Even though the local Sudanese authorities appealed for aid early on, the international organizations failed to take them seriously, as there were no obvious signs of starvation. When malnutrition did occur, the famine had reached an advanced state and was widespread.[23]

Culture Matters, but How?

The World Bank responded to mounting criticism by turning its attention to the social aspects of development. In 1994 it made "social assessment" compulsory for its loan projects, and in 1996 the Bank formed the Partnership for Sustainable Global Growth. For the first time, this demanded institutional reforms that went beyond the economic realm and included practices of "good governance," including transparency and accountability of government and civic participation. The World Bank's 2000 *World Development Report* signaled a new emphasis—along with economic growth—on "empowerment, security and opportunity." Capitalism as a vehicle to development remained unquestioned, but now there was a fresh preoccupation with "social capital."[24] This was coupled with a shift from large-scale projects to smaller-scale ones and entailed a novel focus on participatory practices, in which funds were channeled to local communities with the intention of enabling them to create their own social and economic infrastructures. In the new paradigm, development agendas should emerge from the aspirations and needs of the local people themselves, especially those previously excluded from top-down planning processes. The participatory approach also paid greater attention to "local knowledge" and traditional techniques—in farming or medicine, for example—instead of a single-minded focus on implementing imported know-how.

The innovative spirit of "partnership" signified a step away from the unquestioned belief in the single, linear model with Western countries as teachers, at least in rhetoric. In 2000 the World Bank issued a publication entitled *Culture Counts: Financing, Resources, and the Economics of Culture in Sustainable Development*. In another such endeavor, in 2005, the German development agency GTZ (the Society for Technical Cooperation) and the Goethe Institute, responsible for the dissemination of German culture abroad, initiated a "Culture and Development" cooperation project, arguing "experience has shown that a lack of knowledge and comprehension of foreign cultures and values is one of the main reasons why projects and programmes fail. A decisive factor for successful cooperation is . . . an improvement in the intercultural competence of actors on both sides. Besides knowledge of and respect for the other side's values and attitudes, this includes developing an awareness of one's own culture and values."[25]

To start this process, the GTZ hosted a number of roundtable discussions with its partners around the world to discuss the differing meanings of the term "progress" in the various areas. This was followed by a series of regional conferences, each focusing on a topic of particular relevance to the geographical area, such as "Cultural Aspects of Social Justice" in Latin America and "Cultural Aspects of Corruption" in Asia. Similarly, in 2006 the Swiss Agency for Development and Cooperations started a blog entitled Culture Matters and published a brochure, *Culture Is Not a Luxury*, with a call to all employees to develop a "genuine culture reflex" that not only includes a new focus on "culture" as a way of life but actively seeks to encourage a wide range of artistic expressions in the countries in which the agency is engaged.[26]

With this novel development paradigm, the focus of intervention shifted from an individualistic understanding of society (famously summed up in Margaret Thatcher's phrase "There is no such thing as society: there are individual men and women") to a recognition that "relational and group-based phenomena shape and influence individual aspirations, capabilities, and the distribution of power and agency."[27] Now "culture" mattered "in a very wide range of work—as once 'climate' and, much less long ago, 'political will' and 'good governance' did."[28] Development aid was no longer a technical matter to which culture was extraneous. Rather, culture became something policy had to adapt to but also intervene with. Just how that adaptation and intervention should take place, however, has been the subject of wide-ranging contention, which takes place at two different but overlapping levels. At one level the debate focuses on how culture as a set of values, attitudes, and behavioral norms facilitates or impedes development (the nature of which in this debate is usually unquestioned). The discussion at the other level is much more grounded; it centers on how development projects affect ways of life locally and how by extension to make them more sensitive to local views on the good life.

The first debate goes right back to Max Weber and even earlier, to the late eighteenth century, when Hegel developed his view of world history. Although he postulated that the evolution of the world spirit would take all societies along the same path, Hegel also famously exempted China, which he believed had not been touched by the world spirit. This view of "Oriental despotism," shared by Rousseau, was an early precursor to today's debates about why Africa never appears to move ahead. In the late eighteenth century, China was seen as a rich and powerful country, admired only a generation earlier by Voltaire as the model of an enlightened autocracy. Yet it was obviously impervious to political, economic, and social reforms, which were now deemed necessary in Europe. Many historians have since tried to answer the question of why the industrial revolution and the development of modern capitalism occurred in northwestern Europe, even though many of China's regions had been wealthier prior to it.

The more general of these arguments sought an answer in even earlier times, looking at the development of settled agriculture in the Fertile Crescent, from ancient Mesopotamia to Egypt. The earliest explanations, which focused on climate and geography, recently received an update in the form of Jared Diamond's bestseller *Guns, Germs, and Steel* (1997).[29] Diamond has argued that such ecological factors as the presence of a high diversity of plants and animal species suitable for domestication favored the development of civilizations and technologies, while such natural impediments as mountain ranges or large bodies of water hindered them by blocking trade and the spread of innovations. Once certain societies had achieved food surpluses and high degrees of interaction with outsiders, a long chain of other political, economic, and sociocultural developments followed, which assured that those who got ahead first stayed ahead. The idea that location and climate—through their effects on diseases, transport costs, and agricultural productivity—are the most important variables to explain income levels and economic growth has followers among such influential development economists as Jeffrey Sachs and such anthropologists as Richard Shweder.[30]

Other explanations focused on economic and demographic factors. A number of authors, such as the historian Kenneth Pomeranz, have pointed out that the success of modern European capitalism and imperialism was contingent on access to coerced labor, the epidemiological advantages of Europeans, and the state sponsorship of overseas expansion due to the competition for wealth and power between dynasties and then nation-states, which was absent in China. Pomeranz attributes the actual beginning of industrialization to the lucky availability of accessible coal mining in Britain and the need for better water pumps leading to the application of steam technology.[31]

From early on, there have also been scholars who argued that the divergence in development cannot be explained without taking into account cultural factors. Why, for example, did the Chinese invent gunpowder but had no modern weaponry until their encounter with Western colonialism? Why did they have paper money and a sophisticated banking system centuries before Europe but never developed a capitalism based on a fully-fledged market? Why did they reach Africa in the fifteenth century but attempted neither to colonize it nor to extract its raw materials?

In the account of Joseph Needham, the preeminent historian of Chinese science, this was because of the "'cohesiveness,' anti-individualism, and feeling for 'mutual aid'" and "the absence of a 'military' or 'expansive' ethos" characteristic of the "historic Chinese mind."[32] Needham saw in Mao Zedong's communism an heir to the "intellectual superiority and ethical will with which the Confucian mandarinate had obstructed both capitalism and the seizure of the state by the merchant class" and believed that it may be China's world-role to "restore humanistic values based on all the forms of human experience."[33] Other authors less sympathetic to Mao—including such Marxists as Tőkei Ferenc—developed a similar line of thought: China's "Asiatic mode of production" lacked a competitive spirit (or greed and militarism) and was trapped by a strict social hierarchy and a Confucian disdain for trade.

Popular contemporary arguments focusing on culture as the main variable of development include Bernard Lewis pondering "what went wrong" in the Middle East (see chapter 1) and the views of economic historian David Landes, author of *The Wealth and Poverty of Nations* (published in 1998), who at a 1999 World Bank conference entitled "Culture Counts" referred to "toxic cultures" that impede development.[34] One influential point of view in this debate is represented by Samuel Huntington and another American political scientist, Lawrence E. Harrison. In the preface to their jointly edited book *Culture Matters: How Values Shape Human Progress* (praised by then World Bank president James Wolfensohn and subsequently published in Chinese, Spanish, Korean, and other languages), Huntington developed a comparison between the economic development of Ghana and South Korea, to which numerous commentators have since referred.

In the 1960s both economies had comparable levels of per

capita gross national product (GNP) and a similar division of their economies along primary products, manufacturing, and services. Both were primarily exporters of raw materials and received similar amounts of development aid. Yet thirty years later, South Korea had become the fourteenth most powerful economy in the world, with multinational companies and prominent automobile, electronic, and consumer goods industries. Ghana, however, had achieved nothing of that sort: its GNP amounted only to one-fifteenth of South Korea's. What, asked Huntington, can account for these differences? His answer: The people of South Korea valued thrift and investment, hard work and education, organization and discipline. Ghanaians followed other values. "In short: cultures count."[35]

The view of Africa as a global basket case resonates with the public perception. Since the late 1960s, the continent has been associated in Western media with draught and famine, illness and corruption, terror and debt. Robert Kaplan, an author popular with U.S. policy makers about whom we write more in chapter 3, uses Africa in his book *The Coming Anarchy* as a terrifying model for the anarchy of the post–Cold War world, which he predicts will threaten safety, health, comfort, and civilization worldwide. Why does Africa have the vast majority of countries where illiteracy prevails? Why does it have the lowest life expectancies and highest HIV infection rates? Why does it, with 13 percent of the world's population, account for just 0.3 percent of all Internet connections?

Since World War II, generations have grown up used to seeing Africa as the place that never gets any better—and much of it appears significantly worse off than at the time of independence. Since the early 1950s, $568 billion has been poured into the continent.[36] Jeffrey Sachs, former director of the UN's Millennium Project, and Tony Blair's Commission for Africa are calling for this amount to be doubled. Well, Huntington has bad news for the proponents of more aid. Try as hard as you want, he says, Africa's culture is just not conducive to development, and cultural change is slow. But Huntington does leave a narrow window open. In exceptional cases policies can function to change culture, although perhaps not irreversibly. As an example, he mentions the transformation undergone by Singapore under Lee Kuan Yew's leadership. Knowing Huntington's negative views on "torn countries" and exported values, it would seem, however, that such cultural change would have to take place within the limits set by the civilization. It follows that Huntington's view of development differs from mainstream modernization theory in that he sees development as not necessarily entailing democratization.

Huntington's coeditor Harrison is both more sanguine about the possibility of change and more mainstream in his view of political liberalization, transparency, and so on as forming part of the development package. In the introduction to *Culture Matters*, Harrison outlines an ambitious research program known as the Culture Matters Research Project (CMRP). The project seeks to identify "cultural values and attitudes [that are] facilitators of, or obstacles to, progress" so as to develop "value- and attitude-change guidelines . . . for the promotion of progressive values and attitudes."[37] According to Harrison, "Some 65 experts from 25 countries" ended up participating in the project, which resulted in three volumes published in 2006. Many contributors were very uneasy with the idea of a straightforward link between cultural tradition and contemporary development.[38]

Nonetheless, Harrison claimed that the researchers had come up with a typology of twenty-five factors along which "progress-prone cultures" and "progress-resistant cultures" differed, among them "risk propensity" (moderate in the former but low in the latter), ways of "advancement" (merit-dependent versus relying on family/patron connections), and attitudes to "work/achievement" ("live to work" versus "work to live"). These values are transmitted by such institutions as schools, religion, the media, and political leadership. Having mapped 117 countries by their prominent religion against their economic performance, Harrison concludes that "Protestant, Jewish, and Confucian societies do better than Catholic, Islamic, and Orthodox Christian societies" on "progress-prone Economic Behaviour values." These data, he says, "roundly validate Weber's thesis in *The Protestant Ethic and the Spirit of Capitalism*."[39] This is despite Weber's well-known view that Chinese culture "offered little potential for capitalist development beyond the simple merchant capitalism of trade for profit."[40]

The good news, Harrison says, is that institutions can also change culture. He quotes an aphorism by Daniel Patrick Moynihan: "The central conservative truth is that it is culture, not politics, that determines the success of a society. The central liberal truth is that politics can change a culture and save it from itself." The first sentence appears closer to summarizing Huntington's view (and the view taken in *Culture Matters*); Harrison's most recent book, based on the CMRP and entitled *The Central Liberal Truth* (2006), identifies with the second. Harrison lists a number of cases in which political leadership has successfully altered cultural values. In East Asia, for example, political "encouragement" released a "powerful education/achievement/merit/frugality undercurrent" hitherto suppressed by Confucian (or Marxist) values. "The trigger for the magic in China," he proclaims, "was Deng Xiaoping's 1978 pronouncement, 'To get rich is glorious.'"[41] In Ireland, Spain, and Quebec, initially disadvantaged by their Catholicism, political will managed to change the value profile over the course of several decades by opening up their economies and emphasizing education.

In the end Harrison's view of culture appears tautological. Culture is a prison but a minimum-security one: anyone can escape. Change, it appears, happens because it happens. Spain and Ireland, Harrison admits, changed so much largely because both countries have benefited from massive European Union funding and tourism, and the Catholic church has by now been through decades of salutary decline. The only cultural reason Harrison mentions for what he sees as Chile's uniqueness in Latin America—explaining its entrepreneurialism, low corruption, and the professionalism of its *carabiñeros*—is "disproportionate Basque influence." "Culture" in Harrison's argument seems to play the role of the stone in Hans Christian Andersen's stone soup: if you add enough other ingredients, in the end it becomes quite tasty.

The same uncertainty regarding the meaning of culture has characterized many similar arguments. Daniel Etounga-Manguelle, a former World Bank adviser from Cameroon, has advocated in his call for a "cultural adjustment programme for Africa" reforms in education, politics, the economy, and social relations.[42] A view that subsumes government policies under culture (rather than inquiring into a relationship between them) loses all claims to causality and is for all practical purposes identical to a view that denies culture any relevance at all. For example, policies aimed at stimulating women's entrepreneurship in Zimbabwe encounter the widespread belief that business is an exclusively male activity and that women who try to earn money are immoral and akin to prostitutes. Similarly, traveling—often necessary to find and sell goods—is deemed improper for women, as it involves mingling with (male) strangers. So far, these attitudes, instilled in children from early on, are clearly in the realm of culture, which we understand to encompass ideas, motives, beliefs, and identities that pattern relationships between individuals and groups as well as the everyday practices and strategies humans employ.

Yet how can we separate these cultural factors from those generally seen as economic and social, such as the legal status of women, their role as mothers and heads of family, or the material resources available to them? Under customary law in Zimbabwe, land is owned and inherited by males only, and even the harvested product is men's property. While men are free to go out, women can leave home only for short periods, as they have to care for their families. Formal education also has concentrated on men and leaves many women illiterate and thus qualified only for work at the lowest level of the informal sector.[43] Cultural beliefs regarding gender roles may not be the cause of these "structural facts," but they legitimize and reinforce them.

Let us return to Huntington's oft-cited comparison between Ghana and South Korea. Economist Amartya Sen has called it "a quarter-truth torn out of context." He points out that in 1960— when Huntington says the two countries started roughly from the same base—South Korea had a larger entrepreneurial stratum, a government willing to foster economic growth, a close economic relationship with Japan and the United States, a much higher literacy rate, and a better-developed school system.[44] These in turn were conditioned by the very different policies of the former colonial masters in both countries. Japan, wishing to turn Koreans into fully fledged imperial subjects during its rule from 1895 to 1945, had developed a modern administration and school system and invested in industries. The British had focused on developing infrastructure and the extractive industries but had more interest in preparing Ghana for eventual native rule by building elite political institutions than in universal literacy. We add another difference, perhaps the most important of all: South Korea's close military alliance with the United States in both the Korean and the Vietnam wars, which made the country a major recipient of American funding.

One might argue that several of these differences may nonetheless be linked to cultural norms. Huntington would, no doubt, say that strong government authority and an emphasis on learning are typical of the "Sinic civilization." We do not, of course, argue that cultural factors have no effect on development. For example, belief in sorcery, widespread in many African countries, has led to the disuse of many wells financed by international aid. In a number of cases the wells were believed to be poisoned by jealous individuals, leading locals to continue drinking contaminated river water instead. Similarly, the egalitarian ethos of many traditional lineage-based village societies in Africa or Latin America inhibits economic aspirations. Jackson, a young South African man, told one of us in Johannesburg in 2007 that when he had wanted to upgrade his family house back in the village by replacing the mud floor with concrete, even this minimal attempt at differentiating his household from the others had spurred so much envy and suspicion that he eventually gave up on the project. His behavior was consistent with Anita Abraham and Jean-Philippe Platteau's account of what they called "leveling societies," where private wealth accumulation is seen as antisocial behavior threatening to undermine the dense reciprocal relationships between villagers, who help each other out in times of need. The fear is that once some villagers are wealthy enough to do without these insurance networks, they might refuse to help needy others and thus destroy the fundamental sense of security in the community.[45]

We argue that a mechanistic correlation of "values"—taken at a national or regional level—to development is unproductive, even though it is popular "in international developmentalism because of [its] charming and calibrated mix of thin description with thick prescription."[46] If applied strictly, it lacks explanatory power, as in Huntington's case. Just thinking of East Germany and West Germany or North Korea and South Korea should convince anyone that shared values do not determine economic success or indeed the path of development. In the Soviet Union the republics that had the most prosperous reputation were the Ukraine and those of the Caucasus; now, these republics are largely seen as basket cases (except oil-powered Azerbaijan), while Estonia and Lithuania enjoy close to double-digit economic growth. But if allowed too many exceptions, as in Harrison's argument, this type of cultural explanation becomes meaningless.

Whatever their differences, most contributors to *Culture Matters* agree that such things as "progress" and "development" exist. The waves generated by Arturo Escobar's radical intervention in the development debate have not had much effect on the debate itself because the logical consequence of adopting his viewpoint would have been to stop discussing development altogether. Yet a greater sensitivity to noneconomic indicators is perceptible. Harrison, for example, used the UN's Human Development Index, which takes into account measures of health and education as well as wealth, in his CMRP rankings. Escobar's views are represented by a radically dissenting voice in the volume, that of anthropologist Richard Shweder. Arguing from a consistent cultural relativist standpoint, Shweder rejects any objective measure of development, whether economic or not. What it means to be "modern," he points out, is culture-dependent. There is no reason to assume that technological and material progress is the universal basis of "feeling modern." Most anthropologists would argue that it is so selectively. That is, although there are few places in the world that would not see high-tech as a sign of progress, in many countries— but not all—"successful" people still prefer to live in cottages rather than skyscrapers, and, as the writer Umberto Eco has noted, "Within the western world itself, there are those who primarily wish to live in harmony with an uncorrupted environment, and are willing to relinquish air travel, cars and refrigerators, to weave baskets and travel on foot from one village to another."[47]

Alternative indicators of human well-being are making their way into economics and even politics. A group of economists maintain a Web site called the Happy Planet Index, which ranks countries according to an index calculated by taking into account citizens' life expectancy, their satisfaction with life, and the country's "ecological footprint"—that is, the amount of pollution and rubbish it produces.[48] There are no Western countries among the top fifteen, and some of the top-ranking nations, such as Colombia and Guatemala, are generally associated with poverty and high crime rates. Even such mainstream politicians as the leader of Britain's Conservatives, David Cameron, have begun using the notion of "general well-being" (GWB) as an alternative to GNP.[49] Shweder carries this view further than most. Even long life or health, he says, should not be treated as intrinsically preferable, unless we know that the "communities" whose lives we want to improve value those above other things they might want to achieve. He suggests that richer states should help poorer ones strictly on the basis of local visions of the good life, understood through in-depth ethnographic studies, and not try to foster any "Western" norms of civil society, either in suggesting that different population groups should live together or like each other, or that people organize their private lives in a certain fashion, or that they have private lives at all.[50]

Most anthropologists would disagree with Shweder's radicalism. While the promise of being reincarnated as a Brahmin might be more important for some than an increased life expectancy, one should not come at the cost of the other. It is safe to say that the old Soviet joke—"It's better to be rich and healthy than sick and poor"—is not culture-specific, but nor is dissent from this view. To quote Eco again: "Many mystics could tell me that, between a glutton who lives for 80 years and Saint Luigi Gonzaga, who only survived for 23, it was the latter who had the fuller life."[51] Nonetheless, Shweder's approach has the advantage of inquiring into local views on what constitutes development.

In the case presented at the outset of this chapter, both the Chinese government and the Tibet Information Network claimed to represent the interests of the people whose lives the resettlement project in Qinghai was going to change. The Chinese government promised better land; the TIN, cultural integrity. In the end the decision was fought out between Washington, D.C., London, and Beijing, and though the assessment process carried out by the World Bank included interviews on the ground, we do not know what the locals—and which locals—wanted. If the decision-making process had taken place closer to the ground, it would have been harder for distortions of local interests to occur along the way, and if these interests diverged, there would have been more chance to reconcile them.

Thick Description, Thin Prescription

Questions concerning local interests and ways of "getting things done" are particularly relevant to the participatory approaches, which became the new development orthodoxy in the 1990s. They are also typically the focus of the second culture debate in development. If *Culture Matters* stands for the culture-as-obstacle-or-facilitator discussion, then the volume that encapsulates the effort to take local views on development and real-life interaction between development workers and local social scenes into account is *Culture and Public Action*, the outcome of a 2002 conference organized by two World Bank researchers, Vijayendra Rao and Michael Walton. Most contributors to this volume view culture not as a constant but as a processual variable, not separate from the structural conditions of class and gender and the ideological conditions of politics but interconnected with them.[52] Their culturally informed lens focuses as much on the culture of the local societies "to be developed" as on the unequal relations between them and governments, nongovernmental organizations, or external donors, whose actions are as much guided by cultural beliefs and practices as those of their target societies.

One of the contributors to *Culture and Public Action*, Arjun Appadurai, contrasts their approach to the dichotomy between culture and development in much of the conventional development discourse. He writes: "For more than a century, culture has been viewed as a matter of one or other kind of pastness—the keywords here are habit, custom, heritage, tradition. On the other hand, development is always seen in terms of the future: plans, hopes, goals, targets. . . . [T]he cultural actor is a person of and from the past, and the economic actor is a person of the future. This opposition is an artifact of our definitions and has been crippling."[53] Appadurai points to a paradox: although "plans, hopes, goals, [and] targets" are assumed to be culturally defined, descriptions of culture in development tend to focus on the past and rarely include visions of the future. The confusion of culture with the past leads to the misconception that the desirable future can be attained only by somehow manipulating the values that have been responsible for the undesirable past and present—or not at all. Yet the question development workers actually face in the field is not "How do I change this culture?" Far from worrying about the culture of a nation, even the diversity of a village often proves too daunting. Workers have to figure out how to identify needs, design and carry out improvements, and maintain the results amid the complex realities of local life, characterized by different incomes, occupations, castes, genders, ethnic groups, and classes. Whereas before, consultation for large infrastructure projects usually took place between government officials and development professionals, often far removed from the location of the project, the participatory approach asks them to foster a new partnership with a much broader base in the communities they work in.

Yet how do you identify local needs and interests? Who do you talk to, and who do you enlist in the design, implementation, and maintenance of the project, be it a well, a community center, or a forest management project? Ideally, development workers aim at getting a representative overview of the local social scene. But this is not so easy. Every development project faces at least four hurdles in the way of such local understanding: access to the target population; getting people to talk; the organization's own structure and culture; and the limitations of people's imagination. Let us now turn to each one of them. In the case of the Qinghai resettlement project, the Inspection Panel criticized the World Bank's assessment process for not ensuring that locals were interviewed in an anonymous fashion. It is likely that they had not been able to do so because of close monitoring by the local government. Susanna Price, a "social development specialist" at the Asian Development Bank, describes a typical experience of conducting a social impact assessment in a Chinese village:

> In response to an unusual request from the visiting foreigner, the next stop is a poor household. . . . The inhabitants . . . with courage overcoming trepidation, respond to questions from the foreign visitor. The county mayor stands next to the household head, offering encouragement for his responses, whilst others call out answers if the household head seems to hesitate. . . . Before long, one of the officials looks at a watch, and announces that it is time for lunch. . . .
>
> The foreign visitor is left pondering the value of this small amount of information gained for planning the program. Were those few selected among the poorest households in the township? What factors predominated in their selection? Amid the interventions from high level county officials, were the views of the householders truly articulated? What weight could be placed on information gained in such a context?[54]

But even if formal barriers had not been in place, it is probable that a poor farmer or herder would have been reluctant to talk to them, simply because he would not have known how to do so. Instead, he would have taken them to the party secretary of the village because he had grown up knowing that foreign visitors should be received by persons of authority.

In many villages—such as those in Mali and Niger described by the geographer Jesse Ribot—traditional, often state-backed, power structures may similarly prohibit locals from voicing their preferences openly.[55] While participatory approaches advocate democratic and transparent decision making and the protection of the poor, many traditional villages are characterized by the primacy of personal relationships, loyalty to kin, particularistic ethics, and

respect for traditional authority. Although participatory development methods aim at equally involving all adult members of a
community, any "community" is divided by conflicting interests:
rich versus poor, pastoralists versus settled farmers, men versus
women, or superior versus subordinate ethnic groups.[56] As a result,
the participation process and the implementation of projects are
sometimes threatened by "elite capture."

Any market research agency knows that focus group discussions, even where the participants are social equals, privilege the
opinion of those with more assertive personalities; where power
differences are present, the results will be even more skewed. Yet
focus group–like assessment strategies are routinely used in designing and assessing development projects. When a large participatory rural appraisal (PRA) project, commissioned by Botswana's
Ministry of Finance, sent out teams to visit all villages and hold
meetings, during which the locals forwarded their needs and wishes
to be incorporated into a new development plan, they discovered
that the obligatory village development committees (established as
the local counterparts to outside development agents) were almost
exclusively staffed with members of the dominant ethnic groups.
They also discovered that at village meetings hardly any women,
youngsters, or male members of subordinate tribes dared to speak
out. When, in one unusual meeting, a woman from a marginalized ethnic group complained loudly about discriminatory practices in the village, the chief had her instantly removed from the
meeting place. Even if they were given voice in small-scale work
groups, members of subordinated ethnic groups often sided with
the majority, as they had come to accept their lower status. For
instance, in Botswana the Batawana and Bayei groups traditionally had a master-slave relationship, with the latter—referred to
as Makuba (meaning "useless people")—being denied the right
to own cattle, access to water, and land. Such negative self-images
complete a cycle of repression that is difficult to change, as the
priorities of groups living on the brink of survival often consist of
avoiding risk and maintaining the status quo.[57]

As Jillian Popkins, a social development adviser specializing
in China at Britain's Department for International Development,

cautions, the "instrumental use of participation to build consensus needs to be distinguished from the use of participation to generate alternative narratives of poverty. . . . Without due attention to ensuring that the conditions of the research encounter . . . are made transparent, there is an increased risk that participation becomes co-opted into the service of rationalizing the status quo. . . . [For example,] The use of participation to rationalize the exclusion of attention to gender-based inequities in education on the basis that the views of villagers should be respected makes participation complicit in reproducing social and cultural norms which are at the heart of gender-based poverty."[58]

Rather than employing focus groups or relying on traditional methods of decision making and consensus-building, research that employs the ethnographic method—a longer period of "hanging out" and talking to people in the streets, at the well, or at the karaoke parlor—is much more likely to produce a differentiated understanding of needs and desires, even where not everyone dares speak about them directly. Such ethnographic studies will not focus on "culture" as a separate element, certainly not as a preconceived framework. Understanding "actual patterns of living [will] include all sorts of processes and things that are not normally called cultural—such as class, gender, place, autonomy, sovereignty, resources, trade, and politics."[59] It will thus avoid the pitfall of the "cultural turn" in development debates that Apthorpe cautions against. (Successful examples of such studies are detailed in the book's conclusion.)

The constraints of the routinely employed methods are amplified by the culture of the development agencies. Finding out marginalized people's views is inefficient: it is a lengthy and usually inconclusive process. But development workers have to write clearly defined proposals, work to deadlines, and account for their time. This often leads them to seeking out local interlocutors whose language skills and cultural capital are most similar to the development worker herself and where communication barriers are lowest. As the anthropologist David Mosse has written: "In participatory projects, field staff or project managers hard pressed to meet targets are commonly willing to accept the better-off as their target group (self-presented as the poor)."[60] It is increasingly common for development projects to employ sociologists or anthropologists—the World Bank alone employed more than sixty of them in the early 2000s—to carry out social impact assessment, but they often find it difficult to be reemployed if their views are deemed too far removed from the realities and deadlines of the organization.[61] The fact that the World Bank, the Asian Development Bank, and other development agencies depend on national governments for funding makes it nearly impossible to translate findings critical of these governments into official reports.

One example of the fruitfulness of an ethnographic approach was demonstrated in a report commissioned by the Asian Development Bank and the World Bank's Global Environmental Forum (GEF) in 1999 on a poverty alleviation initiative in the Mount Khawa Karpo area (known in Chinese as Meili Snow Mountain) of northwestern Yunnan Province in China. The initiative, by the Nature Conservancy and the provincial government, aimed to improve livelihoods while conserving biodiversity. The provincial government wanted to include the construction of a road in its strategy, which the Nature Conservancy opposed. The initial document produced by Asian Development Bank and GEF staff, after painting the significance of the region for global biodiversity in vivid colors, noted that "conservation efforts would need to be sensitive to" the livelihood of the local Tibetans' and other ethnic groups' "livelihood needs and development aspirations, and implemented with their cooperation."[62] The chief consultant for the project, an ecologist working for the Nature Conservancy, assembled a team of Chinese conservationist scholars (including a Tibetan from Qinghai) and asked them to "gather as much information about local ideas on conservation and development" as possible using "participatory research methods (interviews, small group meetings, mapping exercises)" and so on, in the target village of Yubeng.[63] To the mind of the team leader, "It was actually similar to the anthropological notion of participant observation: the idea was to live in the village, organize interviews, use translators when necessary, observe behaviors and social actions, and from [there] try to describe the social and cultural life of a particular place."[64]

Despite noting—as social development specialist Susanna Price did—that the process in which the county government mobilized village leaders to assist the research team had "more in common with Chinese Communist Party work team strategies than with the idealized notions of participant observation,"[65] Ralph Litzinger describes the report it produced as "a truly astonishing document" for its "vivid detail" of history, flora and fauna, and "the messy world of village and inter-village conflict."[66] The report did not support the Nature Conservancy's opposition to the road connecting the village with the outside world, but noted that although it was likely that the road would lead to the appearance of mass tourism in accordance with the hopes of the county government, and although tourism would almost certainly endanger local flora and fauna without necessarily producing appreciable income increases for locals, building the road was nonetheless in strong agreement with locals' aspirations. The report concluded with an important question: "Yubeng people have hiked on these mountains for generations. We can't assume they will continue to do so. Why can't they have easier travel alternatives?"[67]

Even if development workers are willing and able to access local views and visions, development agencies face a more fundamental problem: the limited imagination of the very poor whom they want to help. As Appadurai has pointed out, many poor people lack something even more basic than "voice"—the "capacity to aspire." In other words, they lack the ability to imagine different versions of their own future.[68] To return once more to the Tibetans in Qinghai, even if the herder had attempted to formulate his own preferences for the future and the World Bank assessor had had the patience to hear him out, his ideas would have been confined by the few models of success he had seen around him—perhaps a cousin working in a factory in the nearby city or a fellow villager who had opened a small grocery stand. Just as Chinese migrants in Italy, working for years on end in garment workshops that barely make ends meet because there are more and more of them, nonetheless invariably hope to open a workshop themselves when they have saved enough money, herders in Qinghai lack the cultural capital that would give them the vision and the daring to try formulas that others have not.

Repeating the same patterns of escaping poverty not only brings diminishing returns—the fifth nail shop in the village is unlikely to be profitable—more important, it impedes free reflection on just what it is that would make one's life fulfilled. (One might add that this is true not only for the poor: the fact that 90 percent of all Chinese students at Macquarie University in Sydney study accounting is only superficially due to rational decision making based on later chances of employment and permanent residence. Much more likely, students are simply following the only patterns they are familiar with in an environment that does not do much to introduce them to other options.) Thus Appadurai advocates that development projects aim not only at identifying people's aspirations but also at expanding their capacity to develop, deliberate on, and formulate aspirations.

This enabling environment is characterized by the development of rituals and collective actions that help to support social agency at the grassroots level, a resistance to "projectization" (the fulfilling of externally set timelines, project outcomes, and so on), as well as the forging of connections between the poor and policy makers. One example of such building of the "capacity to aspire" is the toilet festival initiated by Mahila Milan, an Indian NGO. Poor slum dwellers, humiliated by having to defecate in public or wait in long lines in front of the few public toilets, have been organized to hold toilet festivals in various Indian cities, during which they exhibit and inaugurate public toilets by and for themselves. The toilets signal a reversal of the standard flows of expertise, as it is the slum dwellers who finance, build, and maintain them, thus experiencing themselves as architects and organizers—not as passive recipients of somebody else's aid project. The NGO responsible for the festivals (as well as for larger housing projects for slum dwellers) explicitly rejects the parameters of development projects, such as external time frames, but instead sees change as a slow and risk-laden process, which involves not only the concrete building toilets and houses but also attention to internal conflict management, as the poor are often inclined to opt out of collective actions in conflict situations rather than work their way through them. This approach involves personally connecting the poor to politicians and officials, who are invited to give speeches and cut the ceremonial ribbon at the festivals, thus associating themselves with and giving recognition to the poor and their grassroots activities.[69]

Yet in most conventional development projects the inability of the subaltern to speak, the hurry of development experts to finish their assignments, and their reluctance to question the authority of self- or government-appointed community spokespeople all impose formidable barriers to finding out "what the locals want."[70] These barriers may run through the whole life cycle of a project. Thus, when outside development agents decide to "empower" marginalized groups, they often meet resistance on the part of traditional power holders. Anita Abraham and Jean-Philippe Platteau have described the case of an NGO that distributed fishing boats, nets, and engines to young people on the Bijangos Islands in Guinea Bissau to help them become independent fishermen. But the local traditional king, himself not a beneficiary, was opposed to the project, as it seemed to challenge his authority. Only one individual managed to withstand his resistance by keeping the equipment and operating it successfully, but soon after, he had to leave the island and resettle on the continent.[71]

Another instance witnessed by Abraham and Platteau involved the introduction of irrigated rice cultivation in Burkina Faso. The villagers were asked to organize themselves into village associations to manage the irrigation infrastructure, collectively purchase equipment, distribute the produce, and run a microcredit association. When they had to select a chairman, a secretary, and a treasurer, the NGO involved in the project soon discovered that in each village, the local chiefs had been elected chairmen and had apparently made all the important decisions without consulting others. In one village the chief refused to disclose the names of credit recipients or the amounts lent, harming the other association members, as the loans were never repaid. He also decided to sell the rice to one trader—his brother—who cheated the farmers by underpaying them. Yet when asked why the villagers did not get rid of their chairman, they answered that this was impossible, as he was their chief.[72] Problems such as these are even more acute in societies that have already become economically differentiated, where the better-off do not feel a sense of responsibility toward other community members. Here, local elites and opinion makers, whose viewpoints and preferences are not necessarily representative of the majority population, use development funds to build and sustain client-patron relationships. In other cases they monopolize the discussions and use international agencies to reinforce and legitimize their own oppressive regimes.

Even if the question "Who speaks for whom?" can be answered, the problem of what outside development agents are supposed to do if their own goals collide with local interests remains. Do you accept and thereby reinforce potentially dysfunctional social hierarchies, or do you try to destabilize them and create alternative ones? Although the latter option might be a deliberate strategy in some cases, it may not always help the project. As we have seen, Simon Harragin linked the failure of Operation Lifeline Sudan's famine alleviation project to its insistence on delivering food relief to the highest-priority targets—the elderly and children—rather than using established distribution channels and risk "elite capture" by the "chiefs." It is not clear, however, that organizations that did go via the chiefs achieved better results. In other words, rather than either privileging existing power structures or always working against them, aid organizations should be mindful that both approaches will favor particular individuals or groups, and that ultimately the choice should depend on the intended goals. Different approaches are called for in different types of aid work. Famine relief, where the goal of saving people from immediate death should override fears of aid dependency, requires different strategies from longer-term development aid, "harm reduction" projects (such as containing the spread of HIV or drug addiction), or coca and opium eradication.

The UNDP's 2004 *Human Development Report* proposed what seems to be a useful rule of thumb: defending tradition should not hold back human development. In the broadest sense, following Amartya Sen and Arjun Appadurai, we can understand "human development" as an expansion of choices of the kind of life people want to live. The weak point of this approach is that these choices do not arise from nowhere: they are "often an aspect of, rather than external to, ideology and power."[73] As critics from the Escobar school are quick to point out, development institutions and the "experts" may seem to be completely open to what their "clients" choose, but in fact the scope of their imagination will now be influenced, in addition to their own life-worlds, by those of the development institutions. No matter how carefully they listen to locals and how culturally sensitive they are, development workers will inevitably privilege particular types of economic practices (such as supporting independent entrepreneurship) and the same forms of social organization (such as NGOs) that have been reproducing themselves globally, as if based on a template, and are unlikely to help their clients imagine choices that depart radically from their own ideals of how individuals should pursue happiness. As the anthropologists Heather A. Horst and Daniel Miller have asked: "Should Jamaican children be said to choose to be educated when educationalists would be just as firm in claiming the necessity of education to the salvation of a population?"[74]

All of this is true. But it does not follow that such an approach amounts merely to instilling a "false consciousness" of the kind that gives a consumer the illusion of choice because she can select from thirty different soft drinks at a supermarket. Besides, consumer choice is not to be dismissed: it often leads to improvements in people's lives that are hard to dispute. It is very likely that, for many Romanian women, being able to use Always sanitary pads instead of stuffing their panties with cotton wool meant as much in 1990 as the first free election.

The Impact of the "Cultural Turn"

Considering all the problems reviewed in this chapter, the question is whether the "cultural turn" in development has made any practical difference. Most of those familiar with the field would agree that attention to culture has grown within certain departments of the main aid institutions, influencing their rhetoric, mission statements, and field manuals, but is still largely absent in the field. In addition, with the ascent of China as a major figure in the aid world, a player pursuing an old-style development agenda based on economic rationality with little interest in sociocultural conditions, a culturally sensitive lens is not likely to become a globally dominant voice anytime soon.[75] Some critics suggest that while attention to culture is necessary, "culturalism" in development will achieve little or perhaps even make matters worse—that is, if culture is simply added to the existing institutional structure as a device of legitimization, without a potential to challenge the basic assumptions and organizational cultures of the big development institutions themselves.

Yet in many cases it seems as if it is less the culture of local communities that stands in the way of development than the culture of the development system itself. On the basis of an ethnography about the ten-year Indo-British Rainfed Farming Project, David Mosse has challenged the idea that "good policy," regardless of its intrinsic merits, is the key to successful development. Rather, he argues, "good policy is unimplementable."[76] Pointing out the complex relationships between univocal and neat dominant policy models on the one hand and scattered, heterogenic practices on the other, he suggests that development practice is predominantly driven by the need of its various actors—government officials and corporations, development agencies and their advisers, local elites and nongovernmental organizations—to ensure continued funding and legitimacy.

Thus, although the threat of African deforestation and "savannaization" is contested among scientists, it is assumed to be high in the development system because the interests of too many players—development consultants, NGOs, local officials who can fine villagers for offenses, villagers who use the threat to the environment as a way to reinforce opposition between savanna and forest dwellers and governments reliant on ecology-conditioned aid—depend on it. The bulk of development work therefore centers around the establishment and maintenance of relationships between different actors necessary to support a project and its narrative. As Mosse has shown, even the villagers in the Indo-British Rainfed Farming Project bought into this logic and saw the established Self-Help Funds not as a way to get microcredits that would stimulate local economic development—their officially stated aim—but rather as avenues to foster good personal relations with the project agency to secure new patrons or the waged labor it provided.[77]

Another example of an aid project whose trajectory threatens to be derailed by the complex obstacles of a poor fit between donor organizations' political goals, the organizational goal of participatory development, "elite capture," and government suspicion is a U.S. AID–funded project to limit overgrazing and improve environmental protection while assuring the continuity of traditional Tibetan lifestyles in the Ganzi Tibetan Autonomous Prefecture of China's Sichuan Province. This example is explored in a brilliant study by anthropologist Gillian Tan. AID, an arm of the U.S. government, approved a budget of $600 million for projects to aid Tibetan cultural preservation, a goal that enjoys obvious political and popular support in the United States. Although the Chinese government did not agree for the project planned for Tibet itself to go ahead, it did consent to one in Ganzi, aimed "to strengthen the capacity of Tibetan communities to meet their socio-economic needs while conserving the environment and preserving their cultural heritage."[78]

The fact that a project funded by the U.S. government to aid Tibetan culture was permitted to go ahead in China marked a major political breakthrough, but the organization carrying it out had to bridge radically differing views of what the project was about. On the one hand, it had to negotiate between the expectations of Tibet supporters in the West, for whom Ganzi was Kham or "Eastern Tibet"; Chinese officials at various levels; and local Tibetans. On the other hand, it had to mediate between Western donors' ideals of cultural preservation and nature conservation and local desires of development. Tan focuses on these dilemmas through the eyes of the Tibetan field assistants hired by the project. They were upwardly mobile, young urban Tibetans with relatively good Chinese educations and some knowledge of English, some with Han Chinese girlfriends, who came back to the countryside to work for the project as much out of a desire to "help Tibetans" and a nostalgia for a pastoral lifestyle as for the pay. Sonam, for example, was asked to conduct a "participatory rural appraisal" with government officials, village leaders, and herders, to convince them to agree to "co-management" of the grasslands. The organization that ran the project was convinced that "co-management" was the key "to protect the rights of nomads, ensuring that they have a greater right towards the continued use of rangelands and that the area is protected from development as a place of natural resource."[79]

Sonam's job was to convince both government officials and herders that co-management was in their best interest—for the government, that it ensured nomads were adhering to grassland policies on herd size and grazing rotation; and for the nomads, that it protected their pastures from being expropriated for infrastructural development. Yet the herders were reluctant, as the plan would have restricted their "access to and use of the grasslands, particularly their access to caterpillar fungus," the gathering of which was an important source of income. The officials were equally uninterested. After an unsuccessful meeting, "Sonam received a letter from the leaders of the nomadic community, brimming with frustration and disappointment. It stated: 'You asked us to think for ourselves what kind of help we needed. When we told you that we needed a school and a road, you told us that we couldn't have those and we should think again.'"[80] In other words, neither herders nor officials were particularly interested in conservation without getting tangible infrastructural improvements in return, but the organization was not prepared to listen to suggestions that it build schools instead. At the same time a village leader told Sonam that "the head of any village association should be his [the leader's] son because then his family could get the direct benefits from the project funds." Eventually, Sonam resigned from the project.[81] Such conflicts are particularly revealing in the context of the battle between Western and Chinese representations of "helping Tibetans," in which both sides accuse the other of doing them a disservice. These accusations became particularly trenchant in the run-up to the 2008 Olympics as the worldwide demonstrations against and in support of China's policies in Tibet showed.

In contrast to a Harrisonian-style cultural determinism, the second debate outlined above does pay close attention to the cultural dynamics of the development regime and the way it interacts with local ways of life. It also firmly acknowledges that social and historical analysis should inform policy design just as much as economic analysis and that recipients of development aid need to be central agents in the formulation and implementation of policy.[82] To this end, the debate calls for an institutional reform of the major donor agencies that would enable decisions to be made not at the headquarters—where they are primarily influenced by political considerations that have little to do with the place where the project is carried out—but close to the project site. The same requirement—to take part in this process locally, rather than predominantly escalating their complaints to the top of a global hierarchy—should be extended to nongovernmental agencies speaking on behalf of local communities.

Yet in order to improve the understanding of local views of the good life and to incorporate "voice," another condition must be met. Here we return to Appadurai's notion of the capacity to aspire. To increase that capacity, the budding aspirations of the local population must be properly assessed through a well-grounded ethnographic study by people whom both the development donor and antidevelopment NGOs can trust. These assessments have to acknowledge that social groups are necessarily heterogeneous—that is, that they have diverse interests and visions of the good life—and that development is not a question of transplanting an intervention that worked in one context (a "best practice") to another, but a social and cultural process that requires slow learning from the ground up.

chapter 3

Culturalizing Violence

As we write this book, the violence in Iraq is the world's most-covered ethnoreligious conflict. Regardless of their political position, Western media and political analysts are largely in agreement that the ongoing fighting is essentially between cultural-historical groups—in most treatments they are called ethnoreligious communities (Sunnis, Shiites, Kurds), and in others they are called tribes. The beginning of American occupation in Iraq, when politicians and the media talked about resistance by "Saddam loyalists," seems a long time ago. The soul-searching produced by the escalating violence among erstwhile supporters of the invasion, as well as among those who have always opposed it but have never expected this amount of carnage, is leading to "calls for an increased understanding of the tribal nature of Iraqi society," as made by a "defense analyst" in Washington, D.C., in February 2006.[1] The CIA has decided to tackle this gap in "expertise" by offering students of anthropology scholarships—something it has not done since the Vietnam War—resulting in an uproar at the American Anthropological Association (AAA).[2]

The idea is to apply the old recipe, familiar from the early-twentieth-century view of the colonial world: the job of anthropologists is to map ethnic diversity out there in the same way as a botanist maps the diversity of plants, and this job must be done to construct a stable administration. Political pundits lament that the United States failed to do its homework earlier and thus repeated the mistakes of Vietnam, where, according to former secretary of defense Robert McNamara, the absence of Southeast Asia specialists resulted in "our profound ignorance of the history, culture and politics of the people," which in turn led to one of America's major political disasters.[3] Now, an increasing number of "analysts" and politicians in the United States, led by Senator Joseph Biden (later to become the vice president), have called for the establishment of Kurdish and Shia states (although some say the Sunnis should be punished by being left stateless).[4] Even those who argue that "only liberals" can win the war talk unreflexively about dealing with "the Shiites," "the Sunnis," and "the Kurds."[5] But is Iraq really best understood as a sum total of groups separated by "deep divides that have long split Iraqi society," divides forcibly obscured by arbitrary colonial borders and then by Saddam's tyranny that now, as *The New York Times* wrote in 2005, finally "burst into full view"?[6] Even in 2007, a BBC/ABC poll suggested that 98 percent of Iraqis thought "it would be bad for the country to separate on sectarian lines."[7]

In chapter 1, we saw that despite the popular view that globalization erodes national boundaries and melts unique local cultures into a rapidly homogenizing mix, governments view the world, for practical purposes, as being made of national cultures and attribute those cultures an even greater importance than before. For Samuel Huntington and his followers, national governments may be weakened by globalization, but national cultures are not. Rather, globalization facilitates the coalescence of nations with similar cultures into "civilizational" entities. The borders *within* these may now be more permeable, but "the great historic fault lines between civilizations are once more aflame."[8] The article in which Huntington made this claim argued that civilizational "fault lines" can sometimes lie *within* national boundaries. He saw these nations—such as Yugoslavia—as composed of ethnic or religious groups belonging to different "civilizations" and prone to violent collapse triggered by inevitable conflict between these groups.

Whether there actually is more ethnic conflict today than a few decades ago is a matter of debate. Some scholars, like Ted Gurr, have argued that local warfare has actually declined compared with the Cold War period.[9] The prominence of the reporting of ethnic conflict in the global media has, however, undoubtedly grown. Some of Huntington's supporters keep a running tab on "ethnic conflicts," attempting to prove that he was right in his prediction that most of these would be across civilizational "fault lines." In his later work, to which we will return in chapter 4, Huntington applied the same logic to Latin American immigrants to the United States, arguing that they and their descendants represented a civilization alien to that of America's "cultural identity."[10]

Huntington argues that *below* the national level, ethnic identity is getting stronger simultaneously to, and for the same reasons as, "civilizational" cohesion above the national level. The contradiction between insisting on "fundamental" cultural characteristics inherent to nations, which cannot be changed "overnight" despite constant demographic change, and allowing for the existence of civilizationally alien groups within the nation is obvious; it can only be resolved by constantly applying shifting, arbitrary judgment to determine who is within the genuine cultural tradition of a nation at any given moment and who is outside. But the emphasis on ethnicity and ethnic conflict fits into a much broader trend, shared by many scholars and activists who are vehemently opposed to Huntington's views.

The Ethnicization of the World

The ongoing celebration of cross-border ethnic "diasporas," the forceful articulation of identities by those fighting for the recognition of indigenous groups' rights, and the mobilization of ethnic symbolism by national governments as diverse as those of China and Bolivia, are all part of an ethnicization of the world. In the post–World War II years the belief was that decolonization, having taken care of national independence movements, would also develop inclusive national cultures. In Benedict Anderson's words, "Mapped Mali would have to find its Malians, mapped Ceylon its Ceylonese, mapped Papua New Guinea its Papua New Guineans."[11] (The fact that sizable immigrant populations, such as Indians and Chinese, were mostly excluded from these national cultures did not at the time worry many people.)

But decolonization was hardly over when ethnicity appeared as a motive of sociopolitical action. Religious, tribal, or linguistic identifications had always existed, but now ethnic groups—claiming a common ancestor, place of origin, similar physical attributes, religion, language, or rituals—voiced their distinctness in a new and highly self-conscious way. Some national governments, which in the 1960s almost universally operated with modernist, secularist, universalist ideologies (although some worked with racialist elements, such as "négritude" in Africa) now use ethnic symbolism to mobilize citizens. In Bolivia ministers in Evo Morales's government ceremoniously chew coca leaves in cabinet meetings, push the introduction of Cosmovisión—a mix of indigenous beliefs they call Bolivia's "traditional religion"—in school curricula, and propagate traditional forms of political organization and conflict resolution. Conversely, some of Morales's opponents have burned Indian ponchos at protest rallies in a similarly symbolic way, suggesting that indigenism may be a double-edged sword that might, if opposition to Morales grows, eventually hurt the Aymara.

Articulation of ethnocultural identity has become a vehicle for the empowerment of marginalized and stigmatized minorities, from Canada's "First Nations" to the Ainu in Japan, the San in Botswana, and the Zapotec in Central America. Claims of disadvantage that may have been formulated in terms of class in the 1960s are much more likely to be made, and responded to, in terms of ethnicity today. They have achieved unprecedented global resonance since the formation in the 1990s of an "indigenous peoples' movement," which succeeded in establishing a Permanent Forum on Indigenous Issues at the United Nations in 2002. The articulation of diasporic identities through global ethnic media and the rise of transnational ethnic organizations—Chinese, Hindu, Turkish, and so on—has added to the new prominence of ethnicity. In Germany, for example, the Polish and Turkish satellite channels are part of the most basic cable package. But although in some cases the new cultural consciousness offers long overdue rights and recognition and makes for a greater choice of legitimate viewpoints, in others it seems to fuel violent ethnic clashes, which explode "naturally" once the restraining forces of such powerful states as colonial empires or Soviet-type regimes retreat or collapse.

As people increasingly see the world as a mosaic of ethnic complexity, the first reaction of media and political "analysts" to almost any violent conflict in the world these days—whether in the civil war in Sri Lanka, the mass killings in the Sudan's Darfur region, or the Aceh Merdeka insurgency in Indonesia—is to look for ethnic, religious, or tribal divisions. Borders, especially those created or maintained by colonial, postcolonial, or state socialist regimes—that is, most borders outside Western Europe and North America—increasingly attract the charge of "artificiality." They are suspected of deviating from the "natural" borders of language (or religion, or ethnicity defined in some other way), much as Johann Gottlieb Fichte had considered the borders between German-speaking states artificial two hundred years ago. In the words of Robert D. Kaplan—one of the most popular writers on foreign policy in the United States and an adviser to both the Clinton and Bush administrations—ethnocultural tensions are leading to an anarchic and violent world in which "national borders mean less. . . . The real borders are the most tangible and intractable ones: those of culture and tribe."[12] A typical comment on laments about Iraq these days is to dismiss Middle Eastern states as "figments of French and British" imagination.[13]

Genocide in Rwanda

Consider the 1994 massacre in Rwanda, in which more than six hundred thousand were killed. In an article in *Foreign Affairs* ("the bible of foreign policy thinking"), security specialist Alan J. Kuperman has summarized the background to the violence.[14] Rwandan politics after independence, he writes, have been "dominated by the Tutsi, a group that once made up 17 percent of the population. Virtually all the rest of the population was Hutu, and less than 1 percent were aboriginal Twa. All three groups lived intermingled throughout the country. During the transition to independence starting in 1959, however, the Hutu seized control in a violent struggle that spurred the exodus of about half the Tutsi population to neighbouring states."[15] The author goes on to describe the division of the Hutu themselves into two regional groups, the majority of which lived in the central and southern part of the country and dominated national politics until 1973, when Juvénal Habyarimana, an army officer from the rival north-western group of the Hutu, staged a coup that shifted power to his region. The domination of the northwestern Hutu triggered resentment from other Hutu as well as from the Tutsi, but large-scale violence against domestic Tutsi disappeared for fifteen years until October 1990, when the Rwandan Patriotic Army, an expatriate rebel force consisting of Tutsi refugees, invaded northern Rwanda. From then on, violence between Hutus and Tutsis escalated, culminating in the monstrous carnage of April and May 1994.

The stress on the deep historical roots of the genocide echoes the line taken by mainstream Western media at the time of the massacre. A news report on the BBC, for example, commented: "Bloody feuding between the majority Hutu tribe and the minority Tutsis has plagued both tiny central African states for centuries."[16] The Canadian newspaper *The Globe and Mail* wrote of a country "torn by years of racial tension."[17] The respected German weekly *Die Zeit* reported: "The roots of the conflict go back many generations, to a time when Nilotic cattle herders migrated from the North into today's Rwanda: the Watussi, later to be called Tutsi. Four hundred years ago they encountered the settled Bahutu, a tribal group of Bantu-speaking farmers. The migrants, who were culturally superior, established a feudal regime over the natives. . . . In 1959, the Hutu rebelled against their masters, the Tutsi. Since then, the Hutu have ruled at the expense of the Tutsi. In 1964, 1973 and 1988, the tensions exploded in bloody tribal wars. Since 1990, Tutsi rebels have been fighting an open civil war against the Hutu government."[18] The article draws a parallel with the biblical story of Abel and Cain, in which the farmer Cain murders his brother, the nomadic herder Abel. "Since that time," the piece continues, "fratricidal strife has made its bloody mark on the history of Rwanda."

Narratives like this, seemingly neutral and straightforward, take categories like "Tutsi" and "Hutu" for granted, implying that they reflect ancient, irreconcilable, and unchanging cultural identities. Western readers react correspondingly, shaking their heads in helpless disgust at yet another round of African tribal warfare. At the time, French politicians and military officers, highly influential in Rwanda and in its neighboring countries in the Great Lakes region, followed the same logic and routinely understood the conflict as identity-driven. A French official of the military cooperative mission, justifying his government's continuing support of the murderous Hutu government and the military cover it gave for the preparation of the genocide, stated: "Since the population of Rwanda is 80 percent Hutu and since in Africa free voting is always ethnic, power has to devolve to the Hutu."[19] In this logic, Hutus killed Tutsis because they were Tutsi. What such accounts fail to acknowledge is that ethnicity is nothing primordial but the product of modern politics. A great body of research points to the fact that precolonial societies in Africa were almost always multiethnic and included a range of competing cultural lifestyles; tribal identities were merely one source of identity among many— and very often not the most important. Identities were constantly in flux as marriage partners were chosen from different groups, people changed territory and professions, and upheld important transethnic social and religious ties.

The image of ancient Africa as a mosaic of ethnic groups originates in the colonial period and is to a large degree a product of the encounter between the colonizer and the colonized.[20] While some historians go so far as to consider "Hutu" and "Tutsi" as complete inventions of the colonialists in conjunction with the Catholic church, there is broad agreement among researchers that French, British, German, and Belgian colonizers were at least responsible for a "hardening of identities" and the simultaneous creation of vast ethnic groups when they used ethnic identity as a political instrument through which to govern.[21] Because of the small number of colonists, the Europeans needed local partners, preferably from minority populations, at their side. When the Germans, followed after World War I by the Belgians, gained control over the Great Lakes region, it was the Tutsi, a minority group of cattle herders, whom they turned to for predominantly racial reasons. The colonial records are full of poetic descriptions: "The race of the Batutsi is without doubt one of the most beautiful and most interesting of Equatorial Africa . . . he is a European under a black skin."[22] While the tall Tutsi reminded the colonists of the images of the pharaohs and fitted romantic notions of the noble savage, the Hutu majority population, predominantly farmers, were described as "negroes properly speaking" with a "round face, thick-lipped mouth" and "squat stature."[23] To recruit the Tutsi to their side, the Belgians gave them privileged access to education and jobs, while the Hutu were discriminated against by such policies as a height minimum for entrance to college.[24]

The rule through ethnic division, practiced throughout the colonies, relied on the premise that each person had a fixed "ethnic identity" and that people could easily be separated from one another. One of the most effective means to know "who was who" was the census, through which everyone was issued an ethnic identity card. A new "imagined community" (Benedict Anderson's famous term) came into being—that of the vast, colony-wide ethnic group. This classification process put an end to the fluid and changeable precolonial ways of group identification and left among others the many children born to mixed Hutu-Tutsi parents in an ambivalent third space. The importance of ethnic identity to the former colonizing powers still seems to hold. When in 1991 the U.S. ambassador in Rwanda suggested that the government abolish ethnic identity cards, his French colleague quashed the initiative.[25]

Yet Hutu and Tutsi share the same language, lifestyle, and religion. Over time, intermarriage has blurred physical distinctions, and Tutsi and Hutu became more economic labels than cultural ones. Because of the racially motivated preferential politics of the colonists, many Tutsis were better off than their Hutu compatriots, and poor Tutsis came to be regarded as Hutus, whereas rich Hutus moved over to the Tutsi identity camp.[26] But the censuses and ethnic passports, together with the colonial discrimination against the Hutu, created a strong sense of distinctive tribal identity. When, after World War II, the colonists set up a quota system to provide Hutu and Twa with equal opportunities in education and employment, ethnic belonging once more became a solid socioeconomic asset. Unsurprisingly, when independence came, the movement to abolish the Rwandan monarchy—occupied by a Tutsi king—was seen not as a constitutional question but as a rebellion along ethnic lines. A large number of Tutsis were driven out of the country into neighboring Uganda and Zaire, while the new Rwandan state was dominated by the Hutu. The remaining Tutsis were discriminated against, and many acquired Hutu identity papers to advance. It was against this Hutu regime that the Rwandan Patriotic Front, a rebel army from Uganda, started its offensive in October 1990, leading to a four-year civil war that formed the prelude to the genocide.

The constructed, even invented nature of ethnicity leaves us with a representational dilemma. Writing about "Hutu" and "Tutsi," are we not reinforcing the very ethnic categories we are challenging? The answer is that *today*, these labels are unquestionably real. As the anthropologist Jean-François Bayart has written, colonized peoples took part in the "formation" of ethnicity "by appropriating the new political, cultural and economic resources of the bureaucratic state. In one of many working misunderstandings, 'Europeans believed Africans belonged to tribes; [whereas] Africans built tribes to belong to' as John Iliffe brilliantly expressed it. The political importance of ethnicity proceeds precisely from the fact that it is an eminently modern phenomenon connected to the 'imported state,' and not a residue or resurgence of 'traditional culture.'"[27]

And, as the anthropologist John Bowen has argued, even though the labels "Hutu" and "Tutsi" only became fixed ethnicities through colonial artifice, they finally became real enough for people to kill for them.[28] Following the work of these authors, we suggest not a rejection of ethnic labels altogether but a differentiated look at the historical record. The record shows that, rather than following "naturally" from clashing cultural identities, it took great political effort from the top to convince people at the bottom that ethnic differences mattered and were worth killing for. The sequence of events in Rwanda from 1990 on tells the story of massive manipulation and instrumentalization of ethnicity, all in the service of a struggle for political power.

The sham started soon after the guerrilla troops of the Rwandan

Patriotic Front had entered Northern Rwanda, when the armed forces of President Habyarimana faked an attack on one of their own military camps in the region, blaming the Tutsi rebels and responding with a village massacre of their own. Similar staged incidents followed, as when in 1992 the state-owned Radio Rwanda announced the "discovery" of a Tutsi plan to massacre Hutus, a false rumor that nevertheless led to the killing of three hundred Tutsis in three days.[29] The mounting pressure against Tutsis was motivated by threats to the president's power, stemming from the insurgency itself as well as from the Rwandan Constitution of 1991, which had established a multiparty system. President Habyarimana responded with a well-planned and highly effective campaign to incite ethnic hatred, which would annihilate not only the domestic Tutsi but also his Hutu opponents.

Philip Gourevitch, who reported on the war for *The New Yorker* and later wrote *We Wish to Inform You That Tomorrow We Will Be Killed with Our Families*—the book that inspired the film *Hotel Rwanda*—provides an account of what followed. While government officials felt restrained by international pressure from publicly preaching ethnic cleansing, they shrewdly used the media, from the state-owned Radio Rwanda and the Radio et Télévision Libre des Mille Collines to local and national newspapers, to do so. To rival the liberal oppositional paper *Kanguka* (Wake up), edited by a Hutu and backed by a prominent Tutsi businessman, which presented an account of Rwandan life not in ethnocultural but in economic terms, the president's wife, Agathe Habyarimana, started a very similarly named paper, *Kangura* (Wake it up)—the "it" here referred to the "majority people." This paper provided the script for the coming Hutu crusade.[30] Its editor, Hassan Ngeze, a former bus conductor, railed against a coming Tutsi supremacy conspiracy that aimed at subjugating the Hutu. His most famous article, "The Ten Commandments," published at the end of 1990 and hailed by the president as proof of Rwanda's freedom of press, was widely circulated and read aloud at public meetings. It pronounced all Tutsi women, reputedly more beautiful than their Hutu sisters, to be Tutsi agents. Hutu men with Tutsi partners were cast as traitors, as were those with Tutsi employees and business contacts. But it was the eighth and most often quoted commandment—"Hutus must stop having mercy on the Tutsis"—that signaled to even the most unsophisticated Rwandan that the last barriers to ethnocide had fallen.[31]

While the airwaves were full of Hutu Power pop songs and hate talk, denouncing the bloodthirsty "cockroaches" (as the Tutsi and the rebel army were called), local and national leaders described the Tutsi at political consciousness-raising meetings as devils, promising those who killed them rich rewards. As a result of the omnipresent propaganda, the ethnic "other" became increasingly dehumanized and, stripped of their individuality, turned into an abstraction. This prepared the ground for the Interahamwe militia, which the president had begun recruiting from criminals and disaffected youth. From 1992, after receiving paramilitary training, these gangs went about systematically killing Hutu moderates and Tutsis. On 4 August 1993 the Rwandan president was forced by international pressure to sign the Arusha accords in neighboring Tanzania, which ended the war between the rebels and the government. The treaty granted Rwandan refugees the right to return to their homeland, prescribed a merger of the two warring armies into a single national defense force, and included a blueprint for a transitional government, with Habyarimana in a largely ceremonial role—all clauses signifying a victory for the Tutsi rebels while stripping the president of much of his powers.

Over the next eight months Habyarimana tried to obstruct the power-sharing provisions of the peace treaty by revving up propaganda against the Tutsi and moderate Hutus. Events in neighboring Burundi played into his hands. There, the newly elected Hutu president was murdered by a Tutsi-dominated military—a real gift for the Rwandan propaganda machinery, which outlined the danger of an approaching Tutsi-governed Ugandan-Burundi-Rwandan empire in vivid colors. When finally, again under international pressure, Habyarimana agreed to implement the Arusha accords, his plane was mysteriously shot down and havoc broke out. Almost immediately the presidential guards, with computer-printed lists of names in their hands, began killing Hutu opposition leaders, human rights activists, and critical journalists. Only then did the youth militia, soldiers, and police go out—armed with swords, spears, and machetes as well as rifles, grenades, and machine guns—to organize mass killings focusing on the Tutsi population. After three weeks more than half of the Tutsi population, originally around 650,000, had been killed. After the end of the genocide, only 150,000 remained.[32]

As beyond understanding as the atrocities committed in the fighting are—sticking bamboo poles up men's anuses or forcing pregnant women to eat the flesh of their dead fetuses—simplistic recourse to "ancient ethnic hatred" does not help. For an approximation to the question "Why did people obey the order to kill?" and especially what enabled ordinary people to commit atrocities to their neighbors and next of kin, modern identity politics seems to be part of the answer, but other reasons are just as valid. As Bayart has written: "This war was social and political as much as it was ethnic."[33] The youth militia at the core of the lynching belonged to an increasingly impoverished population, which had trebled in a little more than a generation and was struggling to survive in the face of civil war, economic collapse, crop failure, and scarcity of land. Half of them were HIV positive and found a new purpose in the militias, where they received paramilitary training, were supplied with busloads of weapons, and were encouraged to view genocide as an entertaining spectacle.[34]

New Yorker writer Gourevitch further described the events: "Hutu Power youth leaders, jetting around on motorbikes and sporting pop hairstyles, dark glasses, and flamboyantly colored pajama suits and robes, preached ethnic solidarity and civil defense to increasingly packed rallies, where alcohol usually flowed freely ... and paramilitary drills were conducted like the latest hot dance moves. The president and his wife often turned out to be cheered at these spectacles, while in private the members of the Interahamwe were organized into small neighbourhood bands, drew up lists of Tutsis, and went on retreats to practice burning houses, tossing grenades, and hacking dummies up with machetes."[35]

Others committed murder out of simple greed. Radio broadcasts as well as politicians promised killers the land and possessions of their victims. Coauthors Catherine Andre and Jean-Philippe

Platteau have found that there were more killings—including within the same ethnic group—where land disputes were involved.[36] They argue, moreover, that Hutu fears of redistribution of wealth to the benefit of the Tutsi as a result of the International Monetary Fund's "structural adjustment policies"—which demanded a greater role for the private sector and curbs on government spending—was the main reason for the outbreak of violence in 1994. Tutsis, pushed out of government, were perceived to dominate the private sector. Finally, some of the murderers settled old scores under the cover of the genocide, and many were caught up and carried away by the killing frenzy, convinced that they would be killed if they themselves did not kill.

In other words, ethnic mobilization—far from being a natural result of history—required both particular socioeconomic conditions and hard work by elites who followed their own interests. As the political scientist Scott Straus has concluded in his recent analysis of the genocide, it was the product of "the combined effects of an ongoing civil war, high levels of state power (and the attendant social pressure), and the existence of a system of ethnic classification."[37] "The term 'ethnic conflict,'" writes anthropologist Thomas Hylland Eriksen, "is an empty vessel, since people do not have conflicts over ethnicity. Ethnic identity or religion instead functions as a symbolic focus . . . and a pretext for transgressing rules and norms."[38] A similar critical reading of events in other conflicts taking place in multiethnic societies reveals that a number of the mechanisms identified in the Rwanda case—the *hardening of boundaries*, the *invention of tradition*, and *mobilization*—are often at work. We now turn to some of these.

The hardening of boundaries. The studies by the Manchester School of anthropology in the mid-twentieth century documented how ethnicity in the African Copperbelt (from Zambia to the Congo) had been articulated by modernizing colonial administrations and capitalism. Colonialists needed to turn farmers dispersed over large territories with little infrastructure binding them together to producers of raw materials supplying a global capitalist market. To do so, they identified and relied on traditional structures of patronage and loyalty to recruit labor. Arriving in the mining towns, these former peasants with little ethnic consciousness suddenly encountered people speaking different languages and behaving in different ways. They used criteria of language and place of origin to classify groups and determine how to behave with them. Thus each group developed its own sense of what was later described as ethnic identity. Because channels of recruitment into specific types of jobs were established in different areas of the colonial territory, a hierarchical ethnic division of labor resulted. Kin structures were used to recruit not only laborers but also warriors, a practice that was later continued by postcolonial warlords and played an important role in the civil wars in Liberia and Sierra Leone in the 1990s.

The elevation of structures of loyalty from the fabric of everyday life into the political and economic fields resulted in the solidification of previously fluid and relational categories of identity. This process was aided by early anthropologists, linguists, and missionaries—who, by mapping languages, customs, and cultural practices, enabled administrators to draw intergroup boundaries—and by the colonial censuses. A whole constellation of India scholars has pointed out the formative role of the All-India Census—which took sixty-one years (1870–1931) to complete—in the creation of an "identity grid" superimposed on a highly complex, locally varying heterogeneity of what the anthropologist Arjun Appadurai has called "practical groupings,"[39] often because of "such practical needs as having to deal with a 'representative' chief or council."[40] Appadurai shows how these categories subsequently "set the stage for the group difference to be the central principle of politics," which led to the principle of proportionate representation in government jobs but also to the establishment of separate electorates for Hindus and Muslims, so that the members of a religious group were only allowed to vote for candidates of that group.[41]

The desire for such mapping and counting was of course more than just an instrument of labor recruitment and efficient administration: it was part and parcel of the modernizing state's view of itself. The census in Yugoslavia was no less instrumental in creating ethnic politics than the one in India. As in the Soviet Union, ethnic labeling was mandatory but the categories had changed. The category "Musliman" was first introduced in the 1971 census; before that, Bosnians of Muslim faith could identify themselves as "Yugoslav," "Croat," "Serb," or perhaps "Macedonian." As Holm Sundhaussen, a historian of southeastern Europe, has pointed out, the fact that "we have no ethnographic map of the Balkans from the early 19th century that we could compare to a present-day map . . . is by no means only a result of statistical lacunae" but also that of a lack of "specific and unequivocal characteristics" that would enable such mapping until well into the nineteenth century. Rather, contemporary accounts used confessional, linguistic, or occupational categories to designate people.[42]

Colonial categories—whether "Yoruba" in Nigeria, "Blacks" and "Indians" in Guyana, or "Indonesians" and "Chinese" in the Dutch East Indies—also formed the basis of anticolonial struggles. These labels were taken on by educated native elites and then successfully communicated, through media and political organizations, to those who were now seen as members of these groups. In many places these classifications have, to a large extent, shaped postcolonial politics. Thus in Singapore each citizen belongs to one of four categories (Chinese, Indian, Malay, Other) that determines the language they must study at school; in Mauritius everyone is Hindu, Muslim, Chinese, or General Population; in Lebanon politics is based on an elaborate set of power-sharing rules between the Maronites, the Sunnis, the Shia, and the Druze, according to proportions defined by the French-administered 1932 census. Colonial classifications have persisted even where the hierarchies between them were reversed after decolonization, such as in Sri Lanka—where the Sinhalese gained the upper hand over the Tamils, favored by the British—and in Guyana or Suriname, where the wealthier Indians (known as Hindustanis in Suriname) lost their political positions to left-wing Creole leaders. In some federal postcolonial states, such as Nigeria, ethnicity was adopted as the foundation for territorial autonomy, resulting in ethnicization as a way to secure control over land.[43]

The invention of tradition. The visceral emotions that came to the surface in the Yugoslav and Rwandan conflicts seem to suggest that millions of people may be bound together by ties of common blood and honor, which, when violated, may provoke them to commit atrocities they would normally consider abhorrent.[44] What turned Radovan Karadžić, a well-heeled, English-speaking psychiatrist, into a mastermind of mass rape? Was it not the same sense of rage that invalidates normal standards of conduct when one's nearest of kin—say, a child—is hurt or killed? Many of us may sympathize with mothers of murdered children who have taken justice into their own hands. For many nationalists the defense of the community or the Fatherland is as natural as a pack of wolves' defense of their offspring or their territory. No wonder that many great nationalist poets, such as Hungary's Sándor Petőfi in 1848, used the metaphor of wolves to call compatriots to arms.

But, as we have shown in chapter 1, the great affective force of belonging to a group wider than one's village is based on a recent invention of common tradition. The systematic process of creating a sense of common culture, set in motion in Europe at the end of the eighteenth century, was exported to the colonies in a way that not only ossified certain aspects of everyday life into formalized and ritualized "traditional culture" but also helped the cementing of ethnic boundaries. Just as they did back in a rapidly industralizing Europe, colonists idealized the village as the locus of authentic tradition—sometimes accompanied by the setting up of European tourism—in an environment characterized by fast-paced social change brought about by colonial modernization. In Africa, "chiefs"—despite their absence in many parts of the continent—came to be seen as part of society's natural structure, with the consequence that the figure of the warlord or the dictator is to this day accepted as part of the African landscape.[45]

As Bayart has pointed out, the colonial idea of an authoritarian African political tradition was successfuly deployed by a number of postcolonial dictators—from the more bloodthirsty, such as Zaire's Mobutu and Central Africa's Bokassa, to the milder, such as Kenya's Daniel arap Moi—who used it both to quash internal opposition and to mobilize people against external threats (often phrased in ethnic terms).[46] In India the idea of a single religion called "Hinduism" (or "Brahmanism") took shape as a result of an encounter between the classificatory endeavors of British scholars and administrators and the response of Indian thinkers and activists. It was Governor-General Warren Hastings who "required in his 1772 plan that in regard to the topics of 'inheritance, marriage, caste, and other religious usages, or institutions, the laws of the Koran with respect to the Mahometans, and those of the Shaster [shastras, or sacred treatises] with respect to the Gentoos [Hindus], shall be invariably adhered to.' This commitment was subsequently extended to other groups."[47]

The ensuing "exchange and translation of texts among British rulers and Indian intellectuals" created a sense of common belonging among religious practitioners who had followed diverse local traditions.[48] It gave munition to the political ideology of Hindutva, the Hindu "communal" nationalism of powerful—now international—organizations such as the Rashtriya Swayamsewak Sangh, the Vishwa Hindu Parishad, and the Bharatiya Janata Party.[49] As in other colonies, this exhange also created the concept and textual body of "customary law" for various groups that became the "essence of local social order."[50] This made a central contribution to the rise of postcolonial ethnoreligious separatisms (such as that of the Sikhs) and gave local, sporadic antagonisms the potential to turn into sustained, nationwide ones.[51]

Mobilization: The case of Yugoslavia. Creating a sense of community, filling it with common symbols and rituals, and sustaining it with institutions is still not enough for violence to erupt. Mobilization of ethnic identity in the service of a violent goal needs an elite seeking to achieve, expand, or maintain power and capable of reaching members of its constituency, as well as a sufficient sense of threat or discontent to make its claims credible. The beginning of the Yugoslav conflicts is generally associated with a 1986 memorandum by members of the Serbian Academy of Arts and Sciences calling the Serbs the "most persecuted people in Yugoslavia."[52] The memorandum came against the background of political ferment and economic decline—including rapidly rising inflation—after Tito's death, when various elites in Yugoslavia's constituent republics were trying to assure themselves a larger slice of a shrinking pie and Gorbachev's perestroika was casting the first doubts on the future of the "socialist system."

The academicians' apocalyptic vision of a nation imperiled was a radical departure from the official Titoist discourse of forward-looking fraternity and brought into the open the much-avoided memory of World War II conflict between the Nazi-allied Croatian puppet regime and the Serb partisans. Their call was picked up by a youngish banking functionary, Slobodan Milošević, who became secretary of the Belgrade branch of the Communist Youth League in 1987 and began his rapid rise to power based on a rhetoric of protecting Serbs around the country. Becoming federal president of Yugoslavia in 1989, Milošević launched his long crusade with an infamous speech commemorating the six-hundredth anniversary of the battle of Kosovo Polje, when Serbs (and others) suffered a defeat at the hand of the invading Ottoman armies. In parallel to this rhetoric, Milošević took steps to strip two ethnically diverse provinces of Serbia—Vojvodina and Kosovo—of their autonomy.

Threatened by these attempts of recentralization, elites in the other Yugoslav republics wasted no time in mobilizing history to their own ends. In Croatia, Franjo Tudjman, a former general, won multiparty elections organized in 1990 with political and financial support from World War II–era nationalists in exile. Like Milošević, Tudjman reached back to wartime history, but instead of dwelling on complicity with the Nazis, he portrayed the Croats as defenders of Christian Europe against the encroachment of Byzantine-Ottoman hordes. He launched a campaign for Croatian independence on the grounds that "Croats belong to a different culture, a different civilization from the Serbs. Croats are people of Western Europe, part of the Mediterranean tradition. . . . The Serbs . . . are eastern people like the Turks and the Albanians. They belong to the Byzantine culture. . . . Despite similarities in language, we cannot be together."[53]

The 1990 constitution defined Croatia as "the national state of the Croat nation." This not only excluded Serbs in Croatia from national membership symbolically but also created a platform for legal exclusion from citizenship.[54] Yet evoking a distinct history was even more difficult for Tudjman and his allies than it had been for Milošević, because Croatia had had no independent modern statehood. Perhaps out of this necessity, they reached back to the wartime puppet state's symbols, and after declaring independence in June 1991, proceeded to rehabilitate it by adopting its coat of arms and naming streets after its ministers. This was a provocation to the Serb population in the Krajina region in eastern Croatia, which had been victim to mass killings and deportations at the hands of that regime. In 1992 rebellious local leaders declared the formation of the Republic of the Serb Krajina. They were propped up by the Yugoslav army sent in by Milošević, setting off the first full-scale war in the history of post-Yugoslav violence.

Politicians on both sides continued the rhetorical escalation, presenting themselves as engaged in an inevitable, historically coded struggle with an enemy bent on annihilating them. Dobrica Ćosić, a writer who briefly succeeded Milošević as president of Serbia, spoke in 1992 of "the . . . people's unconscious, exacerbating antagonism and antipathy, to the extent of mutual hatred and the desire to fight. The tragedy of Serb and Croat is exactly that of Cain and Abel."[55] The cleansing of national histories was accompanied by language cleansing. Whereas previously, Serbs, Croats, and Bosnians were supposed to speak a single language known as Serbo-Croatian or Croat-Serb, each government now set off to compile dictionaries of three distinct languages, claiming that interpreters were needed among them at international meetings. Not surprisingly, the people needed some convincing that this was so. When in 1994 one of us met two Bosnian students studying at the University of Oregon and asked them whether the two of them spoke the same language, they answered "yes" and "no" in unison (the "no" came from the one who described herself as "Croat," while the other simply called herself Bosnian).

Undigested memories of relatively recent wartime atrocities were certainly important factors in igniting hatred on both sides. The political structure of Yugoslavia, in which official "mass organizations" were divided among constituent republics without independent organizations crossing these borders, did not help. But the methodical efforts that had to be made to rewrite history make it clear that hatred was not, as the popular view suggested, somehow coded in the "deep structure" of society, suppressed by Tito for a time but ready to erupt again. Indeed, there had been massive, solid ties, including those of kin, that reached across ethnic boundaries. The anthropologist Robert Hayden has written that the ratio of mixed marriages, especially between Serbs and Croats, rose steadily beginning in the 1950s and reached 25 percent to 35 percent in some mixed towns in eastern Croatia, the very place where the first bloody war was fought.[56]

Intermarriage was most common in Bosnia-Herzegovina, with one estimate putting it at 27 percent of the total by 1992.[57] Bosnia was the most mixed of all the Yugoslav republics, with "Muslims" making up 44 percent of the population in the 1991 census, Serbs 31 percent, and Croats 17 percent. People who called themselves "Yugoslavs" accounted for 6 percent, the highest in any republic.[58] The historian and political scientist Tom Gallagher has argued that it was precisely this mixing that spelled Bosnia's doom. It had no chance of survival because the existence of a mixed state in which Croats and Serbs coexisted would have been a steady refutation of the principles of national purity and historic difference espoused by both Tudjman and Milošević and enshrined in the new constitutions and political frameworks of both states. In 1991 the two leaders agreed in principle on the partition of Bosnia between them, preempting its declaration of independence by a year.[59]

As the anthropologist Tone Bringa has documented, Bosnians after Tito's death were divided about how to deal with ethnicity and nationhood—with only part of the population drawn to reviving nineteenth-century attempts to forge an interconfessional national identity. Thus the decision to establish an independent state in 1992 was primarily a forced move in the face of encroaching Serb and Croat nationalism.[60] The secessionist mobilization of both Croats and Serbs, for its part, had required psychological and historical "work" and was linked to moves by ruling elites in Serbia and Croatia. By the end of 1991 Croat nationalists linked to Tudjman's party in Croatia had announced the formation of the

Croat Community of Herceg-Bosna, supported by the Croatian army. The Serb Democratic Party of Radovan Karadžić had established a separate Bosnian Serb legislature and organized a referendum in which Serbs voted for remaining within a common Yugoslav state.

Against this background, 97 percent of participants in a government-organized referendum—boycotted by the Serbs—voted for independence from Yugoslavia. At the same time the Serbs in Eastern Bosnia declared their own state, the Serb Republic, the Yugoslav army moved its troops across the border and laid siege to Sarajevo, and the three-year war began.[61] Overlooking the besieged city, a Karadžić aide reportedly commented that "down there they are fighting for a single land that will stretch from here to Tehran, where our women will wear shawls, where there is bigamy." In fact, even the remaining population of Sarajevo was heavily mixed (in peacetime, mixed couples were estimated to make up 40 percent) and strongly irreligious (mosque attendance in the whole of Bosnia was reportedly around 3 percent before the war).[62] Gallagher has written that "in order to persuade their men to rape Muslim women, Serb commanders employed historical arguments," drawing parallels between Serb suffering under the Ottoman Empire and the current war.[63]

Despite the success of mobilization—as measured by killings on all sides—pre-1990 accounts of Bosnian life, even in rural areas where religious identity was important to daily life, paint a picture of declining but enduring syncretism and fluidity, rather than that of a contained enmity across clear boundaries. Up to the nineteenth century, numerous families included members of different religions, sometimes for purposes of economic or political expediency. Bringa tells the story of a villager named Atif, who during the sixty years of his life "had been through most of the categories: 'Unspecified,' 'Croat,' 'Yugoslav,' 'Serb' and 'Muslim.' His choice was influenced, first, by official options, and next, by . . . where he lived or where he worked. . . . When he went to Belgrade to perform his military service, he categorised himself as a Serb, since he believed this would make life less complicated in that particular environment."[64] Flexible identities were helped by the fact that

Bosnian names often include elements of both Turkish/Muslim and Christian/Serb origin.

Shrines were sometimes shared by several religions, with one village combining the Orthodox celebration of the Prophet Elijah (Ilin dan) with the holy day of a local Muslim hero called Ðerzelez Alija.[65] When in the mid-1980s Bringa studied a mixed Muslim-Catholic village, she found few intermarriages and a rather conservative maintenance of distinct everyday traditions—forms of dress, coffee-drinking rituals, and shapes of houses—but frequent social intermingling. Muslims had contributed to the construction of a Catholic church, while Catholics had donated funds toward the building of a mosque, and families of both confessions helped build each others' houses.[66] Bringa further commented: "To most Bosnians . . . difference in ethnoreligious affiliation was one of the many differences between people, like differences between men and women, villager and city dweller. It was acknowledged and often joked about but it never precluded friendship."[67]

In 1993, however, this village was entirely cleansed of its Muslim population. The Muslims, who had formerly made up two-thirds of the population, had either fled ahead of the attack of Croat Defence Council forces or been carted off by the attackers to internment camps. Bringa tells us that villagers had continued to live in peace even after atrocities in other parts of Bosnia began, and only a few villagers joined the attackers. The "why" of such sudden fratricidal violence is a question that cannot be circumvented. We have only been able to present a partial answer, and many disciplines—from psychology to economics—continue to search for it. It is clear, however, that whatever the answer is, ethnic cleansing in "Dolina" (Bringa's Bosnian village)—or in Rwanda—did not have the natural inevitability of a mother defending her infant.

The Consequences of Culturalization

The temptation to see culture at the root of every conflict since the end of the Cold War ignores a number of important effects of accelerated globalization since the late 1980s—effects that have changed the social fabric of communities, thrown identities open to contestation, and created fresh insecurities. New moneyed elites have risen in Asia, Eastern Europe, and even Africa. At the same time, satellite television, the Internet, and migration have revolutionized people's ideas of "the good life." Even where actual living conditions have improved, the gap between these and the now-global concept of success is enormous. Twenty years ago, for example, a young Eastern European graduate may have watched the TV show *Dallas* but would not have linked his own aspirations to the lifestyle of Texan oil barons; rather, he looked forward to getting a white-collar job at a university or state-run company and buying a Polski Fiat. His peer in a Chinese village had even more modest ideas of success—perhaps joining the army and visiting the Great Wall.

For today's young Kashmiri farmers and Mauritanian camel herders, it is no longer impossible to imagine themselves returning from Dubai or Paris with the latest iPod, purchasing a house, and receiving the admiration of their fellow villagers. Indeed, they know people who have done just that. The sense of entitlement that arises from a liberated imagination—in Appadurai's terms, an increased "capacity to aspire"—is a double-edged sword: it provides people with more possibilities but, when frustrated, can easily be harnessed by violent agendas. The anthropologist Peter Geschiere has, for example, linked the increase in witchcraft in Cameroon to attempts by those left behind by new economic opportunities to redress their disadvantage.[68] The success of both evangelical Christianity and Islam among marginalized populations both in Western cities and in African slums has been linked to a sense of injustice stoked by expanding knowledge of the larger world. Clearly, such resentments are no less obvious or dangerous than ethnic animosities, yet they are given far less attention.

The routine reduction of political problems and strategies to ethnic affiliation is a dangerous political mistake. It is especially troubling when it guides powerful Western states' interventions, such as the inaction of the French army in Rwanda or the failure of UN peacekeepers to prevent the massacre of eight thousand men in Srebrenica, the last "Muslim" enclave in an area by then run by the Bosnian Serb army. According to Bringa, foreign aid specialists, United Nations employees, and military personnel flew in and out of the war zone holding copies of Robert D. Kaplan's *Balkan Ghosts: A Journey Through History* (1993). Kaplan's dour and hopeless portrayal of the region—filled with such statements as "While the Greeks and the Macedonian Slavs despise each other, as Orthodox Christians they equally despise the Muslim Kosovars"—made the U.S. administration view the Balkan mass murder as somehow inevitable and unsurprising.[69]

A U.S. diplomat told Bringa that the book's "depictions of centuries-old hatred in the Balkans had influenced [President] Clinton's 1993 decision to refrain from military intervention in the war in Bosnia. . . . U.S. Senator Dan Coats acknowledged his debt to the book in a May 1993 speech, in which, in the midst of the shelling of Sarajevo, he characterized the conflict in the former Yugoslavia thus: ' . . . The peoples of the Balkans are bound in the straightjackets of their pasts. They suffer from hemophilia of historical memory: the bleeding will not end.'"[70] Warren Christopher, Clinton's secretary of state, seconded: "The hatred between all three groups . . . is almost unbelievable. It's almost terrifying and it's centuries old."[71] The ideology of irreconcilable historic animosity deployed by the Croatian and Serbian governments in the war fitted neatly with Kaplan's views as well as with Samuel Huntington's theories. As for Bosnia, although Islam played the least part in the violence, especially at its outset, it was supposed to lie on the "bloody border" of that religion. On a map in Huntington's "The Clash of Civilizations," the "civilizational fault line" that divides Europe cuts straight across Bosnia.[72]

In a number of cases overestimating the ethnocultural reasons of a conflict has contributed to the perpetuation of divisions. When U.S. forces occupied Afghanistan in 2001, their assumption was that the stabilization of the war-torn state had to rely on ethnic and tribal authority structures. Although the military authorities portrayed the Taliban—no doubt largely correctly—as loathed oppressors, they paradoxically also identified them with the Pashtu ethnic group that most of them apparently belonged to. In this view it was not just the Taliban but the Pashtu who had been ousted from power and therefore needed to be mollified—while rewarding those groups (the Tajik, the Uzbek, and the Hazara) who had fought against the Taliban. This categorization ignored, however, the fact that many of these labels were locally used in ways that did not fit modern Western ideas of ethnicity. As Bernt Glatzer, a longtime specialist for development aid projects in Afghanistan, has pointed out, "a Tajik in Kabul is a Persian-speaking non-Pashtu Sunni without a tribal affiliation. But for the majority of Kabul's population, ethnic identification plays only a very subordinate role. Differences by class, education and occupation are much more important."[73] Even in the southeastern Afghan countryside, where Glatzer conducted research in the late 1990s, many interviewees refused to answer questions about their ethnicity, calling them nonsense.[74] The political scientist Conrad Schetter has similarly reported that during his travels in Afghanistan in 1997, people named their province of origin more often than their ethnic group when asked who they were.[75]

Yet postoccupation politics placed "tribal elders" and politicians running on ethnic tickets at the center of the new political institutions—the parliament is dominated by three ethnic parties—while champions of nonethnic politics (mostly educated professionals) have been marginalized. Both the modernizing transformation that the country had undergone, in part under Soviet influence in the 1970s and 1980s, and the strong sense of nationhood that arose during the same time as a result of anti-Soviet resistance, has been bracketed in favor of a traditionalist view harking back to the time of the Raj. Today, Afghanistan practices a form of sharia; under King Zahir in the 1970s, it did not. The Taliban are regaining strength. More women are wearing burqas again, where they had not done so before the Taliban. In no small part these developments can be attributed to the overemphasizing of ethnic tradition: the United States, vowing to bring modernity to Afghan society, failed to acknowledge the changes that it had already undergone over the past half century and thereby privileged retraditionalization. In addition, ethnicization is a result of military recruitment along kinship lines, which postoccupation Afghanistan has relied on.

Something very similar is happening in Iraq. According to a

2006 report by the International Crisis Group (ICG) on sectarianism and conflict in Iraq, "With mosques turned into party headquarters and clerics outfitting themselves as politicians, Iraqis searching for leadership and stability in profoundly uncertain times essentially turned the elections into confessional exercises. . . . The secular centre has largely vanished, sucked into the maelstrom of identity politics."[76] Marriages across ethnoreligious lines have disappeared; tribes—first "revived by Saddam Hussein to bolster his regime during the 1990s sanctions decade"—are, with the help of the U.S. military that is hoping to make tribal militias into national police, undergoing a renaissance.[77] But the ICG sees the "sectarian" unraveling of Iraqi politics not as a natural process but in large part as a consequence of recent political moves by both new local leaders and U.S. authorities. The report portrays the relationship between Sunni and Shiites in preoccupation urban Iraq in a way that is quite similar to prewar urban Bosnia: people kept their identities, maintained distinct customs, sometimes disparaged those of the others, but nonetheless readily intermarried. (Intermarriage was especially common among the educated, who were also highly secular, and fear of religious punishment for that has been a major factor contributing to the flight of 40 percent of all professionals from postoccupation Iraq.) Shiites were certainly targeted by Saddam, but they were also co-opted.

At the same time—similarly to the case in Yugoslavia—the repression of old secular social forces (Baath's main rival had been the Iraqi Communist Party) left nothing but religious structures and Kurdish ethnic movements, both supported by exiles, as crystallizing points of resistance. Still, these movements, according to the report, would not have assumed dominance in post-Saddam Iraq if the U.S.-led Coalition Provisional Authority (CPA) had not seen Iraq—in the words of a former CPA official—"as an amalgam of three monolithic communities, and as long as you kept the Shiites and Kurds happy, success was guaranteed, because they . . . formed the majority. . . . This simplistic mindset explains most of the mistakes of U.S. policy. . . . Today we have the sectarian and ethnically-based politics that the U.S. always claimed existed, a self-fulfilling prophecy."[78]

The report argues that the approach of the coalition authorities—which relied on "keeping the Shiites and Kurds happy"
and essentially wrote off the Sunnis as inevitable losers—encouraged ethnic politics and set off a vicious circle. Parties emphasizing (mostly Shia) ethnoreligious identity were allowed control
of key government posts. Ahmed Chalabi, the former exile who
controlled the De-Baathification Council (set up by the first order
of the CPA and in charge of "cleansing" the government apparatus of members of Saddam Hussein's party), "gambled on the
Shiite card to gain power. Moreover, the Shiite parties that rose to
prominence helped to 'sectarianise' the de-Baathification process
by giving Shiite Baath party members within their own community the opportunity to repent" while Sunnis were forced out
of senior posts.[79] Although the report notes that there had been
more Shiite Baath members than Sunnis, de-Baathification has
been used as an instrument to favor the clientele of Shiite parties
for jobs in the public sector. Given the scale of unemployment,
this put Sunnis at an enormous economic disadvantage. As the
journalist Mark Danner has put it, the de-Baathification process
and the dissolution of the Iraqi army (affecting 350,000 people,
most of them non-Sunnis, despite Sunni dominance of the high
command) "appeared to the Sunnis to be declarations of open
warfare against them, convincing many that they would be judged
not by standards of individual conduct but by the fact of their
membership to a group—judged not according to what they had
done but according to who they were."[80]

The Interim Governing Council set up by the CPA was based
on "supposed representation of Iraq's amalgam of communities.
For the first time in the country's history, sectarianism and ethnicity became the formal organizing principle of politics. In the rush
to give an Iraqi face to the U.S. occupation, the CPA fell to default
mode, empowering ethnic and sectarian groups whose presence
in any event accorded with—and may have reinforced—its simplistic view of a society consisting broadly of Arabs and Kurds,
Shiites and Sunnis. 'The Americans played a big role in this new
sectarianism,' said Ismael Zayer, the editor of the daily *al-Sabah
al-Jedid*. 'They characterize the Iraqi people by their sect. They

will ask you: "Are you a Sunni or a Shiite?" Why are they asking this question? Now it has become a trend.'"[81]

The council comprised members from the Arab, Kurdish and Turkoman ethnic, and from the Sunni, Shia, and Christian confessional "communities." At the time the International Crisis Group presciently warned that "the principle behind the Interim Governing Council's composition . . . sets a troubling precedent. . . . This decision reflects how the Council's creators, not the Iraqi people, view Iraqi society and politics, but it will not be without consequence. Ethnic and religious conflict, for the most part absent from Iraq's modern history, is likely to be exacerbated as its people increasingly organise along these divisive lines."[82] Because representatives were chosen from parties that had existed in exile during the Saddam years (most of which supported Kurdish or Shia resistance), they tended to emphasize ethnic or "sectarian" agendas. As government ministries and even army units became party fiefdoms, they too began advancing ethnoreligious agendas.

Armed resistance to the occupation was initially believed to be limited to hardcore supporters of Saddam Hussein. The first major clashes occurred in the Shiite cities of Kufa and Najaf. But after the introduction of the new ethnoreligious policies, the insurgency increasingly took on a Sunni character. The Crisis Group concludes: "A heavy-handed counter-insurgency effort created a self-fulfilling prophecy: raids on towns and villages alienated a Sunni Arab community that then started to express growing sympathy with the insurgents. . . . Rather than keeping latent ethnic and sectarian tendencies in check in its reconstruction efforts, the CPA and its Iraqi allies exacerbated and hardened them, so much so that by the first general elections in January 2005, a perception had taken shape of sharply delineated and roughly homogeneous communities—Sunnis, Shiites, Kurds and sundry minorities—with which Iraqis had begun to identify almost despite themselves."[83]

As in Bosnia, this "perception of homogeneous communities" has translated into a desire to make neighborhoods homogeneous too. Militias are turning Baghdad into a mosaic of "confessionally pure" neighborhoods. The Shia-Sunni division has reproduced itself even in some towns where the population had not previously identified itself in these terms, such as the Turkoman town of Tel Afar. The Crisis Group documents how the situation around Tel Afar, originally characterized by tension between the local Turkoman minority and the Kurdish militias that run the region (and are allied with the Shiite parties in the Baghdad government), has been recast to the outside in the now standard and easy-to-understand terms as a conflict between a local Sunni majority attacking a Shia minority.[84]

Just as politics in postwar Bosnia has been defined by ethnic parties, the 2005 Iraqi elections resulted in a victory by parties defined in ethnoreligious terms. Although such parties had been marginal in the pre-Saddam years, religious networks were the only ones that had survived Saddam's assault on civil society, and they were now newly legitimized by U.S. policy. More educated, more urbane, and formerly more privileged, Sunnis—who may have been overrepresented in the Baathist elite but were probably also overrepresented among secular liberals—have been sidelined. There was in fact no want of secularist parties; but they did poorly, and some secular politicians like the former exile Ahmed Chalabi "draped themselves in religious garb for political cover."[85] The Crisis Group contends that "sectarian identification, previously a taboo, became de rigueur, with Iraqis seeking to discover—in subtle and sometimes not so subtle ways—the ethnic or confessional background of friends, neighbours and visitors."[86] The "sectarian" makeover of Iraqi society, unwittingly engineered by the CPA, in no small part prepared the ground for the rise of Abu Musab al-Zarqawi, the Americans' most wanted man in Iraq who called on Iraqi Sunnis to kill not only Americans but also Shiites.

Although the United States entered Iraq, as it did Afghanistan, with the promise of bringing freedom and democracy—based on the universalist, individualist assumption that everyone, regardless of ethnicity or creed, desires these—its actions have been guided by the most hidebound views on what constituted "Arab culture" (see chapter 1) and by a curiously unquestioned "container view" of Iraq as a fixed set of "communities." In other words, Iraqis were not individuals after all, but preprogrammed automatons executing the double command of "Arabness" and group belonging. This contradiction is quite puzzling. Even though to some extent it mirrors America's own ethnic politics that places every citizen in a neat identity category (see chapter 4), one cannot help but suspect that some of the central figures of the American occupation were Huntingtonian determinists rather than Fukuyamistic neoconservatives: they did not truly believe in the universal desire for individual self-determination, thinking instead that, at the bottom of their hearts, people behave as their cultural traditions dictate.

The ongoing tragedy of the civil war in Iraq is the latest reminder of the grave dangers that can arise when the major powers of the world reduce culture to group identity and—for the sake of convenience—surrender analysis to particular elites that claim to represent the main groups. Christian Caryl, writing in *The New York Review of Books*, has asked the right question: "In our search for authentically Iraqi viewpoints, whom should we be listening to?" Not, according to him, "Riverbend," a twenty-seven-year-old Baghdadi blogger who decries ethnic politics and makes much of her family's Sunni-Shia mix. Because "Riverbend" is unnerved by the sight of self-flagellating Shiites in front of her window, however, Caryl discounts her as an "authentic" Shia—unwittingly demonstrating the influence of the dominant paradigm.[87] Similarly, Jeffrey Gettleman, the author of a *New York Times* article on Somalia, has written that "clan allegiances have always mattered"—and in the next sentence he talks about a man who, in his youth in the 1970s, "did not know which clan he belonged to."[88] Received wisdom about Iraqis being Sunni or Shia as their primary identity, or about Africans belonging to tribes, is so powerful that even such contradictions can be overlooked.

The solution is to resist further privileging the grand narratives of ethnic exclusivism that have already rallied individuals to arms and are likely to serve as the basis for further violence. True, when reports on large-scale conflict begin to arrive from yet another remote place, time to reflect on which group boundaries really matter and what they mean is limited. In today's Iraq the situation is only made worse by the fact that hardly any journalists dare to leave their news bureaus for fear of dying and have to rely on secondhand information gathered by Iraqi aides. Still, mistakes such as those made in Rwanda, Bosnia, Afghanistan, or Iraq can only be avoided if interventions are based not on abstract notions of group culture—whether gleaned from best-selling authors like Robert Kaplan, intercultural gurus like Geert Hofstede, or self-appointed ethnic leaders—but on talking to people on the ground. And that means something more than sending experts to Baghdad to attend meetings that, according to former U.S. diplomat Peter L. Galbraith, "take place within a cocoon so removed from the realities of Iraq as to be worse than worthless."[89]

Belatedly, parts of the Pentagon seem to have recognized this. In 2004 a report to the secretary of defense recommended increasing "ethnographic intelligence," defined as "information about indigenous forms of association, local means of organization, and traditional methods of mobilization."[90] (The chief of the Australian Army, Lieutenant-General Peter Leahy, echoed this call in 2007 when he said that the army needed to tap into anthropology to develop "human intelligence."[91]) In 2006 the Pentagon dispatched five Human Terrain Teams, each of which includes a "cultural analyst" with a master's or PhD in cultural anthropology or sociology and a "regional studies analyst" with a master's or PhD in area studies, on six- to nine-month tours of Iraq and Afghanistan to advise brigade commanders on "the social, ethnographic, cultural, economic and political elements of the people"—specifically, to map social networks that pull locals into insurgencies.[92] A year later Defense Secretary Robert Gates allocated $40 million to increase the number of teams to twenty-eight.[93] The Human Terrain System also incorporates a research center at Fort Leavenworth with a starting crew of fourteen researchers. This center collates all information into a database that "will eventually be turned over to the new governments of Iraq and Afghanistan to enable them to more fully exercise sovereignty over their territory and to assist with economic development."[94]

The idea of a comprehensive cultural compass that will document "the eighty-eight tribes and subtribes in a particular province" sounds perhaps too much like the colonial mapping exercise.[95] It appears to have too myopic a focus on rural resistance to be able to question, for instance, whether the ethnic-mosaic model of representation set up by the U.S. authorities is not actually part of the problem. The new U.S. Army Field Manual 3-24, *Counterinsurgency*, released in December 2006, describes culture as "an operational code that is valid for an entire group of people."[96] Nonetheless, the deployment of anthropologists should go some way in helping to disaggregate lumped-together identity labels and answer specific questions about cultural factors in people's behavior in particular places and situations using the local context, rather than grand and second-hand assumptions.

David Kilcullen, an anthropologist involved with the Pentagon effort, has argued that the more anthropological knowledge is available, the more humane the military operations. Thus "early in the Iraq war, some coalition units alienated friendly communities . . . by arresting innocent bystanders through failure to . . . understand the culture of weapons possession among Iraqi families. Units unnecessarily detained hundreds because they didn't understand kinship systems, and lost track of detainees through misunderstanding Arab naming conventions."[97] While Raphael Patai's *The Arab Mind* (discussed in chapter 1) served as the "definitive guide" to cultural "expertise" for Abu Ghraib investigators and described homosexuality as "hidden from the public eye," Montgomery McFate, an anthropologist instrumental in setting up the Human Terrain Teams, "stressed her success at getting American soldiers to stop making moral judgments about a local Afghan cultural practice in which older men go off with younger boys on 'love Thursdays.'"[98]

According to David Abramson, another anthropologist and analyst with the State Department's Bureau of Intelligence and Research who specializes in Central Asia and Islam, there are now hundreds of anthropologists who work for the U.S. government.[99] But as the anthropologist Roberto González has written, "government agencies may be only the tip of the iceberg. Contractors to the military are probably employing many more anthropologists as the privatization of the military grows apace."[100] Military anthropologists are becoming an organized professional community, with at least one e-mail newsgroup already operating. More texts on culture are being written for soldiers by anthropologists, including the recent *Operational Culture for the Warfighter* that one of the authors describes as "firmly grounded in actual anthro theory."[101]

To most anthropologists, any involvement in military or intelligence operations overseas harks back to colonialism and the Vietnam War (although that history also involves the involvement of such famous anthropologists as Margaret Mead, Ruth Benedict, and Gregory Bateson in the World War II effort) and breaches the relationship of trust that researchers form with their informants. Indeed, the Network of Concerned Anthropologists, based at George Mason University, encourages anthropologists to sign the "Pledge of Non-participation in Counter-Insurgency."[102] In 2007 the American Anthropological Association (AAA) passed a nonbinding resolution calling the Human Terrain System project "an unacceptable application of anthropological expertise" and banning anthropologists from doing secret research (which further alienated many corporate anthropologists, many of whom had already been irked by the AAA's wariness of corporate research).[103] But McFate has sought to rehabilitate her predecessors who were involved in military efforts from World War I to Vietnam. She complains that her academic colleagues "hate her" for her involvement—and slams them for preferring to study the "exotic and the useless" and producing "some of the worst writing imaginable."[104] Sheila Miyoshi Jager, a professor of Asian studies who has been part of the U.S. Army War College's effort to build up a regional studies curriculum, is unapologetic in arguing for a differentiated view of culture so that the United States can then exploit "internal cultural cleavages."[105]

The debate about whether anthropologists should assist in creating a "culturally intelligent military" (a term used by the anthropologist Laura Nader) has just been reopened by what Hugh Gusterson calls the "cultural turn" in the War on Terror.[106] Most of those anthropologists who want to inform government practices insist that it should only be in ways both transparent and public. At the same time, whatever we think about whether the American army should be in Iraq in the first place, turning up our noses at the war simply hands the terrain over to the simplistic culturalism of Huntington and company. There is already a strong demand in the U.S. military to incorporate shockingly simplistic notions of culture into "expert systems" and opt for easy-to-teach cross-cultural curricula that, in Gusterson's words, threaten to evolve into an ethically indefensible "hit man anthropology."[107] Indeed, the Army War College has adopted Richard D. Lewis's *When Cultures Collide* as a textbook.[108]

There is a very real danger that these trends, to which we will come back in detail in chapter 6, will gain even more ground if anthropologists don't learn to tell politicians and military commanders, in plain language and in a critical but constructive way, what they find on the ground. As Richard Shweder, perhaps the best-known anthropologist to publicly oppose the "Pledge of Non-participation," has written: "The real issue for academic anthropologists is not whether the military should know more rather than less about other ways of life—of course it should know more. The real issue is how our profession is going to begin to play a far more significant educational role in the formulation of foreign policy, in the hope that anthropologists won't have to answer some patriotic call late in a sad day to become an armed angel riding the shoulder of a misguided American warrior."[109]

chapter 4

The Challenge of Multiculturalism

Nation-states worldwide have to cope with increasing articulation of cultural diversity in most societies. This is in part the result of an actual increase in human movement and ethnic diversity, but probably more the consequence of the globalization of notions of ethnicity and norms of minority rights. Although the proportion of immigrants in New York's population was higher at the beginning of the twentieth century than it is today (40 percent compared with 37 percent in the 2006 census), it was not until the 1960s that people began to question the assumption that all immigrants eventually take on the language, manners, and aspirations of their new home. Until then, the idea of the "race relations cycle" advanced by Robert Park, the founder of the Chicago school of sociology and the first (along with Florian Znaniecki) to study the lives of immigrants in the United States, remained dominant. According to this theory, every new immigrant group started at the bottom of America's socioeconomic hierarchy and moved up as the next generation assimilated; at this point the lowest rungs of the job ladder passed on to the next group of newcomers.[1]

Park's study, based largely on a sociological investigation of Polish workers in Chicago and their children, reflected more than contemporary assumptions about a natural learning process whereby migrants from lesser-developed, often rural backgrounds pick up the skills and values of the more advanced industrial society: employers and neighbors exerted substantial pressure on newcomers to conform. Henry Ford, for example, had a special training program for immigrant workers that included manners and English-language classes (the first sentence they learned was "I am a good American").[2] Children of immigrants were subjected to merciless ridicule at school, and even if their parents wanted them to retain their mother tongue, they usually wanted to rid themselves of the embarrassing accents, habits, and language of their parents. Some groups, it is true, were deemed unassimilable; but these were denied entry to the United States altogether. The Chinese Exclusion Act (1882) passed by the United States, and similar laws that followed in other countries and colonies, were intended to safeguard the nation from a group seen as carrying moral vices and physical diseases. In other words, although expectations of new immigrants were much lower than they are today—until World War I the United States did not even ask them to be literate, and when Congress, overriding President Woodrow Wilson's veto, did introduce a literacy requirement in 1917, it required only that immigrants read aloud forty words in any language—failure to learn and conform once admitted was seen as a pathology.

The tide began to change in the 1960s under the influence of the civil rights movement in the United States, which highlighted the failure of Park's race relations cycle by pointing to the entrenched discrimination of American blacks and their lack of upward mobility—and the diversification of immigration into Australia, Britain, and Canada after decolonization. Although the civil rights movement started with demands for racial equality, it soon developed a focus on "black pride"—that is, the right to be recognized and celebrated on the group's own, distinctive cultural terms. In the United States the classification of the population into racial groups had a long history, and, unlike in Europe, where such attempts were discredited by Hitler's race laws, the Jim Crow laws, which regulated relations between blacks and whites, remained in force until 1965. The idea that people can be categorized into five "racial" groups, however—Caucasian, Black/African-American, Hispanic/Latino, Asian/Pacific Islander, and American Indian/Native American—instead of disappearing, was picked up by the leaders of the civil rights movement as a tool of empowerment.

As a result, the American politics of ethnic recognition and representation developed along these racial imaginaries—which continue to form the basis of the U.S. Census—and entrenched them further. As Dvora Yanow has written, the American model means that every citizen must have a racial identity, and that this identity is not freely chosen but is limited to the five categories that lump together highly disparate populations: the Mexican avocado picker with the Argentinean banker, the descendant of Haitian slaves with the Nigerian engineer, and the Hmong refugee with the cosmopolitan Chinese businessman. Following the model of the black emancipation movement, the "lumpy" categories provide a way for every American citizen to celebrate his or her history and "heritage." According to Yanow, they also render difference non-threatening and manageable to the state's cultural politics.[3]

The American experience provided a model for new policies of managing diversity in those countries where it was newly emerging. Knowing that they will depend on non-European immigration in the long term, both the Canadian and Australian governments wanted to ensure the mutual accommodation of different ethnic groups—and perhaps limit the success of labor organizing among the growing immigrant working class.[4] The first government to declare its country "multicultural," in 1971, was that of Canada, which had the advantage of a history of bilingualism because of Quebec's French-speaking, and sometimes restive, population. In 1988 the Multiculturalism Act—which declared "the freedom of all members of Canadian society to preserve, enhance and share their cultural heritage" and mandated the active encouragement of that diversity—provided a legal basis for the new policy.[5] Australia repealed its whites-only immigration policy in favor of a policy of multiculturalism in 1973, and in the following year released the National Agenda for a Multicultural Australia, which—while asserting the importance of British heritage to national identity and requiring an "overriding and unifying commitment to Australia"—established three "dimensions of multicultural policy": cultural identity, social justice, and economic efficiency. The policy provided for a framework of government bodies and funding for "community" cultural maintenance, distributed through "community organisations." Britain, similarly affected by immigration from the Commonwealth, also established multicultural policies in the 1970s. Initially, as evidenced by the 1976 Race Relations Act, the goal of these policies was to ensure "racial equality."

Practices of Multiculturalism

The term "multiculturalism" has been used both in a descriptive sense, to refer to the reality of a culturally diverse society, and as the name of an ideology and a set of policies that supports the maintenance of such diverse cultural identities and traditions. Put simply, this view, associated in particular with the Canadian political philosophers Charles Taylor and Will Kymlicka, asserts that in a liberal democratic society everyone must have the right to be both equal and different. The right to difference is asserted through the public representation, and thus affirmation, of that difference, including in core national institutions such as the schools, the military, and the media. Such a society should recognize (a term central to Taylor's philosophy)—that is, publicly affirm and endorse—not only identities based on personal identification and aspirations, as liberal societies have done, but also the identities of groups, especially those that have been discriminated against in the past (such as women, homosexuals, or ethnic minorities), simply because group identity is a crucial aspect of a person's sense of self. Indeed, the single-minded post–World War II focus on a humanity endowed with universal individual rights has been a historical anomaly, triggered by the crimes of Nazi Germany, which were then for the first time called "crimes against humanity."

This approach, which was intended to eliminate once and for all a state's ability to coerce individuals into groups that could then be persecuted, did not, however, extend to colonial subjects. Here, the group identities discussed in chapter 3 remained enforced—and survived decolonization—not only in political representation but also in the codification of customary law for each religious or tribal group. Thus in India, Muslim and Hindu family law continue to differ. In Malaysia and Singapore, the CMIO (Chinese, Malay, Indian, Other) classification, introduced by the British, is the basis for an elaborate politics of representation, including affirmative action in Malaysia for Malays and other Bumiputera (indigenous) groups, as well as ethnically based parties, education, and political patronage networks. Multicultural theorists proposed that this type of group recognition, which can serve to grant some groups special protection or exemption from otherwise universally held norms if these go against their deeply held values, be restored to Western societies. In contrast to the conservative/pragmatic logic of colonial multiculturalism, however, Kymlicka derived this reasoning from the liberal principle of individual freedom, arguing that it is the state's duty to ensure that all citizens can choose their own "conception of the good"—and cultural belonging is an essential context of making that choice.[6]

Kymlicka has summarized the reforms undertaken by countries that adopted multiculturalism as political practice in several points:

- affirmative action programs seeking to increase the representation of minorities in education and employment;
- reserving seats for them in the legislature;
- revising history and literature curricula to reflect the recognition of their contributions;
- accommodating traditional holidays in work schedules;
- revising army or police dress codes to accommodate dress customs;
- harassment codes that prohibit statements offensive to minorities;
- cultural diversity trainings;
- guidelines for the representation of ethnic groups in the media;
- funding public cultural festivals;
- making public services accessible to immigrants who are unfamiliar with the language and institutions;
- and providing bilingual education to their children.[7]

Different countries have picked up different elements of this menu at different times. In the United States, for example, efforts to eliminate the historical disadvantage of the black population were extended from antidiscrimination legislation in the 1970s to affirmative action—that is, the preferential selection of members of underrepresented groups, particularly blacks and later American Indians—for university admissions and public sector jobs. Although "multiculturalism" was never formally adopted by the U.S. government, the new politics of representation went farther than anywhere else: school and university curricula were rewritten to include the history and culture of ethnic minorities; existing museums were restructured and new ones built; and public celebrations, television shows, and magazines devoted to the culture of racial groups proliferated. While Kwanzaa (a holiday celebrating the African-American heritage, created in 1966), Black History Month, the NBA, the Oprah Winfrey Show, gangsta rap, Eddie Murphy's films, and black Barbie dolls have shaped a generation's perception of African-American culture, all groups have developed high-profile public celebrations—from Cinco de Mayo to Chinese New Year.

In addition to this public restructuring of a nation's identity, cultural maintenance was furthered by the introduction of bilingual education for non–English-speaking children in public schools. This was based on a 1974 Supreme Court decision (*Lau v. Nichols*), which declared that the state must provide equal access to education for those who do not speak English.[8] Although the affirmation of multiple cultural traditions has had a positive effect in delegitimizing public racism, its structuring along the lines of the "lumpy" racial categories produced pressure for individuals to behave in accordance with the stereotypical image applied to their "racial" group. If black teenagers were no longer expected to talk and walk "like whites," they were under increasing pressure to behave "like blacks"—that is, like rappers, basketball players, or gangsters. Deviation from this standard can produce reactions of discomfort, as in the case of the film producer who asks, in the Academy Award–winning movie *Crash*, for a scene to be retaken because of an actor who did not talk "black" enough.

The adoption of multiculturalism in Europe has ranged from the experience of the Netherlands, which institutionalized it in the 1980s, to that of Germany, where elements of multiculturalism appeared in federal policy only in the 2000s with the "inter-cultural opening" (*interkulturelle Öffnung*) of public services. Because the emphasis was less on the politics of representation and more on equal access to public services, and since European countries lacked the American tradition of "lumpy ethnicity," these policies have not locked groups into the same rigid boxes as those in the United States. The Netherlands instituted massive state funding for ethnic organizations, broadcasting, and schools, but did not engage in a major reconceptualization of what it meant to be Dutch. Britain's policies, particularly with the advent of prime minister Tony Blair's "Cool Britannia," did focus on changing the representation of the nation as consisting of diverse cultural "communities" in education and the media, adopting, however, a more fluid and differentiated approach to labeling these communities than the United States. Local governments played a major role in implementing these policies. For example, Leicester in the West Midlands, a city with large South Asian immigration, adopted a multicultural policy that had three features: "the pursuit of equality, the employment of black and ethnic staff . . . and policies to celebrate diversity and combat discrimination."[9]

"Creative Cities" and the Management of Ethnicity

The nation-state's encounter with cultural diversity takes place in a number of contact realms. The most direct of these is the realm of cultural policy, which defines what sort of cultural expression the state supports, institutionally and financially. This policy domain, which in the liberal state is both relatively low-profile and of limited reach, is the primary means through which the state can shape the collective identity of its citizens. For example, by encouraging or funding particular kinds of museums, public statues, and forms of artistic expression, the state fosters certain views of the past and present: a focus on the nation, on the locality, or on contact with the outside; a view of the nation that is homogeneous or heterogeneous; a focus on ethnic purity, multiplicity, or mixing and hybridity.

In the 1990s public funding for arts in Australia, Britain, and North America was strongly influenced by a kind of serializing logic. Thus black, indigenous, or Asian artists were eligible for special grants, and public statuary was erected to represent the "cultural memory" of particular ethnic "communities."[10] This trend neatly coincided with the rise of the idea of cultural diversity as a crucial element of successful city planning. Richard Florida's 2002 hugely influential book, *The Rise of the Creative Class*, argued that in order to attract the "creative class" that generates most economic growth in the postindustrial "information age," cities must not only offer a highly developed infrastructure and comfortable living, but also a culturally diverse and tolerant environment that is conducive to trendy lifestyles. In the race to score high on the "creativity scale," ethnic diversity has become an asset for cities as diverse as Birmingham (England), Boston, Rotterdam, and Singapore. As Trevor Jones and Monder Ram, scholars of ethnic minority business, have written: "Birmingham is attempting to make the surreal transformation from nuts-and-bolts-making to post-modernist hedonism . . . the thrust of the campaign is to present the city as a vibrant hub of multicultural diversity. . . . The pivotal resource here is ethnic cuisine—purveyed by the city's innumerable Indian, Pakistani, Bangladeshi, Chinese, and African-Caribbean restaurants and takeaway outlets," especially the Balti Quarter.[11]

Efforts to turn minorities previously considered as problematic or even criminal into tourist attractions have been undertaken even in smaller towns, such as the Sydney suburb of Cabramatta, which took up an "Asian" theme. Such efforts are not without their critics. Jones and Ram have pointed out that in the Birmingham case "this presentation of ethnic minorities as a positive civic resource constitutes . . . a most monstrous re-branding exercise, a cultural U-turn requiring historical amnesia on an heroic scale," considering the degree of xenophobia directed at South Asian migrants and their social deprivation.[12] In Cabramatta, where a Chinese-style archway complete with gilt koalas and a series of matching statues had been commissioned by the local council, and the shop fronts of Freedom Plaza (so named to commemorate the arrival of Vietnamese refugees in the 1970s and 1980s) refurbished in Chinese style, it is not only academics that bristle against this "self-orientalization." In a 2007 documentary, local Vietnam-ese youths deny that the Chinese-style front represents the culture of Cabramatta, and stress instead the common youth culture that unites them with their Lebanese and white peers.[13]

If urban planning is an instrument of nation- and state-building and identity maintenance, education remains the most important one. The citizen-making task of modern public education consists of two components: social "integration"—that is, molding indi-viduals into accepted patterns of behavior formed by the state and elites—and the inculcation of a national consciousness. The school achieves the latter by transmitting a linguistic standard—the national language—and uniform content, as well as unified emotional and attitudinal relations to these. These tasks were first formulated as soon as the idea of homogeneous national cultures appeared, but were not institutionalized until the introduction of compulsory public education. In the French philosopher Rous-seau's words: "It is education that must give souls a national for-mation, and direct their opinions and tastes in such a way that they will be patriotic by inclination, by passion, by necessity."[14]

It follows from its integrative mission that public education tends to treat "otherness" as a deficiency that requires counseling and special care, as deviance or as a risk for the child. Until the 1960s cultural background was only addressed if it was seen as an obstacle to educational success, as with black children in the United States, Gypsies in Eastern Europe, or Aboriginal children in Australia (who were actually removed from their parents so as to eliminate this supposedly negative cultural influence). The civil rights movement changed this too. As mentioned earlier, education became an important arena of multicultural policies. Multicultural (or, as it is sometimes called, "intercultural") edu-cation has three elements: (1) strategies to ensure that linguistic difference does not affect student performance or socialization, including mother-tongue and bilingual teaching, assisted classes, and the employment of interpreters for parent-teacher events; (2) approaches to teaching that are not culturally biased (that is, do not take certain lifestyles or knowledge for granted) and that respect the diversity of parents' preferences in dealing with their children and the school (for example, by visiting those parents who prefer not to come to parent-teacher evenings, and in some cases exempting students from activities to which their parents object, such as sports or sex education); and (3) the representation of students' cultures in the school.

Australia, Britain, New Zealand, and North America have embraced all three prongs of the approach, with an emphasis on the latter two. States mandate both special programs for students whose native language is not English and the teaching of "multicultural perspectives." Ethnic diversity of the student body is seen as an asset that schools often advertise on their flyers. In the classroom teachers are expected to identify and celebrate cultural difference as a way of preparing students for participation in a multicultural society; this is done, for example, through posters and presentations students make about "their culture" and multicultural evenings displaying traditional costumes and dances. Schools are expected to accommodate cultural and religious traditions in food (one London school divides its students into sixteen ethnic groups for purposes of dietary preference), clothing (allowing headscarves or turbans as part of the school uniform), and holidays (allowing students to stay home on major religious holidays).[15]

In Holland and Scandinavia there has been less emphasis on ethnic difference in public education, although the multicultural nature of society is emphasized in the curriculum. Rather, the focus has been on assisted learning for disadvantaged groups, mother-tongue education, and support for schools for immigrant minorities. The Netherlands, for example, established state-funded representative councils for seven ethnic groups (this was formalized in a 1997 law), and has funded more than thirty state-funded Muslim and Hindu schools and even Muslim and Hindu broadcasting corporations. In other European countries multicultural elements have been introduced more recently and more selectively. Thus schools and kindergartens in Germany nowadays incorporate "intercultural learning" into the curriculum by, for example, inviting parents to present their "typical" foods or dress or teach the students a song or dance.

Plural Monoculturalism?

Multiculturalist policies, in their various forms, have focused on the recognition of diversity. This has brought a greater acceptance of multiple lifestyles and norms, thus lifting from more individuals the stigma of deficiency and in principle empowering them to make a greater range of choices about their own lives. But diversity in itself does not ensure mixing. Social inclusion requires interaction, not simply living side by side. When in 2005 five thousand white youths demonstrated to take "their beach" back from Lebanese Australians and assaulted people "of Middle Eastern appearance" in Cronulla, a suburb of Sydney, many commentators pointed to the fact that, although Sydney has one the world's most ethnically diverse populations, the uses of public space in Cronulla are defined by white "surfie" culture, and attempts to encroach upon it can trigger violent reactions. "The city," as the political geographer Engin Isin has written, "is not [just] a container where differences encounter each other; the city generates differences," or can at least accentuate them through the design of public spaces.[16]

Thus designing cities is a form of cultural engineering—sometimes conscious but often unconscious. The prevalent opinion among city planners appears to be that diversity is good but segregation is bad. Yet the urban planning policies inspired by such diversity gurus as Richard Florida, aiming to titillate the tastes of the professional class, disregard trends toward greater residential segregation, which in Britain, according to some researchers, is at an all-time high.[17] Although many Bangladeshi restaurant owners in Birmingham's Balti Quarter express satisfaction with their situation, they depend on hundred-pound-a-week workers, who, like those in London's Chinatown, have little interaction with noncoethnics, tend not to speak English, and often have no legal status. Critics such as Jones and Ram accuse Floridians of providing "a classic justification of social iniquity" by extolling the self-bettering capabilities of ethnic entrepreneurship.[18]

Back in 1984, the sociologist Andrew Jakubowicz had written that the promotion of ethnic entrepreneurship for the sake of productivity turned "super-exploitation, a feature of the migration process from countries with poorly developed industrial sectors," into "a feature to be commended."[19] And the creation of ethnic neighborhoods does not always go smoothly. Despite economic revitalization, tensions have been running high in Rome and Milan, where previously residential urban neighborhoods have been taken over by Chinese businesses.[20] As Amanda Wise has shown, the elderly white residents of Ashfield, a Sydney suburb, have felt alienated by the unfamiliar sights and smells produced after a similar Chinese makeover of their main shopping street, despite council pronouncements celebrating multiculturalism.[21] And, of course, Floridism—although European city boosters latch onto it as public spending on housing is dismantled in favor of a neoliberal market orientation—provides no solution to the failure of modernist housing projects in Europe to further the integration of immigrants. The infamous French suburban *cités*, where high unemployment among residents of largely North African origin has been a source of persistent social tension and intermittent violence, have come to symbolize the lasting socioeconomic disadvantage of immigrant minorities.

For a long time multicultural education seemed to be the way to eliminate these disadvantages by closing the gap in educational achievement and by fostering a tolerant and respectful coexistence of citizens from various cultural backgrounds. In the 2000s, however, it looked as though it had failed in both endeavors. Khalid, a seventeen-year-old Pakistani-Norwegian boy portrayed by the social anthropologist Unni Wikan in her *Generous Betrayal*, speaks Punjabi, Urdu, Arabic, Norwegian, and English—but all of them broken. The Norwegian state provides bilingual education to migrant children based on the observation that bilingualism aids learning. But, Wikan writes, Khalid was miscategorized: although he is from Pakistan, his mother tongue was Punjabi; his parents preferred him to study Urdu because of its greater usefulness and social prestige in South Asia. At the Koran school—also, presumably, subsidized by the state—Khalid learned Arabic. But because of his bad Norwegian, Khalid was ridiculed by his classmates as dumb, and, trying hard to study through most of his school years, he eventually gave up and dropped out in the last year of secondary school.[22]

Wikan's accusation of a "generous betrayal" of migrant children by the multiculturalist state is backed up by the results of the 2003 and 2007 Program for International Student Assessment (PISA) studies, which compare the mathematical aptitude, reading comprehension, science, and problem-solving skills of students nearing the end of their secondary schooling across forty-one countries. The studies, which concluded that schools were failing to reduce social inequalities between families, raised waves of alarm across Europe both in its general outcomes and especially regarding the achievement of migrant children from particular ethnic backgrounds. In Germany, for example, the average PISA reading score of children from migrant families in 2007 was ninety-three points lower than the national average of 495. In Britain, Pakistani and Bangladeshi children remain at the bottom of the educational achievement scale.[23] In the United States, too, achievement gaps between minority and "limited English proficient" students and the average persist, and bilingual education has failed to achieve better English proficiency in the school context.[24]

Even in Australia, a 2008 report by high school principals reported "white flight" from public schools.[25] Adding to the concern were reports of the radicalization and increasing violence among second-generation Muslim youth (underscored by the murders of anti-immigrant Dutch politician Pim Fortuyn in 2002 and filmmaker Theo van Gogh in 2004, and the bombings in the London Underground and the Paris riots in 2005). In a 2007 poll by the British think tank Policy Exchange found that 56 percent of British Muslims between the ages of sixteen and twenty-four believe Muslim women should only be allowed to marry men of the same faith, and 42 percent agree with the statement that sharia law should not be reinterpreted to fit in with Western values.[26]

Critics charge that exempting Amish children from education after the age of fourteen—a decision made by the U.S. Supreme Court in 1972—or Muslim children from all extracurricular activities, instead of facilitating mutual understanding, actually socializes children into viewing society as being divided by regularly confronting them with choices between predefined lifestyle elements: Do you eat pork, attend sex education classes, wear a headscarf or not? The economist Amartya Sen has accused British education of stressing roots at the expense of a tradition of mixing, resulting in what he calls "plural monoculturalism."[27] He notes that multiculturalism in Britain has come to stand for the view that "distinct cultures must somehow remain in secluded boxes." He illustrates this with the following example: "If a young girl in a conservative immigrant family wants to go out on a date with an English boy, that would certainly be a multicultural initiative. In contrast, the attempt by her guardians to stop her from doing this . . . is hardly a multicultural move, since it seeks to keep the cultures separate. And yet it is the parents' prohibition . . . that seems to garner the loudest and most vocal defense from alleged multiculturalists on the grounds of the importance of honouring traditional cultures, as if the cultural freedom of the young woman were of no relevance whatever."[28]

Tolerating Intolerance?

The question Sen puts to multiculturalists is this: "Does it make a difference who chooses the cultural practices—whether they are imposed on young children in the name of 'the culture of the community' or freely chosen by persons with adequate opportunity to learn and to reason about alternatives?" This question encapsulates the tension between multiculturalism's goal of providing different cultural practices with protection and the liberal demand to uphold individual freedoms. Seyla Benhabib, a political scientist, answers it in the affirmative: "It matters a great deal whether we defend culturalist demands because we want to *preserve* minority cultures within the liberal-democratic state or because we want to *expand* the circle of democratic inclusion."[29]

Conservative thinkers have generally rejected multiculturalism as undermining the fabric of common values that holds societies together. Traditional Marxists have opposed it for shifting the focus away from the fundamental problem of class inequalities. Prominent spokespeople for multiculturalism have tended to be liberals. Yet reconciling liberal political philosophy with multiculturalism has been a fraught enterprise. On the one hand, multiculturalism asserts the need for tolerance and affirmation of different cultures in the name of liberalism. On the other hand, by doing so, it creates the need to distinguish people using criteria that are not of their own volition—language, ethnicity, and so on—which goes against liberal principles. It is this tension that has generated much of the liberal criticism of multiculturalism, such as that by political philosophers Brian Barry and Seyla Benhabib.[30] In practice, multicultural politics have often relied on the identification of cultural groups, for how can one assure representation before identifying whom to represent?

This, however, has been a highly problematic process. Who has the right to identify cultural groups? Who has the right to draw their boundaries and speak in the name of their culture? Already Kymlicka—and other theorists such as Chandran Kukathas—stressed that minority groups should be internally free, that individuals should have the right to revise traditional practices or to "opt out." (Indeed, Kymlicka made the internal liberalism of a group a prerequisite for multicultural recognition.[31]) But processes of representation inevitably rely on mediators whose legitimacy is often questionable and result in increased ethnicization that does not necessarily lead to greater understanding or tolerance. As early as 1984, Jakubowicz criticized British and Australian multiculturalism for establishing a hierarchy of "ethnic leaders" who tend to favor certain, often conservative, community organizations.[32]

Another point of liberal criticism came from those who, like Jürgen Habermas, stressed the importance of citizen participation to maintain a liberal public sphere. If in the name of cultural distinctiveness, certain groups—for example, the Amish, or Muslim women—are not expected to participate in public deliberations, does that not lead to the disintegration of the very liberal values that multicultural policies are supposed to serve? When Norwegian youth protection authorities returned fourteen-year-old Aisha from a foster family she was happy in to her abusive parents, who then took her back to their native country, they did so to enable her to retain "her" Arab culture. Unni Wikan, who has described this case, believes that the officials failed to protect Aisha in the same way they would have the daughter of nonimmigrant parents because they were afraid of being charged with racism.[33]

The Headscarf Debate and Similar Stories

The complexity of these issues can be seen in the debate over the Islamic headscarf, which has become a permanent fixture of European newspapers and law courts. This represents the first time European governments have been concerned about their citizens' attire since Peter the Great had Russian courtiers shave their beards, which goes to show just how insecure Europe has become about itself. In France, the epicenter of the headscarf debate, the saga began in 1989, when a school principal in Creil told Muslim students to leave their headscarves at home, citing a 1905 law prohibiting religious symbols in schools. In 1994 the minister of education issued a directive concerning religious insignia in schools—the precursor of the 2004 law, which banned the wearing of Muslim headscarves and other religious symbols at state schools. The law, while widely supported across the political spectrum in France and leading to only minor disputes within schools and a general drop in hijab wearing, was highly controversial not only in Muslim communities across Europe but also among international NGOs such as Human Rights Watch. That organization issued a statement attacking the law as violating religious freedom and children's rights and as being discriminatory against women.[34]

Similar controversies have flared up in a number of European countries. Before the terror attacks of 9/11, only isolated incidents concerning the Islamic head covering of women had been discussed in the media and came before courts. Since then, across Europe "veiling" has been a prominent topic of public debate and legislation. In 2004 local politicians in Northern Italy resurrected old laws against the wearing of masks to ban women from wearing the *niqab* (full-face veil). This was followed a year later with antiterrorist laws passed by the Italian parliament, which made hiding one's facial features in public an offense. Similarly, the Dutch cabinet backed a proposal by the country's immigration minister to ban Muslim women from wearing the niqab in public places. After a ruling by the Constitutional Court in Germany, according to which it was up to the federal states to change their laws concerning the headscarf, several states banned teachers from wearing headscarves, with the state of Hesse applying the ban to all civil servants. When in 2006 three ethnic Turkish members of the German Parliament asked Turkish women to "de-scarf" themselves "as a sign of readiness to integrate," they received threats, whereupon major Islamic and Turkish organizations expressed their solidarity with the three MPs, at the same time emphasizing that they strongly disagreed with the proposal.

The headscarf debate took off even in multiculturalist Great Britain and Australia. In 2005, Australian Liberal MP Bronwyn Bishop called for Muslim headscarves to be banned from public schools. Her proposal failed to attract significant support and was dismissed as impractical by Bishop's fellow Liberal, Prime Minister John Howard.[35] In Britain, which has no regulations on Islamic dress, Commons leader Jack Straw revealed in 2006 that he asked women visiting his London office to consider removing their *niqab*s, as covered faces made relations between communities more difficult. In 2007 the British Department of Education issued a regulation that allows schools to ban the *niqab*.[36]

Over the course of just a few years, the argumentation against the headscarf has changed significantly. The original French argument prohibited veiling as an attack on secularism. Later, however, it came to stand for the oppression of Muslim women and girls. According to this argument, Muslim men forced their daughters and wives into veiling, thereby subordinating and depriving them of the choice to participate in the wider society. By 2005 the veil was being attacked on another account: as a symbol of Muslim hostility toward their Western "host nations" and of a refusal to integrate. Thus one of the Turkish-German MPs calling for the "unveiling" of her Muslim sisters explained that "the headscarf is a means of distancing oneself from German culture and is perceived as a symbol of the repression of women."[37] When the German state of Baden-Württemberg ruled against Fereshta Ludin, a teacher who had refused to take off her headscarf, on the grounds of headscarves violating the neutrality of the state, the court's explicit exemption for Christian and Jewish symbols made clear that the ruling was not, in the first place, concerned with the state's neutrality but with what it saw as anti-integrationist behavior. In Australia, Bronwyn Bishop echoed this sentiment when she said that, contrary to the Jewish skullcap, which "people of the Jewish faith have not used . . . as a way of campaigning against the Australian culture, laws and way of life, [the headscarf] . . . is being worn as a sign of defiance and difference between non Muslim and Muslim students."[38]

Among Muslim scholars there is no agreement as to whether the three verses in the whole of the Koran that mention female body covering mandate veiling, and if so, in which form and to what extent. Numerous Muslim scholars, male and female, from different national backgrounds, have explained that there is no universal prescription. Yet veiling is certainly on the increase, in the Islamic world as well as in Europe. Before the 1980s the headscarf was not prominent in urban Malaysia, Morocco, or Egypt. Turkey and Tunisia had banned it in public spaces and institutions altogether. Its increasing popularity in much of the Islamic world had partly religious reasons, such as the ascent of puritanist Salafi Islam, but was also a political sign of defiance against unpopular secularist regimes, such as the Shah's in Iran and Anwar Sadat's in Egypt. In Europe the headscarf gained new visibility with the arrival of migrants coming from countries with a tradition of veiling, such as Somalia. Yet, similarly to Islamic countries, the prominence of the headscarf among migrant populations is not a relic of old but a recent phenomenon with a range of meanings.

These meanings are hotly disputed. Recent polls, which report a strong increase of hijab wearing among young British Muslim women compared to the older generation, along with heightened levels for sharia law, appear to support an interpretation of headscarf wearing as an attack on Western secularity.[39] Similarly, there certainly are cases of girls and women being forced to wear a headscarf by male family members. This reading is supported by such statements as the recent one by Sheik Taj ed-Din el-Hilali, until recently Australia's top Muslim cleric, who compared women going out without a headscarf to putting uncovered meat in the street. (The sheik was relieved of his position for making this statement.)[40] "Honor killings" and other instances where Islamic codes of honor hinge upon the dress and behavior of women also appear to confirm the relationship between the headscarf and oppression. Yet many girls and women choose to wear headscarves voluntarily. As the French sociologists Françoise Gaspard and Farhad Khosrokhavar have written, it "mirrors in the eyes of the parents and the grandparents the illusions of continuity whereas it is a factor of discontinuity; it makes possible the transition to otherness (modernity), under the pretext of identity (tradition)."[41]

For some Muslim women the headscarf is simply a fashion statement. Others, especially students, self-consciously use it "as a sign of educated urban sophistication," reflecting political awareness and perhaps a rejection of an overly normative Western beauty standard and industry.[42] Yet others wear it as an explicitly political statement to reject what they perceive as the West's anti-Islamic foreign policy and the pressure to assimilate. Merve Kavakçi, who was expelled from the Turkish parliament in 1999 for wearing a headscarf and then went on to lecture at George Washington University, has written that although there are Muslim women who are "forced to cover themselves against their will . . . [f]or women who choose it, the headscarf is an indispensable part of their personal identity." Fereshta Ludin, the German teacher who was expelled from her teaching post in a school in the German state of Baden-Württemberg on the grounds that she represented Islamist tendencies, is a single mother who sends her own child to a Catholic kindergarten.[43]

Many Europeans would probably agree with Jack Straw's argument that the niqab, covering the full face, makes communication difficult and physically separates women from people outside their own communities. Yet although it is fairly widespread in the Middle East, the full veil is only rarely encountered in Europe. Thus, of a million Muslims living in the Netherlands, only a few dozen women wear it. And while the niqab is hardly ever seen in Germany, the German transport ministry recently had to respond to the initiative of a German citizen—obviously worried about

Islamist tendencies—to decide whether women wearing the full veil are allowed to drive cars.

The headscarf debate resonates with public opinion because actors on all sides of the political spectrum feel they have a stake in it. This is in part because public conflicts that involve women and children—"that phrase," as E. M. Forster wrote, that "exempts the male from sanity when it has been repeated a few times"— have a special legal, political, and moral appeal in the argument between the right to maintain cultural traditions on the one hand and individual freedoms on the other.[44] Many conflicts involving multicultural accommodation—such as those that concern the slaughtering or eating of animals, the consumption of drugs, or the treatment of bodies after death—attract far less public attention. Even homicide cases, which account for a large part of legal arguments involving a cultural defense—for example, when a Mexican man shot his poker partner and argued that the latter had insulted him using words that, for a reasonable Mexican, constitute sufficient provocation to violence—go relatively unnoticed unless the victim is a daughter or a wife.[45] On the other hand, so-called honor killings of women by family members, forced marriages, female genital cutting, gang rapes committed by Muslim offenders, and the prenatal sex screening of fetuses never fail to make the headlines. Most of these polemics focus, overtly or implicitly, on Muslims.

In Sweden twenty-six-year-old Fadime Sahindal became a celebrity—and was even invited to address Parliament—after she publicly resisted threats by her male relatives who opposed her relationship with a Swedish man. When her father eventually shot her to death for offending the family's honor, the murder received more media attention in the country than any since the assassination of Prime Minister Olof Palme in 1986. The memorial service was attended by three thousand people, including the crown princess, the president of Parliament, and the archbishop of the Protestant Church.[46] In 2006 a Berlin court sentenced the younger brother of a Berlin-born Kurdish woman, Hatin Sürücü, for the "honor killing" of his sister. Sürücü's father had disowned her after she had left her cousin, whom her parents had arranged her to marry at age sixteen, moved to a home for single mothers, stopped wearing her headscarf, and begun wearing makeup. Although the court failed to prove that the father and the other brothers were implicated in the killings, it was widely perceived that they were, and politicians from both of Germany's main parties suggested that the Sürücü family leave Germany because "they don't belong here," despite being German citizens.[47] Comments by ethnic Turkish teenagers from Berlin's Neukölln district that Sürücü had deserved to die because "she had lived like a German," publicized by the principal of the school they went to, caused even greater outrage, even though when interviewed by the media none of the children said they approved of the killing. In the wake of the Sürücü case and four allegedly similar cases that had occurred in Berlin within as many months, German bookshops filled with books on the subject.

The most discussed of these is *Die fremde Braut* (The Foreign Bride, 2005) by Necla Kelek, a Turkish-born German sociologist, in which she accused politicians and researchers of ignoring the oppression of young women endemic to Turkish culture in the name of political correctness. (In 2006, Kelek released a sequel, *Die verlorenen Söhne* [The Lost Sons].) She argued that Islam was "unintegrable" into Western society, as parents continued to "import wives" for the children, so that "every generation was the first."[48] The publicity Kelek received included a campaign against forced marriage initiated by the minister for integration of the state of North Rhine–Westphalia and mirrored earlier reactions to the film *Submission*, written by Somali-born Dutch MP Ayaan Hirsi Ali and directed by Theo van Gogh, who was later killed by an Islamist.

Hirsi Ali, along with another Somali woman—the fashion model Waris Dirie—is one of the most prominent campaigners against female circumcision, a practice that has spread from parts of Africa and the Middle East to Europe with migration. The severity of the practice varies from making a cut in the prepuce covering the clitoris to the complete removal of the visible parts of the clitoris and the external labia and to the partial stitching up of the vaginal opening. Female genital cutting is generally seen as aimed at depriving women of sexual pleasure and as causing serious harm to their health, sometimes leading to death. The global campaign to end the practice has involved the World Health Organization, UNICEF, the World Bank, the European Union, and both Western and African governments, which have passed such laws or used other laws to sentence offenders. In 1996 the U.S. Congress enacted a provision punishing "female genital mutilation" (FGM) with up to five years in prison as part of the Illegal Immigration Reform and Immigrant Responsibility Act of 1996. In a number of Western countries, including the United States, subjection to FGM is accepted as grounds for granting asylum. In 2007, British police offered a reward of twenty thousand pounds for information leading to the country's first prosecution for female genital mutilation.[49] Similar to the issue of human trafficking, which is discussed in chapter 1, the cause of FGM victims rallies support from a broad range of activists—from the Christian right to the feminist left.

The discourse of protecting young women was invoked by European governments when they raised the age at which visas would be granted to spouses of citizens or residents. Germany raised the age limit to eighteen in 2007 "in order to avoid arranged marriages." Berlin's Neukölln district, which has a large concentration of Turkish residents, recently began a campaign against forced marriage, and the state of Baden-Württemberg initiated legislation to make it a criminal offense (under current law, forced marriage is void). The British government declared that marriage-based visas would not be granted for arranged marriages that involve minors. (In 1999 a Parliamentary committee convened to investigate the prevalence of forced marriage among Britain's Muslim Asian population had estimated that at least a thousand such marriages took place every year.[50])

The French government has announced plans not to automatically recognize marriages with French citizens and, in order to "empower migrant women," to make the women the recipients of welfare payments to families. In Denmark residence permits are now only given to spouses older than twenty-four (provided they "prove" that they have stronger ties to Denmark than their country of origin). One of the most publicized cases involving accusations of forced marriage has been that of Nadia, an eighteen-year-old Norwegian of Moroccan descent. According to Unni Wikan, whose book *Generous Betrayal* describes this case and similar Norwegian cases, Nadia's parents, worried about their daughter's adoption of a Norwegian lifestyle, took her to Morocco to be married against her will. Nadia notified her employer, and Norway initiated procedures to repatriate her, but the family resisted until the Norwegian government threatened to cancel their social welfare benefits. Nadia testified against her parents but pleaded for leniency; eventually, the parents were sentenced to suspended jail terms.[51] The shift in public opinion that these cases represent becomes apparent if we recall that in 1968, a Nigerian student living in London won an appeal against the juvenile court that had removed his wife, whose age was estimated between ten and fourteen. The appeals justice, Lord Parker, took the view that in Nigerian society it was "certainly natural" for a girl to marry at fourteen, and he reminded his audience that Britain only introduced an age limit on marriage in 1929.[52]

Conflicts over the right to maintain cultural traditions or "values" of minority groups often are about the limits of parental authority over their children—including their bodies, behavior, and education. Traditionally, children have not been seen as actors on their own in policy questions. For example, in the case of the Nigerian child bride, Rabi Mohamed Musi, court decisions say nothing about what *she* wanted. The state intervened when it suspected parents or adult guardians of neglect or abuse, but in general family matters remained a "black box." Recently, however, a new view has arisen that endows children with sovereign rights that can sometimes be defended against parental authority. This view has been enshrined in the UN Conventions on the Rights of the Child, which also stated that "states parties shall take all effective and appropriate measures with a view to abolishing traditional practices prejudicial to the health of children."[53]

As the Western liberal state becomes more interventionist (but also attempts to give children a greater voice), parents increasingly deploy cultural rights as a defense against accusations of abuse or neglect. Examples of this include the case of a Latina mother in the United States who was charged with neglect for leaving her two-year-old child in the care of a four-year-old sibling while she was at work, or the Nigerian father who hit his son in a meeting with the school principal.[54] Religious organizations often defend parental authority. In the famous 1972 U.S. Supreme Court ruling on *Wisconsin v. Yoder*, the parents of an Amish girl successfully defended their right to allow their fourteen-year-old daughter to quit school two years before her compulsory schooling ended. Their case rested on the claim that the Amish way of life would be threatened if they exposed their children to the values, practices, and environments of a modern American high school. Christian Scientists have secured a general religious exemption that protects them from prosecution for neglect if they choose not to subject their children to medical treatment.

Child abuse cases that have come before U.S. courts have ranged from parents defending caning with a bamboo rod as a customary Southeast Asian way of disciplining to "coining," a medical procedure used from Vietnam to Indonesia that is not painful but leaves hemorrhages under the skin. In several instances parents lost custody of their small children when they were judged to have touched them in sexually offensive ways. An Afghan man received an initial sentence of three years in prison for kissing the penis of his eighteen-month-old son. A Danish mother was arrested for leaving her fourteen-month-old daughter in a stroller outside a Manhattan restaurant (the baby spent four days in foster care but was subsequently returned to her parents). In both cases the parents argued that what they had done was appropriate in their country of origin.[55]

Across the Atlantic, the Lichtenberg district of Berlin initiated a pilot project, in which sixteen Vietnamese children between eight and thirteen are taken care of by teachers on weekends and taken to the zoo or to the cinema "to give them what their parents withheld from them: a right to childhood and youth." The project followed repeated cases in which local officials prosecuted Vietnamese parents for exploiting "child labor." Although Vietnamese children generally had good marks at school and spoke good

German, they had to help their parents in their shops or restaurants. While some of them, interviewed by media, were quite happy with the situation, others complained that they did not share the freedoms of their German-born peers. Despite their ambivalence, the left-wing newspaper *Tageszeitung* came down strongly on the side of state intervention.[56]

The Cartoon War:
The Clash of Civilizations Comes to Europe?

So far this chapter has summarized a number of high-profile debates in which the traditional culture of migrants was thrown into the spotlight, either by migrants themselves (or people who claimed to speak for them) or by their critics. Nadia's parents argued that their cultural and religious tradition placed the responsibility of defending their daughter from the dangers of immorality on them and thus compelled, or at least allowed, them to coerce her into following them to Morocco. As their plea to the court to consider this as a mitigating circumstance was backed by the victim herself, as well as, in part, by the expert testimony of anthropologist Unni Wikan, Nadia's parents received a very light sentence. The legal anthropologist Alison Dundes Renteln has documented numerous North American cases in which sentences for homicide had also been significantly reduced when the accused managed to convince the court that they had acted under cultural imperatives. For example, in 1985, when Fumiko Kimura, a Japanese-American woman, waded into the Pacific Ocean in Santa Monica with her two children, who drowned, she explained that she had attempted *oyaku-shinju* (parent-child suicide) upon hearing of her husband's infidelity.

Although this practice had been outlawed in Japan, twenty-five thousand Japanese Americans signed a petition asking the district attorney not to prosecute Kimura. The argument that her actions had been culturally mandated to avoid family shame appeared to convince the court, which could have handed down a death sentence but instead sentenced her to one year in jail.[57] In other cases migrants insisted that they must be granted exemption from prevailing standards—such as compulsory schooling, dress or attire codes, or rules on the treatment of animals—because continuing certain practices was vital for the maintenance of their cultural or religious values. For example, a Canadian court has ruled that Sikhs should be allowed to take their *kirpans*—ritual daggers—on board airplanes as long as they are not sharper than the cutlery used on board.[58]

Increasingly, however, it has not been migrants but their critics who pointed to cultural reasons behind criminal or offensive practices—claiming, for instance, that forced marriage, honor killings, or for that matter headscarf wearing are integral parts of "Muslim culture," just as aversion to education and hard work, acceptance of poverty, and lack of ambition and self-reliance are endemic to "Hispanic culture." These attributes are seen to clash with the values of, respectively, European and U.S. society, and when Muslims and Hispanics migrate, they bring the "clash of cultures" with them. Attempting to accommodate these values under the aegis of multiculturalism is not only foolish but also dangerous.

Such claims have come to the forefront of public debates in the post-9/11 world, and in particular in the wake of the London Underground bombings. In the United States, where most of the migrant underclass comes from Mexico, debates have focused in large part on what Samuel Huntington has called "the Hispanic challenge."[59] In Europe, however, the focus has been almost exclusively on Muslims. When it emerged that the terrorists who wished to kill us were not impoverished refugees from Palestine but engineering students from Hamburg and cricket enthusiasts from Leeds, voices previously confined to the xenophobic fringe found themselves in a coalition with critical liberals, former Marxists, gay activists, feminists, and right-wing Christians. "For twenty-five years, we have been naïve and ignorant," commented leading German feminist Alice Schwarzer, apparently speaking in the radical Left's name.[60]

While Europe Slept, by Bruce Bawer, a gay American writer who lives in Norway and blames the European Left for "tolerating intolerance" by appeasing fundamentalist Islam, was nominated for the National Book Critics' Circle Award in 2007, buoyed by "admiring blurbs from well-known conservatives." The president of the Circle's board publicly distanced himself from the nomination, however, calling the book Islamophobic.[61] Bawer might be pleased to find himself in the company of Melanie Phillips, a former writer for the left-liberal *Guardian* and best-selling author of *Londonistan*, but not so pleased to share reviews with Mark Steyn, who, in *America Alone: The End of the World as We Know It*, wrote that the Bosnian Serbs had "figured out" what other Europeans "will in the years ahead: if you can't outbreed the enemy, cull'em." Yet both books were admiringly reviewed by *Vanity Fair* writer Christopher Hitchens, who also invoked the British writer and ex-(?)Marxist Martin Amis in support of his views.[62] The German blog PoliticallyIncorrect.de, only one of several that define themselves as being "against Europe's islamization," received nearly five million visitors in the first seventeen months after its launch in 2006. PoliticallyIncorrect.de is linked to a large network of sites that support American and Israeli policies and are critical of multiculturalism, the "global Left," and "the greens." Beyond that, their orientation ranges widely: they include liberal and conservative, gay, feminist, Jewish, and Christian Right sites as well as the blogs of Bruce Bawer, Melanie Phillips, and Ayaan Hirsi Ali. Three of the sites are entitled "Eurabia" or "Eurabian News" (one based in Germany, one in Spain, and one in the Czech Republic).

The shrill chorus of voices decrying the failure of Western policies—especially their British, Dutch, and Australian multicultural varieties—at integrating migrants and accusing them of undermining the basis of liberal democracy by creating what the German press has called "parallel societies" arises with every new newspaper report of an honor killing, forced marriage, or gang rape. The 2005 "cartoon war" seemed to support the view that the West was embroiled in a clash of civilizations both globally and at home. A Danish newspaper, *Jyllands-Posten*, published a series of cartoons of Mohammed. A group of radical imams in Denmark protested against the publication as offensive to Islam, but the government initially ignored the protest. Five months later, when Danish flags were burning at mass demonstrations in thirteen countries; Danish embassies were being attacked in Jakarta, Damascus, Beirut, and Tehran; and Danish goods disappeared from supermarket shelves across the Middle East, the government could no longer ignore it.

By this time a cartoon debate had unfolded in the European press, which saw the confrontation as one of civilizations. At no previous time had a "clash of civilizations" featured in European headlines so frequently—even though in the highbrow press it was often qualified by a question mark. The televised images of enraged crowds demanding death to the cartoonists—including those in London holding up placards with the words "Behead Those Who Insult Islam" and "Europe You Will Pay, Your 9/11 Is On Its Way"—projected a homogeneous image of Muslims and left those scrambling for anything but a cultural explanation at a loss. Unlike 9/11 and the war in Iraq, it was hard not to see the issue as one of irreconcilable worldviews. Little wonder that the columnist of the *Financial Times Deutschland* wrote: "30 September 2005 [the day of the first appearance of the cartoons] [was] more important for the clash of civilizations than 9/11. . . . Our basic problem is not Islamic fundamentalism but, as Huntington rightly pointed out, Islam itself. It is the daily cultural conflicts that take place in our streets. The French and German dispute about the headscarf ban and the fighting in Paris are heralds of escalating conflict. . . . We Europeans should not evade the clash of civilizations. We should try to win it."[63]

Several European newspapers, although some of them agreed that the cartoons were offensive, felt compelled to reprint the cartoons as a stand for the freedom of speech. Yet an already deeply insecure Europe became even more jittery about possible insults to Islam. A planned production of the Mozart opera *Idomeneo* at the Deutsche Oper in Berlin, in which the protagonist cuts off the heads of Poseidon, the Buddha, Jesus, and Mohammed and presents them as trophies to the audience, was taken off the schedule in September 2006 when the city's police said it could trigger attacks. (It was then reinstated at the insistence of Germany's Interior Minister—ironically, a conservative Christian Democrat who at other times may himself have called the production distasteful.)

In 2005, following the London Underground attacks, the Tate Britain, one of the country's foremost art galleries, scrapped its plan to exhibit "God Is Great 2," a 1991 installation by John Latham, which included copies of the Talmud, the Bible, and the Koran. The artist said his intention was to show the common roots of the three religions, but the Tate's director, Stephen Deuchar, decided that the work could at the time be perceived as deliberate provocation. He said his decision not to show "God Is Great 2" was a result of "unmistakable" indications that displaying it would expose the museum to attacks. But the critic Kenan Malik was not convinced: he suggested it was Tate's knee-jerk reaction that Muslims should feel offended by.[64]

If nothing else, the publicity these stories received strengthened the impression of a Europe only too willing to compromise its values under pressure from an intolerant minority. This was promptly exploited by those who wished to deepen this sense of crisis, presumably to enact even more stringent "integration" measures. In February 2008 a widely circulated e-mail entitled "Disgrace for England" called for signatures to protest the scrapping of Holocaust memorial activities from English school programs, supposedly because they were deemed to "hurt the Muslim population that denies the holocaust." Although the hoax was seemingly obvious, such highly respected liberal intellectuals as the Hungarian philosopher János Kis took the message seriously enough to forward it. And perhaps it wasn't so far-fetched. In 2008 a friend working at a London research agency told us that the funder of a research covering a representative sample of eighteen thousand seven-year-old children vetoed a proposal that the participants receive as a gift a puzzle with a cartoon figure, saying that "some religious groups" may be offended by the depiction of faces.

But a closer look at reactions to the cartoons calls into question the impression of a homogeneous Muslim front and points to manipulation by political and religious elites to ends that have nothing to do with culture. The Danish imams who organized the first protests against the cartoons had reportedly been offended by *Jyllands-Posten*'s earlier description of their Aarhus mosque as linked to Islamist extremism. Snubbed by the Danish government and at first unsuccessful in mobilizing Muslim opinion in Denmark, the radical imams turned to embassies of Muslim countries and religious leaders in the Middle East. Their efforts to attract attention first bore fruit in Egypt, where the government, in the run-up to what was later universally described as a rigged election, needed to shore up its credentials with supporters of the Islamist opposition (which it subjects to continuous harassment and arrests). State-controlled media made the affair known to the Egyptian public, and the foreign minister, Ahmed Aboul Gheit, took the issue to the Organisation of the Islamic Conference (OIC), which has been lobbying for an international resolution to make offending religion a punishable offense and condemned the cartoons at an emergency meeting in Mecca. The Egyptian government paid for the Danish imams' trips to Egypt, Lebanon, and Syria, where they rallied support by showing a file of cartoons that included not just those actually published by *Jyllands-Posten*, but also far more offensive images, such as Mohammed having sex with a dog, which they claimed had been sent to Muslims in Denmark. Yet a month later, with the election over, the Egyptian government took the cartoons quietly off the political agenda.[65]

Just at this time, however, during the annual pilgrimage to Mecca—the largest gathering of Muslims in the world—a Saudi imam called on Muslims to stand up against the insults of the Prophet in front of a live audience of two million and a television viewership of up to a hundred million. Imams in Saudi Arabia are under strict state control, and observers have speculated that the speech may have been intended to bolster the regime's orthodox credentials and to divert attention from the death of 362 pilgrims in a stampede a few days earlier. Soon after, the influential Qatar-based media cleric Yusuf al-Qaradawi issued a call on the Al-Jazeera satellite television channel and his Internet portal (Islamonline.net) to Muslims worldwide to make 3 February a "day of wrath" by taking their anger to the streets. In Indonesia al-Qaradawi's appeal was heard by the Front Pembela Islam (FPI, or the Front of Islam's Defenders), an extremist group that had been campaigning for the strict enforcement of sharia law. A few hundred FPI followers attacked the Danish embassy and demanded that Indonesian newspapers that had reprinted the cartoons apologize. (Later, the English version of *Islamonline* issued a fatwa condemning the violence but approving a boycott of products from countries whose governments have not apologized for publishing the cartoons.[66]) Whereas the Jakarta protests attracted few supporters, more massive ones in Tehran and Damascus could not have happened without the state's consent. Both the Syrian and Iranian governments had reasons to encourage anti-Western sentiments: the former was still being investigated for its role in the murder of Lebanese Prime Minister Rafiq Hariri; the latter was facing sanctions because of its refusal to halt its nuclear program.

Although these details do not deny the existence of a genuine outrage among the world's Muslims, they do show that the street violence that shocked Western audiences was not spontaneous. Nor did it go unopposed. In Beirut, Muslims protected churches and imams tried to calm down the crowds. Imams in Egypt and Jordan, and even al-Qaradawi on *Islamonline*, condemned the violence. In Turkey public anger appeared to be directed not against those who had insulted Islam but against the man who had killed a Catholic priest in the city of Trabzon, putting Turkey on the spot in the Western media (although it later turned out that the murder had been committed by criminals, not Islamists). In Morocco and the rich Gulf states, there were no major street protests at all; and newspapers in some Muslim countries—Morocco, Malaysia, Indonesia, Egypt, Jordan, Algeria, Yemen, and even Saudi Arabia—had taken the risk of reprisals by reprinting the cartoons. Moreover, when in the following year a Swedish local paper published a new cartoon depicting Mohammed as a dog, reactions were muted in the absence of serious mobilization. Sweden's prime minister defended the freedom of expression no less decisively than his Danish counterpart, but he also promptly met with protesting ambassadors from Muslim countries—and the Swedish government does not include anti-immigration parties.[67] Meanwhile, in a BBC World Service poll in Egypt—the country that played a pivotal role in escalating the cartoon war—55 percent of respondents considered freedom of the press more important than social stability (as against 39 percent in Russia).[68]

This indicates that European reactions to the cartoon war might reflect Europe's own struggle with its identity in a multi-polar world. While the reprinting of otherwise offensive or at least not very funny cartoons seemed to arise from a sense that Europe must urgently defend its Enlightenment heritage, British papers refused to carry them, and Prime Minister Tony Blair joined Presidents George W. Bush and Bill Clinton in condemning the images.[69] Just a few months earlier the British government had introduced a Racial and Religious Hatred Bill, which would have made it a crime to publish anything "abusive or insulting" to a religious group. The opposition and well-known public figures, from Rowan Atkinson to Lord Carey, the former Archbishop of Canterbury, opposed the bill. It passed only with an amendment that limited its scope to content that is "threatening" and that has the intention of stirring up religious hatred.[70] But a year after the cartoon debate died down, the UN's Human Rights Council passed a broadly worded resolution, introduced by the Islamic Conference at the height of the controversy. The resolution—supported by China, Cuba, and Russia—says that offending religious feelings causes social disharmony, therefore freedom of expression must be limited to ensure respect for moral traditions and religions. This phrasing suggests that it is not merely the religious beliefs of individuals but also institutions that must be protected from unlimited criticism, while the same protection does not apply to those individuals who are labeled immoral criminals on the basis of not belonging to a particular religion.

Questioning Spokespeople

The controversial nature of the idea that individuals belonging to particular groups should enjoy protections, or exemptions from prevalent norms, that are not available to other individuals is central to many disputes about multiculturalism. As the constitutional theorist Lawrence Sager has put it: "If you are in the grip of culture in the right way, you are entitled to respond to its commands, even at the cost of violating laws that would otherwise bind you; if you are not so situated, you are relegated to the status of an ordinary member of our political community."[71]

There could be two reasons to extend such protection to particular groups: (1) because not doing so would threaten the very existence of a group (more on this in chapter 5), or (2) because the group needs compensation for past disadvantages that continue to affect its equality in society. As we have seen, multiculturalism (along with other measures such as the German law criminalizing the denial of the Holocaust) arose in large part from the latter concern. Critics have pointed out, however, that exclusive attention to cultural groups has come at the expense of protecting the individual freedoms of members of society who are considered vulnerable for other reasons, notably women and children. Moreover, while individuals have attempted to speak in the name of women and children, they could not effectively act as gatekeepers of these two groups—because all of us have had personal encounters with women and children. By contrast, few newspaper readers in the West have ever spoken to a Hmong or a Somali; therefore, public claims about the needs of the Hmong or Somali immigrants tend to be taken at face value if they are made by an articulate member of the respective group.

This is why ethnic organizations and "community leaders" play such an important part in the public representation of ethnic groups. It is they that journalists call when they need a statement about an "honor killing" or a new statistic about school failure rates, and it is they who are in a position to define both the features of the group's culture and the extent of the group itself (that is, who belongs to it and who does not) for public consumption. But in a framework of institutionalized multiculturalism, organizations and leaders are not free to define these matters in any way they wish. In order to be heard—and funded—they must speak the prefabricated language of culture dominant in the media and the specialized government institutions. In a study of Arab American organizations in Detroit, the anthropologist Andrew Shryock has concluded that the multicultural logic of public visibility requires a sanitized and formulaic representation of the group that, although providing a living to ethnic organizations and brokers—consultants, journalists, social workers, museum curators—has little to do with the actual problems of the group, whether socioeconomic problems or internal struggles.

The celebratory nature of multiculturalist representation shields from public view those issues that could be subjected to debate if they were seen on an individual basis—family conflicts over the behavior of women or children, tensions between successful entrepreneurs and poor new arrivals, but also pervasive anti-Semitism and, equally, mainstream hostility toward and suspicion of Arabs that makes breaking out of a disadvantaged socioeconomic niche difficult. Shryock takes a bleak view of what the historian Marilyn Halter has called a "full-blown . . . ethnic revival" that "has been in motion in the United States for more than three decades now, prompting American-born descendants of immigrants to actively re-identify with their ethnic heritages. . . . Even the renowned baby and child care expert, Dr. T. Berry Brazelton felt moved to proclaim: 'Every baby should get to know their heritage.' In the fundamentals of twenty-first-century American childrearing, roots training comes even before potty training."[72] According to Shryock, the "heritage format" prevalent in the United States is "partly false consciousness, partly misdiagnosis and partly moral smugness," and that does not make for greater tolerance and acceptance.[73]

Wikan has described how the Norwegian politics of ethnic representation forces community spokesmen to represent views they (and perhaps others in the group) in fact disagree with, simply because not playing the part expected of them or sending overly differentiated messages carries the risk of losing group representation altogether. Wikan recalls an encounter with an "aggressive Muslim traditionalist," who, after a televised debate in which he defended certain "practices that undermined young people's freedoms and life prospects," privately urged her to help him combat those very practices.[74] This may not be as sinister as it sounds. As Shryock has explained, if you represent a marginalized group in a hostile environment, you may well decide that exposing internal injustices may result in even greater injustice— such as official harassment or demonization by the media—for everyone in the group. Nonetheless, such brinkmanship ultimately undermines spokespeople's authority to define group norms and indeed define the group.

In a very different context—that of Aboriginal life in the Western Sydney suburbs—the ethnographer Gillian Cowlishaw describes a strikingly similar situation. Formulaic reconciliation meetings and "welcome to country" ceremonies at public functions (apparently introduced from New Zealand in the late 1970s) pay respect to the Darug people as "traditional owners of the land" but displace traditional, deeply personal storytelling about kinship and history. "Elders," identified as such by police and hospital liaison officers, claim Darug heritage in spite of the fact that local residents are members of other Aboriginal peoples who migrated from rural New South Wales. (The Darug as a group have not existed in the area for more than a century, and Aboriginal residents question the authority of "elders" on a number of grounds: that it does not extend to members of other "mobs"; that it is irrelevant, unchosen, or altogether "imported.") Site inspections, compulsory before any construction project or archaeological dig carried out on Aboriginal land, employ volunteers who claim Aboriginal heritage as experts. Cowlishaw points out that rather than helping to preserve distinctive local cultural practices and histories—which, in the case of Aborigines, are deeply tied to particular places on the land—this "heritage format" further undermines them while sweeping real problems (joblessness, violence, alcoholism, as well as the continuing hostility and suspicion of the white population) under the rug.[75]

In some situations lives can depend on statements by "community leaders" and "experts." In the 1980s, Kwai Fan Mak, an immigrant from Hong Kong, was sentenced to death by a court in the state of Washington for murdering thirteen people. An appellate court, however, ordered his resentencing on the grounds that when the prosecution portrayed Mak as a cold-blooded "killing machine," his lawyers failed to present "evidence explaining that the defendant's apparent lack of emotion is culturally expected behaviour and not a manifestation of an absence of remorse." The evidence the court was referring to would have been presented by an "expert witness" who had testified that expressing emotions in public was inappropriate for a man in the Chinese cultural context. The court thus acknowledged that the standards of "reasonable" behavior were culturally constructed, that the motives that impel a person to behave in a certain fashion are strongly influenced by culturally divergent beliefs, and that failure to acknowledge this can lead to injustice. This argument saved Mak's life: he was resentenced in 2002 and received thirteen life terms.[76]

But is there, as Renteln has argued in proposing a formalized "cultural defense" in U.S. law, an objective way to tell whether a person is a member of a cultural community, whether a cultural practice or belief indeed exists, and whether it has influenced a person strongly enough at the time when a particular action violating prevalent norms occurs?[77] To take up Mak's example, it is true that in most situations Chinese men are much less likely to publicly express their emotions through facial expression or body language than their American counterparts. But Chinese courts expect defendants to display their remorse by bowing their heads, and although not all do so, expressions of remorse can mitigate a sentence.

Similarly, although a number of defendants of homicide cases in the United States have raised a cultural defense hinging on the concept of honor, and some have even succeeded in substantially reducing their sentence, there is no agreement as to how culturally accepted such killings are. A case in point is that of Dong Lu Chen, whom the New York State Supreme Court sentenced to five years probation for killing his wife after she had confessed to adultery. A best-selling book on the subject, *Forbidden Love*, by Jordanian-born and Australia-based Norma Khoury—supposedly the story of a murdered friend—turned out to be a hoax. Despite that, in addition to generating a handsome income, the work briefly made the author a cause célèbre in the human-rights crowd, suggesting that not only traditional authority figures but also those who feel oppressed by them can sometimes benefit from simplified representations.[78] When Necla Kelek described forced marriages as being endemic to Turkish culture, sixty migration researchers signed an open letter that accused her of blowing marginal practices out of proportion. The Berlin lawyer Seyran Ateş, who represents Turkish women in divorce cases and supports a ban on headscarves, came out in support of Kelek, claiming that 30 percent to 40 percent of Turkish marriages in Germany are forced. Actor Tamer Yigit, however, said he has "never heard" of a forced marriage in Kreuzberg, a Berlin district with a large Turkish population and where he was born.[79]

Where does the line lie between arranged and forced marriage? The former is certainly a dominant practice for a large part of the world's population: it is rather the idea that romantic love must be the basis for marriage that is a novel concept, even in the West. But if the definition of forced marriage is limited to marriage that proceeds despite the active opposition of one of the parties, what do we make of situations where they are unable to articulate dissent in any meaningful way? On the one hand, Western law presumes that minors cannot consent, but undermines that presumption by allowing the marriage of minors with parental agreement. On the other hand, some women may be unable to dissent to their parents' wishes out of fear or simply because the possibility of choice itself does not occur to them. The difficulty of judging such situations, or even of obtaining an unequivocal testimony, is amply clear from the Norwegian case of Nadia, the young woman whose parents took her to Morocco to get married. In the course of the legal process, Nadia retracted her initial statement that she had been abducted, and even after she later came back to it, she was so distraught during the trial that she asked her parents to leave while she testified.[80]

If it is difficult to determine where the line between arranged and forced marriage lies, it can be equally difficult to decide whether sexual intercourse is forced or voluntary. American readers are familiar with the many cases of "date rape," where the contestation of whether a particular behavior indicated consent or not must be seen within the highly culturally specific practice of college partying, in which the daytime rules of behaviour and decision making are temporarily suspended. Members of cultural groups other than American students also often refer to differing sexual traditions when denying charges of rape. In 2006 an Australian court extended to eighteen months a sentence of originally one month in the case where a fourteen-year-old Aborigine girl was raped by a man from the same group. The original sentence was issued after the defendant had argued that the girl "had been promised to him" and that it was therefore his right to "take her" under customary law. In another case in the same year, Queensland judge Sarah Bradley did not impose jail terms on nine Aboriginal youths who gang-raped a ten-year-old girl in Cape York after they used the same defense. In a 2002 case a fifty-year-old Aboriginal man had been sentenced to just twenty-four hours in jail for raping a fifteen-year-old girl. In a 1991 sentence a South Australian judge commented that "there is no crime of rape in your community."[81]

As a remnant of British colonial practice, Australian courts have recognized Aboriginal customary law and have occasionally even used it in sentencing. In 1994, Australia approved a legal amendment that required courts to consider the defendant's cultural background. But this act was reversed in 2007, when the federal parliament passed legislation to prohibit courts from considering "customary law or cultural practice" as a defense or mitigating circumstances for "serious sexual crime and violent crime."[82] Indigenous Affairs Minister Mal Brough said that customary law was stopping people from giving evidence in court when a friend or relative was charged with a crime. He accused "so-called indigenous leaders" of hiding "behind the veil . . . of cultural sensitivity."[83] Central Australia Crown Prosecutor Nanette Rogers also called on the Northern Territory to rein in "mafia-style" customary law, again referring to rape cases. She claimed that "indigenous Australians" asked that the law be applied to Aboriginal offenders in the same way as to whites. Yet earlier, Rogers had supported a different argument: that rape should be punished not because "culture did not matter," but because Aboriginal tradition punished it too.

This argument, advanced by Aboriginal women activists since the late 1980s, maintained that contrary to claims by lawyers for the accused men, Aboriginal custom did not sanction unwanted sex. Externally induced cultural change—the availability of pornography and state or church institutions where young men and women could mix outside the prescribed kinship categories—was causing the rise in rape. This argument pointed out that men and women in these court cases were likely to provide different definitions of "Aboriginal culture"; in fact, some of the men who were given light sentences by courts had subsequently been ostracized in their settlements as a form of punishment.[84] Even so, just as Nigerian child bride Rabi Mohamed Musi's opinion was not cited in the reports on the 1968 British case, neither do we hear the testimony of the Aboriginal girl in the one that triggered the current change in legislation. It is difficult not to conclude that the different treatment of the two cases has more to do with shifts in the political climate and our own standards of moral acceptability than with the actual consent of the victims. Indeed, at the time of the Musi ruling, neither Britain nor any other country had criminalized marital rape—the consummation of marriage, forced or not, was the man's right—so the decision revolved around whether the marriage concluded in Nigeria was valid under British law.

Accusations of forced marriage or forced sex strike a chord in Western society because they pit the right to the free exercise of culture against the freedom of an individual to make his or her own choice, a freedom that is particularly cherished in liberal thinking. It is this type of conflict that has been central for the articulation of nontraditional anti-immigrant agendas. These claim to oppose immigration from certain countries not on conservative but on liberal grounds—not on the grounds that they threaten the cultural purity of the natives but that their cultural claims, if given democratic legitimacy, undermine liberalism. The best known of such movements was the party PFL, headed by the gay Dutch politician Pim Fortuyn. After Fortuyn was assassinated by a Dutch citizen of Moroccan origin, Geert Wilders set up a new party, the Partij voor de Vrijheid (Party for Freedom). The party, which advocates barring all non-Western immigrants for five years and lifting speed limits on motorways, has been leading the polls in The Netherlands.

In the United States a similar figure is the flamboyant Texan politician "Kinky" Friedman, who won 12 percent of the 2006 gubernatorial vote with a platform that included supporting gay marriage and sending ten thousand troops to the country's southern border to keep out illegal Mexican immigrants. The accusation that patriarchal families and organizations oppress women (and female children) and forcibly prevent their integration into Western society while purporting to speak on their behalf is central for such politicians, especially in Europe, but it is also voiced by researchers such as Unni Wikan, the Norwegian anthropologist who has written extensively about migrant women. In France, which has steadfastly resisted multicultural policies and therefore has not provided automatic funding for migrant organizations, there are vocal organizations of migrant women, including the North African feminist group Ni Putes Ni Soumises ("neither whores nor submissive"). That, of all Western countries, the one that has made no concessions to identity politics should display the most diversity of voices among migrant organizations raises further doubts about the success of state multiculturalism.

The End of Multiculturalism?

The anthropologist Thomas Hylland Eriksen sees a change "in the standard presentation of minority issues (enforced marriages rather than discrimination in the labor market; unwillingness to integrate among immigrants rather than demands for cultural rights)" happening since the 1980s.[85] He has linked this change to a shift of focus in policy making to a neoliberal worldview that is centered on the freedom and productivity of the individual and that sees groups as not only unnecessary as mediators or social forms, but also as suspect of limiting the potential of their members. After 9/11, because of the suspicion that ethnic "communities" might be training their children to be enemies of "the West," this ongoing shift has acquired a sudden urgency that precipitated a feverish concern with "integration." Paradoxically, the unprecedented concern with preserving cultural diversity (which is discussed in chapter 5) has been accompanied with a starkly diminished tolerance of substantial differences in moral standards, which in premulticulturalist times appeared quite natural (recall the case of Rabi Mohamed Musi).

The climate of fear generated by the events of 11 September 2001 and the London Underground bombing meant that every further occurrence of violence involving ethnic difference, whether on a large or small scale, was likely to be seen as being caused by it, and thus a confirmation of a need for a stronger hand in enforcing common values. In Australia this happened in December 2005, when five thousand white youths demonstrated with Australian flags at Cronulla Beach in the Sydney suburbs, where several young Lebanese men had assaulted surf lifeguards who had allegedly taunted them with the insult "Lebs can't swim." The demonstrators, in turn, attacked people "of Middle Eastern appearance," and a call for "Leb and Wog bashing day" ("Wog," in the Australian context, refers broadly to Southern Europeans and Middle Easterners) was circulated by SMS (text messages sent by cell phones).[86] The event grew into an occasion for national self-scrutiny, and although mainstream media blamed white extremist groups, it was generally perceived as further undermining the success of multiculturalism. The following year, the government introduced a citizenship test designed to ascertain that migrants know and subscribe to "Australian values." The term "multiculturalism" is still widely used to describe Australian society, but its meaning has transformed into what the political scientist Christian Joppke—along with many Australian critics—has called a "corporate diversity agenda," focusing on the advantages of cultural diversity for economic dynamism but retreating from the strong statements about a pluralism of values.[87]

In 2006 the word "multicultural" was removed from the name of the Department for Immigration and Multicultural Affairs and replaced with the word "citizenship," while local councils have shifted their vocabulary from "multiculturalism where difference is maintained and protected to a more proactive engagement between cultures which emphasizes interaction and the exchange of ideas between different cultural groups."[88] Most Australians today accept living together with people from diverse cultural backgrounds, but do not wish to engage with it actively. The 2005

Australian Attitudes Survey found strong support for maintaining a policy of multiculturalism but an equally large majority of respondents said no to policies providing state support for the maintenance of separate ethnic cultures.[89] Recognizing this fact, government programs increasingly focus on the development of "social capital that builds trust . . . reciprocity and social networks."[90]

The same trend emerged in Europe in the 2000s, as "integration" unseated multiculturalism as the mantra of immigration and minority politics. In 2007, Germany announced a "National Integration Plan," which included measures to improve German-language teaching at an early stage, the "reintegration" of school dropouts, improving the access of elderly migrants to health care, strengthening the "intercultural competency" of local governments, and increasing the representation of migrants and Islam in the media—but also making "behaviour hostile to integration" (*integrationsfeindliches Verhalten*) and "impeding the integration of family members" punishable offenses that can lead to expulsion. President Horst Köhler stated that the country had demanded too little with regard to the integration of migrants and called on the latter to abide by the "civilizational standards" formulated in the Constitution.[91] The Austrian minister of the interior echoed him, claiming that "45 percent of Muslims in Austria are unwilling to integrate, and those who don't want to integrate have no place in Austria." Integration, she clarified, meant accepting the country's values.[92] Italy's Socialist minister of interior, for a change, accused Chinese migrants of refusing to integrate and—referring to ethnic neighborhoods—said Italy would not tolerate "states within the state."[93] When, in 2008, the Turkish prime minister called on Turks in Germany to resist assimilation and on Germany to provide education in Turkish up to university level, his suggestions were met with almost unanimous indignation, even though they were exactly what the European Union recommends to its members as good practice in the protection of minorities.[94]

The new term "hostility to integration" (*Integrationsfeindlichkeit*) has a ring of gravity—it is derived from the word *Feind* (enemy)—and, mirroring *Fremdenfeindlichkeit* (xenophobia or racism), can be used to describe a whole range of behaviors. Many European countries have either developed or are developing "integration courses," increasingly making them compulsory for migrants who apply for permanent residence. Germany is planning a thousand-euro sanction for nonparticipation in integration courses, while the new Swiss integration law includes the threat to withdraw residency permits of those migrants who fail the obligatory language and integration courses. The city of Basel is running a pilot project that offers migrants sixty-six "integration projects." They can become volunteer garbage men—no doubt with the idea that they learn the strict Swiss regime of rubbish sorting—or be trained as intercultural mediators.[95] A core element in the new approach is enforcing the mastery of the national language. The Rotterdam Citizen's Code adopted in 2006 included the precept "We use Dutch as community language."[96] In 2005 a Berlin school whose students are mostly nonnative speakers of German introduced a German-only policy that extends to every interaction at the school, including during breaks. The policy was attacked by Turkish migrant organizations and some media as "forcible Germanization," but held up as a model for giving disadvantaged youth better chances in society by the bulk of public opinion.[97]

The new toughness is related to the fear of *Überfremdung* (overalienation) and "ghettoization" that has long filled Swiss and German tabloids. Even among liberal thinkers who do not want to see immigration curbed, an increasing number have reached the conclusion that multiculturalism has failed. Ian Buruma, a Dutch-American author, and Timothy Garton Ash, a professor of history at Oxford, have both criticized Somali-Dutch ex-MP Ayaan Hirsi Ali for her "Enlightenment fundamentalism" that denounces Islam as inherently oppressive. Nonetheless they agree that "an ideology which holds that people must live in separate communities within a country, should not take an interest in each other and must not criticize each other is both wrong and unworkable."[98] In 2007 the prominent liberal American sociologist Robert Putnam—whose *Bowling Alone* had been a bestseller that earned him audiences with presidents Bill Clinton and George W. Bush—joined Garton Ash and Buruma by releasing, after long hesitation, the results of a survey that suggested that more ethnically diverse American neighborhoods had less civic engagement (voting, volunteering, charities), less communal socializing, more distrust, and a tendency to "hunker down."[99]

Even before the London attacks, Tony Blair's Labor government had called for a new approach to multiculturalism, in 2004. It was to "concentrate on the need to build community cohesion alongside the pursuit of racial and ethnic equality," as well as to define more clearly the obligations of citizenship and develop a shared conception of nationhood.[100] Echoing the 2001 Cantle Report, which had recommended that the "non-white community has to develop a greater acceptance of the principal national institutions," Home Secretary David Blunkett declared that "those who come to our home should accept our norms of acceptability." In 2006 no lesser an authority than Trevor Phillips, the head of the Racial Equality Commission and a close adviser to Blair, declared that Britain was "sleepwalking towards segregation" as it tolerated the proliferation of "black holes into which no one goes without fear," and that "the bridges that so many . . . have laboured to build" were "crumbling."[101]

Three years earlier, following the Cantle Report, whose author wrote that "the concept of nationality . . . should also take its place in the lexicon of cohesion,"[102] Britain had introduced compulsory citizenship education in schools. A further report by Sir Keith Ajegbo, commissioned by the education secretary in the wake of the London bombings, concluded that there was not enough emphasis on UK identity and history in citizenship curriculum. In 2007 the secretary announced that, in accordance with Sir Keith's recommendations, it would become compulsory for secondary school pupils up to sixteen to learn about "core British values" such as free speech, tolerance, and respect for the rule of law.[103] The Conservative opposition went farther, with Shadow Home Secretary David Davis declaring that multiculturalism should be abolished because it had allowed "the perverted values of suicide bombers" to take root.[104]

Some governments begin testing migrants for mastery of the national language and prevailing norms before they arrive. Australia, France, Germany, and the Netherlands have introduced language tests for migrants joining family members.[105] With the exception of Germany, these countries have also started testing potential immigrants on the "norms and values" of the country before entry.[106] The Dutch test includes the screening of a DVD showing two men kissing and a topless woman. If candidates are offended by these images, they are encouraged not to apply for residency. Similar screenings are being devised for applicants for naturalization. After the scrapping of a short-lived test introduced in the state of Baden-Württemberg that included controversial questions such as "Suppose your adult son comes to you and declares that he is homosexual and would like to live with another man. How do you react?" Germany developed federal guidelines for language and citizenship testing. Denmark and the United Kingdom introduced citizenship tests in 2005, while France and Italy—with the Vatican's support—are planning one. Australia, having long served as a model of multiculturalism, based its test, introduced in 2007, on European models but announced a revision a year later as it turned out that every fifth applicant had failed the test.

Most of the tests, introduced or planned, consist of a language exam and questions on national history and/or the arts, political institutions and basic rights and freedoms, and the concepts of rule of law and political participation. The planned German test also includes questions on the welfare state and the responsibility of the individual for the collective good, while the British one requires that applicants know the correct order of St. Andrew's, St. Patrick's, St. George's, and St. David's days and the right thing to do if you have spilled someone's beer in a pub. Germany plans to reduce the period of residence required for naturalization from eight to six years, but only for those who prove their "successful integration" by, for example, participating in associations or charities. Britain, France, and Germany currently have or are planning citizenship ceremonies. Germany wants applicants to sign a declaration of loyalty and acceptance of the liberal democratic system, while France requires the signing of an "integration contract." Switzerland gives the cantons the right to do the same in cases where authorities have established an "integration deficit." (They can do so for a number of reasons—from poor fluency in the local language to criminal activity or protracted unemployment.[107])

From Multiculturalism to "Interfaith Activities"

Considering that 9/11 served as the trigger for this sea change in the European politics of diversity, it is remarkable that in the United States itself, multiculturalism has suffered only minor setbacks. This is largely due to two reasons: that American multicultural policies have been linked to established minorities rather than to recent migrant populations, and that decisions that bear on public policy in the United States are frequently made in courts, which are not accountable to voters, so that the whole process becomes both slower and less predetermined. Several state supreme courts have struck down affirmative action quotas privileging minority students, but—although programs in black history or Asian American literature may be quietly rolled back—there is no serious challenge to the multicultural curriculum, and it is unlikely that the United States picture of itself will ever go back to one of homogeneity.

Some of the European debates have found their way to America. In 2006, for example, a judge dismissed a Muslim woman's demand that she be allowed to wear a niqab (full-face veil) while testifying in court; but there does not seem to be an overall trend away from cultural argumentation in U.S. courts.[108] A campaign against the use of Spanish in public institutions has spread, with twenty-six states and numerous municipalities declaring English the official language, and a similar initiative at the federal level supported by one-third of Congress.[109] In California and Texas— the states with the largest Spanish-speaking populations—a drawn-out battle against bilingual education has made steady advances since the 1990s. In 1997, 29 percent of Californian schoolchildren were enrolled in bilingual classes, a proportion that dropped to 10 percent in 2003. Currently, schools in California must provide bilingual education only if the parents of at least twenty children in a cohort request it and provide a justification.[110] Since 2002, President George W.

Bush's No Child Left Behind Act holds schools accountable for language and learning progress made by "limited English proficient" students and sanctions schools that fail in this. The United States has had a citizenship test since the 1980s, but a 2007 reform introduced new questions dealing with history and the political system to test the understanding of its principles rather than just familiarity with facts. For example, instead of asking "What are the three branches of power?" the new test asks "Why do we need three branches of power?"

In other words, there are few signs that America shares the sense of crisis of multiculturalism that Samuel Huntington relates in his most recent book, *Who Are We?* This is an extended version of his article "The Hispanic Challenge," in which he argues that American values and identity are being eroded by the "irreconcilable differences" between Hispanic and Protestant values and the danger of an "acculturation in reverse" made possible by multiculturalist laissez-faire. By contrast, the dismantling of multiculturalism in Europe is accompanied by a hectic search for common values. The German version of Huntington's question "Wer sind wir?"—with which the *Frankfurter Allgemeine Zeitung* finishes its report on the controversy around the Berlin school that introduced a German-only policy—is echoed across European capitals.

When the parliamentary leader of the Christian Democrats, Friedbert Pflüger, talked about a German *Leitkultur* ("guiding culture") in the Bundestag in 2000, he was widely ridiculed. Today, the thought no longer sounds funny. European states have generally responded to what they see as an integration crisis by attempting to formulate their "values." In 2005 the new president of the Bundestag, Norbert Lammert, urged German society to come back to the "prematurely abandoned" *Leitkultur* debate. In 2006 the efforts of a commission established by Denmark's minister of culture, Brian Mikkelsen, to formulate a national cultural canon to counter the "misplaced tolerance" that had led to the establishment of "a medieval Muslim culture" in the guise of multiculturalism bore fruit. The new canon, consisting of eighty-four works in seven realms (art, film, literature, and so on), is now part of the school curriculum.[111] Interestingly, however, the bulk of Western European efforts to define common values has led not to a cultural canon but to a reassertion of what can be described as Enlightenment values: secularism, equality, freedom of expression, and tolerance of difference—now with a focus shifted from ethnic minorities to sexual ones. Moreover, it is largely conservative politicians—such as the Dutch Christian Democrats and the staunchly Catholic government of Baden-Württemberg, many of whose voters would probably have failed to live up to the tolerance expected in its citizenship test—who have championed the introduction of gay rights into the mainstream of European identity.

As discussed in chapter 1, the alternative vision of European identity—according to which Europeans must return to Christian values to be able to deal with their Muslim fellow citizens' legitimate grievances against a godless world—has gained much less support beyond the papacy and some Eastern European governments. Yet no doubt driven partly by a pragmatic desire to "manage" what is perceived as the Islamic threat, a number of European governments have adopted measures that suggest that they have more trust in an institutionalized "dialogue of faiths," with its inherent contradiction to the concept of society consisting of individuals rather than groups, than in the robustness of the secular values they profess. Even as the British government is engaged in a thoroughgoing reform of multiculturalism, it has increasingly been farming out the task of "community harmony" to religious (notably Muslim, but also Hindu and Sikh) leaders. Germany and even secularist France, which has no equivalent institution for any other faith, have set up government-appointed Islamic councils (respectively in 2006 and 2004) as single Muslim interlocutors on "key questions of living together." The German Islamic Conference has been charged with overseeing the introduction of Islamic religious instruction to state schools, as well as the construction of mosques, seen as "an important step to integration [in making] Muslim communities leave the backyards . . . and document their will to become part of German society for the long run."[112] Germany's interior minister expressed his wish that German Muslims eventually unite in large congregations with a bottom-up structure—"like the Lutheran Church."[113]

Yet the expectation that Muslims—let alone Muslims of different persuasions, such as Sunni and Shia—form a churchlike structure is contrary to Islam. The expectation that the views of millions of people—from Bosnia, Iran, Pakistan, and Turkey—can be legitimately expressed by a religious body that speaks with a single voice is even more unreasonable than the "one ethnicity–one organization" setup in earlier versions of multiculturalism. Quite apart from the undemocratic process of selecting the membership of these councils, their nature means that conservative organizations are able to dominate the agenda—even if, as in Germany, a number of critical individuals, such as Necla Kelek and Seyran Ateç, are appointed to them.

Ostensibly desirous of full Muslim participation in civil society, the Australian government also seems to think that controlling the content of sermons and religious instruction and cultivating "moderate" religious leaders might be a more urgent task. The government appointed a Muslim Community Reference Group in 2005, but the only one of its recommendations taken up by the government was the government-supported training of imams. An increasing amount of federal funding that used to be spent on antiracism programs now went to support "interfaith activities." For example, 30 percent of the Department of Immigration and Multicultural Affairs' funding under the Living in Harmony program in 2005 went to religious organizations. (The Labor government that took office in 2007 seems to be turning away from this.) As the countries that have had multiculturalist policies in the past are also those with a strong tradition of church-run education and health care, it seems a logical choice to many of their politicians to bring Muslims into the fold of institutional politics by encouraging state-supervised arrangements for Muslim schools and hospitals.

The British government, for instance, has been actively promoting "faith schools" for Muslim, Hindu, and Sikh children—a policy forcefully opposed by Amartya Sen, who has called it "not only educationally problematic" but also encouraging "a fragmentary perception of the demands of living in a desegregated Britain."[114] Taking religious leaders as automatic spokespersons

for people coming from a vaguely perceived region is an unde-
clared and erroneous conflation of religion with identity at the
expense of other affiliations ("politics, class, gender, language, literature, social involvements"[115]), no less so than the automatic
privileging of ethnic identity in representing the populations of
Bosnia and Iraq, as detailed in the previous chapter. Incidentally,
this trend is emerging despite a new visibility of "Muslim" politicians across Europe, across the range of mainstream political
parties, whose agendas are not primarily defined by religious or
ethnic issues.

Leave Culture Out or Bring It In?

This new focus on "interfaith dialogue" creates the uncomfortable
impression that the backlash against multiculturalism is directed
more at prohibiting certain kinds of difference than at the examination of how constitutive of particular ways of life those differences
actually are.[116] As Eriksen has pointed out, summarizing Mikael
Kurkiala's article on the "honor killing" of Fadime Sahindal in
Sweden: "'Kurdish culture' did not in any way determine the
actions of Fadime's father" when he shot her, but "his Kurdish
universe offered cultural scripts, one which consisted in killing a
daughter to restore honour."[117] This is a significant difference. If
the former were the case, it would lead to the conclusion that in
similar situations all Kurds are inclined to act in the same fashion;
consequently, they are "unintegrable" in European society, their
children need rescuing, and the only way to make them conform
with accepted norms is through the mediation of cultural or religious brokers, which makes a direct debate with various Kurds
not only unnecessary but perhaps counterproductive.

By contrast, the latter conclusion acknowledges the role of
personal choice in a situation where contradictory emotions and
pressures apply, and it leaves open the possibility of a case-by-case
approach in which the cultural conditioning of actions is taken
into consideration but does not provide absolution from individual responsibility. In this case it is necessary to question the authority of experts and seek a variety of opinions. For example, Western

media debates on "Muslim culture" focus on such questions as whether Muslim women are required to wear a headscarf, rather than on what the choice to wear or reject it means (which is often assumed to be submission to male authority). The original French headscarf ban, as Seyla Benhabib has written, was based not on "individual students' beliefs about what a religious scarf (or, for that matter, yarmulke) meant to them, but on how the school authorities interpreted the scarf's meaning."[118] Under the arrangement that many European governments are now pursuing, organizations such as the Islamic Council will presumably continue to debate in this vein. But, as Will Kymlicka has pointed out, in the debate over the headscarf in Québec schools, the public eventually learned that there is a variety of opinions among Muslims regarding the appropriate behavior of women, and that there is no automatic correlation between the wearing of the headscarf, acceptance of gender inequality, and views on clitoridectomy.[119]

In a study of more than three hundred German Muslim women who wear the headscarf, conducted by the conservative (Christian Democratic) Konrad Adenauer Foundation, 95 percent of respondents said that the most important goal for them was living according to their faith. At the same time, nearly 80 percent—the same share as among noncovered German women—said that it was equally important to be "as independent and free as possible," and more than two-thirds believed that people were equal before God regardless of their faith. And 94 percent agreed with the statement that "in a marriage or life partnership today, it is important that the woman should also be able to fulfil her professional goals."[120] In an ethnographic study of college-educated headscarf-wearing women in Sydney, most informants did not see wearing the scarf as a political statement. Although they emphasized that their Islamic commitment was incompatible with some forms of socializing, they did not feel that the headscarf affected their relations with their colleagues negatively. Rather, many of them commented that it made them feel more confident in the workplace. As one Microsoft employee said: "When I started wearing the veil, I felt more in control and protected, men didn't look at me in a sexual way, I felt respected and that made me feel more comfortable working with men."[121] A university tutor in chemistry explained that she had started wearing the headscarf at nineteen against the advice of her family, who believed she should first achieve "what she wanted in her career."[122] Another had done so out of protest when the school she worked at refused to admit a headscarf-wearing pupil. If one is to believe these studies, the view that the wearing of the headscarf represents a rejection of liberal democratic values, which has been used to justify state and court decisions to ban the headscarf, is unfounded.

In other words, a closer look can help determine where cultural factors play a decisive role and where they do not—such as, according to sociologist Olivier Roy, in the radicalization of Muslim youth in Western Europe. According to Roy's research, it is precisely uprootedness and the loss of Islam's social authority that results in radicalization. Young Muslim radicals tend to be those who have weaker, not stronger, ties with their ancestral culture; they "are not linked to any real community . . . rooted . . . in a given society or culture."[123] Once we have peeled off a group image created by cultural gatekeepers, we usually find a much greater diversity of practices than what public images reduce "a culture" to; but even once we have ascertained that a practice is widely shared and vital to a group, we do not necessarily have to accept it. Despite the fact that multiculturalism has often been presented as going hand in hand with unqualified cultural relativism, its most prominent proponents, Charles Taylor and Will Kymlicka, have argued from the beginning for a hierarchy of values. Taylor acknowledges what Jürgen Habermas, a critic of multiculturalism, has called its "performative contradiction"—that its tenet of the universal equality of values is itself a very particular one.[124] Taylor believes, however, that there is a simple way out of this contradiction: to recognize this particular value as a superior one. He insists that recognition must be *mutual*; the equal terms of multiculturalism require that both parties accept the equality of worth.[125]

Similarly, Kymlicka limits multicultural recognition to those groups that he describes as being structured along liberal lines.[126] Even those cultural claims that have been proven genuinely to represent a shared value within the group should not be granted if they infringe on the freedoms—for example, of expression, movement, or choice—of either a member of the group or outsiders to it. This approach is in fact not far from that of Seyla Benhabib, a critic of multiculturalism, who writes that "norms . . . can be deemed valid only if *all* who would be affected by their consequences can be participants in a practical discourse through which the norms are adopted."[127] Unlike in development projects or military interventions in distant countries, contentions about the cultural rights of immigrant minorities are often highly visible in Western societies and sometimes affect how those societies live. The stakes are not necessarily higher, but they are more obvious. This explains the ambivalence that anthropologists like Unni Wikan, but also public intellectuals like Timothy Garton Ash and Ian Buruma, display.

While condemning Scandinavian states for their "generous betrayal" of Muslim girls, Wikan also argued for a relatively light sentence for Nadia's parents. In her latest book, *In Honor of Fadime*, which focuses on the "honor killing" of Fadime Sahindal, Wikan writes: "Fadime and her parents disagreed about aspects of Kurdish culture. . . . I can understand what they all mean and will then explain why they see things differently. . . . Anthropologists are trained to engage with 'the native's point of view' and then to . . . be aware of the potential for differences."[128] An ethnographic approach creates the kind of practical dialogue Benhabib argues for, and has the advantage of finding out where the infringement on individual freedoms actually takes place—rather than, as in the popular image of Muslims today, assuming that it does. It seems to us that society can accommodate much more free exercise of culture by adults than often presumed.

As Lawrence Sager has written: "Epistemic concerns and the principle of equal liberty counsel that we be slow to judge the unfamiliar, that we take a hard second look at our own factual beliefs and normative judgements before we condemn culturally endorsed practices."[129] Or in Seyla Benhabib's words: "The task of *democratic equality* is to create impartial institutions in the public sphere and civil society where [the] struggle for the recognition of cultural differences and the contestation for cultural narratives can take place without domination."[130] Thus, in the case of the original headscarf debate in France, "even if the girls involved were not adults and in the eyes of the law were still under the tutelage of their families, it is reasonable to assume that at the ages of fifteen and sixteen they could account for themselves and their actions. Had their voices been listened to and heard, it would have become clear that the meaning of wearing the scarf itself was changing from a religious act to one of cultural defiance and increasing politicization."[131] Benhabib continues: "Ironically, it was the very egalitarian norms of the French public educational system that brought these girls out of the patriarchal structures of the home and into the French public sphere and gave them the confidence and the ability to *resignify the wearing of the scarf.* Instead of penalizing and criminalizing their activities, would it not have been more plausible to ask these girls to account for their actions and doings at least to their school communities, and to encourage discourses among the youth about what it means to be a Muslim citizen in a laic [secular] French Republic?"[132]

Female circumcision is another case in point. In many discussions on multiculturalism, from philosophical to legal, this practice marks the boundary between acceptable and unacceptable practices. Most commentators simply assume that no woman in her right mind could voluntarily submit to clitoridectomy, which is seen as a barbaric symbol of the oppression of women with grave consequences for their health. This condemnation goes back to Christian missionaries whose testimony of the practice in Africa during the 1920s and 1930s stands in stark contrast to anthropological accounts of the same period, which described genital cutting—just like male initiation rituals—as an empowering rite of passage. Today, however, the voices of those African women—both in Africa and in the West—who condemn the practice are endorsed, while those that defend it as an integral part of their tradition are dismissed as false consciousness.[133] Yet considering there is a range of genital cutting practices, from making a small incision to sewing up parts of the vagina, and that these obviously have very different consequences, why can't we entertain the possibility that some women may indeed want this operation—

as others want breast enlargement?[134] And if they are adults in a position of informed consent, shouldn't they be allowed to have these procedures performed at a Western hospital? Many would argue that the decisions to get breast implants and to have your clitoris cut are of a very different kind. But are women who are constantly bombarded by media images of the "perfect breast" necessarily more independent in making their choice than those who are told that they are not full women until they have had their genitals cut? As the anthropologist Alex Edmonds has shown, in Brazil it is often mothers who take their teenage daughters to have their first *plástica*.[135]

Of course, the free choice test has to be applied differently to children. It is universally accepted that parents have the right to limit children's freedom and make decisions on their behalf, although where these limits lie is culturally constructed and constantly changing. At the same time, as detailed throughout this chapter, Western states take an increasingly interventionist approach to ensure that children enjoy appropriate welfare and are endowed with the facilities necessary to function in society. In cases where the state considers that the parents seriously endanger the welfare of the children, it can remove them from their families. But what constitutes such an endangerment is culturally constructed. It is often a matter of disagreement not only between migrant families and Western states but also across Western states themselves. When American courts placed in foster care Vietnamese children on whose bodies doctors found marks of "coining" and an Afghan baby whose father had kissed his penis in public, parents successfully appealed these decisions, showing that the practices in question were considered accepted in their cultural environments and did no harm to the children. In the Afghan case this required a demonstration of family photo albums and testimony by a professor of Near Eastern Studies and a religious leader, who explained that in Afghan culture, kissing the penis of a baby demonstrated parental affection.[136]

In the case of the Vietnamese child, the grounds for removing it from its parents was simply a misunderstanding of what had caused the marks on the body; in the case of the Afghan baby, the disagreement was about what the practice meant. The behavior of the Afghan father was beyond the boundaries of the acceptable in the United States, but in Europe this case is unlikely to have attracted any attention.[137] Conversely, the Berlin-Lichtenberg decision to remove Vietnamese children from their parents during the weekends so they can enjoy the benefits of "childhood" would have been unthinkable in the United States or Australia, where the presence of children helping out in the family business is part of the accepted image of immigrant enterprises. Indeed, the Australian government's plan to offer more boarding school places to Aboriginal children has met with criticism from Aboriginal organizations that point out that graduates of such schools "often cannot adjust back to community life."[138] In general, U.S. courts are much more proactive in intervening where they suspect sexual abuse or exploitation than are European governments, but less likely to do so in instances where the accusation is of endangering a child's material welfare.

Lord Malloch Brown, former administrator of the United Nations Development Program and currently Britain's minister for Africa, Asia and the United Nations, believes that "a girl's right to an education will always trump her father's claim to a cultural right to forbid her schooling for religious or other reasons."[139] Amartya Sen has come to a similar conclusion: "Education is not just about getting children, even very young ones, immersed in an old inherited ethos. It is also about helping children to develop the ability to reason about new decisions any grown-up person will have to take."[140] American courts do not always agree, as demonstrated in the famous *Wisconsin v. Yoder* case, where the court ruled in favor of Amish parents who took their daughter out of school, arguing that this was necessary to preserve her religious values. The "ability to reason about new decisions" is also taken away from those children whose parents, citing cultural or religious beliefs, refuse them medical treatment for conditions that could lead to death or permanent physical impairment. There is consensus that in life-threatening conditions the state has the right to intervene, as when a four-month-old Hmong boy in Ohio suffering from cancer had his eyes removed against the parents' objections.[141]

But where the conditions are not life-threatening and parents argue that treatment would compromise their deeply held cultural or religious beliefs, U.S. courts have made divergent decisions. In the case of a six-year-old Hmong child born with a clubfoot who was ordered to undergo surgery by the Fresno County Social Services Department on the grounds that failing to do so would leave him wheelchair-bound, the parents, with support from a shaman and the Hmong Council, argued that surgery would "interfere with the natural order" and could lead to misfortunes for other members of the family. The parents lost the case after a series of appeals all the way up to the U.S. Supreme Court, but they found no doctor willing to perform the operation, presumably because of the emphasis on consent and the related fears of litigation in U.S. medical practice.

Beyond the argument that surgery would be detrimental to their son's and the family's future welfare, the parents' case rested on the claim that performing the surgery would lead to ostracism of the child and the family by the Hmong community, and this would compromise the quality of his adult life. But it is clear that being wheelchair-bound severely compromises the chances of an individual in most societies, particularly so for a low-income child of immigrants in the United States. How can one say which life environment matters more for the future of a person? An adult has the right to decide that the social, economic, and sexual impediments a disability results in within the majority society—which are nearly inescapable—are less important than the acceptance of a small community, which is relatively easy to reject if one so wishes. This six-year-old boy said he did not want to have surgery, but he did not want to be in a wheelchair either, demonstrating that he did not fully understand the choice he was facing. In such situations we believe that state intervention is warranted so as to ensure the maximization of life choices for the individual.

Where children are able to express a choice, it is obviously important to hear them—in contrast to earlier practices that have tended to ignore their preferences. If these wishes go against those of their parents, state institutions sometimes have to decide which side to support. Public schools in Germany have rejected requests by Muslim parents to exempt their children from physical education classes, sex education, and class trips. By contrast, private schools generally grant these requests. Wikan has described a Norwegian case where a school refused to grant exemption from swimming classes. The case attracted wide publicity, with a radio debate between a Muslim organization leader, the student's father, the school principal, and Wikan herself on whether Muslim students should be generally exempted from swimming.[142]

A 1993 decision by Germany's Federal Constitutional Court ruled that Muslim girls may not be forced to participate in coeducational swimming classes above the age of puberty. Jutta Limbach, a judge on Germany's Constitutional Court, has publicly considered exempting Muslim girls from physical education classes. But a 2007 report by the Intercultural Council of the German Ministry of Culture revealed that in fact only few Muslim girls abstain from swimming or P.E. classes.[143] Those whose parents have discouraged them from doing so can gain welcome support from a no-exemptions policy. Surely, school decisions should be made on a case-by-case basis, taking into account both the parents' and the child's wishes as well as ensuring that her school socialization is not significantly disadvantaged. These decisions can be difficult and require familiarity with the terrain. For example, Aihwa Ong, writing about Cambodian refugee families in California, is critical of patriarchal decision making but notes that children—whose fluency in English and familiarity with American institutions puts them at an advantage—learn to manipulate the social services to intervene regularly on their behalf, and such undermining of parental authority leads to dysfunctional families.[144] In any case, religious experts have little place in such decisions, yet they are sometimes granted a lot of it. In the Norwegian debate, for instance, the preference of the girl whose case triggered it was apparently never revealed, even in Wikan's account; and the Muslim spokesman for "the community" told Wikan privately that he did not consider swimming to violate Islamic norms but did not wish to deviate from the role for which he had been summoned.[145]

Here we take the position of legal scholar Lawrence Sager, who has argued against blanket exemptions granted to groups on the basis of culture or religion and, instead, for the protection of individual cultural or religious preferences, whether or not they are legitimized by a group.[146] This is the approach taken in the Rotterdam school described by anthropologists Sabine Mannitz and Werner Schiffauer, where "money obtained from the funds for minority groups" from the state "is used in an ethnically blind way to offer extra provision for pupils who are having difficulties in catching up."[147]

Differing Diversities

There have been several initiatives to reformulate multiculturalism in such a way as to reverse the trend toward pigeonholing. The Parekh Report, commissioned by the British government and released in 2000, and the United Nations Development Programme's 2004 *Human Development Report* both acknowledge the situational, dynamic, and multivalent nature of cultural identification. The UNDP writes, for example, that "cultural liberty is about expanding individual choices, not about preserving values and practices in itself with blind allegiance to tradition. . . . Interest groups led by self-appointed leaders may not reflect the views of the membership."[148] In two reports entitled *Differing Diversities*, the Council of Europe has argued for a reformulation of cultural policy to reflect a social reality that is not reducible to the mosaic-like representation of a number of ethnic "communities."[149] These initiatives have, however, gone largely unheeded in the scramble toward "integration."

The intention to ensure that all of us who are members of the same society share certain values in common is endorsed not only by nationalists who wish to preserve the purity and authenticity of the nation, but also by those liberals who wish to defend the meaning of citizenship as an act of political will and preserve a well-functioning public sphere. Even if we reject paranoid fears of a "Londonistan" or a "medieval Muslim culture" overtaking Denmark, we may be concerned if citizenship is reduced to a question of high or low taxes, easy or difficult travel, and free or expensive education—as is increasingly the case with some highly mobile migrant populations, such as the elite Chinese migrants or Indian IT professionals described by Aihwa Ong.[150]

We agree with Jürgen Habermas that living in a society in which certain common values tie us to our fellow citizens is not only a preferable political model but also a more fulfilling human experience. We even endorse the idea of citizenship testing, as long as the values they expect applicants to embrace contribute to greater tolerance and broaden the range of choices available to all members of the nation, old and new. In this case there is no contradiction between a search for common values and an enlarged menu of choices. Recognizing that choice is not as individualistic a process as it is often perceived to be, but is rather structured by alternative visions of worth, success, justice, or beauty, all of which are collectively produced, the recognition of the multiplicity of such visions should ideally expand, not narrow, choice. We agree with Seyla Benhabib: "If one must choose, I value the expansion of democratic inclusion and equality over the preservation of cultural distinctiveness, but often one can attain both in some measure."[151]

But citizenship tests in themselves are unlikely to provide the glue that will bind people together, and other policies that have been hastily introduced in the name of security and integration have in part done the opposite. Not allowing anyone under twenty-four to settle with her husband in Denmark, or anyone who does not already speak German to do the same in Germany, or challenging the right of an adult woman to wear a headscarf if no one forces her to do so not only generate justified resentment but actually reduce choices rather than expand them. We suggest that, with integration in mind, the politics of recognition become more rather than less important. But they have to adapt to the realities of contemporary migrant lives. Integration policies have tended to operate with the outdated assumption that migrants either accumulate cultural capital by going through the accepted channels of

social mobility in the country they reside in or else become dangerous rejects who blame the West for not giving them a chance. This
is an updated version of the "race relations cycle" in which, ultimately, the only recognized form of success is to join the Rotary
Club and move to a suburban villa with a swimming pool.

The basis of Charles Taylor's philosophy is the idea that identity
and fulfillment depend on recognition by members of the same
society. The reality is rapidly changing, as an increasing number
of migrants live simultaneously in the sociopolitical worlds of
multiple nation-states, which means that even if they fail to
gain recognition *here*, they may be able to do so *somewhere else*.
Moroccan women who clean houses in Italy may not be very interested in their social standing locally if they are certain that in three
years they will return home and enjoy higher respect because of
being able to send their children to university.[152] Chinese traders in
Hungary may display indifference to their vilification as criminals
in the local press as long as the global Chinese-language media cel-
ebrates them as new cosmopolitans and the Party secretary of their
home city congratulates them as contributors to China's modernization.[153] Transnational migrants also tend to remain aloof of
old-style organizational representation. Organizing yet another
lion dance on the Champs-Élysées will not help bind new Chinese
migrants to France, although it may please the Chinese government; French companies offering more jobs to Chinese graduates
might.

Subtle changes in the design of cities and housing, as well as a
preference for mixed-use neighborhoods and particular services,
support for multiethnic residential associations, and dialogue
with ethnic enterprises can be more effective in fostering interactions between different population groups than either the ethnic
rebranding of places or council resettlement projects that in the
1960s moved marginalized ethnic groups into urban high-rises.
Such approaches do not wish to eliminate ethnic neighborhoods,
nor do they aim to emphasize their ethnic uniqueness for purposes
of tourism; rather, they attempt to increase the ways of interaction among residents and visitors by creating or supporting more
diverse uses. Amanda Wise's research in the Sydney suburb of

Ashfield demonstrates how architectural details like shop signs or window displays may encourage or discourage interethnic communication—in this case between elderly white residents and Chinese shopkeepers.[154]

The nearby suburb of Auburn—with a growing refugee population and suffering from "low educational attainment, high unemployment, housing stress, social isolation and heart disease" —decided to increase young (and often unaccompanied) African and Middle Eastern refugee men's access to social networks and resources by funding a "Men's Shed" run by Vietnam War veterans who will "mentor" and work with them.[155] In Lowell, Massachusetts, good public bus service enabled migrants to attend evening English classes in Boston.[156] A report prepared by a group of experts for a coalition of German cities in 2005 noted that the main sources of conflict in ethnically mixed neighborhoods are "dirt, rubbish or noise," and that these can often be eliminated through design. The report's authors propose such practical measures as terraces and gardens that enable privacy, a clear separation between private and public spaces to foster a sense of responsibility, a design that eliminates echo, and frequent rubbish removal. They point out that public spaces should be adaptable to the needs of different users—including large migrant households— and ensure equal access. The design of buildings and apartments should also take into account the diverse needs of population groups and pay particular attention to the access areas, which provide the building with an individual face and should function as places to linger and socialize.[157] The revival of the island of Veddel in Hamburg is an example of a successful private-public partnership to create a mixed-use neighborhood. In 2004 the Hamburgische Wohnungsbaukreditanstalt, a city-owned building society, began renting out renovated waterside apartments in Veddel, a neighborhood with a 60 percent migrant population and a reputation for crime, to students for a symbolic rent of three euros a month for the duration of two years. Working with associations of students, entrepreneurs, landlords, and tenants, the Senate encouraged the opening of cultural spaces, restaurants, and bars.

Rather than engaging in endless discussions about what the

Koran says about martyrs, governments might undertake small changes that expand Muslims' ability to participate in different spheres of life. Despite a shortage of butchers in Germany, there are currently no Muslim butchers because the apprentice test includes carving up a pig. There is no reason why—as the former commissioner for foreigners, Barbara John, has been recommending for years—the same test could not be performed on a sheep.[158] In many instances of everyday life it is easy to recognize the special needs of some Muslims, such as granting religious holidays and providing halal food for workers.

At other times it requires a differentiated approach. Since there is, for example, no standard practice in Muslim-majority countries as to the separation of sexes in a hospital, and since medical professionals have an overriding obligation to serve all patients, calls for establishing separate rules for Muslim patients or medical personnel in the public health care system should be rejected. But if a woman, whether she identifies herself as Muslim or not, prefers to be examined by a female doctor, her wish should be accommodated wherever possible. Yet with the increasing privatization of the health sector, we are certain to witness a market differentiation that will provide a niche for Muslim patients in Europe. One of the first Muslim hospitals is currently under construction in Rotterdam. Here food will be halal, there will be separate wards for men and women, women will be treated only by female specialists, and men only by male doctors. An imam will be present at all times, and Islamic medicines and herbs will be used.[159] If we are guided by the maxim of increased choice, such a hospital will be unproblematic, particularly as its staff will not have to be Muslim itself. Yet there is a fine line to be monitored; this would be crossed if, for example, decisions on medical treatment for female patients would not be left in their own hands but have to be authorized by male members of the family.

chapter 5

Protecting "Indigenous Culture"

In 1970, Paul Simon and Art Garfunkel's *Bridge over Troubled Water* won the Grammy Award for the record of the year. It has remained one of the highest-selling albums since.[1] One of the best-known songs on it was "El Condor Pasa" (also known as "I'd Rather Be a Hammer Than a Nail"), in which Simon and Garfunkel were accompanied by the Peruvian group Los Incas. Unknown to its millions of fans, the American duo were not the original composers of the track, as a letter from the Bolivian minister of foreign affairs and religion to the director-general of UNESCO three years later made clear. In that letter the minister complained that an indigenous folk song from the Andes, which had been rearranged in 1913 by a Peruvian composer and folk song collector, brought American musicians millions of dollars, while the original composers and rightful owners of the song— poor Andeans—were left empty-handed.[2]

The Bolivian government's letter decried the "clandestine commercialization and export . . . of traditional cultures" and pointed out that while tangible heritage was protected by international conventions, expressions such as music and dance were not.[3] This new concern with protecting indigenous culture came against a background of an increasingly commodified world. As the range of consumer goods in free-market economies expanded, objects of popular culture produced by Walt Disney and Levi's were luring Indonesian and Brazilian customers and even made their way to the Soviet black market. A decade later, with the transition of Western societies to a postindustrial phase, the value of designs, information, and knowledge as compared with hardware soared.

As new middle classes emerged worldwide and global trade barriers broke down, the economic significance of branding increased significantly compared with earlier times. Not only was owning a Louis Vuitton handbag becoming the symbol of middle-class status for Asian women, but also more types of goods and services were becoming lifestyle goods. As more companies realized that the money is in brands rather than objects, they scrambled to protect their designs and know-how. In the early 2000s there were 2,315 trademarks on yoga in the United States, a market of twenty million yoga practitioners worth more than $30 billion.[4] As "intercultural communication" became a global industry (explored further in chapter 6), one of its founders, Geert Hofstede, even had his name registered as a trademark.

As new technologies emerged and political controls on imported popular culture weakened, the market for cultural goods—such as films, music, electronic games, and later software—exploded in a way no one could have imagined. In the era of mass-produced DVDs, global MTV, and the Internet, one hit song by Christina Aguilera can immediately reach hundreds of millions of viewers with hardly any manufacturing or distribution costs. Considering that MP3 files and DVDs are also, unlike 12-mm film and vinyl LPs, easy to reproduce and alter, it is no surprise that artists, producers, and distributors are keen to protect their profits and the integrity of their work. Since the 1980s, a movement to expand the scope of intellectual property rights across both time and types of works has seen an "aggressive expansion of copyright, patents and trademarks."[5] The range of patentable things now includes "gene sequences, life-forms, and the manipulation of information in databases" as well as the smell of a car.[6]

The expansion of the free global trade in cultural goods has diverse opponents. As in any other commerce, those who are losing out lobby for protection. Governments worried about the erosion of national culture, and pressured by film companies, broadcasters, and publishing houses to maintain subsidies, argue that cultural goods should be exempted from certain free-market provisions. France has long been known for regulating the quota of foreign-language songs on their airwaves and films in cinemas and on television. Cultural protectionists won a battle in October 2005, when the Convention on the Protection and Promotion of the Diversity of Cultural Expressions was adopted by UNESCO. But the free access movement has been gaining strength, demanding the dismantling of corporate protections on intellectual property, especially in the realms of graphic design, music, and the Internet. Free access activists consider the prevailing system of intellectual property laws a "significant threat to free speech and political dialogue."[7]

A New Indigenous Visibility

An increasingly important voice in the debates about intellectual property is that of indigenous activists. The Zia Pueblo Indians of New Mexico requested the state of New Mexico to pay damages for the unauthorized reproduction of the Zia sun symbol on New Mexico's flag, license plates, and official stationery since 1925. The state legislature refused to award damages but issued an official apology, creating an officially recognized association of the symbol with the tribe.[8] From that point on, the sun symbol has been treated as a commodity. In 2000, Southwestern Airlines received permission from the Zia to display the sun symbol on an airplane, and children from the Zia Pueblo performed a traditional Crow dance as part of the aircraft's dedication ceremony.[9] In contrast to the Zia case, in 1997 an Australian Aboriginal artist, Harold Thomas, successfully asserted his copyright in the Aboriginal flag, which he had designed in 1971 and which the Commonwealth of Australia had begun using as an official symbol in 1995.[10] The difference between the two cases is that whereas the creator of the flag was known and alive, the sun design of the New Mexico state symbols was based on the pattern of a nineteenth-century jar made by an unknown Zia potter.

At the 2004 Grammy Awards ceremony, the hip-hop band OutKast introduced their song "Hey Ya" with an ethereal, Indian-sounding melody. The back-up dancers, mostly African-American women, wore buckskin bikinis and long braids and feathers in their hair, and imitated a traditional Plains Indian tribe war cry.[11] Soon after the performance, the American Indian press reported an outcry from Indian communities over the act: "Complaints ranged from a feeling of violation over the use of Indian symbols, like feathers and war paint, to anger over the perpetuation of tomahawk and tipi stereotypes. The greatest shock came when *Indian Country Today* revealed that the melody piped in to introduce 'Hey Ya' was the sacred Navajo 'Beauty Way' song. According to the Navajo, the song is meant to restore peace and harmony, and it is improper to use the song for entertainment purposes."[12] Despite the widespread complaints, however, no compensation was awarded to Navajos. In contrast, when one of the OutKasts, Andre 3000, criticized the free downloading of "Hey Ya" from the Internet as "straight stealing," he was legally right, even though technically Internet file-sharing is unlikely to be eliminated. But unlike "Hey Ya," and like the Zia sun, "Beauty Way" is not protected by copyright law, as it is not codified in written form and has no known author but has been shaped by generations of Navajos.[13]

"The principal goal of intellectual property laws" as they have been developed in the West, the anthropologist Michael Brown has written, "is to see that information enters the public domain in a timely fashion, while allowing creators, be they individuals or corporate groups, to derive reasonable financial and social benefits from their work."[14] In other words, laws weigh the public benefit of access to an invention or a work of art against the incentive to create them. By contrast, inventions or art whose creator is unknown, those created by groups that are not legally incorporated and whose limits are hard to determine, and those created long enough ago are not protected (that is why patents and copyright expire, so that paper clips and aspirin are now in the public domain). The 1994 Agreement on Trade Related Aspects of Intellectual Property Rights (TRIPS) allows the patenting of only such substances and processes that are new, not found in nature, and are created for commercial purposes. This means, for example, that groups of people who for generations have been collecting knowledge about medicinal plants, selecting them, and administering them—from Yanomani Indians to Swiss herbalists—can get no credit for their knowledge.

Moreover, intellectual property laws—as all property laws in the West—assume the alienability of property, that the creators of works want to allow access to them in exchange for financial compensation or social prestige. Thus, when laws limit access to books, pharmaceuticals, and computer games, their goal is to make sure that people pay for access, rather than to restrict their use to particular kinds of people or situations. But in many non-Western societies, certain types of knowledge are traditionally not deemed alienable, and their protection is not a matter of financial gain but of secrecy, stewardship, or obligation to ancestors or future generations. Thus the Suya Indians in Brazil distinguish between individually and collectively owned songs. The former are said to have been transmitted to individuals from trees or animals and are owned by whoever first performs them. Collective songs, known to have been handed down since mythic times, are owned by different clans, who control their use.[15] Among the Tulalip, an American Indian group, some traditional knowledge—from fishing techniques and herbal medicines to songs and stories—is considered the collective property of the whole tribe, others are the sacred property solely of the one who tells them, and yet others belong to a single family. According to Tulalip tribes policy analyst Preston Hardison, "for tribal members 'owning' something means that they have been charged by the creator with guarding it. They can't sell or trade sacred knowledge; they must protect it."[16] Since the 1970s, indigenous groups have been finding their voices in the international arena, including the formation of a Permanent Forum on Indigenous Issues at the United Nations in 2002. Indigenous identity has become a vehicle for the empowerment of marginalized peoples, from the Lapps of Scandinavia to the hill tribes of Southeast Asia. Between 1970 and 1980 the population of American Indians in the United States grew from eight hundred thousand in 1970 to 2.5 million in 2000, a rate that can only be explained by more people identifying themselves as Indians. Groups that identify themselves as "indigenous" typically describe themselves as the traditional owners of the land and claim that they have a special, spiritual relationship with it.

The new assertiveness of the indigenous movement has several causes. Heightened global sensitivity to the rights of minorities, first generated by the civil rights movement, means that many states have, since the late 1980s, undertaken legal obligations to protect their cultural (and sometimes land ownership) rights and languages. In 1990 the U.S. Congress passed the Native American Graves Protection and Repatriation Act (NAGPRA) and the Indian Arts and Crafts Act. In 1994 the secretary-general of the United Nations, Boutros Boutros-Ghali, declared that "there can be no human rights unless cultural authenticity is preserved."[17] Native claims to land title are now awarded in Australia and Canada, school instruction in South Africa is in eleven national languages, and the European Union has placed improving the living conditions of the Roma (Gypsies) across the twenty-seven member countries on its agenda. Just as important for the empowerment of indigenous movement is the heightened fascination with lifestyles perceived as authentic and close to nature, which many in the West feel humankind must relearn to become whole again.

The diversity and difference that small peoples represent have a strong touristic appeal—and indeed are the major assets of many tourist destinations—that goes well beyond the New Age movement. A sense of an environmental crisis that looms large in public debates in many Western countries has heightened interest in indigenous knowledge of nature. Indigenous peoples are often depicted as living in harmony not only with one another but also with Nature, offering a model for the rest of us to emulate. As Boutros-Ghali wrote: "It is now clearly understood that many indigenous people live in greater harmony with the natural environment than do the inhabitants of industralised consumer societies."[18] In this situation indigenous claims, if they are formulated in a way that is legible for a global audience, have a far better chance of being heard and even financially supported by international organizations or partners in wealthier countries. This means, however, that their claims always sound fairly uniform to the outside world, even if their local agendas actually differ. It has been argued that the Gypsies of Europe are developing a unified ethnic consciousness out of a highly heterogeneous, plurilingual reality under the influence of international activists who want to improve their lot by linking them to European Union funding.

Another reason why native peoples are not so powerless anymore is that some of them have much greater revenues than before. Australian Aboriginal art has been fetching record prices, while money made from gambling concessions has permitted American Indians to hire some of the most expensive and influential lawyers and lobbyists to advance their interests as well as to set up professionally run Web sites.[19] These Web sites project a new level of self-consciousness about the group's way of life and its specificity relative to other groups in society. Out of 193 Native American tribes that had a Web site in 2005, 62 indicated that they maintained specific programs dedicated to the preservation of cultural resources.[20] The Internet has given global voices not only to the relatively well-endowed American Indians but also to previously unrepresented or even unknown groups. Indeed, in some cases it has arguably generated new indigenous identities, such as when online Carib and Taino Indian activists proclaimed that "we are not extinct."[21] It has provided supporters of the indigenous cause with the potential to purchase Venezuelan Indian hammocks or Mongolian yurts, study the Yoruba language, take a virtual tour through a Nairobi slum online, or follow the Lakota dispute about whether Paula Horne is to be held accountable for the exploitation of the Sacred White Buffalo Calf Pipe and, if interested, ring the concerned parties on their cell phones.[22] Perhaps more important, the Internet has forged supranational activist alliances linking groups with very different backgrounds but similar agendas. Thus the Dayaks of Borneo could exchange strategies of resistance to logging with activists in the Brazilian Amazon.[23] Every indigenous group seems to have its overseas activists, from the Friends of Tuva (a small Siberian shamanic people) in the United States to the European Network for Indigenous Australian Rights.

Such initiatives succeed in garnering widespread support and sympathy because of what the director-general of UNESCO, Koichiro Matsuura, has called "a growing recognition that accelerating globalization is placing enormous new pressures upon cultural diversity. . . . These fears, which are widely shared, have stimulated the demand that something must be done before it is too late."[24] The estimate that of the more than sixty-five hundred languages spoken today, only 10 percent will still be used in 2100 understandably spurs people into urgent action. Sir Bob Geldof, for instance, decided to create a "Dictionary of Man," which will "capture 900 of the separate groups of people that anthropologists believe to be in existence" on film and in a digital catalog.[25] UNESCO itself has been at the forefront of efforts to safeguard the world's cultures: it enacted the World Heritage Convention in 1972 to "encourage participation of the local population in the preservation of their cultural and natural heritage [and] encourage international co-operation in conservation of cultural and natural heritage." This was followed, in 2006, by the Convention for the Safeguarding of Intangible Cultural Heritage, which finally addressed the grievances voiced by Bolivia's foreign affairs minister more than thirty years earlier. The World Heritage Convention turned out to be a tourist magnet and was quickly embraced by governments and tourism developers, often bringing millions of dollars and infrastructure to previously isolated and poor regions.

Attention, money, and technology have enabled indigenous peoples to fight assimilative forces and demand control over their "cultural property" with an assertiveness never seen before. In 1995 the Inter-Apache Summit issued a statement "demanding exclusive decision-making power and control over . . . 'all images, text, ceremonies, music, songs, stories, symbols, beliefs, customs, ideas and other physical and spiritual objects and concepts' relating to the Apache, including any representation of Apache culture offered by Apache or non-Apache people."[26] The Department of Cultural and Natural Resources of the Tulalip Tribes in Washington state is in the process of drafting tribal laws to protect traditional knowledge not covered by U.S. and international trademark and copyright law, including unrecorded stories. The department claims that the initiative has been picked up by the World Intellectual Property Organization (WIPO) as a model for other indigenous groups.[27] Other groups are trying to use existing laws to sue corporations for using their symbols, designs, or practices. In a case reminiscent of the Zia sun controversy, an Australian court awarded seventy thousand dollars to seven Aborigine artists for "cultural harm" caused by unauthorized reproduction of Aboriginal designs on carpets. Although Indofurn, the carpet manufacturer, had not violated copyright laws, the court, in a 1995 judgment, accepted the plaintiffs' argument that the patterns could only be used by authorized members of the group and that unauthorized use was believed to cause harm and was sanctioned under customary law.[28]

In 2006, in a development paralleling the OutKast incident, Maori groups, supported by New Zealand's foreign ministry, protested the use of the traditional *haka* dance in a Fiat commercial as belittling of their culture and imperialistic.[29] Some Australian Aborigines have been demanding that didgeridoo manufacturing—a business that sells an estimated twenty million instruments annually—should either be restricted to Aborigines or that part of the profits should be transferred to "indigenous communities."[30] The inhabitants of the Greek island of Lesbos have failed in their effort to prevent the use of the word "lesbian" to denote female homosexuals. In contrast, descendants of an Indian chief are attempting to block the trademarking of his name, Katonah, for a Martha Stewart furniture line. Australian Aboriginal academics have called the trademarking of the word *migaloo* (meaning "white man"), a nickname given by an Aborigine elder to a popular white humpback whale, by a white consumer-goods entrepreneur "cultural genocide."[31]

In one of the strangest cases, reported by a respected small-circulation California newspaper, the *Bolinas Sentinel*, a previously unknown native group calling itself the Indigenous Intellectual Property Liberation Commando claimed that it had taken a prominent scientist hostage and was holding him until WIPO recognized the group's intellectual property rights in sixty-five-hundred-year-old sounds reportedly extracted by Dr. Aquiles Decibile and colleagues from ancient pots in a Belgian laboratory. "The sacred words of our ancestors belong to us, not to him," said the document, copies of which were released to the newspaper by Bolinas authorities.[32] It is true that this story was posted on the

Internet on 1 April, but it does illustrate the nature of some of the battles over cultural rights.

In 2006, Alaskan tribes challenged a *National Geographic* project to collect DNA samples in order to trace human migration because they thought "it could undermine their culture" as, according to their legends, they had lived in Alaska since time began.[33] An Apache tribe in Oklahoma solved the same problem by having geneticists who had acquired blood samples from the tribe to study disease resistance agree that they would refrain from any research that "might contradict traditional views of the tribe's history" (and thereby the idea that Indians have "always been here," which is important for the image of indigeneity). In addition, the tribe will have a share in any profits from the research. Before signing the agreement with the tribe, researchers interviewed up to 20 percent of the adults.[34]

Unlike the Apache case, when the U.S. government filed patents on genetic material taken from the Hagahai tribe in Papua New Guinea and the Solomon Islands in the 1990s, researchers had only asked individuals for their permission. A controversy arose when activist critics pointed out that other tribe members had not been informed that cells containing the genetic information of the group were commercially available for $216 a cell.[35] A similar issue—whether a member of a group has the right to sell his knowledge without the group's agreement—was at the core of an Australian lawsuit in 1998 known as the Bulun Bulun case, in which the court considered whether the member of an Aboriginal community had violated the communal interest of the owners when he sold a design to a textile manufacturer without the permission of elders. Although the court dismissed the case, it also ruled that in general "if the copyright of an artistic work which embodies ritual knowledge of an Aboriginal clan is being used inappropriately, and the copyright owner fails or refuses to take appropriate action to enforce the copyright, the Australian legal system will permit remedial action through the courts by the clan."[36]

American Indian organizations, concerned that the appropriation of traditional rituals—sand painting, Medicine Wheel ceremonies, or sweat lodge sessions—is not only highly offensive but can cause actual harm to "ignorant non-Indians," have lashed out at New Age spiritualists numerous times using highly charged language. "For them," as Michael Brown has written, "the New Age is a kind of doppelgänger, an evil imitation close enough to the real thing to upset the delicate balance of spiritual power maintained by Indian ritual specialists." Thus the Declaration of War against Exploiters of Lakota Spirituality, issued at the Lakota Summit V in 1993, called on "zero-tolerance for any 'white man's shaman' who rises from within our own communities to 'author-ize' the expropriation of our ceremonial ways by non-Indians. All such 'plastic medicine men' are our enemies."[37]

While New Age is no small business, the money involved in it is no comparison to the pharmaceutical industry. When cor-porations registered patents in the United States and Europe for basmati rice and the medicinal use of turmeric, this had the potential of having major consequences for the livelihoods of many South Asians, making the issue important enough for the Indian government to challenge the turmeric patent in 1999 and the basmati patent in 2000, and have several of the patent claims revoked. After a four-year campaign by an NGO coalition with support from the United Nations Development Program, a European patent on the fungicidal use of the neem plant—which had been known in India for centuries—was also revoked. One of the campaigners described the neem as "our sacred heritage" and called the attempt to "take this ancient knowledge away from us . . . blatant and exploitative biopiracy."[38] Accusing multinational companies, particularly pharmaceutical ones, of "biopiracy" has become commonplace not only in the indigenous-rights movement but also, more broadly, among global antiglobalization activists. In India, "Western medical materialism and commercialism" and its exploitation of nature are routinely contrasted to the humanism and ecological awareness of Ayurveda.[39]

Legal Efforts to Safeguard "Indigenous Culture"

In the struggle between indigenous groups and corporations, the former have presented existing legal frameworks as seriously skewed not just in favor of the West, but more particularly in favor of rich people caring about nothing except getting even richer at the expense of poor and marginalized people—and of nature. For example, the report on the Migaloo case accused sixty-four-year-old Brian Meldon of Upper Brookfield (Queensland) of planning to "build a multimillion-dollar empire off the whale's popularity."[40] As far as who has benefited from copyright and patent law, the current system certainly reflects both Western ideas of property and the interests of those with sufficient financial, technical, and cultural resources to maneuver through the legal process. But a series of international conventions have been signed on the protection of cultural property and heritage that have the potential to alter the status quo. A moral shift is already perceptible.

In 2007 the United Nations passed a Declaration on the Rights of Indigenous Peoples, which requires governments to prevent actions that "take away [the] distinct cultures and identities" of indigenous peoples. Under Article 12, "indigenous peoples have the right to their cultural traditions and customs. This includes . . . sacred sites, designs, ceremonies, technologies and performances. Their cultural property shall be returned to them, if it was taken without their permission."[41] Article 29 declares that indigenous peoples "have the right to special measures to control and develop their sciences, technologies, seeds, medicines, knowledge of flora and fauna, oral traditions, designs, art and performances." The declaration gives an edge to the Convention on the Safeguarding of Intangible Cultural Heritage, passed in the same year. The convention allows states to receive global publicity and as a result, often money for such cultural practices as "storytelling, craftsmanship, rituals, dramas, and festivals," and in return, places on them an obligation of protection.

Moreover, as the anthropologist Valdimar Hafstein has written: "Instead of preserving textual or audiovisual recordings of performances, UNESCO's declared objective is now to preserve the enabling conditions of performances—the social fabric and the necessary habitat—and to provide incentives for transmission from one generation to the next. Needless to say, making sure that people keep singing their songs tomorrow is a task of a very dif-

ferent order from that of archiving the songs they sing today."[42]
Prior to this, the Convention on Biological Diversity, signed by
150 government leaders at the 1992 Rio Earth Summit, acknowledged the significance of traditional knowledge in preserving biodiversity and achieving sustainable development and emphasized
the need to ensure that local and indigenous communities retain
control over traditional knowledge.[43]

Besides these and other international conventions and declarations, there is a multitude of regional, national, and subnational
legal initiatives aimed at strengthening cultural property protection, at least symbolically. Thus the new Venezuelan constitution of 1999 guaranteed the "inalienable rights" of indigenous
groups, including the right to protect and practice their culture.[44]
In an example of a state appropriating the indigenous movement,
Bolivia's president Evo Morales, who won the election running
on a platform of indigenous rights, introduced bilingual instruction in schools, strengthening Aymara and Quechua and replacing
Catholic religious lessons with Cosmovisión, which Morales said
was the country's traditional religion. Both Venezuela's and Bolivia's governments engage in a rhetoric of standing up to the dominance of the North, particularly the United States; they oppose
capitalist globalization and make no secret of their disdain for
the international regulations that protect free trade. But even in
countries that have good relations with the World Trade Organi-
zastion, there have been calls to enact legislation protecting indigenous knowledge that contravenes the organization's rules. A New
Zealand researcher and activist, Aroha Mead, has been calling for
the establishment of a Regional Pacific Intellectual Property Office
"to vet patent applications and make sure they conform with
Pacific Island cultural values."[45]

Finally, elements of customary law have been recognized in the
management of such tourist sites as the Navajo Rainbow Bridge
in Glen Canyon in Utah or Ayers Rock in central Australia that
constitute traditional sacred places, either banning visitors from
entering certain areas or encouraging them to keep out. Photography, filming, and "commercial painting" of certain parts of Ayers
Rock is banned as well. In 2003, Anangu tribal elders moved to

stop the publication of the children's book *Bromley Climbs Uluru*, because the book showed photos of a toy bear climbing it, but dropped the efforts after the authors revealed that the photos had been taken before the ban was passed. Four years later, the same elders threatened action against a telecommunications company, Telstra, for featuring a digital representation of Ayers Rock in the virtual world called Second Life, where visitors can fly over the banned areas of the rock and take snapshots.[46] A planned Egyptian law requiring that royalties be paid whenever copies are made of ancient monuments such as pyramids would presumably have even more significant implications—for example, for themed resorts such as the Luxor hotel in Las Vegas.[47]

In many of these initiatives, efforts to protect intangible cultural heritage overlap with those to safeguard tangible property (objects and sites) that have been as prominent in debates about cultural ownership and predate those dealing with intellectual property. Most of the conflicts stem from the age of conquests and concern archaeological discoveries excavated in the Mediterranean, the Middle East, and Central and South America; art taken from Africa and Asia; and objects of folklore collected around the world and now housed in Western museums—mostly outside, but often also inside, the country they were taken from. The archaeologists and collectors of the time did not see their activities as inherently destructive: on the contrary, they were bringing the hidden treasures of the world to the attention of the "civilized" public and protecting them from decay and looting. When Sir Robert Baden-Powell and his cavalry regiment entered the royal palace in Kumasi (part of today's Ghana) on a punitive expedition against the Asante in 1896, he did not see carrying away the art found there as looting but as collecting.[48]

Accordingly, the first initiative to protect art—the Hague Convention for the Protection of Cultural Property in the Event of Armed Conflict passed by UNESCO in 1954 in response to the widespread destruction and looting of art and monuments during World War II, from the looting of European museums by the Germans and Soviets to the destruction of baroque Dresden by the Royal Air Force—was not concerned with the removal of art, only with its integrity.[49] The rationale for protecting art, even when it belonged to the enemy, was that "damage to cultural property belonging to any people whatsoever means damage to the cultural heritage of all mankind, since each people makes its contribution to the culture of the world."[50]

In the 1970s this "cultural internationalist" approach—which saw art and monuments as the common heritage of humankind and found a further expression in the 1972 World Heritage Convention—was challenged by "cultural nationalists," who argued that cultural property is first and foremost the property of the nations that created it.[51] Such calls came both from newly independent nations whose governments were finding that their best-known art was on display in the British Museum or the Musée de l'homme and from art-rich countries such as Italy that felt they were unable to prevent the continuous drain of their art into the international market. Some of their concerns were answered by the 1970 UNESCO Convention on the Means of Prohibiting and Preventing the Illicit Import, Export, and Transfer of Ownership of Cultural Property. This convention stipulated that "cultural property constitutes one of the most basic elements of civilization and national culture, and that its true value can be appreciated only in relation to the fullest possible information regarding its origin, history and traditional setting."[52]

The convention spurred a series of national laws. A number of countries now declare all antiquities that originate within their borders to be state property that cannot be freely exported. In Italy, for example, private citizens are allowed to own "cultural goods" but not to send them abroad.[53] These laws have had a major impact on the international art market by providing a legal means to challenge international art deals and demand restitutions. Recent years have seen a wave of new legal battles between states, museums, and art dealers, which concern sale or transfer not only in recent times but also in the past. A former curator of the J. Paul Getty Museum in Los Angeles is now on trial in Rome, charged with illegally removing objects from Italy. The Getty is also being formally sued by both the Greek and Italian governments for the restitution of various objects, and the Government of Peru has recently demanded the return of some five thousand articles from Yale University that were taken from the ancient site of Machu Picchu in the early twentieth century.[54]

Although China has not made formal demands to restitute artifacts, its State Administration of Cultural Heritage has announced that a new law will ban the export of pre-1911 artifacts altogether. Mexican activists regularly protest in front of the anthropology museum in Vienna, which owns the famous feather crown of the Aztec ruler Montezuma. Afrikanet.info has called an exhibition of art from the African kingdom of Benin, taken by another British punitive expedition in 1897, in the same museum in 2007 "colonial cynicism" and demanded that the objects on display be given back to "their rightful owners."[55]

Despite all this, thousands of artifacts continue to make their way to the displays of art galleries in Geneva, New York, Paris, and Zurich after every major archaeological discovery or armed conflict in a treasure-rich country. In the 1980s thousands of exquisite Djenne-jeno terra cottas disappeared from Mali after their discovery by two archaeologists was made public. They were sold to collectors in Europe and North America before Mali had enacted a law against the export of art objects.[56] In some cases objects restituted to African countries reappeared on the international art market within months. The Royal Museum for Central Africa in Tervuren, Belgium, now opposes further restitutions, citing its experience of returning 114 ethnographic works in 1976 to the custody of Kinshasa Museum, only to see a large number of them stolen amid subsequent political turmoil in the Congo. Yet, although poverty and corruption no doubt play a large part in such failures, we have to keep in mind that even the dapper Italian police are unable to keep the country's cultural relics safe from *tombaroli*, its tens of thousands of museums and churches from theft, its porous borders from illicit export.

In the 1980s indigenous activists joined the chorus of demands for restitution. Their requests were more often directed at governments, collectors, and researchers in their own countries. In part, their arguments were phrased in the language of national heritage, similar to that of Italy or Greece. Unlike the latter, however, they pointed out that some of the objects were of such sacred nature that they should not be displayed at all, or only on certain occasions and to a particular viewership, or else should be left to decay naturally. This presented a new challenge to museums, institutions that are, after all, dedicated to the preservation and display of objects. By the late 1980s museums in New Zealand had removed preserved and tattooed Maori heads from display.[57] In 1991 representatives of the Haisla, an Indian people of Canada's Northwest Coast, demanded that the Ethnografiska Museet in Stockholm give back a nine-meter totem pole, which had been sold—illegally, they said—to a collector in the nineteenth century and was a central attraction of the museum. The Ethnografiska finally returned the pole in 2006 after lengthy negotiations, in which the Haisla agreed—contrary to custom—to build a structure to display the pole rather than simply leaving it to decay, and to supply the museum with a new pole. Until the new structure is built, the pole is being displayed in the Kitimat City Centre Mall.[58]

In the United States the Native American Graves Protection and Repatriation Act (NAGPRA) of 1990 established a legal framework for the repatriation of human remains and ritual objects to Indian tribes that request them, if they can claim direct descent or prior ownership. NAGPRA had wide-reaching consequences for museums, as it extended not only to artifacts but also to notes and sketches made by anthropologists or missionaries. Wariness of possible litigation, but also heightened respect for the indigenous cause, means that museums now had to decide what to do with objects such as the sketches by anthropologist A. M. Tozzer of Navajo healing paintings, made in the early twentieth century. As the original images are traditionally destroyed at the end of the healing ritual, staff at Yale University's Peabody Museum was unsure whether to restore the drawings to the Navajo or let them decompose. Although the Navajo had not made a formal request for restitution at the time (1994), Vernon Masayesva, chairman and CEO of the Hopi Tribe, had already sent a letter to a number of museums, asking them to immediately close down all published or unpublished field data relating to the Hopi to anyone who had not received written authorization from the tribe. A short while

later, the Apache followed suit and asked to control "all representation of Apache culture, including any representations of
Apache culture offered by Apache and non-Apache."[59] If taken
literally, this claim would include Hollywood Westerns like John
Ford's *Fort Apache* as well as the thousands of academic and children's books, such as the best-selling nineteenth-century novels by
German author Karl May, that have included Apache heroes and
villains.

Although the Apache never actually tried to ban *Fort Apache*, a
director would now think twice before making a movie about an
American Indian group without prior consultation. The demand to
control representations has certainly had serious consequences for
scholarship, as it is now illegal to conduct research on an Indian
reservation or in an Australian Aboriginal settlement without
prior permission from the chiefs or elders, who also vet accounts
before publication and tell the researchers what knowledge they
are not allowed to reveal. As a result, the number of Australian
anthropologists who research Aboriginal issues has been declining. Anthropologists who collect tissue specimens or gather information about traditional medicine now routinely face accusations
of engaging in biopiracy even when their motives have nothing to
do with financial gain. Linguists seeking to preserve endangered
indigenous languages may find their work impeded by activists
who insist that language itself is a form of intellectual property to
which native speakers hold implicit copyright.[60] Senior Australian
anthropologists are now not infrequently faced with requests from
young Aboriginals to share the knowledge they gathered about the
past of their people from elders thirty or forty years ago and have
to decide whether or note to share and what sort of information
they feel authorized to part with—even for the sake of the cultural
maintenance of the community they had devoted decades to study.
Matters are further complicated when one considers the rights of
anthropologists who are already dead, such as Tozzer, who gave
his drawings to the Peabody with the intention of having them
preserved.

One way museums worldwide have tried to preempt such
dilemmas was by creating stricter codes of ethics, which require

the establishment of a work's full history prior to considering its acquisition—and withdrawing from a focus on acquisitions in favor of lending. As lawyer Robert Hallman has written: "Objects are assumed to be guilty unless proven innocent."[61] The new policies restrict not only the acquisition and collection of objects, but also their public display. The UK Museum Association's code of ethics endorses removing from public view ceremonial and religious items whose "unrestricted access may cause offence to actual or cultural descendants."[62]

Whose Heritage?

According to Article 4 of the Convention on the Means of Prohibiting and Preventing the Illicit Import, Export, and Transfer of Ownership of Cultural Property, "it is essential for every State to become increasingly alive to the moral obligations to respect its own cultural heritage." The 1970 convention is unambiguous about making nation-states the heirs and guardians of culture. It defines cultural heritage as "created by the individual or collective genius of nationals of the state" and "cultural property found within the national territory."[63] As Kwame Anthony Appiah has written, considering a long and still continuing history of imperialism, violent removal, and looting, it is not surprising that a doctrine has developed through a number of UNESCO declarations holding that cultural property should be regarded as property of its culture. "If you belong to that culture," this doctrine holds, "it is your cultural patrimony, if not, not."[64]

But here is the rub: it is not always easy even for a contemporary artist to decide which nation, or culture, he or she belongs to. Is Chagall a folk artist from Belarus (or Russia, for that matter), a religious Jew whose works should be displayed in Jerusalem, a longtime resident of the French Riviera with an attachment to its Provençal culture, or a cosmopolitan Parisian? Luckily, he has enough paintings to satisfy all these claims. How much more difficult it is, though, to decide the belonging of a fibula from the burial mound of a long-defunct people or the temple of a prehistoric cult in a kingdom that was destroyed two thousand years ago! When the Greek Republic demands that the British Museum send the Elgin Marbles, taken from Athens' Parthenon in 1806, the historical continuity seems relatively straightforward: Athens still exists, and its residents still speak a language that derives from Ancient Greek. But when Lord Elgin took the marbles with him, he duly obtained permission from the Ottoman sultan, to whose empire Athens then belonged. Greek identity—based largely on Eastern Orthodoxy as distinguished from the Islam of the Turkish rulers—had yet to be reconnected with the city-states of antiquity.[65]

When the ruins of the ancient kingdom of Koguryo, located in present-day China and North Korea, were declared World Heritage sites in 2005, demonstrators took to the streets in Seoul protesting China's appropriation of Korean history. For its part, the Chinese Academy of Social Sciences has established a "Serial Research Project on the History and Current Status of the Northeast Border Region," tasked with demonstrating that, quite to the contrary, the culture of Gaogouli (the Chinese spelling of the kingdom's name) was an important constituent of early Chinese civilization.[66]

Who do ancient Nigerian sculptures belong to? Nigeria claims them, but they were produced long before the Nigerian state existed. The people who made the Nok sculptures between 800 B.C.E. and 200 C.E. and the people who commissioned them belonged to societies that no longer exist. But if Nok civilization came to an end and its people became something else, why should Nigeria have a special claim on these objects buried in the forest and forgotten for centuries? The Italian government has persuaded the Getty to repatriate a twenty-three-hundred-year-old Greek vase and an Etruscan candelabrum—one evidently owned by a Roman collector but coming from Greece, and the other made by a people later subjugated and extinguished by Rome.[67] How far back in time do you trace ownership? Most of the treasures of St. Mark's Basilica in Venice come from the Crusades, expeditions not known for the gentle treatment of local populations or art. Should the horses on the roof of St. Mark's be sent back to Istanbul?

As we have seen, indigenous claimants often do not support

national ones. The Monte Albán Museum in Oaxaca wants the Maya treasures of the region back from the National Museum in Mexico City.[68] The Mexican state had appropriated the most attractive items of folk art found all over the country to construct a national cultural identity, but often showed little regard for the livelihoods of their makers, or even violently suppressed their protests. Similarly, the Bolivian minister who complained to UNESCO about Simon and Garfunkel's use of "El Condor Pasa" served the military dictatorship of General Hugo Banzer, which suppressed all dissent and had very strained relations with the Aymara and Quechua Indians, who lived in abject poverty. The meaning of the condor itself had undergone several transformations: once a sacred bird of the Incas, it had served as the symbol of an uprising against white oppressors for the author of the 1913 song and had become a symbol of Latin American unity under the dictators of the 1970s who named Operación Condor—their clandestine cooperation to squash dissent—after it.[69] In Australia the creation of a "national" Aboriginal culture, which has made previously local artifacts like the didgeridoo or dot painting into symbols of indigeneity writ large, sits uneasily with local histories that stress genealogy and make strong distinctions between "mobs."

But although a state's claims to heritage and continuity may often be suspect, they are underpinned by UNESCO's conventions. Yet sometimes states are unable or unwilling to exercise their duty of guardianship, and occasionally even disown and purposefully destroy what the conventions entrust them with protecting. Most of the art and architecture of ancient China, even if it survived Mao Zedong's Smash the Four Olds movement, perished during the Cultural Revolution of 1966 through 1976. During the rule of the Taliban in Afghanistan, keepers of the National Museum in Kabul grew increasingly worried about the fate of its collection of non-Islamic antiquities. They had already heard of century-old texts being burned by Taliban zealots in a library north of Kabul and asked foreign colleagues to help them take some of the antiques out of the country for safekeeping. A Swiss scholar, Paul Bucherer, agreed to do so, and negotiated an agreement with moderate members of the Taliban to ship endangered artifacts to a museum in Switzerland for temporary storage. But UNESCO, citing the 1970 convention, refused permission and accused Bucherer of destroying Afghan culture. Then the Taliban issued an edict against pre-Islamic art, leading to the destruction of many works of art, culminating in the dynamiting of the Bamiyan Buddhas.[70] Only after the destruction of the Buddhas—whose site was subsequently, after the American occupation, declared World Heritage—did UNESCO officials give their approval to Bucherer's small Afghanistan Museum in Bubendorf near Basel as a temporary refuge for endangered artifacts.[71] The collection was returned to the National Museum of Afghanistan in 2007.[72]

If continuity in title is not easy to establish, could the internationalist ideals of the World Heritage Convention and the Hague Convention be taken more seriously? Defenders of the internationalist view hold that cultural property should be there where people value it most, are capable to protect it, and share them with as many people as possible—with the exception of works that cannot be properly appreciated outside their context and objects of ritual or religious importance to living cultures. While exercising much greater caution than in the past when acquiring objects, the major museums of the West—unsurprisingly—subscribe to this view. Nineteen museums, from Chicago to St. Petersburg, signed the Declaration on the Importance and Value of Universal Museums in 2002. The declaration states that objects "become part of the museums that have cared for them, and by extension part of the heritage of the nations which house them. . . . The universal admiration for ancient civilizations would not be so deeply established today were it not for the influence exercised by the artefacts of these cultures, widely available to an international public in major museums. . . . Although each case [of repatriation] has to be judged individually, we should acknowledge that museums serve not just the citizens of one nation but the people of every nation."[73]

Anthony Appiah, grandson of both the ruler of Kumasi and Britain's chancellor and a leading American public intellectual, agrees: "The connection people feel to cultural objects that are symbolically theirs, because they are produced from within a world of meaning created by their ancestors—the connection of art through identity—is powerful. But we should also remind ourselves of other connections . . . connection despite difference. We can respond to art that is not ours. My people, humans, made the Great Wall of China, the Sistine Chapel, the Chrysler Building. The connection through a local identity is as imaginary as the connection through humanity. But to say this isn't to pronounce them unreal."[74]

Commenting on what should be done with the art Baden-Powell took from his grandfather's palace, Appiah has written: "I am not for sending every object 'home.' Many of the Asante art objects now in Europe, America and Japan were sold or given by people who had the right to dispose of them under the laws that then prevailed." If artifacts are returned, we should make sure that they are being returned to people who "are in a position to act as responsible trustees. . . . If an object is central to the cultural or religious life of a community, there is a human reason for it to find its place back with them." When former owners are known and when it is clear that the objects were stolen, we should see to it that they are repatriated. But not all of them: "I actually want museums in Europe to be able to show the riches of the society they plundered. . . . And I'd rather that we negotiated not the return of all objects . . . but a decent collection of art from around the world. . . . We shouldn't become overly sentimental about these matters. Many of the treasures in the Aban (the king's palace) were no doubt war booty as well." And why had the Asante king assembled this huge and very cosmopolitan collection? "Apparently he had been deeply impressed by what he'd heard about the British Museum."[75]

What both the declaration and Appiah point to is the fact that at the time many of the objects now constituting the pride of museum collections and fetching record prices at Sotheby's and Christie's first changed hands, the people who found or owned them were not only unaware of their value on the Western market but simply did not consider them beautiful, interesting, or in any way attractive. In medieval Rome antique temples were taken apart to reuse pillars as building material. Not only Chinese peasants but even state enterprises have for centuries used the bricks of the Great Wall in a similar way. Up to the first half of the twentieth century, the unique manuscripts found in the libraries of Cairo and in the grottoes of Dunhuang (the richest site of Central Asian Buddhist relics)—incidentally documenting earlier eras of a great mixing of Aramaic, Chinese, Greek, Latin, Persian, and Sanskrit learning—were there for the taking by interested scholars from Paris, Budapest, London, or St. Petersburg, so little interest did they generate locally. In 1906, French sinologist Paul Pelliot paid a Taoist master, who had previously used the Dunhuang treasures as presents to Chinese officials, five hundred taels of silver for six thousand documents and paintings.[76]

What revisionists often overlook is that before a global market gradually emerged on the back of maritime trade from the seventeenth century on, the overlap between scales of value that existed in different parts of the world was limited and incidental. Indeed, when Pizarro and Vasco da Gama exchanged their glass beads for nuggets of gold in the New World and the Gold Coast of Africa—images that now stand for all the injustices of colonialism—the beads may well have been more valuable locally than the gold. To pretend that gold, or any other object, has an inherent value, and that the *conquistadores* were simply taking advantage of native ignorance, is a Eurocentric fallacy, though one that Pizarro and his mates doubtless shared. The same is not, however, true for the trading of beads for land, as in this case, as the natives were soon to find out, they were entering a deal whose consequences they did not understand. Obviously, acquiring objects through murder, violence, and theft was not acceptable at any time, anywhere, but today's unified terms of value cannot automatically be projected into the past.

A further problem with a nativist approach to art is that so much of it has been influenced by, or produced for, the outside world. The renewal of fifteenth-century Spanish art took place thanks to Renaissance techniques learned in the conquered Spanish Netherlands. Within a century the same techniques were transmitted to native artists at Spanish missions in South and Central America, resulting in a fusion that produced such art as the statues of the Virgin of Guadalupe, which combined native symbols with Catholic iconography. The kachina dolls, which Vernon Masayesva would now have removed from museums, were already being produced for tourists (including Albert Einstein) in the early twentieth century. Tourists impressed with Hmong textiles in Luang Prabang's market in Laos or with the silver crafts of Maya women in southern Belize are probably unaware that the designs and technologies of these now widespread crafts had been introduced only very recently by Western entrepreneurs or volunteers. Would American Indians who protest the replication of sacred masks be offended by Picasso's borrowing of Congolese masks' shapes in his well-known *Demoiselles d'Avignon*?

The Community Fetish

"Fucking espresso, cappuccino. We invented the shit and all these other cocksuckers are getting rich off it. . . . And it's not just the money. It's a pride thing." In Episode 2 of the first season of *The Sopranos*, the popular soap opera that, some might argue, encompasses New Jersey culture better than any other work of art, Italian-American mobster Paulie rails against the theft of his cultural heritage by the coffee chains that in 1999 were still a new feature of suburban American landscape. Sounds like a perfect example of unacknowledged appropriation of cultural heritage for a profit? But what Paulie does not say is that this essence of Italian culture first became known to Europeans during the conquest of Central America. Tomatoes and peppers also came from the New World, while ravioli and buffalo mozzarella—so the Chinese claim—owe their existence to the Chinese voyage of Marco Polo. What remains of Italian cuisine after that?

The Walt Disney Company, a champion of extending copyright laws and fighting trademark infringements, has drawn most of its recent blockbusters from works of authors either unknown or unprotected by copyright: the tales of the Brothers Grimm, *Alice*

in Wonderland, Peter Pan, the legends of Mulan and Pocahon-
tas, and Kipling's *Jungle Book.* Indeed, Disney appears to systematically trawl the public domain for popular figures and gripping
stories.

Although their supporters are unlikely to see it this way, Walt
Disney, the imagined New Jersey mob, and Native American activists are in a sense rowing in the same boat: they are interested in
creating more instruments to limit public access to cultural goods.
Legal scholar Angela Riley has called for American Indian customary law on cultural property to be codified and incorporated
into American justice so that indigenous groups can enforce their
claims outside their own membership. This is already the case, to
a limited extent, with Aboriginal customary law in Australia.[77]
Similarly, the law professor Susan Scafidi has proposed a new
category of copyright-like protections for cultural products such
as ethnic festivals.[78]

To date, relatively few groups have pursued legal claims seeking
to limit the cross-contextual borrowing of designs by artists. The
Milpurrurru case is one example. In that case awarding damages
seemed reasonable; the patterns whose use the Aboriginal plaintiffs found offensive were not publicly available, as they were
deemed sacred, so their sudden appearance in the commercial
realm may well have been perceived as theft. But in other cases,
where the design or information whose circulation the spokespeople for a group wish to suppress is already in the public realm,
or where there is dissent within the group, such a decision would
be much more controversial. If decisions like that in the Bulun
Bulun case became the norm, as Riley and Scafidi wish, then any
Aboriginal artist who either inadvertently uses a pattern from the
sacred realm or does not feel committed to the norms imposed by
the elders is likely to face punishment. Such problems are further
complicated by the fact that, as the anthropologist Jennifer Deger
has documented, the extent of the sacred is undergoing rapid
change and reinterpretation in Aboriginal communities. While
elderly Yolngu keep the prohibition on viewing photographs of a
dead person, younger people, on the contrary, have made it part
of the mourning ritual.[79]

Critics of the restrictionist trend point out that creativity depends on mixing. This is perhaps most obvious in music. Jazz depends on improvising upon musical traditions from around the world. Contemporary sampling music does not even have an "original core," but is completely made up from sound bites from other music. There is no literature without intertextuality and no art or philosophy without borrowing. As *The Simpsons* said: "If you take our right to steal ideas, where are they going to come from?"[80] Riley has commented that incidents "involving theft of indigenous peoples' traditional knowledge and the blatant appropriation of culture have become more widely acknowledged."[81] But although similar practices *by* indigenous peoples are not so widely acknowledged, that does not mean that they are less widespread (in fact, they are a staple of anthropological research). Coca-Cola bottles have been used on the Ryukyu Islands in Japan as fertility symbols.[82] In Bhutan, Ethiopia, and Mexico they regularly serve as containers for water offered in temples and churches. The Mexican writer Carlos Monsiváis has described with some regret how in the 1980s the organizers of the annual Holy Week ceremony in a small town in Veracruz state petitioned the mayor and the priest to be allowed to have the Smurfs and the Gremlins instead of Roman legionnaires, who meant much less to them, as the evil characters in the dramatization of the crucifixion. Indian dancers worshipping the Virgin of Guadalupe replaced traditional masks—which were sold to tourists—with those of Batman and Spiderman.[83]

The Aboriginal paintings in acrylic that now sell for hundreds of thousands of dollars are an invention of the 1970s based on Western art formats. Today they are imitated, among others, by some Balinese villagers who have found that they sell better than other designs. Should these villagers be punished for misappropriating Aboriginal patterns when—as the Indonesia scholar Adrian Vickers has shown—their own traditional dances, now performed for tourists, owe much to German artists who settled in Bali in the 1920s?[84] Rap is a good example of appropriation in both ways: first the American music industry picked it up from ghetto streets and created its media stars with it, both white and black; then marginalized populations around the world, from colored South Africans to Eastern European Gypsies, appropriated it as an instrument of fighting for recognition. To take an earlier example, it is well known that van Gogh (Vincent, not Theo) was inspired by, and copied, the rich colors of Japanese woodblock prints called *ukiyo-e*. But these colors, notably Berlin blue, had only become popular in late nineteenth-century Japan and were imported from Europe.[85] *Ukiyo-e*, now often featured as a symbol of Japanese culture (such as Hokusai's prints of Mount Fuji), had been regarded in Japan itself as a rather vulgar art form until it became admired in Europe.

Proponents of stricter protections want to level the playing field by making "borrowing" from poor people as sanctionable as "borrowing" from rich companies. But it requires a difficult balancing act to protect minority populations while maintaining the flow of information necessary to liberal democracy and human creativity. Moreover, what legal principle will prevent other social groups—based on ethnicity, religious affiliation, lifestyle subculture, or political agenda—from advancing similar claims?

The Church of Scientology, as Michael Brown has pointed out, has for a long time been involved in legal battles with Web site owners who have put their "sacred knowledge" online and used similar legal reasoning to that of American Indian tribes.[86] If Alaskan natives can persuade researchers who investigate their genome to refrain from publishing findings that contradict their ancestral myths, then surely Christian groups can impose on scientists the demand not to disseminate conclusions that support the theory of evolution. The Ethio-Africa Diaspora Union Millennium Council, a Rastafarian organization, plans to get in touch with WIPO to protect Rastafarian intellectual property. According to the council's chairman, this may include the colors of the Jamaican flag as well the word "iPod."[87] Will Pitjantjatjara Aboriginal artists, the marketing of whose paintings has been aided by the resemblance of their traditional red-yellow-green color sequence to the "global African" color, be among those sued? Scottish crofters[88] are looking into asking the United Nations to recognize them as an indigenous people based on their distinctive relationship to the environment and the land, so they can have a greater say in government. Indeed, since cow herding techniques in Costa Rica have been recognized by UNESCO as Intangible Cultural Heritage, the road seems open for the crofters' recognition.[89]

The cherished cultural heritage of one group is sometimes the nightmare of another. Thus the Orange Order's annual marching rituals in Northern Ireland can rightly be described as an important part of "the culture, tradition and heritage of Ulster Protestants." Yet given their role in the political climate of sectarian civil war and their part in the glorification of centuries of colonial oppression, should they be formally recognized and protected?[90] Similarly controversial are many other traditions, such as Somali clitoridectomy, the Afghan burqa, and Japanese whale-hunting, all of which have many supporters who argue that these traditions are central to their way of life and in need of protection in the face of attacks by Western globalization. If the Makah Indians of Canada, the Faroe Islanders of Denmark, and some Inuit groups have been granted an exemption from the international whaling ban, should the Japanese not enjoy the same treatment just because they are more numerous and richer? Such cases are not all hypothetical. In 2008 an Australian judge allowed a Sydney-born teacher who admitted to having forced an eleven-year-old Torres Strait Islander boy to perform oral sex on him to present evidence in support of a cultural defense even though the defendant was not a Torres Strait Islander. The judge accepted the teacher's argument that he had "genuinely believed what he was doing was culturally appropriate" to uphold the traditions of the boy's native community.[91]

The problem with these propositions is not that they sound outrageous to many Western readers. The "heritage-ization" of living cultural traditions runs the danger of depriving individuals of their choice in whether to follow them or not. If residents of World Cultural Heritage towns are now only allowed to build houses using traditional materials and conforming to the style of old buildings, it is not impossible that for people within the purview of a World Intangible Heritage designation, if they live in an authoritarian country and generate tourist revenue, it will be difficult not to participate in the dances or ceremonies that received heritage status. In the Northern Laotian town of Luang Prabang, a World

Heritage site since 1995, one of the central attractions is the early morning almsgiving to local monks. According to an online guide to Luang Prabang, when a number of monks fell ill after having consumed unsuitable offerings, resistance among them grew to continuing the tradition. "However, the government has made it clear that the monks have to continue the tourist pageant or risk being replaced with lay people clothed in saffron robes in order to keep appearances and thereby keep the tourist dollar rolling in."[92]

In China, where state control over representations of ethnic and religious culture is strong in general and particularly so when it comes to Tibetans and Uyghurs, a sometimes restive Muslim ethnic group in the northwest, the government's successful application to have twelve Uyghur *muqam* (chants) declared as World Cultural Heritage raises much stronger concerns about control of the practice. In Australia the spread of Aboriginal performances at public functions has meant that young men often perform dances that have traditionally been reserved for elders. The anthropologist Gillian Cowlishaw has documented this in Western Sydney, to the embarrassment of older Aborigines who dismiss "textbook learning" as well as the idea that ceremonies can be revived at places with which they have had no connection.[93]

In other countries it may not be national governments but local interest groups that force "heritage-ized" traditions into a standard mold. As the folklore scholar Dorothy Noyes has shown, the granting of Intangible Cultural Heritage status to the Patum —a popular festival of medieval origins in Berga, a Catalan town—resulted in the suppression of other forms of dissent and diversity through the homogenization and bureaucratization of the festival, and eventually in the withdrawal of those very people who had helped revive it after the Franco dictatorship. The Patum case demonstrates that the actors most savvy in global dialogue will be the first to advance claims, whether or not they are locally regarded as authentic or representative.[94] The initiative to apply for heritage status came from a newly established foundation, the Patronat, formed by members of the local elite who were not performers of the Patum. Their application, approved by UNESCO in the first batch of designations in 2006, argued that the Patum was "threatened by transformation, distortion and loss of value" because of "urban and tourist development that tend to reduce the Patum to a mass phenomenon. These factors risk denaturing the Patum ritual by encouraging its organization in areas and at dates that are not authentic. Moreover, the hundred-year-old Patum figures that require care and restoration by artisans who possess specific secular knowledge and know-how risk being replaced by modern replicas devoid of all artistic and historical value."[95]

Noyes argues, however, that it is the Patronat—a self-appointed coordinating body accepted as representing "the community" by UNESCO and the Spanish government—that has been responsible for the bulk of commercialization and distortion. As Noyes explains, "UNESCO will give the valley to the irrigators. That is, a tradition is not 'protected' if its practitioners simply continue to do what they do."[96] Although in the past the Patum has had no coordinating body, the Patronat—which has obtained funds to develop plans, register a trademark to license T-shirts and sparkling wine with the Patum label, and hire a historian to determine "the true origins of the Patum"—now has physical and organizational control of the elements of Patum and threatens to take action against unauthorized commercial users of the festival's imagery. The winner of a poster competition who put his design on a T-shirt is now being sued by the Patronat.[97] A music group that had been participating in the Patum for thirty years has been denied the use of Patum's great bass drum for a recording. Permission to take out certain costumes for use in photography have been denied to rivals of the photographer allied to the festival.[98] In this controlled atmosphere, exchanges with the neighboring village of Manresa, which has a similar festival, may well come to an end after centuries of mutual exchange and borrowing.

The Patronat has introduced a point system to designate festival administrators, a honorific office accorded to four newlywed couples. Points are awarded for having been born in Berga and having been married in church.[99] The Patronat is clearly interested in strengthening an image of tradition conforming to the stereotype of a strongly Catholic, sedentary rural society, but Noyes points out that the town has a large immigrant population and a working class that is historically anticlerical. The Patum has historically served as a means of incorporating new Berguedans into full community membership, and in particular to provide a place in society for unruly young men. But now that folklore holds political and economic opportunities—participants are now recast as artists and invited to other festivals—tensions increase about who can participate. Opportunities for those with a low social status are becoming fewer. For example, professional craftsmen are now replacing volunteers who have for decades participated in restoring the Patum figures. As a result, many locals fear that their festival will be turned into "frozen heritage."[100] Thus, the ironic result of Heritage protection in the case of the Patum seems to be the gentrification of a practice that has, if we are to believe Noyes, previously been vibrant and inclusive. This danger is inherent in the trend to equate the cultural property of indigenous groups with "heritage," thus emphasizing continuity and homogeneity at the expense of flexibility and difference. Maintaining "heritage" becomes not only a right but also an obligation of indigenous "communities." The Convention on the Safeguarding of Intangible Cultural Heritage stresses that sustaining the community is a precondition for maintaining heritage.[101]

The embrace of "the community" is part of a broader shift in policy making, described by the social theorist Nikolas Rose, toward communities as a tool of managing populations.[102] In the mainstream of Western society (and, lately, China), communities are spoken of as residential units of civil society, but indigenous groups are supposed to form "communities" on the basis of common descent. (The same approach to immigrant groups, as discussed in chapter 4, is increasingly rejected by the postmulticultural state.) There are community development programs, community development or liaison officers, community police, and Community Studies.[103] In the world of indigenous rights, "community," as the sociologist Tony Bennett has remarked, "has constantly to be rescued from its imminent disappearance or, because the perceived need for community often precedes its existence, to be organized into being."[104] The indigenous "community" is the idealized locus of authenticity and solidarity, which has a legitimate desire to satisfy its economic needs but insists on having its way of life preserved. It is also pictured as living in harmony with nature, although locally, disputes between environmental conservationists and native populations—about matters that range from overgrazing by Indians in California to hunting in the Kalahari Desert and logging in the Tibetan areas of China—are the rule rather than the exception.[105]

Although every few years Hollywood unfailingly releases another film with Steven Seagal defending Alaskan natives from the encroachment of oil companies, some Alaskan peoples have in fact supported drilling. The creation of Native-controlled corporations under the Alaska Native Claims Settlement Act has become a way for some timber companies to circumvent curbs on logging.[106] Nonetheless, the "pastoral vision" of the Native who is one with Nature is so powerful that the chiefs of the Goshute Indians in Utah have been able to argue—despite protests from the state's governor—that their reservation is the best place for a nuclear waste dump (which would bring in subsidies and jobs).[107] The uranium, they argued, comes largely from Navajo mines, and it should now return to Indian land to rest.[108]

This view is reflected in the arguments of cultural protectionists Angela Riley and Susan Scafidi. Riley believes that unlike "top-down legal systems, tribal laws reflect tribal economic systems, cultural beliefs, and sensitive sacred knowledge in nuanced ways that national and international regimes simply cannot."[109] This argument reflects four problematic assumptions. First, it sees the "tribe" as existing separately from the outside world, as if members of its "economic system" were not also participants in that of the United States, and as if they could not embrace the cultural beliefs of both. Yet, as for many Indians, for the Tulalip, who are at the forefront of the codification of customary law, their casino is a major source of income, and as in many parts of mainstream America, Pentecostalism is growing strongly. The Chumash Mission Indian tribe, as Riley herself writes, devotes part of the "booming" revenues from its Chumash Casino Resort to develop a ten-week course to teach Chumash Inezeno to tribal members.[110]

Riley emphasizes that rather "than seeking to commercialise traditional knowledge, indigenous groups generally desire to assert ownership and control over it in order to protect it." Yet, she neglects evidence to the contrary—for instance, the fact that traditional healers have in the past been relatively well paid for their services.[111] Ironically, Riley uses the example of Hopi kachina dolls to prove that "sacred elements" of culture may not be sold, even by members of the group, ignoring the flourishing kachina trade that has existed since the early twentieth century.[112]

In a more recent case, Tommy Kapai, a Maori activist, "decided to trademark certain Maori words and iconic symbols . . . to hopefully hold on to them for Maori for ever so they wouldn't end up like the other lost languages of the world." Kapai supports a legal initiative, known as the Wai 262 claim, to prevent the trademarking of Maori words or concepts by non-Maori companies without "prior consent from Maori." Yet to offset the costs of this protectionist exercise, he licensed these brands to a number of companies: for example, Moemoea ("to slumber") and Awhi ("to embrace") became bedding and furniture brands. Kapai says that whenever he "was approached by a Maori company to use our brands, they were always given the green light at no cost," while the licensing fees from non-Maori companies went in part to pay royalties to the Maori designers. Nonetheless, he acknowledges that other Maori resented the commercial success of his trademarking initiatives.[113] Clearly, the idea that "tribal culture" is somehow untouched by contemporary market relations and therefore needs to be protected from them is hard to reconcile with the perfectly legitimate demand that members of "tribes" should be able to take advantage of these very relations to improve their lot.

As for the second problematic assumption of Riley's, she assumes that there is a coherent set of "tribal laws," corresponding to an equally uncontested set of values, that one need only codify. But in fact Australian lawyers active in native land claims point out precisely that what constitutes "evidence" for an Aboriginal group often fails to convince the judge because it rests on contradictory oral accounts. Moreover, often there is internal disagreement on what constitutes "tradition" itself. As Vine Deloria

Jr., a Standing Rock Sioux who has served as executive director of the National Congress of American Indians and was also a professor at the University of Colorado, told *New Age Retailer* magazine, when the Northern Plains spiritual leaders "issued a code of conduct to prevent further exploitation of ceremonies . . . they were immediately criticized by some Indians, who claimed they had received their ceremonies from different elders. So, not even Indians can figure out how to curb abuses."[114] Similarly, when the Association of Traditional Healers of the Navajo Nation was asked to issue a list of recommended chanters, herbalists, and hand tremblers to curb the influence of so-called plastic shamans (fake healers), they were unable to do so, because, as the *High Country News* reported, "no one agrees on the qualities that make a true healer."[115] The Hopi tribe has gone through a decades-long split between a "traditionalist" and a "progressivist" faction, and ironically the former camp prevailed in part because they made more effective use of the Internet in attacking their adversaries.[116]

Riley's third problematic assumption in advocating greater authority for tribes over their members who might be offending against customary law is that what is "consistent with the community's values" or "good for the community" is good for every member. The supremacy of the collective that she promotes would mean that tribal courts would treat members in a way quite different from mainstream American courts' defense of individual rights. Yet, it seems, for those who belong there would be no choice: "It is up to each individual tribe"—with the elders as guiding figures—"to determine which activities it seeks to incentivize and which activities it hopes to deter."[117]

As argued in previous chapters, an approach that limits choice based on belonging to a group does not serve the interests of liberal society. And as in our discussion of the multicultural state, we need to ask the question of who determines belonging to the group. This is the fourth problem with Riley's approach. Some American Indian tribes, using the criterion of the Jim Crow laws, will enroll members who have one-sixteenth of Indian "blood." Others are more purist, however. In the Cherokee elections of 2007 so-called Black Cherokees or Cherokee Freedmen—the descendants of slaves who found refuge with Indian communities—were not allowed to vote.[118] As the anthropologist Adam Kuper has written, in Labrador, an urban resident who speaks only English can be granted aboriginal rights if he can prove some Indian ancestry, but white settlers who have intermarried with Inuit, share their life-style, and are bilingual are regarded as squatters.[119]

The Side Effects of Safeguarding Culture

The codification of traditional ethnobotanical and medical knowl-edge takes place in parallel to that of traditional festivals and ceremonies, but for different reasons. Here, what is at stake is "preemptive protection" from possible future patents filed by "biopirates." The Convention on Biological Diversity and the Convention to Safeguard Intangible Heritage place the responsibil-ity for protecting "their" traditional ethnobotanical and medical knowledge with nation-states. Article 27.3 of TRIPS allows "devel-oping nations" and the African Union to develop their own pro-tection frameworks for traditional knowledge. These conventions encourage states to create inventories and databases of traditional knowledge to protect them from the reach of corporate exploita-tion. Having learned a lesson from the costly and lengthy process of challenging foreign patents on the medicinal use of turmeric and the fungicidal properties of neem, the Indian government launched two gigantic projects of "defensive publishing." First, it has created a Traditional Knowledge Digital Library of thirty-six thousand formulations used in classical Ayurvedic medicine. Second, it is having a twelve-volume seventeenth-century Dutch botanical text, the *Hortus Indicus Malabaricus* (The Indian Malabar Garden), translated to prove the long history of Indian knowledge on the medicinal uses of plants.[120]

These internationalist initiatives were intended to do the opposite of what both corporations and indigenous activists tend to want: to counter, in the name of the nation, the trend toward the further privatization of knowledge by placing it in the public domain. The financial implications of these efforts are substantial, as the market of proprietary Ayurvedic medicine alone was estimated at one billion dollars in 2008.[121] Yet the projects encountered resistance from some Ayurveda practitioners, for whom they meant loss of control over traditional knowledge. The Ezhava Social Reform Movement, which claims traditional ownership of the botanical knowledge written down in the *Hortus Malabaricus* in the name of the Ezhava caste, whose physicians provided most of the information to the Dutch compiler of *Hortus*, opposes the distribution of the translation outside India and instead calls for the "repatriation" of the original Latin text.[122] Practitioners of the *shuddha* (pure) branch of Ayurveda, who refuse to adopt any of the terminology of biomedicine and have opposed the industrial manufacturing and standardization of Ayurvedic formulas, condemn the Traditional Knowledge Digital Library as a contamination of Ayurveda: "In their view, sacred Ayurvedic texts should not be defamed by exposing them to secular or public scrutiny."[123]

Comparable controversies surround the protection of yoga. After a number of legal conflicts between the Los Angeles–based Bikram Yoga Corporation, run by an Indian entrepreneur, and other American yoga studios over the filing of copyrights on postures and breathing exercises, Indian gurus felt the need to proactively register intellectual property rights claims related to yoga exercises to secure continued free and open access. The Indian state is now also engaged in creating a National Yoga Database.[124] Anthropologists Sita Reddy and Alison Fish, in their analyses of these disputes, point out that the Indian state's efforts to codify traditional knowledge transform its very nature by turning knowledge (of the hands-on kind that James Scott has called *metis*) into information, isolating it from its spiritual base, stripping away its oral tradition, and turning it—in Scott's phrase—into "standardized formulas legible only from the center."[125] Thus for many traditional healers active plant ingredients are only one part of a complex health regime, which comprises medicinal incantations, spiritual cleansing exercises, or massage.[126] The National Yoga Database reduces and standardizes a highly heterogenic and multilayered body of knowledge. It contains only a few thousand postures and their explications, a limited number considering that the Bihar School of Yoga alone claims to use tens of thousands of asanas (postures). Only the tangible aspects of yoga, those that have been popularized globally as the essential representations of yoga—such as yogic texts and asanas—are included in the digital library, thus privileging certain yogic traditions over others (for example, those that emphasize abstinence or trance).[127]

Digital archives for traditional medicine being set up in South Africa and Brazil, among other places, as well as "cultural archives" such as the one initiated by Bob Geldof and the BBC, thus have a limited use. They might be able to prevent corporations from further encroaching on the public sphere and to document some aspects of existing cultural diversity. They can also be useful in providing differentiated access to traditional knowledge by respecting indigenous canons of confidentiality. Thus a new archive of the Mukurtu-Wumpurrani-kari, an Aboriginal group, enables precisely graded access to knowledge by making certain parts of the database accessible only to certain predefined gender, family, age, or ritual affiliation groups.[128] But expecting too much of documentation and overlooking its transforming effect on the nature of knowledge is, as Michael Brown has written, "mistaking the map for the territory."[129] Attempts by earlier generations of anthropologists to salvage what they saw as disappearing cultures by documenting them did not halt cultural change and loss, although they did sometimes prove useful for indigenous activists who used anthropological accounts for cultural revival. Thus some American Indian groups are using older linguistic anthropology texts to find out about their language and teach it to the younger generation.[130]

As these examples as well as the case of the Patum show, it is difficult to come up with mechanisms safeguarding culture that are not accompanied by a whole tail of unintended consequences. Mechanisms that seem straightforward and sensible on paper soon take on a different life of their own once turned into practice. The same pitfalls can be documented for some of the benefit-sharing schemes, which are increasingly popular in the pharmaceutical industry. Many of these schemes indicate positive departures toward a more equitable distribution of profits from traditional knowledge without binding the hands of inventors or marketers. In May 2007 the cosmetics company Aveda presented its successful collaborations with indigenous groups, which it called "stewards of the earth," at a United Nations Forum on Indigenous Entrepreneurship. Aveda first entered into a partnership with the Yawanawa, a people dwelling in the Brazilian rainforest, in 1993 to cultivate *uruku*, a plant producing a red dye used in Aveda make-up. With the company's support, the Yawanawa built a village and planted the *uruku* on their land. In 2004, Aveda established the Songman's Circle of Wisdom, a sustainable business protocol with the Kuktabubba Aboriginal community to supply sandalwood. The company helped the Aborigines gain land rights and access to natural sandalwood resources, and as a result the Kuktabubba's income has risen sevenfold.[131]

Benefit-sharing arrangements comply with Article 2 of the Convention on Biological Diversity, which requires states parties to implement such schemes "between the providers and users of traditional knowledge." But they are not without their own pitfalls and problems, many of which have to do with defining the group that should benefit from the utilization of knowledge—in other words, the attribution of cultural authority that we have grappled with throughout this book. Traditional medical knowledge can be attributed to hereditary holders of medical knowledge (who, in India, have remained identifiable as groups because of the caste system) or to the traditional owners of the land that produced the substance in question. In either case corporations inevitably deal with smaller groups that purport to represent the beneficiaries but whose authority is often contested.

Sita Reddy has illustrated these problems with the case of Jeevani, an Ayurvedic drug developed with medical knowledge from the Kani tribe in southwestern India. Three Kani informants provided information on the tonic qualities of the *arogyapacha* (*Trichopus zeylanicus*) plant to researchers from the Tropical Botanical Garden and Research Institute (TBGRI) under a profit-sharing agreement according to which 50 percent of the licensing fee and 2 percent of royalties would be paid to the Kani for eight years. The agreement seemed like a laudable effort at benefit-sharing and was indeed praised by WIPO as a model. But the Kani Samudaya Kshema Trust, formed to administer the process, had only five hundred members and was treated with "enormous suspicion" by other Kani, who refused to attend its meetings.

This suspicion arose in part because TBGRI, unaware that the traditional political system of the Kani no longer commanded full support, assumed that it had to negotiate with the hereditary tribal chief rather than elected local governments (*pancayat*). As a result, its negotiations were largely limited to one of the three *pancayat* in which Kani lived. Meanwhile, the Kani share in the profits was reduced when the state forest department claimed a share, arguing that the plant could only be grown in its forests. As a result, while "payments continued to be made into the Trust . . . the Trust itself lost any legitimacy to distribute" them.[132] Finally, Kani *pancayat* leaders and a group of tribal healers announced that they would not renew the license for Jeevani. In the middle of all these disputes, nobody thought of applying for a patent or trademark, and "a leading U.S. food supplement manufacturer and vitamin store chain" managed to secure trademark rights for it "without technically infringing on IPRs of the original drug."[133]

The safeguarding of culture is no easy and straightforward matter. Almost all aspects of it can be and are contested. Those who call for increased protection for indigenous cultural property generally argue—or imply—that indigenous groups deserve more such protection than others. The argument for greater protection is rarely made explicit, but four elements that contribute to it can be identified. The first two elements—that the distinctive culture of indigenous groups is in greater danger of disappearing than that of others and that their disappearance would be an inherent loss to the cultural wealth of humankind—reflect positive goals, but they rest on the same flawed understanding of culture that allowed mass murder in Rwanda. Cultures cannot be safeguarded by legal mechanisms; they are dynamic and changing, in a way that is not a zero-sum game. Contrary to the claim of a Tulalip spokesman that "we could be out of ability to practice our culture within the next twenty-five years," culture is not an expendable resource.[134] Today, UNESCO monitors cow herders in Costa Rica to ensure they do not deviate from their traditional practices—enshrined as intangible heritage—too much. How much is too much?

Not only do industrial cultures stand to profit from a vibrant and open public sphere; so do indigenous cultures. Their "cultural survival" depends on adaptations and exchanges with other societies, as demonstrated by the American Indian tribes that have used gambling revenues to support language and culture courses. The world is much more complex than the picture of indigenous groups subjected to "cultural genocide" by corporate interests. Anthropologists have shown how newness comes into the world out of the contact between local and global; how indigenous cultures use globally circulating goods, ideas, and institutions—in Marshall Sahlins's words—"to become more like themselves."[135] We should not automatically call all the influences going the other way "stealing."

The other two claims that—often, though not nearly always—are invoked in the argument to grant indigenous cultural property increased protection run into problems of a different nature. These claims can be summed up in this way: first, that "traditional owners of the land" inherently have more rights than latecomers; and second, that their lifestyles are precious because they reflect a "natural state" of humanity. If one took the first claim literally, then one would find oneself in the camp of Western anti-immigrant parties. (Sometimes such crossovers do occur; as Adam Kuper has noted, the founder of the prominent indigenous-rights group Survival International later became leader of the Countrywide Alliance, a movement opposed to the ban on fox hunting in Britain that is generally seen as being on the extreme right of the political palette.[136])

Of course, in reality, claims of indigeneity are only accepted as legitimate when they come from groups that can convincingly present themselves as historically marginalized. (When white South African Boer farmers claimed indigenous status, for example, it was intended, and perceived, as a provocation.[137]) Such claims do not necessarily rest on a longer historical presence compared with other population groups, but they are typically produced by a history of conflict with the modernizing state, whether colonial or not.[138] But even though claims of indigeneity often deserve sympathy as an instrument of compensating severely disenfranchised populations, their recognition, anthropologically speaking, is uncomfortably arbitrary. While we may treat implied or sometimes explicit claims of moral superiority with generosity when they are made by—or, more often, on behalf of—vulnerable groups, this does not make them more credible.

Today, when indigenous groups do participate in a global exchange, the goal should be to create a system of cultural protection that takes into account the interests and values of all sides. But claiming monetary compensation based on projecting today's unified terms of economic value onto past transaction—remember Pizarro's encounter with the Indians?—while at the same time demanding that the past's differing spheres of value be respected in the present (by limiting the circulation of particular kinds of knowledge) appears inconsistent. Discursive and legal maneuvers that would place "indigenous communities" outside nation-state constitutions in some ways while preserving the full range of protections offered them by these constitutions are obviously problematic. Creating a whole new system of protective laws, adding them to the existing ones (many of which, such as those governing the Internet, are not enforceable in the first place, or only enforceable at an excessively high cost for individual freedoms and privacy) seems to be the wrong path.

Moreover, as the historian James Suzman has noted in his study of the San in southern Africa, "a focus on indigenousness" in complex societies of poor people "may well reinforce the very structures of discrimination that disadvantage these people in the first place."[139] More generally, as Michael Brown has written: "One must ask whether the world will be a better place if we replace one expansive flawed, ethnocentric system by a thicket of small-scale, flawed ethnocentric systems whose sole value is that local communities are familiar with them."[140] And some acknowledgment should be made of the seemingly obvious fact—one that is central to the argument of this book—that cultural diversity is not limited to ethnic diversity. If this is so, then neither nations nor indigenous groups can be seen as the sole repositories and guardians of cultural heritage. This in turn means that institutional, financial, and symbolic support for cultural preservation should not be the exclusive preserve of representatives of national or ethnic entities.

As we have shown, a legal approach to heritage protection makes dealing with claims on a differentiated, case-by-case basis difficult. Yet it is intuitively obvious that the grievance of poor people deprived by a corporate drug patent, based on medical information they provided, of affordable access to a drug they have always used should be treated differently from protests against OutKast's appropriation of an American Indian war cry. Although patents and trademarks may actually have the power to prevent individuals from continuing to practice their traditions, unauthorized borrowing of tunes or patterns does not. Overall, the approach that seems most promising is that advocated by Michael Brown: to place the emphasis on acknowledgment—whether material, as in the case of benefit-sharing practices for patented drugs, or symbolic, as in the case of using a traditional song or image in a film or book.

chapter 6

The Age of "Cultural Competence"

Jürgen Schrempp, chairman of DaimlerChrysler, comes into the company's "War Room" in Stuttgart, the department that assembles and analyzes strategic information for the corporation. "I need something about Shintoism and Hinduism and how they get along," he says to an analyst. Within an hour the team has come up with the relevant information from its huge database. It takes another hour to prepare it in graphic form. They are ready to brief Schrempp. The most important tenets of both religions and their relationship to each other are projected onto the screens of the "war room." Schrempp looks satisfied. The team leader asks what he needs the information for. "I've been thinking about sending a Japanese factory manager to a plant in India," he replies. "But now I know that I'd better drop the plan." The briefing convinced him that "Shinto culture" and "Hindu culture" do not go together.

In the 2000s the terms "intercultural communication" (IC) and "intercultural competence" are everywhere. Look for a job online, and you will find that "intercultural competence" is part of the routine qualifications, just like knowledge of English or the "ability to work independently." It is something not just expatriate marketing managers are supposed to have, but also engineers at a rural German light bulb plant or teachers in a London suburb. And for those who do not, there is a bewildering choice of trainings, courses, texts, kits, and videos, available from consulting companies, universities, business magazines, and publishers. It is hard to avoid taking part in an "intercultural communication" training if you work for Exxon or Motorola, Boeing or Ford, Nokia or PepsiCo, DaimlerChrysler or Siemens. After the merger between

Daimler and Chrysler, more than three thousand employees took part in the "Effective Negotiations with American/German Business Partners" training. In a 2007 poll of twelve hundred "global executives" by the consultancy Bain & Co., 91 percent of the respondents felt that "culture was as important as strategy for business success."[1]

As a city employee in Europe or a nurse, you are also increasingly likely to be sent on one of these trainings. The Peace Corps runs Culture Matters workshops; international development agencies offer their staff culture and language trainings; even the U.S. Department of Defence (DOD) is suddenly promoting "cultural knowledge." The U.S. Air Force, Navy, and Marine Corps have all introduced "intercultural curricula" in their training facilities, are planning to set up full-blown cultural learning centers and are hiring anthropologists at their existing colleges. In 2004 the Pentagon sponsored "the Adversary Cultural Knowledge and National Security Conference, the first major DOD conference on the social sciences since 1962."[2] A report entitled *Fire, Ready, Aim* suggests that IC has come to the Air Force big time:

> Recent operations in Iraq and Afghanistan underscore the . . . need to be able to interact effectively across cultural boundaries. . . . The prisoner abuse at Abu Ghraib remains a well-known case in point where cultural dissonance was fundamental to the transgressions committed there. . . . The ranking Democrat on the House Armed Services Committee, Representative Ike Skelton (Mo.), . . . sent a letter to Defense Secretary Rumsfeld urging him to invest in cultural awareness training. He wrote, "In simple terms, if we had better understood the Iraqi culture and mindset, our war plans would have been even better than they were." . . . Air Force Chief of Staff General John Jumper . . . in a June 2004 speech . . . said that expanding cultural sensitivity was more compelling than the technical aspect of learning languages.[3]

Four other military authors, after stating that there was now "broad agreement . . . that many, if not most, of the challenges we face in Iraq and Afghanistan have resulted from our failure early on to understand the cultures," went as far as claiming that "conducting military operations in a low-intensity conflict without ethnographic and cultural intelligence is like building a house without using your thumbs: it is a wasteful, clumsy, and unnecessarily slow process at best."[4] In 2007 the U.S. Naval Academy introduced a four-week "total immersion" program for midshipmen (naval cadets) to live with foreign families speaking only their languages. In the Marine Corps every Marine officer is now required to have language skills and country expertise to qualify for promotion. According to an article released by USINFO, the State Department's foreign information service, "As an example of what can go wrong when people are not culturally aware, [Paulette] Otis [of the Marine Corps Center for Operational Learning] mentioned the Marine/Navy task force that quickly steamed to Sri Lanka after the 2005 tsunami and began to off-load relief supplies to people on the beaches. 'What they didn't realize,' she said, is that 'they were giving the supplies to the Tamil Tigers [a rebel insurgency group] and Sri Lanka's government objected.'"[5]

"Cultural competence" is the subject of several different but partly overlapping fields of expertise, each of which has its own institutional logic and ideology. In this chapter we consider, first, the most omnipresent of these: the world of IC consulting. We then briefly discuss ethnic marketing and diversity management and finally look at the application of the intercultural perspective in public health.

Intercultural consulting and training has become a rapidly growing industry that has now developed its own internal specializations. Although "how to do business with . . . " trainings remain the most popular, predeparture, reentry, and conflict resolution trainings for corporate managers have also become commonplace. Intercultural professionals working with foreign students at universities hold their own annual conferences. A company contracted by the German Foreign Ministry offers children of diplomats moving overseas a special program, called SMOOTH Moves.[6] Relocation companies—yes, those that move your furniture—provide tips about "cultural confidence" in their newsletters. Intercultural Press has more than a hundred titles in stock, ranging from *The*

Art of Crossing Cultures to culture-specific guides (*Learning to Think Korean*) and intercultural advice for specific professional settings such as global call centers and health care providers.[7] Universities offer degree programs in intercultural communication, intercultural management, and diversity management.

Engineers, microbiologists, language teachers, tour guides, even relocation managers with a high school degree can all become credible cultural trainers by virtue of their international experience ("I have lived in . . . ") or their ethnic background. The usefulness of their services is only rarely questioned, such as when an investigation into embezzlement at Volkswagen revealed that the company's top human resources manager, Peter Hartz (later responsible for reforming Germany's social security system), had paid more than four hundred thousand euro to Adriana Barros, the mistress of VW's trade union head and a former holiday-camp animator from Brazil, for work in "intercultural relations."[8] Those who make it to the top of the IC world become real celebrities. In the spring of 2002 a display rack with a single book dominated the social sciences section of the venerable Waterstone's bookstore in Goodge Street, London. The book, replete with grammatical mistakes and spelling errors, was Fons Trompenaars's *Did the Pedestrian Die? Insights from the World's Greatest Cultural Guru*. Trompenaars, holder of a PhD from the prestigious Wharton School at the University of Pennsylvania, has been ranked the twenty-fifth "most influential living management thinker."[9] His company, Trompenaars Hampden-Turner Consulting, advises many Global Fortune 500 corporations. His best-selling book, *Riding the Waves of Culture* (1997), has sold more than 120,000 copies in nine languages, including Korean, Turkish, and Chinese.[10]

This attests to the global spread of the IC business. Originating in the United States in the 1980s, it reached Western Europe and the rest of the world in the 1990s. The Society of Intercultural Education, Training, and Research (SIETAR) was founded in the United States in 1974; the first overseas chapter was established in Japan in 1985, followed by Europe and Indonesia in the 1990s, India in 2006, and the Middle East in 2007. China has no SIETAR chapter, but the demand for intercultural training is rising: in 2006 the Delegation of German Industry and Commerce in Shanghai offered, for example, a two-day training entitled "Bridging the Cultural Gap" for the fee of three thousand yuan, the monthly salary of many white-collar workers in the city. Computer manufacturer Lenovo, which has bought IBM's personal-computer business, has a course designed to help Chinese managers to "talk more openly and . . . oppose their colleagues."[11]

The reasons for the IC boom are, at least in part, obvious. The latest wave of globalization has meant that an increasing number of businesses—no longer only very large ones—rely on manufacturers overseas, try to sell their goods and services worldwide, outsource production and back-office support, and have a more ethnically diverse workforce even at their headquarters. In the neoliberal mind-set of maximizing productivity and lifelong learning, cultural difference appears as a technical obstacle that good management should eliminate. It's become business magazine common sense that cultural friction costs money. A widely cited study claimed, for example, that as many as 70 percent of expatriate managers in "developing countries" fail to complete their terms because of lack of cultural adjustment. Surely, avoiding such waste is worth the intercultural trainer's fee? If customers have doubts, intercultural trainers are quick to dispel them.

A training on Chinese culture for German participants began with the announcement: "For us, Chinese culture is unfathomable. Especially central is the taboo of losing face. Therefore thorough intercultural preparation, which explains the essential cultural standards of the Chinese, is a must." When a participant asked whether unreserved curiosity and an unprejudiced willingness to learn would not also be a good way to prepare for living in China, the trainer—Juliana Roth from Munich University's department of intercultural communication—replied: "You've got the wrong idea there. Cultural differences must not be treated lightly. Believe me, I can tell you from my personal experience that an unprepared stay in China can come to a deadly end."[12]

The figure of the successful manager—and increasingly, the successful person writ large—now includes confidently negotiating one's way around the world, and that requires conscious training

from early on. Because of China's central position in business scenarios for the twenty-first century, New York hedge fund managers
and French IT professionals are hiring Chinese nannies for their
children. In 2006 a Hamburg doctor and his wife moved to Kuala
Lumpur for two years, just to provide their children with what
they believed was a good international education in an environment where they can become familiar with Chinese culture.
China's new elite is equally concerned with raising a cosmopolitan
offspring: more than a hundred thousand children from mainland
China now study in secondary schools in Australia, the United
States, and Britain. At the tertiary level "international education"
is increasingly a must for any university as the function of education shifts "from the goal of constituting national subjects allied
by common values" to the neoliberal ideal of shaping flexible and
productive individuals who can maximize their advancement and
happiness wherever they want.[13] In the 2006–2007 academic year,
240,000 Americans and 75,000 Germans were studying abroad,
and there is an increasing proliferation of "global learning" initiatives that involve completing one's degree in several countries.

One of several programs offering a semester aboard a ship that
calls at different ports of the world, The Scholar Ship—a U.S.-
based venture sponsored by Royal Caribbean Cruises—offers its
students "intercultural communication" skills. Its lofty objectives,
as formulated by its associate vice president for academic affairs,
trained as an aerospace engineer, include "identifying the ways
in which enhanced intercultural competencies can be harnessed
through teams working in the natural and social sciences towards
the creation of a better world for all."[14] A 2005 report from the
global consultancy McKinsey, *China's Looming Talent Shortage*,
identifies the lack of a "cultural fit" with multinational employers
as one of the key problems of Chinese graduates.[15] Both Macquarie University in Sydney and Tsinghua University in Beijing
have "global leadership" programs.

In addition to various international education schemes—which
now include offering degrees through branch campuses in the
students' native countries, known in the trade as "offshore education"—there has been a slow but fundamental change in cur-

ricula, reflecting a concern with preparing students for a global career. Many universities—for example, Columbia in New York City—have special committees charged with making their curriculum more "international." In Germany many federal states, following the advice of the Standing Conference of Education Ministers in 1996, have included "intercultural education" in their curriculum guidelines, and teacher manuals explain that "information about life in all the different cultures are an essential element of learning."[16]

The Bill and Melinda Gates Foundation and others have donated $8.4 million to a campaign by Asia Society to create new public secondary schools in the United States with an integrated global focus; ten have opened since 2004, including two in New York, and up to thirty more schools are expected by 2013. In one of those schools, students in an English class have been asked to "write a journal entry from the perspective of a Kenyan villager returning home after the elections." The mother of one of the students commented that this was "an improvement over the show-and-tell multicultural activities in past years. She recalled sending her kids to school with Oreos and red, white and blue T-shirts"—standing for the United States—"when they were asked to bring food or wear clothing from their culture. . . . 'I mean, occasionally we'll eat a Greek cookie, but we're not sitting around singing Greek songs.'"[17]

Clearly, the idea of "global learning"—which in the United States follows the earlier wave of curriculum reform to reflect greater representation of ethnic minorities (discussed in chapter 4)—is a positive one. Even if the driving force behind it is individual desire to maximize one's chances in a global economy, the promise it makes—to educate individuals who are better informed of the global problems of the environment, poverty, and health, and who are more aware and tolerant of diverse ways of life— should be taken seriously. When the Berlin municipal government's Vocational Information Centre teaches apprentice carpenters the ecological consequences of the logging of tropical hardwood in Malaysian or Brazilian rainforests, chances are that they will feel more responsible for their part in an important global process.

When students of fashion design at London's famed St. Martin's School of Art have to spend their Mondays taking courses in "cultural studies," it may not influence their designs but could make them more sensitive to the social context of fashion.

If a shipload of American undergraduates gets to see life in African and Middle Eastern ports and has a genuine opportunity to get to know locals, they may well turn into professionals with greater empathy and more support for their government's engagement with the world. But often, the concepts used in preparing them for such encounters actually work against a greater understanding: The Scholar Ship, for example, includes Samuel Huntington's *Clash of Civilizations* in its curriculum—and not with a critical approach. In the worst case, if taught to think about large parts of the world in stereotyping ways, students may find engaging with the infinite variety of individual experiences behind the broad facade of a "national culture" or religion more difficult than if they had been taught nothing. Nonetheless, in general, the idea of "intercultural learning" in education—particularly in ethnically relatively homogenous states—has had the beneficial effect of expanding students' knowledge beyond their home countries and questioning the single national perspective on history and society. In the corporate world, partly because of its demand for quick fixes, the effects of IC's advent have not been so clearly beneficial. Next we turn to the examination of the central tenets of IC that are embraced from corporate "war rooms" to the Peace Corps.

Riding the Waves of Culture: Hofstede™ and the 7D Models

The most cited figures of IC today are the Dutchmen Geert Hofstede—who has registered his name as a trademark—and Fons Trompenaars.[18] The work of both men relies on identifying and "measuring" a series of cultural variables that, Hofstede and Trompenaars maintain, can be usefully compared across societies. This approach goes back, on the one hand, to the teachings of anthropologist Edward T. Hall as initiated at the Foreign Service Institute in Washington, D.C., in the 1950s, and on the other hand, to the methods of social psychology. At the request of the Foreign Service Institute, Hall developed a practical approach to sensitize future diplomats to cultural differences that obstruct communication. He divided societies into those with high versus low "context," those with "monochronic" versus "polychronic" time systems, those with higher and lower needs for personal space, and those with higher and lower speed of messages (referring to the formation of social networks).

"Low context" societies were those where people compartmentalized interaction in various personal and professional settings, and since that meant having less background knowledge about those outside their immediate circle of relatives or friends, they required more information to complete a task. Thus a Chinese employee could be given much simpler verbal instructions than an American because the intense social interaction between manager and employee would create much tacit understanding between them. Similarly, a "monochronic" time system means a compartmentalized management of tasks, where scheduling and precision punctuates the natural rhythm of human interaction, distinguishing work time from leisure. A "polychronic" time system refers to dealing simultaneously with a range of matters and people and to a greater tolerance of delays.

Hall was the first to call the attention of nonanthropologists to the culturally constructed nature of ideas about time, privacy, and nonverbal communication. Many of his insights reflected the reality of different work cultures and were unquestionably useful. Hall did not offer simple, quantitative matrices to apply to the societies he described; he did not explicitly divide the world into regions colored differently based on whether they were high or low context. But by describing culture as a "silent language," a code that could be cracked; by using exotic, untranslated concepts from the Japanese; by routinely writing about "the Americans" and "the French"; and by insisting that "like oil and water, the two systems" (monochronic and polychronic time) "don't mix," Hall prepared the ground for those who made the next step: self-styled cultural translators who divided the world into a patchwork of cultural boxes with quantifiable variables of difference.

The idea of such variables came from social psychology, a discipline that relies on the quantitative analysis of large-scale opinion surveys and on controlled experimentation in laboratory settings, and cross-cultural psychology. Cross-cultural psychology, a subfield of social psychology that acquired its own identity in the early 1970s, proceeds by identifying a number of universal dimensions of behavior, such as individualism or respect for authority, and tests them comparatively across different groups, revealing quantitative variations in reactions to particular situations through such statistical methods as factor analysis.[19] The set of cultural variables is sometimes derived from cross-national surveys, but very often it is simply assumed. In other words, while cross-cultural psychology generally assumes that particular cultures (that is, nations or ethnic groups) can be distinguished by core sets of values, it is interested not in establishing what these values might be (and hence, whether they indeed form a coherent set or not) but in how behavior varies across what are assumed to be cultures driven by different values.[20]

The study that in many ways formed the basis of contemporary IC was Hofstede's questionnaire survey of work-related values among eighty-eight thousand IBM employees in more than fifty countries, conducted between 1967 and 1973 and published as *Culture's Consequences* in 1980. For example, the question used to rank societies on "power distance" was: "How frequently, in your experience, does the following problem occur: employees being afraid to express disagreement with their managers."[21] Claiming that "data obtained within a single MNC [multinational corporation] does have the power to uncover the secrets of entire national cultures," Hofstede proceeded to develop a system of five "cultural dimensions" that identifies and quantifies "value orientations" in different societies.[22] He saw culture as "the collective programming of the mind that distinguishes the members of one group or category of people from others."[23] This "programming" is acquired through socialization in a particular country and has the same fundamental nature as the forces of physics.[24]

The five cultural dimensions, measured on a scale from 0 to 100, are "power distance," collectivism/individualism, masculinity/femininity, uncertainty avoidance, and long/short-term orientation. To focus on one of these variables, the "collectivism" dimension means an orientation toward the expectations and norms of the "we-group" (such as kin) and strict differentiation between it and outsiders. By contrast, in individualistic societies, individuals are expected to be concerned primarily about themselves and their immediate family members, and the distinction between the in- and the out-group is weak. "Power distance" denotes acceptance of hierarchy versus preference for egalitarianism. Thus Americans are individualists with a small power distance; Chinese, collectivists with a large power distance. Hofstede then proceeds to group countries into clusters on his five-dimensional value map. Writing about the "spirit of Asian capitalism" in such articles as the much-cited "The Confucius Connection: From Cultural Roots to Economic Growth" (written with Michael Harris Bond in 1988), Hofstede echoes Huntington's terminology of civilizations (or, rather, the other way around).

Trompenaars's model is very similar to Hofstede's. He and his collaborator, Charles Hampden-Turner, use seven rather than five "cultural dimensions" (table 2). Like Hofstede's name, these seven dimensions are a registered trademark. Trompenaars's study, published in *Riding the Waves of Culture*, was based on a questionnaire administered in 1993 to fifteen thousand managers and administrative staff working in corporations in fifty countries. He found that Americans and Europeans are "universalistic," Chinese "particularistic." This is because Westerners think in a logical and linear fashion and make sense of the world using abstract concepts. Chinese thinking, on the other hand, is intuitive, nonlogical, and nonabstract. Dutch and Swedes are "neutral" because they consider the control of emotions as a sign of civilization and deem it inappropriate to exhibit them in work relations, whereas Italians and Southern Europeans are "affective" because they show their feelings openly in the workplace as well as at home.

Clearly, Hofstede and Trompenaars owe their "dimensions" and the idea of cultural "programming" to Edward Hall. Hall's views were inspired by the "culture and personality school" of anthropology that flourished at Columbia University in the 1940s

Table 2. Trompenaars Hampden-Turner's
"seven dimensions of culture"

1. Universalism versus Particularism
   What is more important—rules or relationships?

2. Individualism versus Communitarianism
   Do we function in a group or as an individual?

3. Specific versus Diffuse Cultures
   How far do we get involved?

4. Affective versus Neutral Cultures
   Do we display our emotions?

5. Achievement versus Ascription
   Do we have to prove ourselves to receive status
   or is it given to us?

6. Sequential versus Synchronic Cultures
   Do we do things one at a time or several things
   at once?

7. Internal versus External Control
   Do we control our environment or work with it?

Source: From http://www.thtconsulting.com/Content/cont042.htm (accessed 17 January 2007).

and 1950s and included such influential scholars as Margaret Mead and Ruth Benedict. Benedict's report on Japan for the Office of War Information, which formed the basis of her famous book *The Chrysanthemum and the Sword* and detailed the divine status of the emperor in Japan's cosmology, convinced the U.S. government not to prosecute Emperor Hirohito for war crimes. Benedict's and Mead's success in making the American public aware of cultural difference—such as Mead's intervention in the public debate on education and sex roles—was an important public corrective to the global role the U.S. government was embarking on in the postwar era. The two scholars influenced the thinking of millions of Americans and provided intellectual ammunition for the antiwar movements of the 1960s. But at the time, anthropology—in the words of Mitchell Hammer, an intercultural trainer recalling Hall's significance—described "patterns of human interaction as it exists within a particular group of people and within another group." In Hammer's view Hall's innovation was to look at interaction *between* human groups: "that's what intercultural communication was about."[25]

But if Hall's foregrounding of national cultures was understandable in the context of the 1950s, in the immediate aftermath of World War II and a period that had seen the climax of ideologies of national purity and unprecedented restrictions on migration, it lost much of its purchase in the thirty years before the publication of Hofstede's first book. In those decades, as communication and migration across borders increased, anthropologists began paying more attention to cultural change and cross-fertilization over history, realizing that cultures previously depicted as static and monolithic entities were not only being now influenced from the outside but had in fact always been so. Beneath their facades of homogeneity lay conflicts between individuals and groups who had quite different views on and uses for common cultural practices. Anthropologists now paid as much attention to conflict as to integration within cultural groups, and began asking by what mechanisms the fiction of unity had been maintained. Japan scholars such as Helen Hardacre and Tessa Morris-Suzuki showed that the Japanese culture reflected in Benedict's work—who herself could not visit Japan because of the war and relied on secondary sources such as letters by Japanese POWs—reflected a relatively recent construct of Japanese culture, promoted by the state since the mid-nineteenth century to counter a sense of humiliation before a technologically superior West.[26]

At the same time, anthropology also underwent a more fundamental epistemological change, beginning to see itself—as Clifford Geertz famously wrote in 1973—no longer as "an experimental science in search of law but an interpretive one in search of meaning."[27] Soon, as the anthropologist Matti Bunzl has put it, "ethnographers would no longer provide data for a broadly comparative 'science of man' but, rather, evidence for the specificity of all cultural configurations. . . . [James] Clifford identified and championed this very development when he noted the general trend toward a *specification of discourses* in ethnography: who speaks? who writes? when and where? with or to whom? under what institutional or social constraints?'" Going farther than Geertz, Clifford argued that culture was "neither an 'object to be described' nor a 'unified corpus of symbols and meanings that can be definitively interpreted,'" but "contested, temporal, and emergent."[28]

In the 1980s Hofstede's view of the world as a mosaic of distinct national cultures thus already appeared to anthropologists as outdated. Perhaps for that reason, Hofstede himself in his later work dismissed anthropology as concerned with "marginal groups and . . . problems which for society as a whole are fairly trivial."[29] But it is not only anthropologists who are critical of national cultural dimensions. In a lead article in the influential journal *Human Development*, psychologist Per Gjerde recently criticized cross-cultural psychologists for creating a new set of stereotypes by "mistaking passports for cultural categories" and failing to pay attention to individual variation, power structures, conflicts within groups, and historical change.[30]

Yet for Hofstede and his followers, "cultures" constitute clearly demarcated, static entities. Cultures are like onions: their outer layers, such as the clothes one wears or the music one listens to, may change—for example, as a result of globalization—but their inner cores of values, in the words of Marieke de Mooij (whom Hofstede praised as a pioneer in the field of culture and marketing), "have not become global . . . and are not likely to change during our lifetime."[31] These cores are firmly linked to national belonging. As Hofstede has admitted, his "idea of dimensions of national cultures has become part of what Kuhn called 'normal science'"—that is, the generally accepted paradigm of truth.[32] Hofstede equivocates about whether these dimensions should be seen as standing for national cultures in their entirety and criticizes others for oversimplifying his approach: "Some people have tried to imitate my approach cheaply for commercial purposes. . . . At times my supporters worry me more than my critics."[33] He even adds that he used to write "CULTURE DOESN'T EXIST" on the blackboard for his students. Yet, although a number of books in his vein acknowledge cultural variation within societies, this squeamishness gets lost in what filters down to the Web sites, training manuals, and university curricula.

Clicking, for example, on "Australia" in the long list of countries featured on Hofstede's own Web site leads to the following text: "The Geert Hofstede analysis for Australia reflects the high level of individuality Australian's [sic] hold dear. . . . This individuality is reinforced in Australian's daily lives and must be considered when traveling and doing business in their Country [sic]. Privacy is considered the cultural norm and attempts at personal ingratiating may meet with rebuff." It is fair to describe Hofstede's approach, then, as national cultural determinism.[34] IC books invariably acknowledge the existence of other variables—such as age and gender—somewhere in the introduction, only to forget about them completely in the body of their analysis. When they do give internal cultural variance any further thought, it is mostly variance between ethnic or language groups (such as French versus German speakers in Switzerland, African Americans versus Latinos in the United States.)[35] Despite the faddish appeal of "lifestyle groups" in marketing—one company divided Chinese residents of San Francisco into five "clusters," from Young Literati to Money & Brains—interculturalists spare them no thought.[36] The idea of a national culture, as the management professor Brendan McSweeney wrote in a devastating but elegant critique of Hofstede, does not differentiate the New York City Young Marxist Club from the Keep America White Cheer-Leaders Club in Smoky Hill, Kansas.[37] The privileging of the nation as the unit of analysis—which we discussed in chapter 1—is a choice made by the analyst rather than a given: any other classification may have produced significant differences in responses as well.

The historical examples Hofstede himself provided in support of his findings cast further doubt both on his method and on the causal link between national belonging and thinking, but they can be entertaining. In one of these examples, Hofstede links Freud's theories to his roots in Austrian culture, which "is characterized by the combination of a very low power distance with a fairly high uncertainty avoidance. . . . The low PDI [power distance index] means that there is no powerful superior who will take away one's uncertainties: One has to carry these oneself. . . . High UAI [uncertainty avoidance index] indicates an intolerance of deviance. . . . a very high MAS [masculinity] score sheds some light on Freud's concern with sex."[38] Yet, as McSweeney writes, Adolf Hitler, another Austrian of Freud's generation, "unhesitatingly argued for submission to a 'powerful superior.'" Leopold von Sacher-Masoch, also an Austrian and known as the godfather of masochism, appeared to enjoy "voluntary submission to humiliations administered by fur-clad women." Finally, Felix Salten, though also a pornographer, wrote "the extremely successful asexual animal novel *Bambi*." In other words, material both to support and to refute Hofstede's inferences (intolerance of deviance, high masculinity, low power distance) can easily be found in a nation of (today) nine million, and indeed even within the writings of one person. McSweeney concluded:

> A genuinely open exploration of the conditions of possibility and the possible influences on Freud's theories would surely consider his birth and early years in Moravia (then part of the Austro-Hungarian Empire but now in the Czech Republic); his family and school backgrounds; his later education; his class; his Jewishness; the extensive anti-Semitism in Vienna; his relationship with his wife and children; those he analysed; his network of friends—Austrian and non-Austrian; the significant age gap between his parents; his non-religious upbringing in a turbulent turn of the century imperial city (Vienna); the decline of the Austro-Hungarian Empire; what he read; his mentors, and so on, and so on. Linking a national cultural dimension with the views of a writer is an easy but facile "game" to play. It is as intellectually spurious and equally invalid as the statement that Freud developed his theories because he was born on 6 May and therefore was a "Taurus."[39]

National cultural determinism is the main conceptual weakness of mainstream interculturalism. It also rests on a weak methodological foundation. The IBM study that has been the urtext of most IC work for more than a quarter of a century was done on a relatively small sample in most of the included countries: only in six countries (five of them in Western Europe) did the number of respondents exceed a thousand. In fifteen of the countries sampled, the numbers were under two hundred.[40] Moreover, most respondents were in sales and marketing. Numerous quantitative studies, both before and after Hofstede's, have been at loggerheads with his conclusions. For example, a 1999–2000 survey entitled "Good Government, East Asian and Nordic Perceptions" found that among respondents in Japan, Korea, Taiwan, and Denmark, "hard work" was least important for the Japanese, "creativity" was rated highest in Korea and lowest in Denmark, and "obedience" was more important for Danes than for any of the Asians.[41] (These results, of course, may say more about the value of surveys than about the values surveyed.)

Sampling problems aside, questionnaires and formal interviews reflect how people see themselves and want to be seen by others, not their complex, often contradictory behavior. In other words, they "measure" perception, not practice, and miss the messiness of everyday life that the following "culture cameo" nicely describes. Anthropologist Raymond Apthorpe recalls how, when living in a Taiwanese village, he was offered a dish of buffalo stew. Having been told previously by the villagers "We don't eat buffalo meat, it is our culture not to eat buffalo, they have worked hard for us," Apthorpe asked the cook:

RA: So, this is buffalo stew.
Man: Yes, it is.
RA: I thought I had learned from you that you do not eat buffalo meat.
Man: Yes, we don't eat buffalo.
RA: But this is buffalo stew.
Man: Yes, but it is not our buffalo, it was our neighbour's.[42]

Surveys also fail to capture the influence of politics and the historical moment on *both* what people say and what they do.

To illustrate this, McSweeney comments on "the radical decline in church attendance in post-Franco Spain and [its] considerable increase in post-Soviet Russia," both linked to the end of regimes —one of which strongly promoted, and the other suppressed, religion. Clearly, any survey conducted in Francoist Spain or the Soviet Union that included a question on religion would not have yielded results that were independent of state coercion.[43] In another poignant example of the fallacy of "national culture," McSweeney points out that "although Hofstede depicted Yugoslavia as having a high level of Collectivism, a strong degree of Uncertainty Avoidance, and being very Feminine . . . it violently disintegrated into a number of separate states. And we are now, consistent with his claims, supposed to believe that the national cultures of each of these states: Serbia, Croatia, Kosovo, Bosnia, and so forth, are identical to each other. Such an idea beggars belief, but if it is not true, then what was really identified/measured as the 'national culture' of Yugoslavia —indeed of every nation— by Hofstede?"[44]

Cultural dimensions are ill-equipped to deal with change, whether political or social. According to Hofstede, Venezuelans have a low level of tolerance for uncertainty. "In an effort to minimize or reduce this level of uncertainty," he writes, "strict rules, laws, policies, and regulations are adopted and implemented. The ultimate goal of this population is to control everything in order to eliminate or avoid the unexpected. As a result of this high Uncertainty Avoidance characteristic, the society does not readily accept change and is very risk adverse [sic]."[45] Last we checked, this text was still on Hofstede's Web site, a decade into President Hugo Chávez's "Bolivarian revolution," which introduced radical land and oil industry reforms.

In a study of U.S.-Mexican joint ventures, business academics Rao and Teegen expected to find that Mexicans, who score extremely high on Power Distance, would dislike the participatory management techniques introduced by the Americans.[46] But where such techniques were implemented, "employees seem[ed] to enjoy the interactive process with their bosses and it helped them in terms of their satisfaction and morale." Because of Mexico's high collectivism index, a differentiated reward scheme based on performance appraisal was expected to be unpopular, but the authors found that this too was not the case. In China, another highly "collectivist" country, performance-based pay is in fact more prevalent today than in the West, so that the income of a junior manager or a journalist often depends primarily on bonuses. Rao and Teegen conclude from this that "Mexicans are slowly moving from their traditional human resources practices." They point out that Mexico scores quite differently on the Hofstede and Trompenaars scales. In Trompenaars's study, conducted in 1994 (twenty-five years after Hofstede), Mexicans are particularistic, individualistic, and high on the achievement dimension. But both Hofstede and Trompenaars claim that "core values" do not change over a lifetime. For if they do, how much are their dimensions, which purport to be predictive, worth in rapidly changing societies? Although Rao and Teegen's results beg this conclusion, caught up in the orthodoxy of IC, they do not draw it.

The similarities between the Hofstede-Trompenaars and the Huntington models of culture are obvious: the major difference is that while Huntington warns us of the clash of civilizations, the interculturalists offer their services to prevent it. Gary Weaver, a professor of intercultural communication at the School of International Service at American University, likens cultures to icebergs, whose invisible parts clash when they get too close to each other.[47] The role of the interculturalist is to prevent that clash, but sometimes his clients might decide that the risk is too high for them to take.

This was apparently the case when DaimlerChrysler's former CEO gave up on sending the Japanese manager to India when his advisers' graphs showed too much of a gap between the beliefs of the Shinto and Hindu religions, which Schrempp obviously saw as proxies for Japanese and Indian culture respectively. Some historical reading would have quickly revealed, however, that the central status these two religions now enjoy in the imaginary of the two nations is a product of late nineteenth-century politics. As detailed in chapter 3, the idea of "Hinduism" emerged as "a composite portrait of various, sometimes contradictory traditions, but also as an incipient reality" from the encounter between colonial efforts to classify the Indian population and local reactions to it.[48] Similarly, the modernizing Japanese state "can be said to have created Shinto as its official 'tradition'" out of a loose system of animist beliefs and ancestor worship existing in syncretism with different strands of Buddhism and lifted it to the center of its nationalist ideology.[49] Though this state Shinto, which was instilled in every school student between 1890 and 1945 through the reading of the *Imperial Rescript on Education,* promoted devotion to the emperor and unquestionable deference to the nation's common good, it is extremely far-fetched to extend these doctrines to the everyday behavior of all Japanese people today.[50] Though a concern with differences between the organizational cultures of DaimlerChrysler's Japanese and Indian branches is legitimate, the reduction of individuals to carriers of a putative state religion can lead to absurd situations like the following. A Japanese student at Macquarie University in Sydney took a linguistics class that focused on the cultural aspects of language. One day, the lecturer asked him to demonstrate how Japanese people greet each other. Atsushi lifted his hand, wiggled his fingers, and said "Hello." Not satisfied, the lecturer insisted: "No, I mean how do you greet people in a formal situation?" Atsushi shrugged and repeated that this was how he greeted people. Getting annoyed, the lecturer— who was of course expecting Atsushi to perform a bow—said, "Okay then, how would you greet the emperor?" Atsushi, feeling harassed, responded that he would prefer not to meet the emperor. Finally, the lecturer was obliged to perform the bow herself, but Atsushi felt stereotyped and kept complaining about the incident for weeks.

Intercultural trainers are not always averse to forcing the desired cultural characteristics onto resisting participants either. Thomas Hüsken, in a critical account of IC in German development aid, describes the experience of an Arabic employee of the German Foundation for International Development who participated in an intercultural training before taking up a position in Yemen. Because of his background, he was to personify the Hofstedean attributes of Arabic culture. The man, however, kept contradicting the trainer: "I studied in the GDR [East Germany] and have worked nearly 25 years as a journalist. I am a Syrian citizen and, why not, an Arab too, but I am also an intellectual and a cosmopolitan person. . . . I had not felt as humiliated and offended in a long time as at that training. The Germans could not understand why I was being so defensive. After all, it was supposed to be about understanding me better. . . . The trainer and the participants let me know that I should quit the training. I wasn't being open enough. It was horrible."[51] An Egyptian development worker related a similar story: "I was horrified to be described as the member of a 'collectivistic culture.' The trainers ascribed to us characteristics that have nothing to do with me or my compatriots."[52] In these cases the trainings designed to facilitate intercultural communication precipitated the breakdown of such communication before they were even over.

"Chinese Culture": IC versus Life

Let us test the assumptions of IC on the example of the cultural entity it is most preoccupied with these days: the Chinese. "I can live anywhere in the world, but it must be near an airport," said a Chinese hotelier in San Francisco to the anthropologist Aihwa Ong.[53] This quotation captures the contemporary image of the Chinese as the *homo oeconomicus* that roams the world in search of profits, passports, property, and prestigious schools for his children. Since the late 1980s, this picture of the flexible capitalist has replaced the older cliché of the take-out or laundry man, which had in turn arisen in place of the colonial-era image of the Chinese as coolie or mandarin.

The tens of millions of overseas Chinese—estimates vary between thirty-five million and fifty million—have come to stand for a new transnational capitalism. They are represented as a globally spread but closely knit diasporic community whose behavioral norms and values are not only central to their own success but are also essential knowledge for Westerners who want to succeed in doing business with or teaching them. A wide range of manuals, trainings, and consultants caters to that need—from airport book-shops to corporate HR divisions. As a random example, let us look into Intercultural Press's *Encountering the Chinese: A Guide for Americans* by Hu Wenzhong and Cornelius Lee Grove.[54] As far as IC manuals go, this is a very practice-oriented book, with only a minimum of theoretical pretensions, the key one being that China is a collectivistic society and the United States is an individ-ualistic society, and it is from this that the book deduces most of the practical differences.

Of course, the perception of Chinese society as collectivist and hierarchical has been around for a long time. But it was Hofst-ede's study that provided this view with the respectability of man-agement science. In the 1990s Hofstede's findings were used as quantitative support for the cultural explanations for the success of overseas Chinese, which, as we showed in chapter 1, arose in business schools in the context of the economic miracle of the "Asian Tigers" (Hong Kong, Taiwan, Singapore, and South Korea—the latter not ethnically Chinese but dominated by a "Con-fucian ethic"). Politicians, journalists, and business-school pundits succeeded in convincing the world that there was a distinct set of cultural values—often glossed as "Asian" but really understood as Chinese in origin—that went back to Confucius and explained such economic phenomena as high savings rates, long working hours, and the prevalence of family businesses.

Numerous Western and some Asian authors have addressed this correlation between cultural values and economic growth, among them such economists as Murray Weidenbaum, a top adviser to Ronald Reagan who now has his own Weidenbaum Center at Washington University; such sociologists as Ambrose Yeo-chi King, former vice chancellor of the Chinese University of Hong Kong; and such management specialists as Gordon Redding, cur-rently director of the Euro-Asia and Comparative Research Centre at INSEAD, one of the world's most famous business schools.[55] By the end of the 1990s, as foreign investment and economic growth in China itself increased, the attention of IC pundits shifted to China. Yet they continued to refer to Hofstede's study, carried out twenty years earlier in three historically and politically very different societies—Taiwan, Hong Kong, and Singapore—with fewer than a hundred respondents in the latter two places!

All three societies in the Hofstede survey had scored high in the dimensions of Collectivism and Power Distance, but the base in both Singapore and Hong Kong was too small for statistical analysis. To make the research more robust and to exclude a possible Western bias in the original questionnaire, social psychologist Michael Harris Bond, in consultation with Hofstede, asked scholars from Hong Kong and Taiwan to devise a Chinese Values Survey. The survey, conducted in twenty-threes countries, confirmed the latter's conclusions but introduced a fifth "dimension," called Confucian Dynamism. This dimension entailed a long list of values, including persistence, industriousness, benevolent authority, loyalty to superiors, harmony with others, pragmatism, thrift, wealth, patience, respect for hierarchy and tradition, protecting "face," resistance to corruption, family orientation, high work morale, and patriotism—a list that, as we have seen in chapter 1, mirrors the image China's government promotes.[56]

In keeping with this scheme, *Encountering the Chinese* begins with a section entitled "Group Cohesiveness in Contemporary China," followed by "Three Fundamental Values of the Chinese." The first section explains that the Chinese always live in a group (family, school, workplace, neighborhood), and "very few significant relationships occur beyond the boundaries of these primary groups."[57] This corresponds to the high Collectivism index in Hofstede's model, which is supposed to reflect putting the interests of the group ahead of the individual's and clearly differentiating between relationships within and outside the group (whether family or nation). Unquestioned loyalty to the group is rewarded by lifelong protection. In the second section, based on Hofstede and Bond, the authors add "high power distance" and "intragroup harmony" to collectivism to make up the three fundamental Chinese values. They emphasize that "people are comfortable with an unequal distribution of power and thus do not try to bring about a more nearly equal distribution."[58] This argument, as we have seen in chapter 1, is frequently deployed by authoritarian Asian politicians, but it also appears frequently in the "doing business with the Chinese" literature. In *The Bamboo Network*, coauthors Murray Weidenbaum and Samuel Hughes write about an overseas Chinese network of business relationships throughout Southeast Asia, glued together by a "Confucian tradition [that] is remarkably persistent; it inculcates loyalty to a hierarchical structure of authority, a code of defined conduct between children and adults, and trust among friends. The closely related virtues of pride in work and disdain for conspicuous consumption are especially beneficial to rapid economic growth."[59]

The premise of Bond's work is even more questionable than that of Hofstede's. Unwittingly, he comes close to acknowledging that his discourse is one in which, by citing a psychological experiment here and a Confucian classic there, banalities are packaged as scientific achievements. Thus Bond acknowledges that his conclusions echo those made long ago by such authorities as the missionary Arthur Smith, author of *Chinese Characteristics* (1894), but—unlike his—those had been "episodic and unsystematic, lacking the synthesis and the power to predict that are the hallmarks of scientific theorizing."[60] The Rev. Smith's book, for example, contains this passage: "Lying . . . duplicity, lack of sincerity and obsequious accommodation are national traits that fly in the face." Compare to this a quote from a 1984 study by Bond and coauthors: "As expected in the East, there are more rules about . . . maintaining harmonious relations and restraining emotional expression." Yet there is no experimental evidence cited for this. As a matter of fact, a 1972 study of kindergarten children in Taiwan concluded that they were more prone to expressing anger (but less likely to express sadness) than their American peers. This does not mean that the stereotype of the poker-faced Chinese is always wrong; it just points to the fact that rules about controlling emotional expression do not apply in all situations.

The view that Chinese people are naturally "cohesive" also ignores the political dimension: the fact that government enforces "group cohesiveness" for keeping control. For example, the ten-household responsibility system, in which every one of ten households can be held responsible for each other's transgressions, was used as recently as the late 1990s in some coastal areas to reduce illegal emigration. Neighborhood committees are the basic unit of Communist Party control; typically, these consist of old crones who endeavor to stamp out vice by peering into residents' kitchens. Although such systems of surveillance have a long tradition in Chinese history, they are not a natural result of collectivism but a well-honed state instrument that capitalizes on such universal emotions as fear and envy and on the lessons of state-instigated neighborhood terror from the Cultural Revolution that still live in the collective memory. Other examples of group cohesiveness cited by the authors are true for Europe as well as China and seem unusual only for Americans (for example, that children stay in the same class collective as long as they are at one particular school and that they are supported by their parents until they graduate from school, rather than holding part-time jobs).

The feeble foundations of the Hofstede-Bond corpus do not prevent business writers from using them to accentuate the uniqueness of Chinese culture. Some carry this exoticizing to absurd levels. Marieke de Mooij, for example, has written about "Asians not being able to think in opposites."[61] A 1996 training video by George Renwick, a well-known interculturalist, bears the telling title *Chinese Cultural Values: The Other Pole of the Human Mind.* To pick a more recent work, the popular former premier of Western Australia, Geoff Gallop, wrote the foreword to Yow Yit Seng's *The Chinese Dimensions: Their Root, Mindset, and Psyche,* in which "concepts peculiar to the Chinese psyche are explained in an easy-to-understand manner, centering on yin-yang, the five determinant elements and the *I Ching* [a classic text on divination]. Collectively they impact on a whole spectrum of uniquely Chinese cultural practices such as the Chinese zodiac, fengshui, pillars of destiny analysis, divination, self-cultivation as well as Chinese medicine."[62]

The tendency to portray Chinese culture as the inscrutable Other of the West is reflected in the widespread use of untranslated Chinese terms, presented as lacking equivalents in the English language. One such exercise is a book by Stella Ting-Toomey and Ge Gao, *Communicating Effectively with the Chinese,* whose chapters have such titles as Gan Qing (emotions), Ke Qi (politeness), and of course Mian Zi (face).[63] One of the buzzwords of the trade, *guanxi*—to which *Encountering the Chinese* also devotes a section—means "personal connections."[64] Yet even an authority such as the respected political scientist Lucian Pye—a former president of the U.S. Association of Asian Studies—has claimed, in a report prepared for the Rand Corporation, that *guanxi* had no English translation. He warned American negotiators that their Chinese counterparts will, in social interactions, aim to create a sense of long-term obligation, where expectations of reciprocity were unclear.[65] Sociologist Ambrose King linked *guanxi* to Confucian teachings about society and constructed a complicated theory, only to come up with such platitudes as "'walking through the back door' (*tsou hou mên*) is widely known to be the most effective and necessary way to get things done through personal networks (*kuan-hsi [guanxi]*)."[66]

Zha Daojiong, a professor of international relations at Peking University, criticizes such literature as serving "the purpose of promoting . . . cultural gaps . . . not minimizing them."[67] Aihwa Ong has written that, thanks to the feverish activity of IC consultants—both Chinese and Western—in Shanghai, Western employers, when faced with a high turnover of local managers, low regard for corporate rules, and the use of a corporate position for personal business deals, take it for "Chinese culture or guanxi"—that is, greater loyalty to one's personal network of friends than to the corporation—even though it is the opposite: "a precipitous embrace of neoliberal values of self-management and risk-taking."[68] Souchou Yao, who studied ethnic Chinese businessmen in the Malaysian state of Sarawak, points out that "the logic of network building, in fact, cannot be primarily about maintaining the status quo. It is also frequently about ruthlessly pruning the deadwood of guanxi connections while actively pursuing politically and economically more useful ones—even among non-Chinese."[69]

Confucian-capitalism pundits often point to the ubiquitous Chinese family firm, with its flexibility, internal loyalty, kin-based hierarchy, and low overhead costs, as the expression of such values as group orientation and filial piety. Management professor

Gordon Redding has written about the "benevolent paternalism" of the Chinese family firm, in which individual family members work not for individual benefit, but for the long-term well-being and mobility of their family.[70] Sociologist Gary Hamilton has claimed that "Chinese organizational principles rest upon inviolate social relationships; people must obey the 'internal dictates' of those relationships."[71] "But how," Souchou Yao asks, "are abstractive philosophic principles transmitted to the present as 'inviolate social relationship'? What makes people submit themselves with pathetic compliance to these 'internal dictates'?"[72] Anthropologist Susan Greenhalgh, in a study of twenty-five family enterprises in Taiwan, found that "division of labor in these firms was not a natural reflection of tradition but a political construction of the family/firm head, who was pressed to build his firm out of family resources by several features of the national and global political economies. I argue that the Confucian thesis is a form of Orientalist economics that arose in the context of, and in turn supported, a very conservative politics."[73]

While Greenhalgh's concern, as a feminist anthropologist, is with uncovering the exploitative side of family enterprises, researchers of management, coming from very different premises, have also come to conclusions that contradict the supposed cultural uniqueness of Chinese family firms. Business professor Phillip Phan and his collaborators have studied how Chinese-owned family businesses in Hong Kong and Thailand manage succession. They found that the expectation of business founders to be able to pass the business on to a relative, as well as the preference for selling the business to an outsider versus closing it, were quite divergent. Contrary to their expectation that "the Asian family business would be more homogeneous *a priori*, due to the widespread influence of Confucian values that permeate overseas Chinese businesses . . . [t]he results clearly attest to the fact that we cannot treat all overseas Chinese businesses as homogenous, something that the literature"—they refer, among others, to Redding—"has consistently done. . . . but that generalizing to business owners about succession requires . . . the careful examination of the type of firm, the [political and macroeconomic] context in which it is competing, and the nature of the family members' contributions. Thus, in the light of this research, the general models that are now popular in the literature appear to be oversimplifications of a complex phenomenon."[74]

In fact, the line between "network-based" and "market-based" business relations is a subtle one. Relations between employees and employers are rarely governed by pure economic rationality, even in the West. Think about the case of Volkswagen's Peter Hartz with "intercultural manager" Adriana Barros described earlier in this chapter. Here, the company secretly paid a total of more than two million euro over a period of years to keep its trade union boss happy. Business transactions between Western companies frequently develop into long-term relationships that are often valued over cost-effectiveness. When Procter & Gamble moves into a new market, for example, it prefers to work with market research agencies and advertising companies that it has an established relationship with, although local companies often charge much less. Public contracts in Europe are often accompanied by accusations of nepotism, and a common defense is that the government must consider not only the financial cost but also the previous record of the bidder. And who could get an article published in *The New Yorker* without prior connections? (Not us.)

If the Hofstede-Bond model often fails to account for the behavior of overseas Chinese businesses, it also proves naive when the apparent cohesiveness, harmony, and family orientation of individuals is subjected to closer scrutiny. One of us has been studying contemporary Chinese migration to Europe since the early 1990s. At the level of media and organizations these migrants tend to display a remarkably homogeneous set of images and texts, which correspond to the state-sponsored discourse of patriotism and unity. A large part of the globalized Chinese media sphere—which includes satellite television, thousands of newspapers, and the Internet—circulates images of hard-working, dynamic, and prosperous Chinese businessmen, from IT entrepreneurs to pig farmers, and contrasts them with those of an anemic West (or worse, an uncivilized South). Chinese migrant organizations have put up an increasingly convincing display of Beijing-oriented patriotism in worldwide demonstrations protesting

NATO's bombing of the Chinese embassy in Belgrade in 1999 and in a global network of groups opposing Taiwan's independence.[75]

Nonelite first-generation migrants, such as market traders in Eastern Europe or garment workers in Southern Europe, often do not speak local languages and have limited contact with local society, so a degree of identification with this public arena of "Chineseness" is not surprising. Still, while public narratives underscore the distinctiveness of "Chinese values," private conversations display a more varied attitude: selective identification but also criticism, and in some contexts the adoption of viewpoints and lifestyle choices associated with their local neighbors. People may invoke the discourse of group solidarity strategically, when they want to convince a business partner that he is getting a good deal. (For example, a businessman booking a banquet at a Chinese restaurant may be told: "We will make sure to host you enthusiastically. We can't let Chinese lose face!")

Yet it is a typical complaint among migrants that Chinese businesspeople are too individualistic: very often, they would name the Jews, the Vietnamese, or the Arabs as those who are truly united and therefore, unlike the Chinese, defend themselves successfully against police harassment. Many Chinese prefer to live in places where there are few other Chinese around. Ji Dongtian, a former Propaganda Department official in China who became a newspaper editor in Hungary, described his appreciation from the freedom of various forms of peer surveillance: "There are no Party cells here, no labour unions, no Youth League, no Women's League, no work unit, no street committee. . . . Nobody meddles if you go to the red-light district or to the casino or join up with a woman. You can taste freedom here."[76] Ji's is not a political statement—he has maintained good connections with the Chinese embassy—but a social one. He expresses his relief at freedom from the ties of reciprocal obligations.

Souchou Yao has pointed out that both well-known "self-made" business leaders and struggling village shopkeepers, speaking in public, often refer to the "Chinese spirit" of hard work, perseverance in adversity, and care for one's employees as the key to success. The same is true of Chinese entrepreneurs in Hungary. As Yao notes, the literature on "Confucian capitalism" arose on the basis of migrant and diasporic entrepreneurs, whose very specific situations of leaving a generally humble existence in China and having to create new livelihoods in an alien and often hostile environment understandably give prominence to stories of succeeding against the odds—whether to derive gratification from one's success to an audience in China that has traditionally looked down on uneducated traders or to be heartened by the promise of an eventual success.[77] Yet Confucian-capitalism pundits (not unlike European anti-Semites earlier) confused the specificity of the migrant predicament with the cultural essence of a people.

Examining actual behavior uncovers yet another level of complexity. Ethnographic material makes it clear that many migrants fulfill certain expected obligations to kin but try to evade others, and that there is a fairly general desire to withdraw from group scrutiny and pressure. The Zhaos, an urban professional couple who migrated to Hungary in the early 1990s, were followed by four siblings with their spouses, and it was expected that the couple would take care of their accommodation and provide them with initial capital and business opportunities until they could stand on their own feet. They did so, despite the fact that during this period they had a baby and faced a battle against deportation. The help they provided included letting the relatives use the couple's stands at a market to sell their goods, even though they could have made money renting them out; moving out of their apartment so a sister and her family could stay there; repeatedly bailing out a brother who was a professional gambler; and even, they say, taking the blame for a violent crime committed by Mr. Zhao's brother, which eventually resulted in Mr. Zhao's sentencing and deportation. Thus far, the Zhaos' behavior had been straight out of *Encountering the Chinese*. But after her husband's forced departure, Mrs. Zhao, resentful of the relatives, cut her contacts with them and moved to another place. Miss Li, a former college teacher who had come to Hungary at around the same time, provided only minimal assistance to relatives. She let her sister work at her company when the latter first arrived. Miss Li did not go to her father's funeral in China—traditionally an extreme violation of filial piety—because she had business to attend to in Hungary. Family conflicts arising from unmet expectations to help relatives are very common among Chinese in Eastern Europe.

As for *guanxi,* the cultivation of personal ties with officials and corporate managers, involving extensive dinner invitations, is a prominent feature of the way Chinese businessmen and women advance their lives in Europe. A researcher in Hungary in the 1990s, after having been treated to one or two dinners, would often be asked: "Do you know anyone in the interior ministry who could help with visas?" But one does not need cultural explanations to understand that a group of people in a vulnerable legal situation and in a generally xenophobic society—not speaking the language, deprived of information, not knowing the legal environment and having to rely on local middlemen for even trivial everyday matters such as renting a flat—attempt to rely as much as they can on the few channels available to them to gain access to resources. Efforts to maintain a long-term relationship also depend on the social status of the person a migrant is dealing with. Mr. Zeng, a well-known restaurant owner in Budapest, routinely pays his Hungarian lawyer more than she asks, but he is such a pinchpenny with workers that once, when he moved, the relocation company's workers left him in the middle of the street after an argument over what amounted to a couple of dollars. In Hungary as in the jungle of Borneo, while "Chinese traders are wont to regard reliance on social networks as . . . simply the normal Chinese way," it is in reality selectively deployed to overcome the disadvantaged status of the Chinese: as noncitizens in Hungary and as non-Bumiputra ("non-natives") in Malaysia.[78]

What about conflict avoidance? Relations with non-Chinese generally conform to this image, but not necessarily because this is an inherent characteristic of Chinese culture. When suffering some harm from locals, especially authorities, Chinese in Eastern Europe rarely report to the police or sue. But this is hardly just a cultural characteristic, as the assumption is that authorities are usually biased in favor of the Hungarians, and police are likely to retaliate if sued. Regarding conflicts among Chinese, several people said that they wish they could turn to the police, but they have no confidence in their effectiveness and are afraid that an investigation might turn against them. In other situations, such as debt collection, they do not like turning to legal means for a variety of reasons: because they fear retaliation, because they want to maintain long-term business relations, or because the business transactions are not documented in a fashion required by Hungarian law to bring a lawsuit. Familialism, collectivism, ethnocentrism, and conflict avoidance describe the behavior of Chinese migrants in some situations but not in others. To analyze when they do and when they do not means to analyze the contradictions between what is said in public, voiced in private, and actually done. This can only be done by taking into account the social and political contexts that IC generally leaves out of its considerations.

Of course, for some overseas Chinese, nationalism is a deeply felt sentiment. For others, it is brought out by the mistreatment and discrimination they experience at the hands of local authorities and residents. Yet for others, it is a tactical choice. For importers whose competitiveness depends on access to goods, capital, and business information in China, displays of patriotism—such as joining organizations, appearing at protest meetings, and writing articles in newspapers—help establish contacts with Chinese officials and garner invitations to investment fairs organised by Chinese authorities. For students, they facilitate getting a government job when returning to China.

Some interculturalists recognize, if not the flawed nature, then at least the insufficiency of the "dimensions" approach. Alois Moosmüller, a professor of intercultural communication at the University of Munich, has pointed out the danger of seeing culture as essential and primordial and has devoted research to the effects of national stereotyping in German-Japanese joint ventures.[79] Hofstede himself, as discussed earlier, expresses distaste for some of his more commercially oriented epigones and their lack of research rigor. For example, he quotes a study that checked the claim—stated in thirty-one different management articles—that 70 percent of expatriate managers fail at finishing their terms abroad due to cultural incompatibility. This strong argument in favor of IC training turned out to rest on shaky legs indeed: the only empirical base for the thirty-one publications was one study for which the data were collected in the late 1970s.[80]

Internal criticism is yet to trickle down to business schools. When Phillip Phan, a professor of management at Rensselaer, submitted an article analyzing the differing dynamics of international expansion among European low-cost airlines, peer reviewers who missed culture from his paper told him to brush up on his Hofstede. In corporations, trainings and consultancies based on Hofstede might reign supreme. (To pick a random example from our recent incoming mail, a four-hour seminar offered by the Department of Professional Development/Global Expertise of the renowned Ludwig Maximilian University in Munich promises, for 220 euros, to teach participants about "the Chinese understanding of time and authority" and "about the collectivistic and person-oriented tendency of your [Chinese] counterpart."[81]) As the maestro himself wrote, Hofstede's work has "become part of intercultural training programs and of textbooks and readers in cross-cultural psychology, organizational psychology and sociology, management and communications."[82] In the 1990s and early 2000s the Social Science Citation Index registered an average of ninety-four citations of Hofstede's *Culture's Consequences* annually (nearly all in management and psychology), far exceeding the number required to be considered a "super-classic" and still growing every year.[83]

While Hofstede retains a certain "scientific" clout, the most popular intercultural consultants are Trompenaars Hampden-Turner, warriors of the cultural box according to whom individuals who do not seem to fit with the well-defined cultural characteristics of their societies are best avoided: "Foreign cultures have an integrity, which only some of its members will abandon. People who abandon their culture become weakened and corrupt. We need others to be themselves if partnership is to work."[84] Trompenaars Hampden-Turner's list of clients is a showcase of Fortune 500:

ABN AMRO, AstraZeneca, BT, Exxon Mobil, General Motors, Heineken, KPMG, and many more. Trompenaars's fans are found not only in the West: Singapore's senior minister Lee Kuan Yew—who shared a conference platform with him—is among them, as is Layla, a trainer and reviewer for Amazon.com from Dubai.[85] Nor is it just large multinationals that require the services of cultural consultancies. While these often employ such expertise in-house, medium and even small businesses increasingly feel compelled to rely on interculturalists if they want to succeed in a global market or just manage their own workforce. Every week, the German branch of SIETAR receives several requests for intercultural trainers from such companies. These trainings are mostly specific to a particular national culture, in the context of a relocation, merger, or negotiation process. They typically provide clients with a compass or kit, which, armed with Hofstedean or Trompenaarsian "dimensions," makes culture "tangible and measurable, not 'touchy, feely' or 'vague.'"[86]

A DaimlerChrysler manager preparing for a move from Germany to China had, for example, to undergo two trainings: one specific to his job—where, because his supervisor was going to be an Englishman, his German culture was juxtaposed to both Chinese and British cultures—and one for his family. The former, which used the popular Cultural Navigator, first determined the manager's personal "orientation" along a number of scales, such as "high-context" in communication, equality-oriented in power relations (that is, low power distance), cooperative rather than competitive, and so on. This was then compared, in a "gap analysis," to the attributes of Chinese and British (as well as German) culture, and recommendations offered about overcoming the possible problems arising from the "gaps" between these. The recommendations were rather general and often tautological. As the manager was determined to be oriented toward equality while Chinese culture valued hierarchy, he was told to "respect authority with deference based on position, social level and education" and "learn the markers of power, status and associated behaviours that operate in hierarchy-oriented environments."

Ethnic Marketing

The assumption that group culture defines behavior—in this case, that of consumers—is also the basis of another large area of corporate activity: ethnic marketing. "Ethnic marketing" is a term that covers both the targeted development and marketing of products to specific, predefined ethnic groups (such as the development of cosmetics lines and Barbie dolls for American blacks in the 1990s) and the identification and marketing of products associated with such groups to the general population (such as the explosion of kosher foods and restaurants and klezmer music records[87]). In addition, it refers to the hiring of employees belonging to particular ethnic groups for sales and marketing jobs targeting those groups, as well as to public-relations activities such as the sponsorship of ethnic events and organizations or preferential supplier arrangements. Avon's market share in America's inner cities improved after it hired more black and Latina managers.[88] DaimlerChrysler has a special scheme for Minority Retail Dealers (only open to general managers belonging to the respective minority). In 2006 it promoted the new Jeep Commander in a Missy Elliott clip for the African-American market and in "motivational speeches and performances" by American Indian rapper Litefoot to residents of more than two hundred Indian reservations. The company also sponsors dozens of minority organizations in the United States, from the Dearborn Arab Festival to the Jewish Federation of Metropolitan Detroit.[89]

Like IC, ethnic marketing is a widespread corporate trend. Bank of America and the U.S. Postal Service both have departments of ethnic marketing.[90] For smaller companies there are consultancies such as EMG, a "100% Hispanic owned and operated, full-service agency that specializes in building strong and profitable brands . . . that are culturally relevant to the Hispanic community."[91] Although there is an obvious overlap between the concerns of ethnic marketing and the more general subject of IC—the global expansion of production, workforce, and markets—the former refers mainly to diversity within a particular nation-state and has its origins in the specifically American politics of ethnicity. In its birthplace, the United States, ethnic marketing is primarily focused on the institutionalized categories of African, Asian, and Latino/Latina Americans, but is in constant search for more narrowly focused target populations. Thus Intercultural Niche Strategies, a company that develops ethnic marketing strategies for major record labels, found 350,000 Galicians in the United States as a target for a Chieftains album of music from Galicia.[92] Curiously, one of the effects of heightened attention to Muslims has been their "discovery" as a distinct market, notably of halal foods (foods that correspond to Muslim rules of purity) and loans that satisfy Islamic rules on interest, by multinational consumer goods companies and banks.[93]

In Germany ethnic marketing mainly targets ethnic Turks and Russian speakers. In France, which has never embraced multiculturalism and where the concept of ethnic marketing has generated unease because of how it divides the population into "racial" groups, half a dozen books on it have nonetheless been published, and it seems to thrive on the Internet. In Brazil, which has traditionally lacked clear-cut ethnoracial categories, the recent emergence of an *afrodescendente* movement modeled on black American politics of identity has created what the press kit of a black beauty pageant labeled a "new market niche of 36 million black and mulatto beauty product consumers" that "practically did not exist five years ago."[94] Indeed, the anthropologist Alexander Edmonds believes that the invention of racial segmentation in market research and the advent of ethnic marketing—"a new visualization of the consumer"—in the 2000s is playing a pivotal role in shaping new forms of racial identification that are potentially transforming social relations in Brazil.[95]

Like IC, ethnic marketing is built on the premise that ethnic groups share cultural preferences. In its original context these groups are drawn primarily from the ethnic labels institutionalized in the U.S. census, and the emergence of ethnic marketing in the 1990s is closely linked to the politics of minority representation that were at their height during that period. The employment of black managers might be good for business, but it also made the company look better in the eyes of a public that sympathized with affirmative action.

While greater attention to the skincare needs of a black woman or to the food preferences of a recent Armenian immigrant is a good thing, ethnic marketing also solidifies "lumpy" institutionalized categories of American identity politics (see chapter 4) by creating powerful images of what a successful Latina "homemaker" or Jewish family looks like.[96] Every race and ethnicity is supposed to possess its own distinct beauty. Making an individual choice to ignore such standards of racial aesthetics and lifestyle preferences—for example, opting out of the professional African-American woman look—can lead to accusations of make-believe and "passing" by other members of the "community."

On the outside, identification of large ethnoreligious groups with certain stereotypical lifestyle choices—such as "Jews eat kosher food" and "Muslims don't eat pork"—can result in distorted images that, as we have seen in chapter 4, have the potential of increasing segregation. As one commentator on Altmuslim. com wrote regarding the introduction of halal food in supermarkets: "The only plausible reason I could see halal going mainstream . . . is . . . if it had a neat twist on the 'organic' . . . I would rather it go mainstream than becoming a tool of self-ghettoization." Another poster suggested that halal should rather stand for "animal rights, environmental protectionism, human rights" than for Muslim religious ritual.[97]

At the very least, ethnic marketing ignores people's evolving choices and their desire to mix and match elements from various ethnic and lifestyle repertoires.[98] Hiring "ethnic" employees to deal with "ethnic" customers may increase profits in the short term, but the assumption that communication across ethnic barriers is somehow problematic, which such practice implies, presents a bleak view of the future and may ultimately be counterproductive. At McKinsey the idea of assigning Indian consultants to Indian customers is "old thinking" that inhibits creative solutions. The pitfall of imprisoning individuals in prefabricated lifestyle boxes can be avoided only by using a more ethnographic approach, which is discussed in the book's conclusion.

Diversity Management and the "Intercultural Opening" of Government

"No matter who you are, you're going to have to work with people who are different from you," says a top manager at IBM. "You're going to have to sell [to] people who are different from you, and buy from people who are different from you, and manage people who are different from you."[99] While corporations expect their employers to understand markets, consumer behavior, and workplace relations in Berlin as well as they do in Bahrain, they are also confronted with the cultural pluralization of their workforce and their shareholders. Like states that put a different spin on the culturalist discourse when designing their international engagements (see chapter 1) versus managing their own populations (chapter 4), many corporations have come to regard workforce diversity as key to creativity and competitiveness. Companies from General Motors to Philips celebrate "diversity" and have declared cultural diversification of their top managements a goal. Yet at the same time, in a study of unsuccessful mergers, two-thirds of the managers interviewed put failure down mainly to cultural differences in management style. Heterogeneity may be the new ideal, but only if it is properly managed. That is why DaimlerChrysler has Global Diversity Councils and IBM, a president of Global Workforce Diversity.

Apart from playing a role in recruitment and promotions, a central element of diversity management is sensitizing employees to difference, and particularly to prejudice against and stereotyping of minorities. Because the rise of "diversity management" was directly linked to affirmative action initiatives that had grown out of the civil rights movement in the United States (see chapter 4), the emphasis is not on national cultures but, more broadly, on ethnicity, "race," gender, and sexual orientation, in ways that export constructs specific to America's minority politics across the globe.

Thus Deutsche Bank has global employee support networks for women, gay, lesbian, bi-, and transsexual employees, as well as ethnic minorities. More recently, however, the emphasis in hip management journals and high-end knowledge-economy companies has shifted from respect for group sensitivities to creative and irreverent mixing: "The hybrid is hip. Mighty is the mongrel," writes Pascal Zachary in *Fast Company*. "Forget the original, the primordial, the one. . . . Mixing . . . spawns creativity, nourishes the human spirit, spurs economic growth, empowers nations. Racial, ethnic, and national categories no longer impose fixed barriers or unbending traditions."[100]

By 1999, 60 percent of consultants at McKinsey, including the chief partner, were from outside the United States. Each national office is annually evaluated by someone from somewhere else— Düsseldorf by San Francisco or Mexico City by Paris. Rather than celebrating coziness within an ethnic or national group, "there's an obligation to see things from other points of view," a McKinsey partner says.[101] A cause célèbre of corporate renewal through hybridization was Stefan Marzano's relaunch of Philips's design in the 1990s by turning a largely Dutch team into one of thirty-three nationalities.[102]

If raising productivity requires a diverse workforce, then you want to avoid hiring bigots, and if you already have, you want to change them. This is why part of the diversity exercise is testing employees and applicants for "intercultural sensitivity" or "intercultural competence." Most of these tests come up with a numerical score intended to measure an individual's ability to work with cultural difference. One of the well-known tests is the Intercultural Development Inventory, developed by Milton J. Bennett and Mitchell Hammer. In this model an individual is assessed on five different scales corresponding to particular cognitive mechanisms, and on each scale located at one of six stages of intercultural sensitivity, from "denial" to "integration" of cultural difference. Generally, these tests deal with individual attitudes rather than group cultures; as such, most have little use for Hofstedean "dimensions." Leading authorities on diversity management, such as Taylor Cox Jr., tend to focus on differences in perception, influenced by the relative status of two individuals as much as their "core values." Thus Cox discusses the differing evaluation of a promotion policy by black and white American employees in a company and interprets them primarily as a result of minority-majority power dynamics.[103] Although he includes a broader set of factors influencing behavior in organizations, Cox does rely both on "dimensions" (taken from Hofstede, Hall, Bond, and others) and on summary statements about "Asian" or "African-American" values (by authors such as Redding) when he discusses culture.

In the European context diversity management has taken a somewhat different spin, as it is related to the sudden diversification of the workforce due to migration and globalization rather than to the elimination of the historically subordinate position of long-standing minorities. Thus its role is primarily in ensuring equal access of individuals to jobs and leadership positions, rather than in the collective celebration of diversity. A similar logic is behind the transformation of a European public administration that still carries much of the legacy of the nineteenth century's homogenizing effort of nation-state building. In the United States citizens have generally less to do with the state, and local administration has traditionally been far more flexible and independent of the center. For a Spanish-speaking American, it would have been quite common until recently to come into contact with state officials only when getting a driving license, and this he could do in his native language. Recent initiatives to legislate about language at the state level are a backlash against precisely this tradition.

This transformation received its strongest impetus from the European Union's Racial Equality Directive and Employment Equality Directive, issued in 2000. The Racial Equality Directive, which "gives protection against discrimination in employment and training, education, social security, healthcare and access to goods and services," compelled a range of public institutions to scrutinize the way they deal with a greater share of migrants among their clientele—a process called "intercultural opening" in Germany.[104] In chapter 4 we saw the range of problematic encounters between the government bureaucracy and migrants' cultural practices: youth offices dealing with circumcision, courts ruling on arranged marriages, and police alerted in cases of disorderly conduct or child neglect. Already in 1997, the number of migrant children taken into foster care in Germany was double that of German citizens.[105]

Creating "intercultural competence" in these organizations is intended to prepare officials for such situations but also to encourage them to reach out to a more diverse constituency, as with German youth officials who are now supposed to visit with Turkish mothers at kindergartens rather than wait for them to show up in their offices. In addition to greater equity, "intercultural opening" is supposed to serve the new ideology of security: the new ideal is that of the community police officer who can walk into a gambling den in London's Chinatown or visit the home of illegal immigrants in Rotterdam and find out about brewing trouble without creating fear in his or her informants. "If you don't know who you're dealing with, you don't know what you're dealing with, you won't know how to deal with it" is the title of the Race and Diversity Strategy of London's Metropolitan Police for 2006 through 2009. Although ethnicity ("race") is—for political as well as historical reasons—the most substantial concern of the police, and "race relations training" is a compulsory element of the program, the strategy emphasizes that "diversity" refers not only to race but to a variety of other considerations, including disability and age. In this respect diversity trainings in public institutions tend to differ from IC. Since, in this scene, trainers come from a greater variety of backgrounds—IC, antiracism, social work—the content of the trainings is less standardized. In general, however, they place far less emphasis on "cracking cultural codes" and far more on making individuals aware of the diverse factors that influence the behavior and judgment of both their clients and themselves.

In Germany materials on "intercultural competence" in public organizations, commissioned by city governments, trade unions, and charities, often explicitly warn against taking a national view of culture and overemphasizing the role of cultural difference. Gari Pavkovic, the Integration Commissioner for the City of Stuttgart—where the automobile factories attracted a large migrant population beginning in the 1960s—has been influential in shaping a training approach that deals first with migrants' life stories, the social situation of the family, and the minority-majority power dynamic, and only then turns to culturally defined values.[106] Thus training guidelines developed for the Nuremberg branch of the Arbeiterwohlfart, a provider of social services, dismiss the usefulness of "intercultural trainings" developed for businesses in the field of social work as "very doubtful," since "the danger of creating new stereotypes and clichés is very high. Social work . . . on the contrary, is about dialogue and dismantling stereotypes. . . . Culture consists not only of elements such as nation and ethnic group, but also age, gender, education, religion, and economic circumstances."[107]

Trainers should create awareness of these diverse factors by asking such questions as "What does a peasant from the Bavarian mountains have in common with, say, a teenage hip-hopper from Berlin? 'German identity'? And what does she share with a Portuguese peasant?" Perhaps more than with the hip-hopper, the author suggests. In his view "intercultural competence in this context should be understood as the ability to perceive differences and accept them on an equal footing." The trainings therefore should consist of three modules: development of intercultural competence in this sense; transmission of knowledge about the specific background of migrant groups; and practice-oriented training that teaches the case worker to inquire into the individual and situational contexts of cases she encounters. The broad context of the "home culture" of a migrant should, the author advises, be taken into consideration only in the final step of the analysis.

This is also the approach taken by the authors of the manual "Fit and Competent for an Intercultural Future," one in many such initiatives by the German confederation of trade unions.[108] Warning against "statements such as 'because of their culture, all Chinese people have a collectivistic view of society' or 'Americans are individualistically oriented,'" their manual instead analyzes "critical incidents," specific conflict situations between particular individuals such as a Turkish woman passenger and a German bus driver or a Moroccan immigrant and his friend who is an immigration official. In one such critical incident, traffic police in Germany stop a car carrying a group of ethnic Turkish friends for a routine check. After the police ask for the driver's papers, all of the friends get out of the car and surround the police, explaining that everything is in order. One of the policemen feels threatened and orders the company back into the car, giving one of them a shove. The friends begin to shout that the police are manhandling them only because they are foreigners. The situation escalates, and the police radio for reinforcement.

The authors present the situation from the standpoint of both sides. For the police it is unusual and threatening that instead of the driver alone, the entire company gets out of the car and surrounds them at a close distance, talking loudly. The travelers react the way they do because—due to their personal experiences in Germany or stories told by others—they feel unfairly singled out as foreigners and because it feels natural to them to act collectively in situations of threat. Thus the authors suggest that this conflict arises due both to the specific dynamics of a minority-majority relationship and to a cultural difference between "individualistic" and "collectivistic" orientations to problem solving. They stress, nonetheless, that although "collectivistic" patterns are more typical of Muslim countries and "individualistic" ones more typical of Western Europe, they do not "rest on national boundaries but arise from the history of collective experiences." These patterns "are influenced by the politics, economy etc. of a country, but they can also differ considerably within a country, a village, a family and so on." Indeed, the title of the case study, "Real Friends Stick Together," is written in a Bavarian dialect, making the reader see the young Turks as Germans from a particular region, rather than as exotic foreigners. As a solution to the conflict, the authors recommend that the police allow the entire company to get out of the car, but request that only the driver speak and that the others stand somewhat to the side, explaining that threatening the police is "not acceptable anywhere."[109]

"Cultural Competence" in Public Health

Health is an important sphere of public services as well as of people's lives, and it is one that has in the West undergone a major shift with the "cultural turn." Along with education, the health differential between the white and black populations was an early concern in the United States.[110] In Europe attention to disparities in accessing public health services arose as a result of increased awareness of migration in the 1980s. But it was not until the late 1990s that the conceptual framework of "cultural competence" became part of the teaching and practice of medicine. This time the concern was not only about inequalities in health indicators and access to health care; it was also a reflection of a new perspective that entered medicine from anthropology and history and saw health and illness as conditions that were not biological universals but were differently defined and experienced by people in different places and at different times. Hysteria or "mad travellers disease" were the subject of many medical handbooks in the nineteenth century but have disappeared from the medical vocabulary since.[111] Depression, however, is a condition that entered clinical handbooks only in the twentieth century and is still mostly unknown as such outside the West. (After a Korean-American man killed more than thirty students at Virginia Tech in Blacksburg on 16 April 2007, some commentaries focused on the lack of cultural competence necessary to diagnose depression in East Asian patients.) To compound the complexity, it turns out that peoples from different ethnic backgrounds can have different biological reactions to antidepressants.[112]

These fundamental insights—also related to the growing popularity of non-Western medical treatments in the West—met with practical and high-profile concerns arising from the reality of more and more people from different cultural backgrounds sharing hospital wards and corridors, sometimes leading to conflicts. In 2003 loudly mourning relatives of a Gypsy woman who had died at a Hungarian hospital were beaten and arrested by police after they refused to obey hospital staff's orders to leave. The prime minister suggested that separate "mourning rooms" should be set up in hospitals to cope with such situations. In 2006 a French Muslim man attacked a gynecologist in a Paris hospital after he had examined his wife, despite their demand to be treated by a female doctor, prompting the prime minister to appoint a panel to examine religion in hospitals.[113]

All of these factors resulted in the emergence of a new paradigm in health care, which Harvard medical anthropologist Arthur Kleinman has summed up as the recognition that "culture influences the experience of symptoms, the idioms used to report them, decisions about treatment, doctor-patient interactions, the likelihood of outcomes such as suicide, and the practices of professionals."[114] This paradigm fitted in a broader trend toward "patient-centred care," which in turn, apart from recognizing the importance of patient satisfaction for health, was undoubtedly motivated by an increasingly litigious American medical environment. Many discussions in U.S. literature on cultural competency in health therefore revolve around the issue of informed consent to treatment, such as in situations where family members or the patient herself may not want to be told about all possible risks and prefer to leave responsibility for the choice of treatment with the doctor.

Although Kleinman is considered one of the intellectual fathers of medicine's cultural turn, much of the institutional change that has taken place can be linked to the publication of a singularly influential book: Anne Fadiman's *The Spirit Catches You and You Fall Down*. Published in 1997, it has accomplished a rare feat: the book has sold more copies on Amazon than the first Harry Potter book (not to mention Samuel Huntington). Its pirated copies are peddled on Cambodia's beach, but it has also been adopted as required reading at medical schools and been celebrated in mainstream medical journals. The book inspired the Association of American Medical Colleges (AAMC) to convene an "expert panel on cultural competence," charged with making recommendations on the medical school curriculum. The AAMC panel defined cultural competence as "a set of . . . behaviours, knowledge, attitudes, and policies . . . that enables effective work in cross-cultural situations."[115]

The Spirit Catches You tells the story of Lia Lee, born in Merced, California, in 1992, to a couple of Hmong refugees from Laos. At three months she had the first of a series of strong seizures. Because the Lees did not speak English, it was not until their third visit to the hospital—when the doctors themselves witnessed the fit—that she was diagnosed with epilepsy and prescribed a regime of medication (which, during the course of her treatment, was to change twenty-three times). Her seizures continued, and from blood tests the doctors found out that the parents had not administered the drugs properly. (They did not realize that the Lees could not read either the labels or the numbers on the thermometer or the clock.) After a protracted period of what the doctors called "non-compliance," the child protection office was called in, and for a year Lia was placed in foster care. When she was finally allowed back home, the Lees were instructed to follow a simplified drug regime, and they complied. At age four, however, Lia suffered a disastrous seizure, which left her brain-dead.

In Fadiman's view Lia's life "was ruined . . . by cross-cultural misunderstanding" between American doctors and Hmong parents.[116] What the doctors diagnosed as a neurological disorder caused by an electrochemical storm inside Lia's brain, stirred up by the misfiring of aberrant brain cells, the Lees believed to be *qaug dab peg* ("the spirit catches you and you fall down"). They thought that Lia's soul had been frightened when her sister slammed the door very loudly, fled her body, and been snatched by a spirit. Although they did not comply with the drug regime prescribed by the doctors, they—both unemployed—spent thousands of dollars on healing amulets, pig sacrifices, and on flying Lia to a famous *txiv neeb* (shaman) in Minnesota. They also felt that Lia's fits might be a mark of distinction, because, according to Fadiman, "Hmong epileptics often become shamans."[117] From the parents' perspective, child neglect, which the doctors charged them with when Lia was placed in foster care, was incomprehensible; on the contrary, they felt that the medicines, prescribed by doctors who understand nothing about the soul, made her condition worse.

As a way to minimize the possibility of such misunderstandings occurring, Fadiman recommended the integration of traditional medical knowledge into the treatment, so it complements rather than competes with biomedical knowledge. She advocated the utilization of assertive bicultural interpreters who are positioned as equals to the doctor and work within the belief system of the patient. Further, to make the treatment of Hmong patients more culturally competent, Fadiman suggested that families be involved in all medical decisions; that visitors gain twenty-four-hour access to patients; that shamanic rituals be allowed to be performed in hospitals; and that doctors avoid undercutting the traditional power roles of the father.[118]

The book's gripping narrative appealed to readers who empathized with both sets of well-intentioned people—doctors and parents—even as they witnessed the child being swept toward the inevitable, tragic conclusion. It became popular in medical schools because, coming at a time when the impersonal technicalism of medicine was being criticized, it uncovered structural deficiencies in health care, particularly the lack of interpreters and cultural mediators that could help bridge the gap between clashing understandings of health. Its publication marked the beginning of a trend that involves the publication of numerous manuals on "cross-cultural care" and trainings for doctors, nurses, and pharmacists. The *Diagnostic and Statistical Manual of Mental Disorders*, the most commonly used reference book of American psychiatrists, has included a glossary of culture-bound syndromes and idioms of distress since the mid-1990s.[119]

Since 1997 the California Department of Mental Health requires mental health care providers to report the ethnic composition and linguistic competence of health care personnel. The U.S. Liaison Committee on Medical Education implemented a standard for cultural competence in 2000, defining it as the requirement for "faculty and students [to] demonstrate an understanding of the manner in which people of diverse cultures and belief systems perceive health and illness and respond to various symptoms, diseases and treatments," as well as "to recognise . . . gender and cultural biases in health care delivery."[120] In 2004 a report on the death of an Afro-Caribbean schizophrenic during a "restraint procedure" in England made twenty-two recommendations to ensure that the treatment of all mental health patients meets statutory obligations. The first of these was mandatory cultural competence training for all managers and clinical staff.[121] In the same year the European Union launched the Migrant-Friendly Hospitals Project, aiming at improving interpreting services, providing better information to migrants, and—based on North American and Australian models—training staff in "cultural competence."[122]

Generally, "cultural competence" programs and manuals endeavor to accomplish three aims: (1) to provide information on particular "racial" or ethnic groups, their health status, and their traditions of medicine; (2) to provide practical information on matters ranging from diet to mourning customs; and (3) to increase the cultural sensitivity of practitioners. The specific orientation of the programs varies, as there are now numerous consultancies specializing in "cross-cultural health care." *The Multicultural Health Series*, a training program produced by the California Endowment, a private charity, together with health insurance provider Kaiser Permanente, is used in a number of university hospitals in the United States. It includes ten videotaped "critical incidents"— cases of miscommunication between patient and doctor—each featuring a patient from a particular ethnic or religious group, ranging from a Navajo elder to an Orthodox Jewish woman and an Armenian child. Participants are then asked to discuss the cases to uncover what went wrong and why. They are asked to pay attention to the speech patterns and nonverbal communication of both patient and doctor, and encouraged to interpret these in terms of differing "world views" (including those underlying Western biomedicine).

Participants are then provided with information on cultural practices and world views—for example, they are told that traditional Navajo speech patterns are slower, that the Navajo have sacred numbers and healing ceremonies, and that they are reluctant to talk about death—as well as on the health status of particular ethnoreligious groups (mortality due to tuberculosis among American Indians is 500 percent higher than the United States average). Finally, participants develop solutions for each case—such as rescheduling an operation to avoid an inauspicious number or offering a "Consent Not to Be Informed" form instead of a consent form (to accommodate the patient's reluctance to discuss the possible consequences of the operation).[123] While the starting point of each analysis is a specific set of circumstances, the explanation often rests on highly generalized statements about the ethnic or national group. In India, "[p]regnancy is expected early in the marriage, and if a woman is slow to conceive, she is viewed very negatively by the husband's family"; and "when a Navajo is sick, it is because he or she has offended one of the spirits." [124]

A large number of trainings focus on Muslim patients. The Australian organization Mission of Hope ("Muslim Community Solutions for Health and Well-Being") conducts workshops on "Raising Your IQ (Islamic Quotient)."[125] The brochure *The Muslim Patient: Intercultural Understanding and Questions of Medical Ethics* by Stecher Consulting, a Swiss hospital consultancy, calls the topic "a burning problem."[126] As part of the Migrant-Friendly Hospital project, the Emperor Francis Joseph Hospital in Vienna organizes special birth preparation courses for Turkish women.[127] The focus on Islam is not only due to the large numbers of migrants from majority-Muslim countries in Western Europe, but also to highly publicized conflicts related usually to male doctors treating female patients. The programs tend to focus primarily on religious prescriptions and proscriptions regulating fasting, food, medication, personal hygiene, and the contact between the sexes—all of which directly affect treatment and hospital routine—and underpin their explanations with quotes from the Koran.

Contrary to the recommendations of the French College of Gynaecologists and Obstetricians—which, in relation to the 2006 assault mentioned earlier in this chapter, affirmed that "male and female doctors would treat patients whatever their sex"[128]— a manual for intercultural care at German hospitals insists that "strict guidelines for opposite-sex contacts must be unfailingly observed," to the point of avoiding handshakes.[129] Manuals typically point out that doctors must warn patients if the medicines they prescribe may contain substances derived from pigs—such as gelatin—and often recommend the setting up of prayer rooms.

Discussions of matters such as how belief in the evil eye affects psychological treatment or how to handle the appearance of large crowds of visiting relatives also come up regularly, but often they are also linked to religious commandments.

How do we evaluate the rise of "cultural competence" in public health? There is little question that health care practitioners should understand what the patient is experiencing and ensure that she is clearly informed—at any rate, if she wishes to be. The training of interpreters with special skills and the recommendation, made by Fadiman and subsequently adopted by U.S. medical bodies, to use an interpreter who is of the same sex as the patient but not a family member, are likely to advance this goal. Furthermore, it is likely that if, as Fadiman and in her wake the AAMC recommend, the patient believes the illness is caused by supernatural influences, or wishes to pursue a traditional treatment, encouraging him to talk about these rather than attempting to suppress them (as long as they do not intervene with the biomedical treatment) will create trust and increase compliance. But involving the entire family in making decisions about treatment may or may not correspond to the patient's wishes. To take a different type of issue, there is nothing wrong with pharmaceutical companies developing drugs that are free of pork derivatives, but what if a Muslim patient wants to be provided with a much more expensive alternative at public expense? If Scientology is banned in Germany in large part because of claims, denied by the church, that it does not allow patients to seek medical treatment for certain illnesses, should then the choice of patients from ethnic minorities who refuse particular treatments on a religious basis be respected? Conversely, should the request of the adherent of a New Age movement to be given only organic food in a hospital receive less consideration than a Jewish patient's request for kosher food? Similarly to the cases discussed in chapter 4, the line is admittedly arbitrary, but it has to be drawn based on a careful analysis of the validity of cultural claims and without limiting individual choice.

The AAMC warns that "cultural competence is complicated: Health-care professionals must be educated to avoid stereotyping, but to also be aware of normative cultural values that can affect informed consent."[130] It describes cultural competence as a combination of attitudes (such as curiosity, empathy, and respect), knowledge (of "styles of communication, mistrust/prejudice, autonomy vs. family decisionmaking . . . traditions and customs," and so on), and skills.[131] Similarly, the American Medical Student Association notes that "services should be adapted to meet the needs of the group and the individual based on identity, degree of assimilation and subcultural grouping."[132] The usefulness of such an approach is obvious, but cross-cultural manuals and trainings developed for medical practitioners do not always help in developing it. Overwhelmingly they refer to (national or ethnic) cultural tradition, rather than its current context, and treat individuals as carriers of a stable set of beliefs derived from that tradition, regardless of the reality of their personal circumstances, which are obviously shaped by their divergent migratory experiences.

In *The Spirit Catches You and You Fall Down*, Foua and Nao Kao Lee become representatives of a group culture whose resistance to assimilation, to Fadiman, is "almost like a genetic trait, as inevitable in its reoccurrence as their straight hair or short, sturdy structure."[133] The implication is that any Hmong who shows up at a hospital will adhere to the same set of beliefs and will behave in a similar way. Yet it is doubtful that the majority of American Hmong cannot read a clock. A Hmong American critic of Fadiman, Mai Na M. Lee, writes that "Hmong people," far from seeing *qaug dab peg* as a possible honor that can indicate shamanic gifts, they "fear epilepsy the most." She accuses Fadiman, whose portrait of the Hmong in America is one of a culture deliberately isolating itself from the American mainstream, of romanticizing a "stereotype which comes to us from the dawn of Chinese history."[134] Vilma Santiago-Irizarry has made similar charges about three programs targeting "Latino" mental health care patients in the United States.[135] The same can be said about much of the *Multicultural Health Series*. In the context of India's population the claim that "pregnancy is expected early in the marriage" may be overwhelmingly true because educated urban residents whose views may no longer correspond to the tradition are a small minority. But in the United States it cannot be assumed that the visitor to the doctor's office is the wife of a Tamil farmworker from the San Fernando Valley rather than of a software engineer in Silicon Valley, and the two would likely hold very different views about family planning.

The anthropologist S. Agnes Lee and the public health official Michelle Farrell have found that most cross-cultural health manuals are "primarily lists of characteristics for particular races and ethnic groups."[136] This "trait list approach," as Arthur Kleinman has called it, typically relies on research done in the country of origin, often a long time ago.[137] For example, the section on Filipino Americans in *Transcultural Health Care* (1998) is based on studies of the Philippines, rather than of Filipino Americans.[138] But traditions even in the country of origin have often undergone dramatic change that manuals fail to reflect. For example, Cambodian women—similarly to Hmong—are often described as preferring to give birth at home.[139] But a growing network of nonprofit clinics in Cambodia is rapidly changing the situation.[140]

Many manuals relish the description of traditional medical practices and present the migrant's encounter with Western biomedicine as a culture shock. But in fact, in both China and South Africa, antibiotics nowadays are used alongside with, and often preferred to, traditional remedies, so that Australian physicians used to treating recent Chinese migrants are more concerned about their tendency toward the haphazard use of strong antibiotics than with their preference for teas and ointments. In the case of "Islamic health" the religious focus obscures not only individual differences and the role of migration, but also the ethnic diversity of Muslims and indeed much of social reality. It is naive to expect that quotes from the Koran—themselves, of course, interpreted in numerous ways by different strands of Islam, as the highly divergent attitudes to artificial insemination in Islamic countries demonstrate[141]—are equally sufficient to explain the behavior of a Indonesian *haji* and a secular Bosnian or Moroccan in a Swedish hospital.

The focus on culture can also mislead doctors into looking for a cultural rationale where there is none. Kleinman has described the case of a HIV positive Mexican-American man who failed to take his son, also infected, to the clinic for regular treatment. The personnel at the clinic, culturally sensitized, assumed that this was because he had "a radically different cultural understanding" of the illness. As it turned out, however, his understanding of AIDS was no different from that of other patients, only he had to work late shifts as a bus driver.[142] "Probably the most essential clinical check," Kleinman concludes, "is not to do harm by stereotyping patients."[143]

That a misplaced respect for real or perceived cultural tradition can harm the people it is intended to benefit is the argument of Peter Sutton, one of the best-known anthropologists of Aborigine life in Australia. The health gap between the Aboriginal population and the rest of Australia is one of the most dramatic in any society: the life expectancy of Aborigines is about twenty years less than the national figure. Guilt for the forcible assimilation and "civilizing" policies practiced until late into the twentieth century has cast a long shadow over the political treatment of Aboriginal culture and history and resulted in a proliferation of symbolic acts of recognition, such as acknowledging the traditional owners of the land through flags and ceremonies. But, unlike with American blacks, the new politics has not led to a narrowing of the socioeconomic gap. On the contrary, life expectancy in some Aboriginal communities has in fact decreased. Sutton charges that the concern with giving Aborigines a political "voice" has obscured "very basic things such as domestic sanitation and personal hygiene, housing density . . . alcohol and drug use . . . [and] the social acceptability of violence. . . . There is no empirical evidence for irredentist politics [that is, efforts to reverse the inequality of the Aboriginal population's rights] as a cure for extreme rates of renal failure, ischaemic heart disease, and domestic homicide."[144]

In Sutton's view *both* the consequences of colonialism *and* the "continuation of past practices" such as the cohabitation of large groups "under changed and now often inappropriate conditions" (that is, in concentrated settlements of people who have in the past led a nomadic lifestyle) should be held responsible for the health gap, and guilt for the assimilationist policies of the past cannot mean a taboo on attempts to change hygiene practices. Sutton writes: "If people don't *assimilate* themselves to certain blanket-washing and other relevant practices then their children are more likely to get scabies and hence more likely to suffer kidney disease. . . . Unless there is cultural adaptation to the biological features of fixed housing and repeatedly used and shared bedding, the perpetuation of cultural practices and beliefs appropriate to the old semi-nomadic camping style, but now mixed up with fabrics and buildings, will continue to [do] great harm to people's kidneys."[145] Sutton argues against "encouraging the perpetuation of traditional aetiologies of disease" through the employment of Aboriginal traditional healers in hospitals, a practice now introduced in some rural institutions as an effort to accommodate traditional beliefs. If people are encouraged to maintain their belief that "most serious illnesses and most deaths are due to the ill-will and sorcery of other people," he points out, then they are unlikely to comply with doctors' recommendations. This goes against the very logic of setting up a public health care system in the first place.

Sutton's charges point to the limits of accommodating cultural difference in public health. There will be little dispute over hospitals finding creative ways to accommodate the large number of people visiting Turkish patients. Accommodating the persistent Chinese and Vietnamese tradition not to take a shower or bath in the immediate postnatal period, even if it means a nurse having to clean the pubic area before the doctor's examination, can help avoid severe distress that sometimes results in sickness and fainting. In some instances conjoint treatment, which integrates Western medicine with traditional healing, can be advisable. But patients do not always want to be treated differently. Thus an ethnographic study of Vietnamese and Lebanese dialysis patients in Western Sydney showed that in the course of this treatment— perhaps because there are no particular Vietnamese or Lebanese beliefs or practices associated with it—the patients downplayed the cultural requirements associated with them (such as halal) because they "didn't want hospital staff to impose ethnic labels on them . . . for fear of discrimination. Instead they wanted to be recognised as 'Australians' and therefore be entitled to the same rights as other citizens." The South Western Sydney Area Health Services Plan states that it is "mandatory for a multicultural institutional environment to be created which assumes cultural diversity," but some patients "commented that the hospital staff did not need to know about their culture as they were *patients* now."[146]

Moreover, where an understanding and flexible approach can make a major difference for the better, a fossilization of traditions may do the opposite. When a German volunteer doctor who tells a patient at an Aboriginal clinic in Alice Springs to wash her hands regularly after using the toilet is rebuked by her supervisor for interfering with the Aboriginal way of life, we have to question the notion of "cultural sensitivity" that includes personal hygiene in the definition of Aboriginal culture.[147] It seems unlikely that pressure by the state-supported health system to change this practice has harmful effects on other, broader aspects of Aboriginal culture, while its continuation is almost certainly harming people's health. In Ecuador attempts by indigenous activists to set up a public health program staffed by traditional healers, midwives, and bonesetters have been rebuffed by villagers who felt that "activists were out of touch with local health needs and were all too willing to dismiss the political-economic realities of sick bodies in the name of *interculturalidad*."[148]

Cultural Competence in the Balance

In health, as in business and public administration, the focus on "cultural competence" has had some positive effects, both at the level of fostering a more open, creative mind-set and of providing practical information. It is useful to know that one should not wash a car in the street in Germany,[149] pick one's neighbor's flowers in America,[150] or stress one's skills too confidently when applying for jobs in China.[151] For a recently hired Chinese or American flight attendant at Lufthansa, the intercultural competency test's question about what films are inappropriate to be shown to children provides useful learning: they invariable choose those that show sex, while the correct answer, in Germany, is those that contain violence. When a U.S. Army captain in Iraq complains, "I've never been given classes on how to sit down with a sheik," or an infantry commander—after having stormed

a village—ruefully observes, "What I lacked was cultural awareness," they have a point.[152]

The problems arise when this practical advice is linked to a
fiction of unchanging national or ethnic cultural values, either by
decontextualized and often spurious surveys or by simple article
of faith. The authors of *Encountering the Chinese* go on to say:
"You must not openly admire the appearance of a member of the
opposite sex . . . such a compliment could easily be interpreted
as a sexual overture."[153] In fact, whether such compliments are
appropriate or not depends on the situation, but they are certainly
more common than, for example, in the United States. In some
cases they *are* sexual overtures (and in many cases it is deemed
normal that sexual overtures are part of the business conditions).
In other cases they may be intended as flattery. Thus advice must
be context-specific. The Chinese candidate who applied for a job at
an Australian university and introduced himself with the sentence
"I am a hard worker and a fast learner" had learned that he had to
market himself aggressively in the individualistic West, yet he did
himself a disservice. Had he been given the wrong advice? No—
it had just failed to specify that different work subcultures can
diverge quite strongly, even within a single institution, let alone a
society.

Intercultural communication rests on the premise that cultures
can be learned. They cannot—or not at the national level most intercultural manuals operate at. Organizational cultures are much more
legitimate objects of comparison, because they serve as actual
frameworks of day-to-day encounters, sufficiently removed from
the putative immutabilities of the nation for researchers to acknowledge their changing nature. For the same reason the "critical
incident" approach can be useful if it resists the temptation of
unnecessary gesturing toward national culture. In good manuals
critical incidents reveal individuals not as culture zombies but as
actors who deploy cultural difference (or similarity) strategically
to achieve their aims. As the trainers Petra Haumersen and Frank
Liebe have pointed out in a book on intercultural mediation—yet
another booming subfield of IC—members of structurally weaker
groups tend to emphasize group identity and disadvantage to

strengthen their position in an argument ("that's what you would say as a white man, isn't it!"), while members of stronger groups emphasize the individual aspects of the case and tend to downplay structural power inequalities ("this has nothing to do with being white, let's talk about the damage your dog caused").[154] Yet even where the intention is to sensitize people to dealing with cultural difference (and its conscious manipulation), trainers fall back on the schematic world of "cultural dimensions" all too often.

Arthur Kleinman contrasts the "trait list approach" with the "explanatory models approach" he advocates. The trait list approach asks health practitioners to take into account the view of "the Hmong." Kleinman's ethnographic approach asks them to take into account the view of the patient (admittedly, this gets more difficult when the patient is a child: this is a problem we dealt with in chapter 4). To that end, Kleinman proposes a set of questions doctors should ask their patients:

- What do you call this problem?
- What do you believe is the cause of this problem?
- What course do you expect it to take? How serious is it?
- What do you think this problem does inside your body?
- How does it affect your body and mind?
- What do you most fear about this condition?

Suppose little Lia Lee's doctors had asked these questions. They would have found that Lia's parents believed her soul had been stolen by a spirit and feared that it might not find its way back into her body without the help of a shamanic ceremony. Knowing this may have created a new relationship of trust between doctors and parents, which in turn could have led to greater "compliance" with medical treatment.

Like the best approaches to diversity training and management, Kleinman calls on those engaged in the encounters to listen and watch carefully, and use their observations to build an understanding of the cultural dimension of what is going on—rather than deducing their interpretation from the view of "a culture." In the conclusion we review successful examples of just such an approach.

Conclusion

The Ethnographic Approach

The introduction to this book discusses how a number of factors contributed to the emergence of a world in which "culture," and especially cultural difference, were accorded an unprecedented place in everyday life and official policies, advancing to a major explanatory paradigm for socioeconomic and political development and change. These factors include the American civil rights movement and the globalization of identity politics; the growth of nationalist movements after the end of the Cold War; increasing ethnic diversity of nation-states because of migration; and corporate globalization, the rise of "symbol analysts," and the "cultural turn" in science. We have explored the way this paradigm works in very different realms—from the international down to the interpersonal level. Even though each of these realms follows different internal logics and dynamics—for example, corporate mergers obviously operate with a terminology and set of values that is different from those of international aid or immigrant integration—the way they understand and use the concept of culture shares a number of flaws.

Misunderstanding Culture

First, *culture is too often described as constituting bounded, homogenous units.* This view is as fundamental for Geert Hofstede's concepts of intercultural communication or Lawrence Harrison's typology of "progress-prone" and "progress-resistant" cultures as it is for Samuel Huntington's vision of "clashing civilizations," Raphael Patai's and Bernard Lewis's portrayals of "the Arab world," or the stilted multicultural ideologies that Amartya Sen dubbed "plural monoculturalism." Despite their radically different political agendas, Robert Kaplan, with his view of the Balkans as a region of "ghosts" that arise from their graves to avenge the eternal ethnic enemy, and indigenous rights activists who see the "tribe" as existing separately from the outside world share this assumption.

Second, *culture is often depicted as unchanging.* Both Hofstede and Huntington see cultural change as superficial, not affecting the "core" of national cultures (or civilizational values). If it does affect that core, then this, according to Huntington, has dangerous consequences. For Hofstede and Fons Trompenaars, who work at the individual level, such cultural change creates people who are best avoided by the businessperson because they are unfit to represent their countrymen. The idea of an unchanging cultural essence is central to the discourse on "Asian values" and to Patai's and Lewis's views of Arab/Islamic culture, which rely on projecting ancient philosophical or religious texts onto today's social realities and postulating that they must have explanatory power. As we have already noted, the idea of historical continuity—"they have always hated each other, therefore they still hate each other"—plays an important part in popular explanations of ethnic conflict, not only by such observers as Kaplan, but also by those who work to arouse and legitimize ethnic hostilities in the first place. And the view of tribal cultures as unchanging and hence in danger of running out—as the spokesman of the Tulalip tribe put it, that "we could be out of ability to practice our culture within the next twenty-five years"—is so well-established that it is echoed in UNESCO's Convention on the Safeguarding of Intangible Cultural Heritage.

Third, once cultures have been portrayed as constituting distinct and fixed units, it is often asserted that some *cultures are incompatible with others.* Huntington's thesis of clashing civilizations is the best-known expression of this view, but the propensity to attribute conflicts to historic ethnic hatreds, or the assertion of

Necla Kelek and many others that Islam is "unintegrable" into Western society, spring from the same root. The threat of carelessly managed cultural encounters turning into cultural collisions is also important in legitimizing the intercultural communication industry.

But if cultures can be incompatible, then *mixing them up can be dangerous*—even if, at first, everything seems to be going well. This fourth argument, while more politically divisive and therefore less popular than the first three, still enjoys rather wide currency. It is most often heard from opponents of immigration such as Samuel Huntington, who sees mixing up people from different "civilizations" as a recipe for trouble. For Huntington states such as the former Yugoslavia that have the misfortune of sitting atop "civilizational fault lines" are "candidates for dismemberment." States that abandon "their" civilization and try to belong to another (Mexico, Russia, or Turkey), or where the mixing of ethnic groups belonging to different civilizations reaches a certain threshold (the United States), are "torn countries" of a different kind: they suffer from "cultural schizophrenia." Like American multiculturalists, political leaders outside the West who "infect" their countries with "the Western virus" therefore do so at their own peril. At the interpersonal level intercultural communication guru Trompenaars advises businesses against relying on cultural "hybrids." "Foreign cultures have an integrity," he has written, "which only some of its members will abandon. People who abandon their culture become weakened and corrupt. We need others to be themselves if partnership is to work."[1] Finally, the argument that mixing with the cultural mainstream endangers the cultural integrity of indigenous people is not uncommon among indigenous rights activists.

For those who accept these four premises, culture is a collective attribute that encages individuals and determines how they will behave. For Hofstede this is a good thing because it makes dealing with foreigners calculable; for Harrison, it is bad because it may mean that the culture of a society must be changed before development can be achieved. This argument—that, for example, a Mexican is compelled by his culture to react violently to certain kinds of provocations, or that a Muslim or a Japanese person has no choice but to defend the honor of the family in particular circumstances, even if it is against the law—is also at the root of many a cultural defense.

This image of culture tends to lead to one of two kinds of reaction: uncritical celebration of cultural difference or its pathologizing. But, as we have argued throughout this book, this image conflicts with reality. The boundaries of cultural units, whether in Africa or the former Yugoslavia, are often recent constructions. Internally, the membership of cultural groups is heterogeneous and there is hardly ever agreement about what constitutes tradition and what symbols mean. Indeed, who belongs to the group is itself often open to contestation. People act with the knowledge of cultural norms and scripts that come from a variety of sources: the village, the state, the ethnic or indigenous group, the world as transmitted through television. Which of these norms and scripts they follow depends on sets of circumstances—including the individual's own intentions and inclinations, the historical and political circumstances—that are unique in each case. As Thomas Eriksen has written: "'Kurdish culture' did not in any way determine the actions of Fadime [Sahindal's] father" when he shot her, but "his Kurdish universe offered cultural scripts, one of which consisted in killing a daughter to restore honour."[2] Cultural identification is situational, dynamic, and multivalent. Hofstede's onion metaphor is faulty: the onion, as Peer Gynt—the hero of Henrik Ibsen's eponymous drama—has pointed out, has "layer upon layer but no (single) core."[3] Cultures change and new ways of life can both conflict with old ones and support them, as casino revenues support Native American heritage conservation efforts.

As Unni Wikan has pointed out, it has by today become quite accepted for teenage girls to have boyfriends in some villages of Turkish Kurdistan, although not among Kurds in Norway.[4] While Saudi women on planes to Europe can be seen peeling off their *abaya*s to arrive in London clad in jeans and T-shirts, Turkish girls going back to Germany from a vacation in Istanbul get rid of miniskirts and put on conservative clothing in time to meet their parents at Stuttgart airport. The time-capsule treatment of culture in diaspora is intended to counterbalance the undesirable effects of mixing. But mixing, not isolation, is the norm: cultures are, and have always been, engaged in exchanges—both equal and unequal. Global ideas and goods are appropriated for local purposes. Cultural differences are neither to be celebrated nor to be pathologized: understanding them requires a careful, case-by-case approach.

That the effects of culture are so widely misunderstood is due to a range of reasons. A genuine desire by governments, corporations, or individuals to be open-minded and sensitive to the needs of others (or at least to present oneself as such) plays as large a role here as strategic misrepresentation by political and business elites. "Asian," "Western," and "Pacific values," Eurasianism, and "the Arab mind" have served as rallying cries for cultural conservatives, helped governments quash dissent and dispel challenges to foreign policy, and fueled the "war on terror." Cultural mobilization and mapping has been useful in governing colonies, fighting for resources in times of uncertainty and scarcity, and securing the power base of warlords. In its standardized format identity politics has aided the media visibility of politicians and the emancipation of subordinated groups that have been able to reap material and symbolic benefits from essentialized representations and the myth of indigeneity; but it has also helped neoliberal states to "govern through community," contradictory though this may be to their ideal of individual responsibility and action.[5]

Finally, the idea of cultures as "collective programming" that is "tangible and measurable, not 'touchy, feely'" has provided a range of professionals and academics with a decent livelihood.[6] And because most people in the West—including decision makers and editors—have little knowledge of or personal experience with Arabs, Hmongs, or Aleuts, they have not questioned the "evidence" at the basis of experts' claims: the one 1950s study that Patai used to underpin his claims about Arab attitudes toward masturbation or the study of IBM employees from the 1970s that provided the foundation for Hofstede's and his followers' claims about national cultures. Apart from all the specific methodological flaws of these

studies, they have a common problem: they are based on ideological constructs—as in the debate about the "real" nature of
Islam—and not on real people.

Of course, going around gatekeepers is not easy. As we have
seen in the earlier discussion of participatory approaches in development, even when explicit efforts are made to access local views,
power structures on the ground often prevent project leaders from
hearing the voices of anyone but community spokespeople. Institutional pressures tend to cement the "community fetish": though
the redistributive functions of institutionalized multiculturalism
may be disappearing, it has left behind an entrenched "culture of
cultures," from which organizations and leaders are perhaps even
less likely to stray now that they fear losing their share of a diminishing trickle of funding.

The price we pay for misunderstanding culture is more than
just wasted money. In the cases of conflicts that are judged to be
culturally coded and therefore politically irresoluble, it is human
lives. In the case of authoritarian regimes that enjoy Western
support in the name of cultural integrity, it is the demise of human
rights as a factor in foreign policy. In the case of some development projects, it is the loss of chances for those who do not
benefit from current power arrangements on the ground. In the
case of "heritage-format" multiculturalism, it is the abandonment
of struggling or dissenting members of a group "because it is their
culture." As Andrew Jakubowicz wrote in the mid-1980s: "A sufficiently moderate level of racist propaganda and racialist-tinged
social dialogue engenders not a resistance but an accommodation,
which sees the most important cleavages to be those of culture, of
belief, of colour. In the minority communities many of the rights
gained as a result of indigenous working-class struggle fragment
and dissolve in the name of 'cultural appropriateness.' The rights
of workers . . . are eroded and replaced by a 'cultural predilec-
tion for hard work.'"[7] Across the board, the most worrying consequence is less, rather than more, understanding and tolerance for
"other cultures." The misrepresentation of the cultural dynamics
of groups and societies ultimately risks destroying cultural diversity per se.

Although cultural pigeonholing does not correspond to historical reality, it may yet become a self-fulfilling prophesy. In some cases it seems to have done so already. If we are to believe a Brazilian marketing company, the "new market niche of 36 million black and mulatto beauty product consumers . . . did not exist five years ago," before the concept "afrodescendente" was imported from the United States.[8] "Plural monoculturalism" in British schools, Amartya Sen has charged, socializes children into seeing society as divided—and has perhaps contributed to rising militancy among young Muslims. Most tragically, if the International Crisis Group is right, the U.S. government's belief in Iraq's sectarian divisions being at the bottom of all conflict is in part to blame for the spiral of violence that now seems to be leading to a future of partition.

Should we not, then, reject the "cultural turn" as counterproductive and expel "culture" from the vocabulary of governments and corporations? To an extent, this is what anthropology did in the 1990s. Indeed, one of the programmatic writings of the decade was Lila Abu-Lughod's "Writing against Culture." In it, she argued—reflecting the profound influence of French philosopher Michel Foucault that marked anthropology during this period— that anthropologists must avoid generalizations not only because they are inaccurate, but because they, as is any expertise proffering itself as "objective," are an instrument of power that serves to place the observer in a privileged outside position of authority, masking her own inevitable bias. Because unmasking hidden hierarchies of power behind statements of authority was now a central concern of anthropology—as it has been in this book— anthropologists must not themselves fall into the trap of creating such hierarchies.[9] Although Clifford Geertz had "challenged . . . the idea that culture determined behaviour . . . [he had] nonetheless asserted its existence and relevance in the strongest terms."[10] But Abu-Lughod argued that the very concept of culture was irredeemably imbued with "coherence, timelessness, and discreteness" and was fundamentally a "tool for making 'other,'" and the job of anthropologists was now to unmask and deconstruct it.[11]

These ideas were central to the development of anthropology throughout the 1990s, especially in the United States. Distaste toward appearing as experts in any context—not just in corporate or military contexts—became part of the disciplinary socialization of anthropologists almost as much as the instinct to seek out and "deconstruct" the realities of power behind any authoritative pronouncements about people, cultures, medicine, or science. The word "culture" itself made roomfuls of anthropologists squirm in their seats—for good reason. As the world outside anthropology was undergoing a "cultural turn," anthropologists, not coincidentally, were otherwise engaged, leaving "experthood" to social psychologists, political scientists, lawyers, and philosophers. Quietly but definitively, they refocused a discipline not long ago preoccupied with enduring traditions of exotic tribes on the interaction between global forces and local ways of life. These ethnographies that recognized the transitory and contested nature of cultural logic in human interactions and did not presume to be final, nonetheless offered powerful interpretations of cultural practices that were, *at that moment*, characteristic of certain groups of people and not others. During a decade when most commentators saw globalization as an erasure of difference, these ethnographies—many of which have been cited throughout this book—provided early explanations for the highly specific, uneven, and divergent ways in which global processes affected populations and produced unexpected results.

Awareness of cultural differences is necessary for any attempt to understand the workings of a globalized world; it is the exclusive focus on a single unit of analysis—the nation, or religious or ethnic group—that is wrong. No doubt, national laws, schools, and media shape people's cultural norms; but they are not nearly sufficient to understand a person's behavior in a particular situation. It is necessary, as Ulf Hannerz has advocated, to bring people back in.[12] The same plea is made by Amartya Sen in his recent book *Identity and Violence*. Sen asks his reader to finally stop debating the "real" nature of Islam: the world's 1.2 billion Muslims, he writes, have other things to worry about than being Muslim. They belong to different nations, are heads of families, teenagers, poor and rich, abstinent and alcoholics. Whoever views Muslims as a coherent group mistakes an ideological construct for reality.[13]

In the preceding chapters, we have contrasted the dominant view of culture as a "box" with approaches that "bring people back in." In chapters 1 and 4 we suggested that an approach to area studies that takes into account external influences—as Mahmood Mamdani and Olivier Roy did in analyzing the roots of Islamic militancy in Pakistan and Europe respectively—is more fruitful than one that treats cultural "areas" as self-contained entities. In chapter 3 we cited work by Tone Bringa and the International Crisis Group on the political and social dynamics that led to the mobilization of ethnicity and religion in the Bosnian and Iraqi civil wars. Elsewhere, we mentioned Amartya Sen's and Arjun Appadurai's individual-centered approaches to development; Unni Wikan and Andrew Shryock's detailed studies of the everyday realities of multiculturalism; Sita Reddy and Alison Fish's equally detailed examination of how people get involved and implicated in codifying cultural heritage; and German approaches to urban planning that start with examining the daily experiences of individuals in a housing complex.

In chapter 6 we wrote about the tendency to recognize that attitudes to work, illness, housing, business, and warfare have a strong cultural aspect, and we cited studies of Chinese businesses by Susan Greenhalgh and Yao Souchou, as well as some "intercultural opening" manuals and Arthur Kleinman's questions for health professionals, as positive examples. In this final chapter we come back to the ethnographic method in more detail and suggest that it can offer a way out of the culture trap.

Ethnography in Product Development: An Alternative Approach to Culture

In recent years ethnographic approaches—that is, approaches that build their understanding of culture from the close observation of individuals in groups—have been adopted in some development, health, and even foreign-policy contexts. But the only arena where they have become widely accepted, indeed fashionable, is corporate product development—from jeans to houses to computer software. Perhaps because this work is politically uncontroversial and there is little at stake apart from corporate profit, there are not as many gatekeepers and spokespeople with their own agendas standing in the way of researchers wanting to "hang out" and observe. Indeed, the company Trendwatching.com markets its list of photo, video, and map feeds, allowing users to "peek into" the lives of consumers, as "virtual anthropology." The company's Web site reads: "Be on the ground in the new super states of China, India, Russia, and Brazil, connect to the vibrant emerging economies of Turkey, South Africa, and the Gulf states, immerse yourself in the established yet bustling centers of art, retail, fashion, and finance like New York, Tokyo, and London: it's all at your fingertips if you further develop your VIRTUAL ANTHROPOLOGY web."[14] The introduction to a study of young adult news consumption conducted by the Associated Press in 2007 enthuses: "An analyst on the planning staff suggested doing an 'ethnography' . . . and after a quick Google search to understand exactly what that meant, we decided to give it a try. To be frank, our expectations were modest. . . . In the end, it was as transformative as it was fun."[15]

That consumer-goods companies should be interested in cultural difference is easy to understand. As products invented for a Western market go global, how do you adapt and sell them to people who spend most of their income on rice, milk powder, and dried fish, buy soap by the slice, and find cosmetics indecent? As corporations expanded their markets, they found that the 1980s ideology of "one product for the whole world"—advocated by such marketing authorities as Harvard's Theodore Levitt—rarely worked.[16] Despite what the common-sense logic of globalization dictated, they were faced with the task of adapting their products to local needs. And even products that actually *were* global adopted different marketing strategies—like the Michelin tire man performing the "*wai*" greeting in Thailand—to appear local.

To understand the needs and desires of consumers, companies have long used qualitative and quasi-ethnographic techniques such as household visits and diaries to complement questionnaire surveys and focus groups. With their global expansion, however, there has been a shift from social psychology to anthropology as the main disciplinary inspiration in corporate research. Ethnography is "in." Corporate anthropologists from Intel or Matsushita spend months with bakers in an Osaka hotel or with computer-using households in China to understand consumer needs.[17] Hip anthropological consultancies (some owned by marketing firms) compete with more conventional market research agencies in providing product development advice. As a result, corporate ideas about culture tend to be more experiential and contextual than in many other areas we have reviewed.

Xerox began hiring anthropologists to work in consumer research back in the 1970s, but it was not until the mid-1990s that the trend spread to other large corporations, many flush with new-economy money. A 1996 article in the trendy business magazine *Fast Company* counted General Motors, Intel, McDonnell Douglas, and Nynex among the employers of anthropologists.[18] Today, these include Whirlpool, Nokia, Wal-Mart, Wells Fargo, JC Penny, Philips, Andersen Consulting, DaimlerChrysler, Ogilvy & Mather, Microsoft, and Yahoo. At Sapient, a technology consultancy in Cambridge, Massachusetts, a team of seventy anthropologists advise clients on how to design user-friendly products.[19] Intel, which set up several specialized ethnographic research teams, such as the Digital Home Group and the Digital Health Group in 2004, went on a hiring spree two years later, recruiting over a hundred more anthropologists and other social scientists.[20] A poll of twelve hundred "global executives" by the consultancy Bain & Co. in 2007 found that 35 percent of them used ethnographic methods.[21] Corporate ethnographers are fast acquiring a professional identity. Since 2005, they gather for annual conferences, called EPIC (Ethnographic Praxis in Industry Conference).

The adoption of ethnographic methods was triggered by a recognition that conventional surveys, focus groups, and user tests carried out in laboratory conditions often failed to reflect how consumers behaved and thought at home. A number of American women were invited to participate in a focus group discussion —the usual method to assess advertising—for an insecticide company. Even though the women had been recruited on the basis of having dealt with insect infestations, when the moderator began asking questions, none of them admitted ever having had rodents or cockroaches in their homes. It does not take an anthropologist to guess that the women were afraid that admitting to having pests at home would make them look unclean, yet these types of basic mistakes are not infrequent in marketing research.[22]

As Genevieve Bell, a senior anthropologist with Intel's People and Practices Research Group, has said: "When we first started to develop a sense of the consumer market we were using a set of traditional market research tools: calling people on the phone, using market research surveys, demographic profiling. All those things are good at telling *what people say they are doing*. They don't tell you *why* they are doing them; they don't tell you *how* they do them. Nor do they tell you what they *actually are doing*. . . . [Ethnography] gives us a powerful voice for thinking about our consumers, in their own voices, in their own language, from their own perspective."[23] Elsewhere Bell added: "Malaysians love cell phones with integrated Mecca compasses, produced by LG Electronics. . . . The latest products also ring at prayer times. Nobody with a standard questionnaire from the U.S. would have ever thought of coming up with such a product. Genevieve Bell asks the rhetorical question: Would you ever have thought of including in a questionnaire such questions as: Do you use your cell phone to find a religious location?"[24]

When Anne Kirah began working as a design anthropologist at Microsoft, she soon found that processes that had worked well with a thousand test users in the lab worked with none of the forty families she visited in their homes. Kirah videotaped a very angry customer who didn't manage to set up the system. The video helped convince Microsoft's management "that people who signed up for usability lab assessment were not average people, but rather techno hobbyists who knew something about usability."[25] After this, the focus of the company's product testing changed from abstract "users" to real people. This, Kirah explains, "means looking at people who are at a basic level focused on everyday aspirations and motivations. For instance, a new mother needing support in trying to figure out the best diaper to buy, or a lonely person looking for someone to love. We look at patterns across life stages, within life stages, across cultures and within cultures, and we make design recommendations based on the themes that emerge."[26]

When Microsoft's MSN Messenger was not succeeding in Japan, Kirah's team went over to find out what was happening. "It turned out that in Japan," she explained, "synchronic communication (interrupting people) is considered the rudest form of communication possible. So we made Messenger asynchronic, which means that you can send a message even if the other person is not online. However, doing this, we realized that this intervention, which originated from a culturally specific need, was also meaningful to the rest of the world. In the end we changed the platform globally."[27] Nokia's user researchers typically rent a house together in the place they are investigating and cycle around with an interpreter. Sometimes they live with locals. One study of mobile phone use took the researchers to both urban and rural areas of Indonesia and Uganda. In Uganda they discovered that phones were used for banking in an unexpected way: "Someone is in Kampala and wants to send money to a cousin living in the countryside. The cousin doesn't have a mobile phone, but a local village kiosk operator does. So the Kampala person buys a pre-paid card but instead of using it himself he calls the village kiosk operator and reads out the number so that he can top up his phone (he will then give the money to the cousin)."[28] This insight led to the establishment of a new financial services unit.

Ethnography led advertising agency Ogilvy & Mather to discover that young women in Tokyo discotheques refreshed their makeup on an hourly basis.[29] Ethnographers from Vigilante, a U.S. advertising agency, spent several days "hanging out" at laundries talking to customers.[30] Intel's anthropologists found that some Chinese families took their mobile phones to temples to be blessed or burned paper cell phones in funeral rites, and that European families and friends spent a lot of time in their kitchen, so home computers had to be small enough to fit there.[31] The adoption of ethnography in corporations meant recognizing that letting consumers tell manufacturers which categories they found meaningful was better for business than imposing laboratory-developed categories on users. An example from *Harvard Management Update*: "Toothpaste marketing used to be about fighting cavities and whitening teeth. But ethnographic research found that . . . people were really concerned with gums, their tongue, the whole mouth. Toothpastes such as Colgate Total, which purports to 'continue to work even after you stop brushing,' are designed to appeal to this broader concept of dental care."[32]

In some cases this approach has led to abandoning categories drawn from the "heritage approach" to indigenous cultures. In 2004, for example, Procter & Gamble hired two anthropologists to look into South African beliefs and treatments concerning household health care. The assignment was based on the assumption that South Africans held a set of traditional beliefs on illness that was distinct from Western biomedical logic and thus had to be tackled if P&G was to be successful in marketing its over-the-counter drugs. The researchers familiarized themselves with the large body of work on traditional African medicine, presented by the South African government as something like Chinese medicine—a complete healing tradition that presents an alternative to the Western medicine system. Most of this work described traditional African medicine as focused on supernatural agency, where healing is accomplished by removing impurity or disequilibrium from the patient's mind and body.

Subsequently, the anthropologists spent time (between three and six hours) with twelve black, colored, and Indian households in Johannesburg and Cape Town, learning about patterns of everyday life, looking into medicine chests, talking about illnesses and treatments, and witnessing medicinal preparations. They found that people accorded traditional medicine no privileged status. Some rejected it completely, but for most it was one treatment possibility among a whole range of available traditions—from Western scientific medicine to old Dutch and herbal remedies. All households had huge medicine chests at home, in which ginger, garlic, gum leaves, and aloe vera were placed next to Vicks VapoRub (a product now made by P&G but first introduced in South Africa in the 1930s), aspirin, and old Dutch cough medicine. When none of this worked, people said they sought the help of a state-funded clinic, a doctor, or a traditional healer.

The householders view of health care was pragmatic rather than ideological. One woman claimed that "for chest infections you must have antibiotics," but she also insisted that herbs to prevent diarrhea had to be picked before sundown. Dispirin, a soluble aspirin, was boiled with fresh ginger or ginger beer to make a fever-reducing hot drink. A popular headache powder was mixed with Valeine and applied directly to the body as a remedy for painful joints. Especially popular were medicines that not only worked but also left a "feel" of their effectiveness, such as "burning" and sweating, like VapoRub. Informants saw illness as something that could have spiritual origins, but could also be caused by climate, heredity, stress, diet, the environment, or other people. They also preferred to know what they took rather than rely on the opaque mixture of herbs prescribed by traditional healers. Whatever increased their personal autonomy and choice was deemed superior. In short, the research found traditional African medicine to be a political and scholarly abstraction rather than a description of actual life.[33]

Most ethnographic studies undertaken by corporations tend to last weeks rather than years, as do those by academic anthropologists. Some critics have charged that in many cases such techniques as online focus groups or in-store "intercept interviews" have simply been relabeled "ethnographic."[34] It is not surprising, then, that some studies lack sufficient context to interpret the findings. One large research project carried out by BBDO studied daily rituals across countries to detect regularities that could be of use to marketers and product developers. The researchers observed five thousand people over nine months and came up with findings such as "49% of Chinese eat on the way to work (against a global average of 17%)."[35] An online discussion of these data led some researchers to think that China was a good market for drive-through fast food. But for someone familiar with Chinese eating practices—notably the importance of meals as social events—it is clear that this is not the case. In other words, the statement "49%

Chinese eat on their way to work" is only useful once you know what and how they eat.[36]

Yet unlike in ethnic marketing, which is based on prefabricated categories of ethnicity, most corporate studies that call themselves "ethnographic" develop their ideas about culture from what they observe. In some instances the desires or behaviors they unearth are shared across national spaces—one imagines this would be the case, for example, with media consumption—but in other cases they are specific to particular local (sub)cultures. In yet other instances, new product ideas have nothing to do with cultural differences and categories at all. There is nothing especially "Ugandan" about mobile phone banking, nor is the frustration experienced when installing a computer software limited to a population group. Indeed, product innovations created on the basis of observing a particular group often turn out to be useful in others. This approach to culture—observing a practice, understanding its meaning for those engaging in it, relating it to larger social and cultural forces, and being as alert to common patterns as to difference—is, in fact, very close to the contemporary approach of academic anthropology. No longer attempting to describe *cultures*, realizing that culture is neither fully integrated nor necessarily territorial, that it is transitory and contested, they nonetheless insist on the importance of the *cultural* to the way particular groups of people, at particular times, manage their lives and respond to social, economic, and political challenges.[37]

The Ethnographic Method in Other Realms

The appeal of ethnography has begun to make its impact in the other areas we have discussed. William Callahan, a professor of political science, used fieldwork at three locations in Thailand to argue against the "bamboo network" view of overseas Chinese. He demonstrated that the international networks of local Sino-Thai merchants had very different orientations. While those in Bangkok were creating more and more contacts with China, those in Phuket mostly networked with Chinese in Malaysia and Singapore. Those in rural Mahasarakham Province were actually opposed to the opening of the national economy and, like Thai nationalists, saw "outsiders as immoral competition. . . . Rather than being evidence of an invisible empire of diasporic Chinese entrepreneurs who constitute the largest economy in the world, or of a neo-national economic culture, this group of businesspeople is simply trying to keep the caravan traders out."[38] While Callahan has called for the adoption of the ethnographic approach in international relations research, psychologist Per Gjerde recently advised his colleagues to move toward a "person-centred cultural psychology" by paying more attention to individual variation, power structures, conflicts within groups, and historical change.[39]

Ethnographic techniques are also gaining popularity with development agencies. Some of these are "one-minute ethnographies." Grameen Bank—whose founder Muhammad Yunus received the Nobel Peace Prize in 2006 for his efforts to fight poverty—has bankers from Washington, D.C, and Brussels interested in the work of microfinance institutions spend a day with a poor female borrower in rural Bangladesh to get a glimpse of the kind of lives the bank's clients lead and the choices and challenges they face. In a much more ambitious project, the United Kingdom's Department for International Development (DFID) funded a study on the benefits of emerging information and communication technologies (ICT) for poor societies. The researchers spent approximately one year living in the kind of households they studied. The findings challenged, among other things, plans by the Jamaican government to levy a special tax on telecommunication companies that would be spent to enable mass access to the Internet by equipping more schools with computers and enhancing virtual teaching resources. Daniel Miller and Heather Horst, authors of the Jamaica report, found, however, that because of security fears, computer access in schools was highly restricted and only available to high-achieving children, many of whom came from higher-income families and had access to the Internet at home anyhow. Furthermore, secondary school children in Jamaica were often poorly motivated and frequently dropped out of school.

Yet these same children discovered a new interest in schooling when they reached their late twenties and early thirties. Miller and Horst proposed therefore that the government channel more resources into adult education (evening schools and educational television). They also suggested that the cash-strapped government purchase lower-tech computers that lacked the capacities needed for the latest online games, and that it use high-quality existing Web sites and put money into "kitemarking" (that is, portals that identify useful and high-quality resources), instead of investing in new educational content. In addition, the authors commented critically on the emphasis on "community computing," a variation on the development sector's obsession with "the community" (see chapter 5). The Jamaican government had received large loans from the Inter-American Bank and the United Nations Development Program to set up "community computers," but Miller and Horst found that these—in post offices and libraries—had never become popular, in part because the government and organizations are generally distrusted and venues associated with them were unpopular, and in part because Jamaicans placed a premium on privacy. Even cybercafes enjoyed only limited success.

At the same time, the authors also suggested a number of ways in which support for mobile telephony—a technology the government had ignored—could further development goals. The researchers found that Jamaicans generally preferred oral communication, and cell phones were immensely popular (there were two million subscriptions for a population of 2.6 million). They recommended, for instance, that clinics use text messaging to remind women when to return to clinics for contraceptive injections or tablets; that the police be issued mobile phones to fight crime; and that the government offer support for providing limited Internet access through the phone. More broadly, Miller and Horst found that, contrary to conventional wisdom, ICTs do not necessarily have a positive impact on employment and income generation for the poor. In the poor households they studied, the cell phone proved vital in income distribution but not generation. On the one hand, more than half of household income was derived through social networks and personal contacts rather than through employment or work. On the other hand, phone use helped the long-term maintenance of large but shallow social networks that could be called upon in times of crisis. Cell phones also facilitated access to remittances from the Jamaican diaspora. The people who did use ICTs for entrepreneurial purposes (traders or drivers, for example) were those that already possessed regular employment.[40]

Another report that resulted from the DFID project, on Ghana, showed that Internet users in an Accra slum used the Internet exclusively to chat with foreigners whom they were unlikely ever to meet. The report profiled a fourteen-year-old girl, Asma: "She seems to believe that there is something intrinsically enriching about being in direct contact with foreigners and the Internet is the most direct access imaginable to innumerable legions of the foreign." But Asma has no awareness of the existence of "the Internet" in the sense of a World Wide Web or information source: "There was exceptionally low awareness of even the existence of websites."[41] Yet much government policy on ICT was based on information provision through Web sites, despite the fact that the majority of Ghanaian users never visited them. The government and NGOs focused either on simply the provision of infrastructure and hardware without attention to the institutional and practical contexts of use, or on the cultivation of computer literacy and software development that did not connect clearly to the way large numbers of current users understood these media. Accordingly, the authors of the report recommend that public information posters drawing attention to useful Web sites and how to access them be displayed in cafes, schools, churches, and clinics, and that "information intermediaries"—such as local teachers, religious figures, health workers, cafe owners—be involved.

The DFID reports are significant because they challenge some of the received wisdom of the development industry. They are able to do so because their access is not constrained by the straitjacket of specific projects; rather, they rely on "greenfield" research. In this respect they are similar to a recent report on Islamic community life in Berlin, prepared for the city's Senate Commissioner for Integration and Migration. Conducted against the background of public fear surrounding mosques and Koranic schools as obstacles to integration at best and security threats at worst, the report, based on participant observation, found that while most (though not all) Koranic schools had separate instruction for girls and boys, the justification for this was mostly pedagogical (to avoid distraction) rather than religious. They also found that approximately as many schools taught in German as in Turkish.[42]

Other examples of ethnographic research being successfully employed in the development sector are in public health. Australia's development aid organization, AusAID, and the World Bank commissioned anthropologist Alexander Edmonds to investigate why bad health indicators persist in the Solomon Islands while existing health care provisions are underutilized. Similarly to the Procter & Gamble study on South Africa, Edmonds found "medical pluralism"—that is, the coexistence of biomedicine and *kastom* (traditional medicine). As in South Africa, the

> first resort for treating minor illnesses (fever, diarrhoea, but also malaria) is generally kastom medicine prepared at home, or self-medication with Panadol or chloroquine using home supplies. . . .
>
> A *kastom illness* locates the cause in the social and spiritual sphere, for example . . . social disputes or sorcery. . . . It will generally require a kastom treatment. . . . A *medical illness* is understood to emanate from inside the body or be caused by a pathogen and can be cured by *either* kastom medicine or biomedicine. [43]

But "sorcery can be involved in illnesses that are recognized as having a biomedical explanation," such as malaria. Some *kastom* doctors "advise patients to use clinics to diagnose some illnesses (cancer, diabetes, TB, STIs) and then return to them for the appropriate treatment."[44] Barriers preventing patients from going to clinics are not cultural: rather, they include large distances, high transportation and treatment costs, stock-outs of medicine, rudeness from nurses, and long waits. Thus, against the conventional understanding that *kastom* is an obstacle to the effective delivery of biomedicine, Edmonds concluded that as "kastom is often a malleable concept, it might be possible to redefine it in some areas through open discussions of health risks."[45]

In an earlier report on the underutilization of health care facilities in East Timor (a fifth of poor households have never used the health care facility closest to their house), Edmonds had found that Timorese believe injections to be more powerful than orally administered medicine and that patent antibiotics (available at private clinics) are more powerful than cheaper (or free) generics available at the government facility, leading to resources being wasted on more expensive pharmaceuticals.[46] Foreign and Timorese medicine are seen as complementary, but hospitals are seen, especially by peasants, as places for dying, not for curing. There are fears that there will be no transportation back home, delaying quick burial that is important so that "crying" can be done and the spirit find rest. For these reasons, by the time the patient finally comes to the clinic, it is too late. Edmonds found: "Nurses complain of a vicious circle whereby users do not have confidence in biomedicine and delay seeking care, thereby prejudicing the success of treatment and confirming belief in inadequacy of biomedicine."[47]

A general feature of such studies is that "culture" as a national trait or that of an ethnic subgroup is rarely deemed relevant. Researchers inquire into the causes and meanings of behavior (in Edmonds's case, the avoidance of health care facilities that results in the inefficiency of foreign aid) and find that some of it has to do with traditional cultural norms and beliefs, some with beliefs that emerged very recently, and some with "hard" factors that are in no way cultural.

Now that as many anthropology PhDs end up in the corporate world and in government positions as in academia, applied anthropology is getting much more attention, but also critique. Anthropologists working for the military, such as Montgomery McFate, get most of the flak, but corporate anthropologists also have to defend themselves against accusations that they are helping companies to sell products to people who do not really need them, may not be able to afford them, and may even be harmed by them. "One-minute ethnographies" are also frequently subjected to scorn in academia, and the ability of ethnographers embedded in administrative command structures to influence decision making is far from clear. In a paper for the U.S. Army War College, Sheila Miyoshi Jager, a professor of Asian studies, pointed to the prevalence of a static view of culture in army reports and blamed it on an excessive focus on tactical operations at the tribal level. She wrote: "The innovative insights about cultural knowledge adapted in operations and tactics by our military leaders have so far not yielded *any* comparable innovations from our political leaders."[48] Despite these criticisms, we believe that the spread of ethnographic (or even paraethnographic) methods represents a step forward from the current enchantment with culture as a container.

The Culture Clinic

A central argument of this book is that it is more helpful to see the dominant understandings of our world as a result of a number of specific intellectual and political trends that have led to today's culturalism. Nonetheless, today, the container view of culture is what anthropologists call a "social fact." Claims attributing a particular failed development project, an unsuccessful merger, or a murder to "culture" may be erroneous, but government officials, corporate executives, and judges will have to deal with them and determine their basis. Too often, this is done with the help of weekend trainings or manuals that attempt to outline the cultural tradition of a national group. What is needed instead for culturally informed, context-sensitive, and productive outcomes is an awareness of and sensitivity to cultural differences and local contexts, values, and practices as well as a critical ability to question the implicit and explicit assumptions behind cultural claims and the power dynamics that they may be concealing.

Wherever possible, the merits of cultural claims should be examined in their context, not in the courthouse or the boardroom. This means going to a development project site in Africa, a military base in Afghanistan, a school in Berlin, or a factory in China with someone trained in ethnographic methods. Here are two examples of this "culture clinic" approach. For two years Jasmin Mahadevan conducted an ethnographic study of the department of objectmaking improvement (OI) of a German high-tech company operating in Germany and India. The aim of the research was to identify cultural barriers to the cooperation of the 450 engineers working at different locations within the OI department. Mahadevan found that most engineers saw the tensions between the German and Indian organizations as having nothing to do with culture. The new Indian branch was taking jobs and competencies away from the German headquarters. With the opening of the Indian branch, the German department had stopped hiring new employees and invested only in Bangalore. Many visible conflicts in the German headquarters occurred at the engineers/management interface. Thus there was a latent conflict between engineer culture and management culture.

But these conflicts were generally downplayed by both sides with reference to the long (more than a hundred years) shared history of the company, for whom many employees had worked for a long time. Instead, the company's human resources department interpreted the tensions as a cultural conflict and offered intercultural trainings. Although these were rejected by engineers in both Bangalore and the German headquarters as irrelevant (which HR evaluated as a sign of lacking "social competence" on their part), some engineers nevertheless started using the terminology of intercultural conflict. It was those individuals who feared being made redundant once the Indian branch was fully operational who were most active in "othering" their Indian counterparts by referring to the presumably "completely different system of time" that would make joint project planning impossible. Those who did not stand to lose much through the transfer of competence, however, recognized their Indian counterparts mainly as "engineers like us" and attributed problems to physical distance as well as to the newness of the Indian employees. Mahadevan concluded that contrary to HR's evaluation, the main fault lines lay not between Indian and German engineers—they were (potentially) united by "engineering culture" ("good engineers" were for both groups people who are able to recognize faults in the technical system)—but between the "losers" created by the company's globalization and the other employees, as well as between those who were new to the organizational culture and had not adopted its rituals (such as reaf-firming to each other the shared company heritage) and the old employees.[49]

In another example where cultural difference turned out to be less important than assumed, Clemens Dannenbeck and Hans Lösch studied the lives of ethnically diverse youth in a low-income Munich neighborhood. They found that Turkish and German youth in a club targeting underprivileged families did not mainly perceive each other in terms of their ethnicity. More important were such personal attributes as likeability and capabilities. Ethnic Turks and Germans shared a lot of their everyday lives—in school, at work, and in the street. Lacking language skills was a problem, but on a number of occasions it was bridged by Germans learning Turkish. Monika, a young ethnic German girl, had an ethnic Turkish boyfriend. Although he was bilingual, they frequently "hung out" with his male friends, who spoke mainly Turkish. To know what was going on and to keep some control, Monika learned the language. Yet this was perceived as a problem by her school principal, who described Monika as a very nice and active girl whose only problem was that she "went out with Turks." As in this case, it was overwhelmingly adults (politicians, parents, teachers, and social workers) who tended to see young people pri-marily through the lens of their ethnicity.

One day a conflict during a party ended in a knifing. Initially, various interpretations of the conflict were given. The teachers who had arranged the party mainly blamed organizational shortcom-ings (such as overcrowding and having no weapons search at the entrance). Some youths saw the conflict as a result of sexual provo-cation. But after some time an ethnic explanation emerged as the "official" one: the conflict was framed as one between a Kurd (the young man who produced the knife) and a Turk (the victim). According to this interpretation, the conflict was bound to occur, simply because Kurdish and Turkish youths were let into the party. Eventually, the young people themselves adopted this interpre-tation. The Turkish-Kurdish fault line, which according to the researchers had not previously been important for most of the youths, was then turned into a social fact to be taken into account in all further events organized by the youth center.[50]

It is impossible to devote two years to studying each cultural claim. Sometimes the resources are not available even for two weeks. What to do in such cases? To enable professionals to critically interrogate projects and policies, a tripartite checklist of questions, not unlike those Arthur Kleinman has recommended putting to patients, might help:

- What explicit and implicit statements about culture are involved, about which groups?
- What are the fault lines along which groups are defined and differentiated?
- Are you overlooking important differences within (or across) these groups?

Dominant categorizations of people into nations and religious or ethnic groups are of only limited value for explaining, let alone predicting human behavior. There are just too many internal differences and cross-group links, and for most people group membership is just one of many determinants of identity. So statements about the culture of one of these big groups in a newspaper article or at an intercultural workshop should set off alarm bells. If, for instance, a journalist tries to convince you that the two hundred lashes of the whip to which a twenty-year-old rape victim was sentenced in Saudi Arabia in 2007 has to do with "Muslim culture," ask yourself how likely it is that men and women, grandparents and teenagers, workers, lawyers, writers, residents of Mecca, Tangiers, Cologne, and Detroit all share the same values and will behave alike in similar situations.

Or, if you are a judge in a European country, and a Nigerian woman accused of causing her two sons bodily harm by making incisions on their faces argues before your tribunal that she did so to ensure that they be considered fully grown men in Nigerian society when they reach adulthood, find out how widespread such scarification is in today's Nigeria, whether it is limited to some remote regions or is also common in Lagos and Abuja and whether it is practiced by all social classes. You might find out that the scars are not an integral and necessary part of contemporary Nigerian culture but a niche phenomenon. As the children are respectively nine and fourteen years old, you can ask them where they see most of their lives in the future. If they have spent most of their childhood in Europe and do not plan to return to a Nigerian village, it would appear reasonable to prevent the mother from further scarification, as it can be argued that facial scars might make life in Europe more difficult. In a real case a British judge sentenced a mother for such scarification but imposed no punishment on the grounds that she had been unaware of breaking the law.

- Who is making the statements about culture? Why might they be making them?
- On whose behalf are they speaking—explicitly or implicitly? What lends them authority to do so?
- Why are they able to voice their opinion? Whose voices are not heard?

Most of the time cultural characteristics become the center of discussion, it is claims by spokespeople of particular "communities" or "experts" we rely on. Question their authority! Are they self-appointed, democratically elected by a majority of those they speak for, or do they have some other source of real legitimacy? Can they credibly represent nondominant members of the group—for example, women, children, homosexuals, or the disabled? If your Chinese business partner uses "Chinese culture" to explain working conditions in his factory, ask yourself why he does so and how he knows. If the village head in Africa tells you the well you came to build must, according to tradition, be in front of his compound, talk informally to other villagers and find out if this belief is shared.

Had American occupation authorities in Iraq subjected the claims of Shiite parties to power to this type of questioning, they would have found that these parties and their representatives owed their positions not to tradition but to the destruction of civil society under Saddam. Perhaps the American authorities might have hesitated to deepen the divisions of Iraqi society by endorsing their power claims. Had the judge who ruled in the case of Fumiko Kimura, the woman who drowned her children in the Pacific Ocean, found out that mother-child suicide was no longer widely accepted or legal in Japan, he may not have let her walk free. Had UNESCO's experts who recognized the Patum festival in Spain as World Cultural Heritage made more effort to find out the background of the organization they were dealing with and realized that it had not in fact been central to the festival before, they may have thought twice before giving them the authority to control it. And had Jürgen Schrempp known that the popular perception of Hinduism and Shinto as the bases of Indian and Japanese national cultures, respectively, were largely twentieth-century creations, he may not have used them as the basis of his decision not to send a Japanese manager to India.

· Are the statements that are being made about culture empowering or oppressing the groups and individuals involved (which ones)?
· How free are members of the group to change or decline norms?
· Do they open up or shut down options of dissent (or exit) within the group?

If we recognize in principle the existence of a wide range of different cultural values and practices as a positive factor that contributes to human development and makes the world more enjoyable, then we must refrain from rejecting the unfamiliar without due consideration. An arranged marriage may not be an option for you, but it would be wrong to denounce all arranged marriages as forced and forbid your neighbors from practicing them. The test is not whether we find a practice acceptable for ourselves, but whether those who follow it do so freely. If they do, you may still, in some situations, decide not to support it if it is incompatible with your goals. For example, if it turns out that the village head is right, you must build your well in front of his house, and subordinate groups have internalized their lack of say in the matter, but you represent an organization that insists on participatory development and democratic decision making, then it may be perfectly justified to go around existing power structures and empower other groups. If you do so, however, you must be aware of the potential consequences the shift in power relations may have.

This book has made clear the preferences that have guided us in deciding which claims—by cultural relativists (speaking on behalf of cultural rights and specificity) and cultural universalists (speaking on behalf of universal rights and individual freedoms)— we consider acceptable. With Amartya Sen and Seyla Benhabib, we take "human development" to be the expansion of choices of the kind of life people want to live. We acknowledge that these choices do not arise from nowhere; rather, they are culturally influenced and therefore informed by belonging to a group or groups. The distinction between free choice and coercion is never absolute. Having said this, however, we believe that the freedom of individual choice should always enjoy priority over group cohesiveness. Cultural diversity is valuable not per se but as a vehicle to enable as many human beings as possible to live their lives in a way they find good and right.

Notes

Preface and Acknowledgments

1. Hannerz 2004, 232.
2. Besteman and Gusterson 2008, 63.
3. The blog is available at http://culturematters.wordpress.com.

Introduction

1. Ilves, quoted in Bissell 2007.
2. Pobłocki 2002, 163.
3. Fisher 1998, 37.
4. Johnson 2000, 158.
5. Anderson 1983.
6. Schein 2005.
7. Kemper 2001.
8. Hammonds 2000.
9. Lee 2004. *The International Journal of Cultural Policy*, in which this article appeared, has been published since 2002, another sign of increased interest in cultural policy as an element of governing.
10. The policy address is available at http://unpan1.un.org/intradoc/groups/public/documents/APCITY/UNPAN007457.pdf (accessed 1 November 2006).
11. Bourdieu 1986.
12. Friedman 2004.
13. "U.S. Study Abroad Increases by 9.6%, Continues Record Growth," Institute of International Education. Available at http://opendoors.iienetwork.org/?p=69735 (accessed 1 November 2006).

14. Hugo 2005.
15. See the Web site of the Yew Chung school at http://www.ycef-sv.com (accessed 30 October 2006). Unfortunately, this link is no longer available.
16. Reich 1992.
17. Stearns 2003.
18. For the obesity gene, see the "Obesity Gene Map Database" at http://obesitygene.pbrc.edu/ (accessed 27 October 2006). For the human cooperation gene, see Ridley 1997.
19. This Maurer comment is on the dust jacket of Besteman and Gusterson 2005.
20. Sahlins 1993, 19.
21. Yanow 2002.
22. Morris-Suzuki 1999.
23. Kharmawphlang et al. 2004.
24. Benhabib 2002, 3.
25. Schönhuth 2005, 45. Antweiler 2003, 41.
26. Eriksen 2006a, 41.

1. Clashing Civilizations

1. Bush, quoted in BBC News 2005a.
2. Currie 2005.
3. Arrighi 1994.
4. Kennedy 1993, 16.
5. Huntington 1991.
6. Huntington 1993, 23.
7. Möser 1986, 123.
8. Fichte 1808, "Speech 13," 408.
9. Williams 1983, 89.
10. See Lawson 2006, 131–36, for

an overview of national character
studies.
11. Morris-Suzuki 1995.
12. Smith 1991, 76, cited in
Lawson 2006, 113.
13. Pobłocki 2002.
14. Huntington 1996, 156.
15. Huntington 1993, 22.
16. Ibid., 31 and 34–35.
17. Huntington 1996, 183.
18. Huntington 1993, 42.
19. Huntington 1996, 154.
20. Huntington 1993, 35.
21. Huntington 1996, 225, 234.
22. We thank our master's students
Anupom Roy and Atsushi Murata
for providing this information on
Bangladesh and Japan.
23. Yuen 2003.
24. Xian Yu n.d.
25. Debreczeni József, Élet és Iro-
dalom (Budapest), 4 May 2004, 7.
26. Guo 2004, 61.
27. For example, Fang, Wang, and
Song 1999. See Garver 2001.
28. Sheng and He 2006.
29. Ibid.
30. Zhenduo 2007.
31. Zakaria 1994, 111.
32. Ong 2005, 24, 16.
33. Hofstede and Bond 1988.
34. Weber 1951.
35. For examples of such literature, see chapter 6. The anthropologist Souchou Yao (2002, 6) credits
Herman Kahn's World Economic
Development: 1979 and Beyond
(Boulder, Colo.: Westview Press,
1979) with having started the trend.
36. Zakaria 1994.
37. Sen 1997.
38. Drake 2003, 39.
39. Weisman 2006.
40. Sztankay 2007.
41. Xinhua News Agency 2006.
42. Shishin interview in Barnaul,
28 September 2004, in Breidenbach
and Nyíri 2008, 135.
43. Popkov 2005.
44. Oldfield 2001, 104.
45. Ibid., 105.

46. Moiseev 1999, paraphrased in
Oldfield 2001, 105.
47. Lomanov 2005, 74–76.
48. Berman 2001.
49. Titarenko 1996, quoted in
Lomanov 2005, 75–76.
50. Lawson 1996.
51. "It's as if the [Indian] civilization was always born to be a front-
running civilization," the brand
manager commented (Giridharadas
2007). The Giertych report is in
Giertych n.d.
52. Available online at http://www.
insaf.pk/Forum/tabid/53/forumid/1/
tpage/1/view/topic/postid/44984/
Default.aspx#44984 (accessed 31
December 2008).
53. Available online at http://www.
unaoc.org/aoc.php?page=2 (accessed
6 June 2008).The Alliance of Civilizations had its first, highly publicized
meeting in 2008.
54. Jung as cited in Broder 2006.
55. See the International Progress
Organization online at http://www.
i-p-o.org/civilizational_dialogue-
roster.htm (accessed 5 March 2007).
56. K. Brown 2005.
57. Huntington 1993, 24. The
anthropologist Dru Gladney (1998,
116) has drawn a parallel between
Huntington's definitions of a civilization and Stalin's definition of a people.
58. Huntington 1996, 41.
59. Huntington 1993, 34.
60. Huntington 1996, 154.
61. Anderson 1983, 14.
62. Hobsbawm and Ranger 1983.
63. Morris-Suzuki 1995; Yoshino
1999.
64. Jensen 1997.
65. The Analects, Book 11, translated by D. C. Lau (London: Penguin,
1979), 109.
66. Bell 2006.
67. Sen 2006b.
68. Ong 1999, 55.
69. Huntington 1996, 307.
70. Giertych n.d.
71. Jakubowicz 1984, 37.
72. Casanova 2006.

73. Gledhill 2007. Selected results of the survey have been published in Esposito and Mogahed 2008.

74. Verhofstadt 2006.

75. College van Burgemeester & Wethouders 2006.

76. Lawson 2006, 152.

77. Chua 1995, 27.

78. Yao 2002, 9.

79. Huntington 1991, 108.

80. *Straits Times*, 14 December 1993, 29, cited in Yao 2002, 11.

82. *Straits Times*, 13 September 2003, H10, cited in Yao 2002.

82. Lackner 2007, 499.

83. Cheng 1995, quoted in Song and Sigley 2000, 55.

84. Guo 2004, 62.

85. Ibid., 63, 64.

86. "Jilie jingzheng beijing xia fangdichanye ruhe kaifahao wenhua zhi hun" (In fierce competition, how should real estate business develop the spirit of culture?), 29 October 2006, available online at http://www.zhihui114.com/news-1.asp?id=4303 (accessed 18 March 2007).

87. Kim 2004.

88. Chan and Zhu 2003.

89. Fu and Choy 2004.

90. Yang 1994.

91. Costello, Smith, Brecher 2007.

92. "Wal-Mart China Corporate Social Responsibility" is available online at http://www.wal-martchina.com/english/community/community.htm (accessed 3 September 2007).

93. Trompenaars 2002, 7.

94. Huntington 1993, 45.

95. Ibid., 31, 35.

96. See http://www.jihadwatch.org.

97. Lewis 1990, 60.

98. Whitaker 2004. Patai's *The Arab Mind* (1973) was updated in 1983 and republished in 2002 and 2007.

99. Patai, quoted in Hersh 2004.

100. Patai 2002, 144.

101. Patai 2002, cited in Whitaker 2004.

102. The article from *Die Weltwoche* is cited in Widmer 2004.

103. Anderson and Stansfield 2004, 77.

104. Inhorn 2003.

105. Patai 2002, cited in Whitaker 2004.

106. Gledhill 2007.

107. See the "Pew Global Attitudes Project 2005," available online at http://pewglobal.org/reports/display.php?PageID=801 (accessed 11 May 2007).

108. Wynn 2007, 147ff.

109. Lewis 1990. Bernard Lewis has reaffirmed his view of the clash of civilizations as the key to international relations policy in many publications since. See, for example, Lewis 2003.

110. Lewis 2002a, 159.

111. *Newsweek* interview, cited Hirsh 2004.

112. Preface in Lewis 2002a.

113. Lewis 2003.

114. Ibid.

115. Ibid.

116. Lewis 2002a, 7.

117. Bulliet, cited in Hirsh 2004.

118. Alam 2003.

119. Hirsh 2004.

120. Said 1979, 317–18.

121. Gerecht 2006.

122. Andoni 2002.

123. "Vice President's Remarks at the World Affairs Council of Philadelphia Luncheon Honoring Professor Bernard Lewis," 1 May 2006. Available online at http://www.whitehouse.gov/news/releases/2006/05/20060501-3.html (accessed 13 May 2007).

124. Wolfowitz, speaking via video phone at a special ceremony held in Tel Aviv to honor Lewis in March 2002, cited in Andoni 2002.

125. Cited in Robin 2004.

126. Cited in Hirsh 2004.

127. Lewis 2002b.

128. Hersh 2004.

129. Lagouranis and Mikaelian 2007, 17.

130. Tony Lagouranis commenting on "Some General Thoughts about

Anthropology, Interrogation, and Torture," *Savage Minds*, 13 September 2007. Available online at http://savageminds.org/2007/09/09/some-general-thoughts-about-anthropology-interrogation-and-torture/ (accessed 12 October 2007).

131. McCoy 2006, cited in González 2007, 17.

132. De Atkine 2002.

133. Ibid.

134. Ibid.

135. Ibid.

136. Whitaker 2004.

137. De Atkine 2002.

138. Ibid.

139. Fukuyama 2004.

140. Rosen 2007.

141. Luxenberg 2004. Noted in Kristof 2004.

142. Abu-Lughod 2002, 784.

143. Prewitt, as quoted in Guyer 2004, 500.

144. Appadurai 2001, 7.

145. Mamdani 2002; Coll 2005, 180.

146. Rashid 1999.

147. Quoted in Coll 2005, 182.

148. Ibid., 104.

149. Mamdani 2002, 770.

150. Hannerz 2004, 231.

151. Letter to President Clinton, 26 January 1998. Available online at http://www.newamericancentury.org/iraqclintonletter.htm (accessed 22 March 2007).

152. Rice, cited in Nordlinger 2002, 36.

153. Fukuyama 2002, 4.

154. Barber 2001.

155. Lawson 1996, 171.

156. Keesing 2000, 234.

157. Ibid.

158. Guillermoprieto 2006.

159. Perdue 2005, 100–2.

160. Triandis 1990.

161. Lawson 2006, 162.

162. "Rede von Bundesaußenminister Steinmeier anlässlich der Eröffnung der Frankfurter Buchmesse" (Speech of Foreign Minister Steinmeier at the opening of the Frankfurt Book Fair), 3 October 2006. Available online at http://www.auswaertiges-amt.de/diplo/de/Infoservice/Presse/Reden/2006/061003-Buchmesse.html (accessed 13 May 2007).

163. Ibid.

164. "Umfrage: Franzosen und Deutsche klar gegen EU-Beitritt der Türkei" (Survey: French and Germans clearly oppose Turkey's EU accession), *Spiegel Online*, 13 December 2004. Available online at http://service.spiegel.de/digas/servlet/find/ON=SPOX-332559 (accessed 13 May 2007). Unfortunately, this article is no longer available.

165. Casanova 2006.

2. Culture

1. Mallaby 2004, 56.

2. Ibid.

3. Fox 2005, 307.

4. Quoted in Mallaby 2004, 57.

5. Mallaby 2004, 57.

6. Litzinger 2003, 3.

7. Ibid., 28.

8. Shi 2008; Paul Cohen, personal communication, 16 January 2008.

9. Oakes 1998.

10. Chen 2006.

11. Wei 2003.

12. Bettina Gransow, e-mail to Pál Nyíri, 29 April 2007.

13. Leslie 2006, 113–27, 192–214.

14. J. Taylor 2007, 4.

15. Truman, quoted in Esteva 1996, 6.

16. We thank one of our anonymous reviewers for pointing this out.

17. Cited in Watts 1999.

18. Easterly 2006a.

19. Escobar 1995.

20. Cited in Ferguson 1990, 25.

21. Ibid., 69.

22. Ibid., 169–227.

23. Harragin 2004.

24. Watts 2001, 285.

25. GTZ and Goethe-Institut 2006, 8.

26. The *Culture Matters* blog is

online at http://www.culturematters.
ch/en/Home (accessed 29 March
2007). Swiss Agency for Development 2003, 4.

27. Rao and Walton 2004, 359.

28. Apthorpe 2005, 131.

29. Jared Diamond, *Guns, Germs,
and Steel* (New York: W. W. Norton,
1997).

30. Gallup and Sachs 1998.
Shweder 2003, 354–56.

31. Pomeranz 2000.

32. Needham, cited in Cowling
1993.

33. Ibid.

34. David Landes, *The Wealth
and Poverty of Nations* (New York:
W. W. Norton, 1998). World Bank
2000, 30.

35. Huntington 2000, xiii.

36. Easterly 2006b.

37. Harrison 2000, xxii and xxxii.

38. Ibid. See, for example, the
contributions by Chua Beng Huat
on Singapore, Robert P. Weller on
Taiwan, and Nicolai N. Petro on
Russia in Harrison and Berger 2006.

39. Harrison 2006.

40. Weller 2006, 121.

41. Harrison 2006.

42. Etounga-Manguelle 2000.

43. Chitsike 2000.

44. Sen 2004.

45. Abraham and Platteau 2004,
220–22.

46. Apthorpe 2005, 132.

47. Eco 2001.

48. See the Happy Planet Index
at http://www.happyplanetindex.org
(7 April 2008).

49. Cameron, as mentioned in
"Happiness (and How to Measure
It)—Affluence," *The Economist*, 19
December 2006. Available online at
http://www.glaserfoundation.org/
program_areas/pdf/Happiness_and_
how_to_measure_it.pdf (accessed 5
January 2009).

50. Shweder 2004.

51. Eco 2001.

52. The anthropologist Raymond
Apthorpe (2005) has pointed out

that this hands-on attitude to cultural
factors is not altogether new. It was
present, though not articulated as
such, in development projects from
the 1950s through the 1970s.

53. Appadurai 2004, 60.

54. Price 2004, 68–69.

55. Ribot 1998.

56. Mompati and Prinsen 2000,
626.

57. Ibid., 627–31.

58. Popkins 2004, 83, 85, 94–95.

59. Apthorpe 2005, 137.

60. Mosse 2004.

61. Leslie 2006, 143.

62. Quoted in Litzinger 2003, 12.

63. Ibid., 22.

64. Ibid., 23.

65. Ibid.

66. Ibid., 24.

67. Ibid., 29. The irony is that the
project did not eventually go ahead,
not because the recommendations
were inconclusive but because the
Asian Development Bank did not see
sufficient guarantees that the loan
would be paid back.

68. Appadurai's approach and the
term "capacity to aspire" is inspired
by Amartya Sen, himself a contri-
butor to *Culture and Public Action*.
Sen's approach, first developed in
*Poverty and Famines: An Essay on
Entitlement and Deprivation*
(Oxford: Oxford University Press,
1982), argues that development
should be measured against the
concrete capabilities people have.
Thus it is not enough for people to
have the right to vote; they also need,
for example, to be educated enough
to make a choice and they need transportation to the polls. This view is
developed into a theory of human
rights in Martha Nussbaum's *Sex
and Social Justice* (Oxford: Oxford
University Press, 1999).

69. Appadurai 2004, 70–80.

70. "Can the subaltern speak?" is
Gayatri Chakravorty Spivak's famous
phrase (from her "Can the subaltern
speak?" in Cary Nelson and

Lawrence Grossberg, eds., *Marxism and the Interpretation of Culture* [Urbana: University of Illinois Press, 1988, 271–313]).

71. Abraham and Platteau 2004.
72. Ibid, 220–21.
73. Horst and Miller 2006, 173.
74. Ibid.
75. Nyíri 2006.
76. Mosse 2004.
77. Ibid., 16
78. Tan 2007.
79. Ibid.
80. Ibid.
81. Ibid.
82. Rao and Walton 2004, 361.

3. Culturalizing Violence

1. Stallworthy 2006.
2. The AAA established a committee in response to concerns about CIA advertising to members and other post-9/11 security-driven efforts and programs. See Albro 2007.
3. McNamara 1995, 322.
4. One of these analysts, Peter L. Galbraith (2006), who served as the first U.S. ambassador to Croatia, has argued that the United States should not repeat the same mistake as it did with Yugoslavia, where it initially clung to the idea of a unitary state despite the reality of an ethnic split. Kurth 2006.
5. Beinart 2006.
6. Tavernise 2005.
7. "Why They Should Stay," *The Economist*, 15 September 2007, 13.
8. Huntington 1993, 35.
9. Gurr 2000.
10. Huntington 2004.
11. Anderson 1998, 65.
12. Bissell 2006. Kaplan 1997, 132.
13. Beinart 2006.
14. Quoted from the *Washington Post* on the *Foreign Affairs* Web site, available at http://www.foreignaffairs. org (accessed 29 November 2006).
15. Kuperman 2000, 95.

16. "Rwanda President's Plane 'Shot Down,'" BBC World Service, 6 April 1994. Available online at http://news.bbc.co.uk/onthisday/ hi/dates/stories/april/6/newsid_ 2472000/2472195.stm (accessed 4 December 2006).
17. "Hutu, Tutsi Bitter Enemies: Background," *Globe and Mail* (Toronto), 8 April 1994.
18. "Jeder gegen Jeden" (All against all), *Die Zeit*, 15 April 1994, 11.
19. The French official is quoted in Bayart 2005, 21.
20. Anderson 1998; Bowen 1996.
21. On the Catholic church, see Chrétien 2003. On the "hardening of identities," see Amselle 1996.
22. Gahama 1983, quoted in Malkki 1995, 53–55.
23. Ibid.
24. Bowen 1996, 6.
25. Gourevitch 1999, 88.
26. Ibid., 3.
27. Bayart 2005, 29–30.
28. Bowen 1996, 3.
29. Gourevitch 1999, 93.
30. Ibid., 86.
31. Hintjens 1999.
32. Kuperman 2000.
33. Bayart 2005, 23.
34. On the HIV infection rates, see ibid.
35. Gourevitch 1999, 92.
36. Andre and Platteau 1998.
37. Straus 2006, 226. We thank Katrien Gedopt for this reference.
38. Eriksen 2006a, 107.
39. Appadurai 1996, 127. See, for example, Cohn 1987, Guha 1983, and Chakrabarty 1988.
40. Pels and Salemink 2000, 26.
41. Appadurai 1996, 130–31.
42. Sundhaussen 2007, 303.
43. Mamdani 1998.
44. "The Invention of Tradition" is borrowed from the title of Eric Hobsbawm and Terence Ranger's 1983 work.
45. Bayart 2005, 25–30.
46. Ibid., 38.

47. Mansfield 1993, cited in
Benhabib 2002, 93–94.
48. Pels and Salemink 2000, 28.
49. The "invention" of Hinduism
has a large literature. Pennington
2005 and Lorenzen 1999 are recent
examples.
50. Pels and Salemink 2000, 28.
51. For examples from the Pacific,
see Keesing 2000.
52. Gallagher 1997, 51.
53. L. Cohen 1993, 208.
54. Hayden 1996, 790.
55. Ćosić, quoted in L. Cohen
1993, 282.
56. Hayden 1996, 789.
57. M. Thompson 1992, 91. The
number of mixed marriages is difficult to estimate. Hayden (1996, 789)
writes about 15.9 percent "mixed"
children, whereas according to
Gallagher (1997, 69), 40 percent of
Sarajevo's and 8 percent of Bosnia-
Herzegovina's population lived in
mixed marriages.
58. Bringa 1995, 26.
59. Gallagher 1997, 58.
60. Bringa 1995, 33–35.
61. Ibid.
62. Gallagher 1997, 63, 69, citing
Vulliamy 1994, 49.
63. Gallagher 1997, 62.
64. Bringa 1995, 29.
65. Ibid., 17–18.
66. Ibid., 67–75.
67. Ibid., 83.
68. Geschiere 1997.
69. Kaplan 1993, xxvii.
70. Bringa 2005. Kaplan's influence
on Clinton is confirmed by several
authors (e.g., Campbell 1999).
71. Christopher in an interview
on CBS, 28 March 1993, quoted in
LeBor 2006, 49.
72. Map in Huntington 1993, 30.
73. Glatzer 2003, 19. In the 1920s
the Soviet Union had similarly turned
the Tajiks from a Persian-speaking
urban elite into a territorial nation
when it created a separate Tajikistan
and Uzbekistan as part of its strategy
to suppress resistance by traditional
rulers.

74. Ibid., 22.
75. Schetter 2005, 70.
76. International Crisis Group
2006, i.
77. Ibid., 26.
78. Ibid., 8.
79. Ibid., 10.
80. Danner 2006, 94.
81. Quoted in International Crisis
Group 2006, 10–11.
82. International Crisis Group
2003, ii.
83. Ibid., 11–12.
84. Ibid., 21.
85. International Crisis Group
2006, 22.
86. Ibid., 13.
87. Caryl 2007. Riverbend's
comments are a fascinating parallel
to those made by an engineer in a
Shiite village in the late 1950s to
American author Elizabeth Warnock
Fernea (1969). The engineer found
self-mortification "primitive" and
blamed the British for having encouraged it to accentuate differences
between Shiites and Sunnis.
88. Gettleman 2007.
89. Galbraith 2006, 29.
90. Simons and Tucker 2004, 5.
91. Allard 2007.
92. Kipp et al. 2006, 9.
93. Rabie and El-Maghraby 2007.
94. Kipp et al. 2006, 14.
95. Packer 2006.
96. U.S. Army 2007, 3–8.
97. Kilcullen 2007.
98. McFate, as paraphrased in
Shweder 2007.
99. J. Thompson 2007.
100. González 2007, 18.
101. Holmes-Eber and Salmoni
2008. Paula Holmes-Eber, "New
Book: Operational Culture for the
Warfighter," e-mail to the Mil_Ant_
Net discussion group, 24 July 2008.
102. Available online at http://con-
cerned.anthropologists.googlepages.
com/ (accessed 9 October 2007).
103. Glenn 2007.
104. J. Thompson 2007 and
McFate 2005.

105. Jager 2007, 9.
106. Nader 2006 and Gusterson 2006, quoted in Albro 2007. This is true in the United States and to some extent in Britain and Australia.
107. Gusterson 2006.
108. Jager 2007, 26n12.
109. Shweder 2007.

4. The Challenge of Multiculturalism

1. Park 1950.
2. Meyer 1980.
3. Yanow 2002. See also Nobles 2002.
4. Jakubowicz 1984.
5. Department of Canadian Heritage 1988.
6. This "conception of the good" is in Rawls 1999. Kymlicka 1995a, 82–84.
7. Kymlicka 1995b, 163.
8. Stewart 1993, 41–43.
9. Singh 2004, 59.
10. Assmann 1992.
11. Jones and Ram 2007, 50.
12. Ibid., 54.
13. Lau, Pehk, and Stockey-Bridge 2007.
14. Rousseau 1953, 176.
15. On the London school, see Mannitz and Schiffauer 2004.
16. Isin 2002, 283.
17. Johnston, Poulsen, and Forrest 2005.
18. Jones and Ram 2007, 64.
19. Jakubowicz 1984, 33. A better-known Marxist critique of multiculturalism is by Slavoj Žižek (1997).
20. Rosenthal and Povoledo 2007.
21. Wise 2005.
22. Wikan 2002, 124ff.
23. See http://www.pisa.oecd.org (accessed 19 December 2007).
24. Fix 2005.
25. "White Flight Leaves System Segregated" 2008.
26. Policy Exchange 2007.
27. Sen 2006a.
28. Ibid.
29. Benhabib 2002, x.

30. Barry 2000.
31. Kymlicka 1995a, 153.
32. Jakubowicz 1984.
33. Wikan 2002, 103.
34. Winter 2006.
35. *Crikey* newsletter, 10 November 2005. *Crikey* is a popular independent Australian online news service, based in Melbourne, Victoria. See http://www.crikey.com.au.
36. BBC News 2006c.
37. Lau 2006.
38. *Crikey* newsletter, 10 November 2005.
39. BBC News 2007b.
40. BBC News 2006b.
41. Gaspard and Khosrokhavar 1995, 44–45. Translation in Benhabib 2002, 97.
42. Abu-Lughod 2002, 786. The anthropologist Lila Abu-Lughod has drawn on her own ethnographic work as well as that of Fadwa El Guindi.
43. Kavakçi 2004, 66–67.
44. Forster 1961, 180.
45. *Trujillo-Garcia v. Rowland*, California, 1992; cited in Renteln 2004, 34.
46. Kurkiala 2003.
47. Beikler 2007.
48. Mathé and Weber 2006.
49. BBC News 2007e.
50. Wikan 2002, 249n21.
51. Wikan 2002.
52. *Alhaji Mohamed v. Knott*, cited in Renteln 2004, 116–17.
53. The Convention on the Rights of the Child is available online at http://www.unicef.org/crc/.
54. Renteln 2004, 55.
55. Ibid., 59 and 245n56.
56. Mai 2006.
57. Renteln 2004, 25.
58. Ibid., 153.
59. Huntington 2004, 30–46.
60. Schirrmacher 2006, 45.
61. P. Cohen 2007.
62. Hitchens 2007.
63. Münchau 2006.
64. Malik, quoted in Kolbe 2006.
65. The account in this and the

following paragraphs is based on
Hansen and Hundevadt 2006,
Thumann 2006, Howden and
Hardaker 2006, and Van Doorn-
Harder 2006.
66. "Are Violent Protests Against
Anti-Prophet Cartoon Acceptable?"
7 February 2006. Available online
at http://www.islamonline.net/
servlet/Satellite?pagename=IslamO
nline-English-Ask_Scholar/FatwaE/
FatwaE&cid=1139318348431
(accessed 1 November 2007). We
thank Lisa Wynn for this reference.
67. "Gone to the Dogs," *The Economist*, 15 September 2007, 62.
68. Available online at http//news.
bbc.co.uk/1/shared/bsp/hi/pdfs/10_
12_07_worldservicepoll.pdf (accessed
12 January 2008).
69. BBC News 2006a and
VandeHei 2006.
70. Racial and Religious Hatred
Act 2006. Available online at http://
www.opsi.gov.uk/acts/acts2006/
20060001.htm (accessed 7 October
2007).
71. Sager 2000, 206.
72. Halter 2007, 201.
73. Shryock 2004.
74. Wikan 2002, 152–53.
75. Cowlishaw 2008.
76. *Kwai Fan Mak v. Blodgett*,
cited in Renteln 2004, 40–42.
77. Renteln 2004, 207.
78. Fickling 2004.
79. Zekri and Maier 2005.
80. Wikan 2002, 180–81.
81. Murphy, Robinson, and Koch
2008; Shah 2002; and Lloyd and
Rogers 1993, 161.
82. "Australian Law Should
Apply to All: Brough," Karvelas
2007, "The 7:30 Report," ABC TV,
23 May 2006 (transcript available
online at http://www.abc.net.au/7.30/
content/2006/s1645722.htm).
83. Kirk 2006.
84. Lloyd and Rogers 1993. The
authors note that the Aboriginal Legal
Aid Service, founded by the government in part to help the recognition

of Aboriginal traditions in courts,
has been criticized for "twisting"
traditional law in the interests of
male defendants.
85. Eriksen 2006b.
86. Guilliatt 2005.
87. Joppke 2004.
88. Auburn Council 2007, 60.
89. Goot and Watson 2005.
90. Auburn Council 2007, 16.
91. "Köhler mahnt Ausländer"
(Köhler warns foreigners), *Spiegel
Online*, 1 December 2004. Available
online at http://www.spiegel.de/
politik/deutschland/0,1518,330542,
00.html (accessed 15 January 2009).
92. "Prokop Defends Integration
Statement," Ö1 Inforadio, 19 May
2006. Available online at http://oe1.
orf.at/inforadio/64373.html?filter=1
(accessed 28 August 2007).
93. "Italy: Milan Police Clash
with Chinese," *New York Times*, 13
April 2007. Available online at http://
query.nytimes.com/gst/fullpage.htm
l?res=9C0DE4D9133FF930A25757
C0A9619C8B63&fta=y (accessed 15
January 2009).
94. *Migration und Bevölkerung*
2008a.
95. Stefanidis 2006.
96. College van Burgemeester &
Wethouders 2006.
97. Mönch 2006.
98. Buruma 2007.
99. Putnam 2007.
100. Singh 2004, 56.
101. Phillips 2005.
102. Cantle 2006.
103. BBC News 2007a.
104. BBC News 2005b.
105. *Migration und Bevölkerung*
2007a. After the introduction of
the language test, family-sponsored
migration to Germany dropped by
40 percent. In the first court test of
the new legislation, an Indian wife
of a German man sued the state after
being denied a visa on the basis of
lacking language skills—and lost.
106. *Migration und Bevölkerung*
2007c.

107. *Migration und Bevölkerung* 2008c.

108. Applebaum 2006.

109. U.S. English, Inc. 2007.

110. *Migration News* 2003.

111. Bartmann 2005.

112. *Migration und Bevölkerung* 2008b, 1.

113. Ibid.

114. Sen 2006a.

115. Ibid.

116. "Leave Culture Out or Bring It In?" is borrowed from the title of Eriksen 2006c.

117. Ibid.

118. Benhabib 2002, 98–99.

119. Kymlicka 1995b, 175.

120. Nungeßer 2007.

121. Ouazzif 2007, 31.

122. Ibid., 33.

123. Roy 2005, 6.

124. Habermas 1990.

125. Taylor 1994.

126. Kymlicka 1995a, 153.

127. Benhabib 2002, 11, italics added.

128. Wikan 2008, 183.

129. Sager 2000, 205.

130. Benhabib 2002, 8, italics in original.

131. Ibid. Namely, the public would have found out that the girls decided to defy the school order on their own initiative, after consulting with a Muslim-rights organization, rather than following the wishes of their parents.

132. Ibid., 117–18, italics in original.

133. Shell-Duncan and Hernlund 2000.

134. Obermeyer 1999.

135. Edmonds forthcoming.

136. *State v. Kargar*, cited in Renteln 2004, 59.

137. Legal anthropologist Alison Dundes Renteln (2004, 60) believes, for example, that "it is probably advisable to discourage touching [of the genitals] that is deemed inappropriate in the United States because children who are at least partly Americanized will feel humiliated if they are touched in this manner."

138. ABC News 2008.

139. Malloch Brown 2004, v.

140. Sen 2006a. Benhabib (2002, 124–25) has made a similar argument.

141. Renteln 2004, 63. In the United States, although courts do not accept cultural arguments in life-threatening cases, they do accept religious arguments based on the statutory exemptions granted Christian Scientists. Although these exemptions protect parents from having their children subjected to forcible medical treatment, they do not exempt them from charges of homicide if the child dies (Renteln 2004, 65–67).

142. Wikan 2002, 148–49.

143. *Migration und Bevölkerung* 2007b.

144. Ong 2003.

145. Wikan 2002, 148–49.

146. Sager 2000.

147. Mannitz and Schiffauer 2004, 75.

148. UNDP 2004, 4.

149. Bennett 2002; Ellmeier and Rásky 2006.

150. Ong 2006.

151. Benhabib 2002, x.

152. Salih 2003.

153. Nyíri 2005a.

154. Wise 2005.

155. Rudolph 2008.

156. Ray 2005 and Germain 2005.

157. Schader Foundation et al. 2005.

158. Appenzeller, Burchard, Grunert 2002.

159. "Rotterdam to Have Islamic Hospital," *NIS News Bulletin* (Netherlands), 28 September 2006. Available online at http://www.nisnews.nl/public/280906_2.htm (accessed 16 September 2007).

5. Protecting
"Indigenous Culture"

1. For example, *Rolling Stone*'s 2003 special issue, *The 500 Greatest Albums of All Time*, ranked the record number fifty-one.
2. Hafstein 2006.
3. Ibid.
4. Fish 2006, 191–92.
5. Coombe 1991, cited in M. Brown 1998, 196.
6. M. Brown 2005, 44.
7. M. Brown 1998, 196.
8. Ibid., 197; Watkins 2005, 82.
9. Watkins 2005, 83n33.
10. Ibid., 83n31.
11. Riley 2005, 70.
12. Ibid.
13. Ibid., 80.
14. M. Brown 1998, 196.
15. Seeger 1997.
16. Quoted in Kapralos 2007.
17. Boutros-Ghali 1994.
18. Ibid.
19. M. Brown 1998, 219.
20. Riley 2005, 101.
21. Forte 2006.
22. "Welcome to Mji wa Huruma Village, the First Slum on the Internet!" Available online at http://www.pips.at/huruma (accessed 26 November 2007). "DLN Issues: The Selling of Indian Culture," Dakota-Lakota-Nakota Human Rights Advocacy Coalition. Available online at http://www.dlncoalition.org/dln_issues/selling_indian_culture.htm (accessed 5 October 2007).
23. Keck and Sikkink 1998, 121–63; and Conklin 1997f.
24. Hafstein 2006.
25. BBC News 2007d.
26. M. Brown 1998, 194.
27. Kapralos 2007.
28. *Milpurrurru and Ors v. Indofurn Pty Ltd* in Blakeney 1995.
29. *Corriere della Sera* (Rome), 7 July 2006. Also in *New Zealand Herald*, "Italians Drive Ahead with Car Mate haka," n.d., available

online at http://www.nzherald.co.nz/nz/news/article.cfm?c_id=1&objectid=10389619 (accessed 20 January 2009). The commercial can be seen at http://www.youtube.com/watch?v=QIgksCRFwnI (accessed 20 January 2009).
30. European Network for Indigenous Australian Rights 2003.
31. Murphy 2007. "Elders Angry at Migaloo Hijack," *Gold Coast Bulletin*, 2 June 2007.
32. "Scientist Who Recovered Ancient Sounds May Be Hostage of Shadowy Terrorist Group," 1 April 2006. Available online at http://www.williams.edu/go/native/ancientsounds.htm (accessed 28 August 2007).
33. Kapralos 2007.
34. Cohen 1998.
35. "Hands Off Our Genes, Say Pacific Islands," *The National* (Port Moresby), 27 May 2007. Available online at http://www.thenational.com.pg/032107/column6.htm (accessed 20 January 2009).
36. *John Bulun Bulun & Anor v. R & T Textiles Pty Ltd*, in *Australian Indigenous Law Reporter* (1998) 3 AILR 547.
37. The "Declaration of War against Exploiters of Lakota Spirituality" is available online at http://www.aics.org/war.html (accessed 15 April 2007).
38. Reddy 2006, 173.
39. Bode 2007.
40. "Elders Angry at Migaloo Hijack," *Gold Coast Bulletin*, 2 June 2007. Unfortunately, this source is no longer accessible: http://www.gcbulletin.com.au/article/2007/06/02/5518_news.html.
41. The UN's Declaration on the Rights of Indigenous Peoples is available online at http://www.un.org/esa/socdev/unpfii/en/declaration.html (accessed 5 October 2007).
42. Hafstein 2006.
43. The text on the Convention on Biological Diversity is available

online at http://www.cbd.int/conven-
tion/convention.shtml (accessed 5
October 2007).

44. Kapralos 2007.

45. "Hands off Our Genes, Say
Pacific Islands," *The National* (Port
Moresby), 27 May 2007. On "Pacific
Islands values," see the discussion in
chapter 1.

46. Canning 2007.

47. BBC News 2007f.

48. Baden-Powell 1900, chapter 13.

49. The text of the convention
is available online at http://www.
icomos.org/hague/hague.convention.
html (accessed 7 October 2007).

50. Hallman 2005, 216.

51. On the "cultural internationalist" approach, see Merryman 1986.

52. The text of the Convention on
the Means of Prohibiting and Preventing the Illicit Import, Export, and
Transfer of Ownership of Cultural
Property is available online at
http://portal.unesco.org/en/ev.php-
URL_ID=13039&URL_DO=DO_
TOPIC&URL_SECTION=201.html
(accessed 20 January 2009).

53. Cuno 2001, cited in Appiah
2006, 39.

54. Appiah 2006, 38.

55. Opoku 2007.

56. Appiah 2006, 38.

57. Hanson 1989.

58. Rozental 2007.

59. M. Brown 1998, 194.

60. M. Brown 2004.

61. Hallman 2005, 205.

62. Jenkins 2005.

63. Article 4 of the Convention on
the Means of Prohibiting and Preventing the Illicit Import, Export, and
Transfer of Ownership of Cultural
Property is available online at http://
portal.unesco.org/en/ev.php-URL_
ID=13039&URL_DO=DO_TOPIC
&URL_SECTION=201.html
(accessed 20 January 2009).

64. Appiah 2006, 38. Other criticisms of UNESCO's culture concept
include Arizpe 1998, Wright 1998,
and Eriksen 2001.

65. Herzfeld 1982.

66. Ahn 2007.

67. Appiah 2006, 39.

68. Watkins 2005, 80.

69. Hafstein 2006.

70. Appiah 2006, 40.

71. Ebener 2001.

72. Micah 2007.

73. The Declaration on the
Importance and Value of Universal
Museums, cited in Hallman 2005,
216.

74. Appiah 2006, 41.

75. Ibid.

76. Yeh 2006, 10–11.

77. Riley 2004, 75–76.

78. Scafidi, cited in Riley 2004.

79. Deger 2007.

80. Sorry, we lost the reference.

81. Riley 2004, 69.

82. Daniel Miller, personal communication, 1992.

83. Monsiváis 1994. Thanks to
María José Cruz for bringing this
article to our attention.

84. Vickers 1989.

85. Bincsik 2006.

86. M. Brown 1998, 199.

87. Henry 2007.

88. You don't know what that
means? Nor do we!

89. BBC News 2007c.

90. M. Brown 1998, 50.

91. Murphy et al. 2008.

92. The "Luang Prabang Travel
Guide" is available online at http://
wikitravel.org/en/Luang_Prabang
(accessed 7 October 2007).

93. Cowlishaw 2008.

94. Noyes 2006.

95. See http://www.unesco.org/
culture/intangible-heritage/38eur_
uk.htm (accessed 28 November
2007).

96. Noyes 2006, 35.

97. Ibid., 39.

98. Ibid.

99. Ibid., 40.

100. Ibid.

101. Hafstein 2006.

102. Rose 1999.

103. Ibid., 175.

104. Bennett 2000, 1422–23.

105. See, for example, Krech 1999.

106. Dombrowski 2002 and Kuper 2005, 207.

107. On this "pastoral vision," see M. Berman 1983.

108. "Indianerstamm will Atommülldeponie" (Indian tribe wants nuclear waste dump), *Newsletter des Verlages für Amerikanistik* (Wyk auf Föhr), August 2002. Unfortunately, this link is no longer accessible: http://www.amerikanistik-verlag.de/news-aug-2002.doc (accessed 29 November 2007).

109. Riley 2004, 69.

110. Ibid., 110.

111. Ibid., 88.

112. Ibid., 121.

113. Kapai 2007.

114. Deloria Jr., quoted in Hemachandra 2003.

115. Quoted in Donovan 1997.

116. Landzelius 2006, 13.

117. Riley 2004, 90, 122.

118. "Cherokee Tribe Reinstates Blacks," *New America Media*, 3 July 2007. Available online at http://news.newamericamedia.org/news/view_article.html?article_id=bd8b0521f87 3436b06547cd272ceefcf (accessed 9 October 2007). The tribal "citizenship" of some Freedmen was reinstated after they sued the tribe.

119. Kuper 2005, 210–11.

120. Reddy 2006, 163, 174.

121. Ibid., 167.

122. Ibid., 168–73.

123. Ibid., 175–76.

124. Fish 2006.

125. Scott 1998, 333.

126. Reddy 2006, 165, 175.

127. Fish 2006, 201.

128. Christen 2007.

129. M. Brown 2005, 48. The phrase is an allusion to James Scott's *Seeing Like a State* (1998).

130. Downey 2007.

131. Aveda 2007.

132. Reddy 2006, 179.

133. Ibid.

134. Quoted in Kapralos 2007, 2.

135. Sahlins 1993, 17.

136. Kuper 2005, 218.

137. Ibid., 203.

138. Kuper (2005, 210) has pointed out, for example, that the ancestors of the Innu Nation of Labrador in Canada only appeared there eighteen hundred years ago, displacing and assimilating other ethnic groups.

139. Suzman 2003. African states were among those—along with Australia, Canada, New Zealand, and the United States—that moved to postpone voting on the Declaration on the Rights of Indigenous Peoples at the UN General Assembly.

140. M. Brown 2005, 53.

6. The Age of "Cultural Competence"

1. "Management Tools 2007: An Executive's Guide," available online at http://www.bain.com/management_tools/home.asp (accessed 6 April 2007).

2. McFate 2005.

3. The report is cited in Rothstein 2006, 1.

4. Kipp et al. 2006, 8, 11.

5. J. Thompson 2007.

6. SMOOTH is an acronym of the German words for "self-confidence," "motivation," "organization," "openness," "tolerance," and "home."

7. Storti 1990, Kohls 2001, Granered 2004, and Chong 2002.

8. Kaufmann 2007.

9. See the Thinkers 50, online at http://www.thinkers50.com/?page=home, 2005 (accessed 15 January 2007).

10. See "About Trompenaars Hampden-Turner Consulting" at http://www.thtconsulting.com/index1.html (accessed 15 January 2007).

11. "Bold Fusion," *The Economist*, 17 February 2007, 68.

12. Hüsken 2006, 118.

13. Ong 2006, 154.

14. See "More Masala for the

Melting Pot: Sharing Cultures and Competence for Collaboration," available online at http://www.sietar-europa.org/files/SIETAR_India_congress2006_programme_and_registration.pdf (accessed 16 January 2007).

15. The McKinsey report is available online at http://www.mckinsey.com/mgi/reports/pdfs/China_talent/ChinaPerspective.pdf.

16. Cited in Mannitz 2000, 8.

17. Quoted in Hu 2008.

18. In 2007, Google Scholar yielded 4,334 citations of Hofstede's 1984 classic *Culture's Consequences,* as compared with 3,651 for the 1973 work *The Interpretation of Culture* by Clifford Geertz, who is generally regarded as the best-known anthropologist of recent decades.

19. The *Journal of Cross-Cultural Psychology* was founded in 1970, the International Association of Cross-Cultural Psychology in 1972. In 2006 the International Association of Cross-Cultural Psychology awarded Geert Hofstede Honorary Fellow status.

20. See, for example, Triandis 1977.

21. Hofstede 1984, 73.

22. Hofstede 1980, 44.

23. Hofstede and Hofstede 2004, 4. This definition of "culture" has been reproduced in countless business texts—for example, in Pauline Weetman, Paul Gordon, and Clare Roberts's standard *International Financial Reporting: A Comparative Approach* (Upper Saddle River, N.J.: Pearson Education, 2005), 190.

24. Hofstede 1984, 14.

25. Quoted in Dahlén 1997, 102.

26. Hardacre 1989 and Morris-Suzuki 1995.

27. Geertz 1973, 5.

28. Bunzl 2008, 55–56, quoting Clifford 1986, 13, 19.

29. Quoted in Baskerville 2003, 11.

30. Gjerde 2004.

31. Hofstede 1998a; and Mooij 1998, 47.

32. Hofstede 2002, 1356.

33. Ibid., 1356–57.

34. Hofstede's Web site is http://www.geert-hofstede.com. McSweeney 2002a, 92.

35. Weaver 2005. See also Weaver 1997.

36. Weiss 2000.

37. McSweeney 2002a, 101.

38. Hofstede 1980, 375.

39. McSweeney 2002b, 1367–68.

40. Hofstede 1980, 411.

41. Helgesen 2001.

42. Apthorpe 2005, 137.

43. McSweeney 2002a, 110.

44. Ibid., 111, citing Hofstede 1980, 222, 165, 279.

45. Available online at http://www.geert-hofstede.com/hofstede_venezuela.shtml (accessed 4 February 2007).

46. Rao and Teegen 2001.

47. Weaver 2005.

48. Pennington 2005, 5.

49. Hardacre 1989, 3.

50. Yoshino 1999, 13–14.

51. Hüsken 2006, 113.

52. Ibid., 118.

53. Ong 1999, 135.

54. Hu and Grove 1998.

55. Weidenbaum and Hughes 1996a; Seagrave 1995; and Redding 1990.

56. Bond 1986, 9–10.

57. Hu and Grove 1998, 2.

58. Ibid., 7.

59. Weidenbaum and Hughes 1996b (excerpted from *The Bamboo Network*).

60. Bond 1986, 216.

61. Mooij 1998, 109.

62. Yow Yit Seng, *The Chinese Dimensions: Their Root, Mindset, and Psyche* (Selangor: Pelanduk Publications, 2006). Available online at http://www.yitseng.net/chinese%20dimensions/ (accessed 4 February 2007).

63. Gao and Ting-Toomey 1998.

64. Hu and Grove 1998, 63–66.

65. Pye 1992, 89ff.
66. King 1991, 63.
67. Zha 1995.
68. Ong 2006, 223.
69. Yao 2002, 143.
70. Redding 1990, 3.
71. Hamilton 1996, 47.
72. Yao 2002, 14.
73. Greenhalgh 1994, 746.
74. In Butler et al. 2001.
75. Nyíri 2005b.
76. Ji 1996.
77. Yao 2002, 30ff.
78. Ibid., 158.
79. Moosmüller 2000.
80. Hofstede 1998b.
81. Gregor Sterzenbach, "'Ni hau, Herr Kollege!'—Erfolgsfaktor Interkulturelle Kommunikation" ("Ni hau, colleague!—Intercultural communication as a success factor), 18 April 2007.
82. Hofstede 2002, 1356.
83. Baskerville 2003, 3.
84. See Trompenaars Hampden-Turner Consulting online at http://www.7d-culture.nl/ (accessed 15 January 2007).
85. Hampden-Turner and Trompenaars 2001. See Layla's reviews online at http://www.amazon.com/gp/pdp/profile/A3HOWFKT1ELU2J/ref=cm_cr_auth/103-1702765-6616609 (accessed 15 January 2007).
86. "How We Do It." Available online at http://www.thtconsulting.com/ (accessed 17 January 2007).
87. Halter 2002, 111–15.
88. Ibid., 30.
89. DaimlerChrysler Corporation 2006.
90. Halter 2002, 57, 73.
91. See Ethnic Marketing Group online at http://www.emgad.com (accessed 4 February 2007).
92. Halter 2002, 126.
93. Amanullah 2007.
94. Edmonds forthcoming.
95. Ibid.
96. Dávila 2001.
97. Comment to Amanullah 2007.

98. In a study conducted for a consumer goods company, Patricia L. Sunderland and Rita M. Denny (2007, 218–20) found that middle-class black and Latina American women felt that conspicuously "black" or "Hispanic" products were not only condescending but also marked the rest of a company's products as "for whites," thus having the effect of alienating the very market those products had been designed to attract.
99. Hammonds 2000.
100. Zachary 2000, 272.
101. Ibid., 280.
102. Ibid., 282.
103. Cox 1994, 142ff.
104. "The Racial Equality Directive 2000/43/EC" is online at http://web20.s112.typo3server.com/fileadmin/pdfs/Reports/Directives/2000-43_en.pdf (accessed 18 January 2007).
105. Kircher n.d.
106. Pavkovic 2001.
107. Kircher n.d.
108. Dälken and Heidari 2004
109. Ibid., 17.
110. A recent example is Braithwaite and Taylor 1992.
111. "Mad travellers disease" was an illness only described in France, which manifested itself in sudden, unexplained, and compulsive travelling (on foot or by rail), of which the patients had only a vague recollection. See Hacking 1998.
112. Kleinman 2004, 952.
113. "French Panel Recommends Measures to Keep Religion out of Hospitals," *International Herald Tribune*, 29 January 2007.
114. Kleinman 2004, 951.
115. AAMC 2005, 1. We thank Benji Phillips for this reference.
116. Fadiman 1997, 262.
117. Ibid., 21.
118. Ibid., 266.
119. Mezzich et al. 1999.
120. AAMC 2005, 1.
121. Blofeld 2004.
122. "Project Summary: Migrant-

Friendly Hospitals Project," 2005.
Available online at http://www.mfh-
eu.net/public/files/mfh-summary.pdf
(accessed 30 January 2007).

123. Gilbert 2005, Module 1.

124. Ibid., Modules 7 and 1.

125. For example, at the Liverpool
Hospital Conference Centre, Liverpool, New South Wales, 6–8 July
2006.

126. Ilkilic n.d. The brochure
is based on a book by Ilhan Ilkilic
(2002), a Bosnian.

127. Heller 2005.

128. "French Panel Recommends
Measures to Keep Religion Out of
Hospitals," *International Herald
Tribune*, 29 January 2007.

129. Becker, Wunderer, and
Schulz-Gambard 1998.

130. AAMC 2005, 2.

131. Ibid., 3.

132. American Medical Student
Association n.d.

133. Fadiman 1997, 13.

134. Lee n.d.

135. Santiago-Irizarry 2001.

136. Lee and Farrell 2006, 9.

137. Kleinman and Benson 2006.

138. Lee and Farrell 2006, 9.

139. Rice 1999.

140. Dugger 2006.

141. Inhorn 2003.

142. Kleinman and Benson 2006.

143. Kleinman 2004, 953.

144. Sutton 2005, 2.

145. Ibid., 8–9.

146. O'Callaghan 1998.

147. Sabine Boes, personal communication, December 2003.

148. Pribilsky 2008, 105.

149. Federal Commissioner for
Migration 2005.

150. Language and Orientation
Resource Center, *Your New Life in
the United States,* quoted in Fadiman
1997, 186.

151. Hu and Grove 1998, 51–58.

152. McFate 2005, 25.

153. Hu and Grove 1998, 51.

154. Haumersen and Liebe 1999.

Conclusion:
The Ethnographic Approach

1. Trompenaars is at http://www.
7d-culture.nl/Content/cont043.htm
(accessed 20 January 2009).

2. Eriksen 2006c.

3. In Scene 5 of Act V, Peer
describes the onion in this way:

What an enormous number of
sheaths!
Isn't the kernel soon coming to light?
I'm blessed if it is! To the innermost
centre,
It's nothing but sheaths—
each smaller and smaller—
Nature is witty!

In a different context, Peer Gynt's
onion appears in anthropology in
Eriksen 1997, 119.

4. Wikan 2002, 104.

5. Rose 1999.

6. See "How We Do It," available
online at http://www.thtconsulting.
com/main/research.php (accessed 17
January 2007).

7. Jakubowicz 1984, 33.

8. Edmonds forthcoming.

9. Abu-Lughod 1991, 137–62.

10. Bunzl 2008, 56.

11. Abu-Lughod 1991, 147.

12. Hannerz 2004, 231.

13. Sen 2006b.

14. See "Virtual Anthropology,"
online at http://www.trendwatching.
com/trends/VIRTUAL ANTHRO-
POLOGY.htm (accessed 24 October
2007; italics in original).

15. Associated Press 2007, 3.

16. Levitt 1983.

17. For a review of the evolution of ethnographic approaches in
consumer research, see Sunderland
and Denny 2007, 25–41.

18. Kane 1996.

19. Walsh 2001.

20. Johnson 2006 and Fitzgerald
2006.

21. The results of the survey are
available online at "Management
Tools 2007: An Executive's Guide,"

http://www.bain.com/management_tools/home.asp (accessed 5 October 2007).

22. Muoio 2000.

23. Genevieve Bell's biography is available online at http://www.liftconference.com/person/gbell (accessed 20 January 2009).

24. "Ethnologen helfen westlichen IT-Firmen, den Zukunftsmarkt Asien zu verstehen" (Anthropologists help Western IT companies to understand Asia, the market of the future), Antropologi.info, 14 September 2005. Available online at http://antropologi.info/blog/ethnologie/ethnologie.php?p=1336&more=1&c=1&tb=1&pb=1 (accessed 5 October 2007).

25. "Experientia interviews Anne Kirah," October 2006. Available online at http://www.experientia.com/en/interviews/kirah/ (accessed 5 October 2007).

26. Ibid.

27. Kirah, quoted in Tett 2005.

28. "Nokia's Design Research for Everyone," Business Week, 14 March 2007. Available online at http://www.businessweek.com/innovate/content/mar2007/id20070314_689707.htm (accessed 5 October 2007).

29. "So helfen Ethnologen mit Big Brother Videos bei der Marktforschung" (Here's how anthropologists help with Big Brother videos in market research), Antropologi.info, 28 April 2005. Available online at http://antropologi.info/blog/ethnologie/index.php?p=1218 (accessed 5 October 2007).

30. Muoio 2000.

31. Tett 2005 and Walsh 2001.

32. McFarland 2001.

33. Jones 2006.

34. Sunderland and Denny 2007, 14.

35. Emma Hall, "Do You Know Your Rites? BBDO Does," Advertising Age, 21 May 2007, 22.

36. Ibid.

37. This distinction is made in Appadurai 1996.

38. Callahan 2003, 508.

39. Gjerde 2004, 7.

40. Miller and Horst 2005.

41. Kwami and Chandola 2005, 5.

42. Spielhaus and Färber 2007.

43. Edmonds 2006, 8.

44. Ibid.

45. Ibid.

46. Edmonds 2005.

47. Ibid, 8.

48. Jager 2007, vi.

49. Mahadevan 2007.

50. Dannenbeck and Lösch 2001.

Bibliography

ABC News. 2008. "Boarding Schools Not the Answer, Indigenous Group Says." 31 March.

Abraham, Anita, and Jean-Philippe Platteau. 2004. "Participatory Development: Where Culture Creeps In." In Vijayendra Rao and Michael Walton, eds. *Culture and Public Action*, 210–233. Stanford, Calif.: Stanford University Press.

Abu-Lughod, Lila. 1991. "Writing against Culture." In Richard Fox, ed. *Recapturing Anthropology: Working in the Present*, 137–162. Santa Fe, N.Mex.: School of American Research Press.

———. 2002. "Do Muslim Women Really Need Saving? Anthropological Reflections on Cultural Relativism and Its Others." *American Anthropologist* 104, no. 3: 783–790.

Ahn, Yonson. 2006. "The Korea-China Textbook War—What Is It All About?" *History News Network*, 3 June. Available online at http://hnn.us/articles/21617.html (accessed 30 July 2007).

Alam, Shahid. 2003. "Bernard Lewis and the New Orientalism." *Counterpunch*, June 28. Available online at http://www.counterpunch.org/alam06282003.html (accessed 13 May 2007).

Albro, Robert. 2007. "Anthropology's Terms of Engagement with Security." *Anthropology News* 48, no. 1: 20–21.

Allard, Tom. 2007. "Islamist Insurgents Doing Well, Admits Army Chief." *Sydney Morning Herald*, 25 October. Available online at http://www.smh.com.au/news/federalelection2007news/islamist-insurgents-doing-well-admits-army-chief/2007/10/24/119294115 3902.html (accessed 25 January 2009).

Amanullah, Zahed. 2007. "The New Halal (and the Non-Muslims Who Love It)." *Altmuslim.com*, 30 April. Available online at http://www.altmuslim.com/a/a/b/2476/ (accessed 25 January 2009).

American Medical Student Association. N.d. *Cultural Competency in Medicine.* Available online at http://www.amsa.org/programs/gpit/cultural.cfm (accessed 12 June 2007).

Amselle, Jean-Loup. 1996. *Mestizo Logics: Anthropology of Identity in Africa and Elsewhere*. Stanford, Calif.: Stanford University Press.

Anderson, Benedict. 1983. *Imagined Communities: Reflections on the Origins and Spread of Nationalism*. London: Verso.

———. 1998. *The Spectre of Comparisons: Nationalism, Southeast Asia, and the World*. London: Verso.

Anderson, Liam, and Gareth Stansfield. 2004. *The Future of Iraq: Dictatorship, Democracy, or Division?* New York: Palgrave Macmillan.

Andoni, Lamis. 2002. "In the Service of Empire." *Al-Ahram Weekly*, 12–18 December.

Andre, Catherine, and Jean-Philippe Platteau. 1998. "'Land Relations under Unbearable Stress: Rwanda Caught in the Malthusian Trap." *Journal of Economic Behavior & Organization* 34, no. 1: 1–47.

Antweiler, Christoph. 2003. "Anthropologie gewaltsamer Konflikte: Konfliktmotoren und Gewaltmotive" (The anthropology of violent conflicts: Motors of conflict and motives of violence). *Entwicklungsethnologie* 12, nos. 1 and 2: 26–73.

Appadurai, Arjun. 1996. *Modernity at Large*. Minneapolis: University of Minnesota Press.

———. 2001. "Grassroots Globalization and the Research Imagination." In Arjun Appadurai, ed., *Globalization*, 1–21. Durham, N.C.: Duke University Press.

———. 2004. "The Capacity to Aspire: Culture and the Terms of Recognition." In Vijayendra Rao and Michael Walton, eds. *Culture and Public Action*, 59–84. Stanford, Calif.: Stanford University Press.

Appenzeller, Gerd, Amory Burchard, and Brigitte Grunert. 2002. "Müssen Ausländer sich anpassen, Frau John?" (Mrs. John, must foreigners fit in?) *Tagesspiegel* (Berlin), 6 October.

Appiah, Kwame Anthony. 2006."Whose Culture Is It?" *The New York Review of Books* 53, no. 2: 38–41.

Applebaum, Anne. 2006. "Veiled Insult." *Washington Post*, 24 October, A19.

Apthorpe, Raymond. 2005. "'It's [the] Culture, Stupid!' Why 'Adding Culture' Is Unlikely to Make Any Serious Difference to International Developmentalism." *Asia Pacific Journal of Anthropology* 6, no. 2: 130–141.

Arizpe, Lourdes. 1998. "UN Cultured." *Anthropology Today* 14, no. 3: 24.

Arrighi, Giovanni. 1994. *The Long Twentieth Century: Money, Power, and the Origins of Our Times*. London: Verso.

Assmann, Jan. 1992. *Das kulturelle Gedächtnis: Schrift, Erinnerung und politische Identität in frühen Hochkulturen* (Cultural memory: Writing, remembering, and political identity in early high cultures). Munich: Beck.

Associated Press. 2007. *A New Model for News: Studying the Deep Structure of Young-Adult News Consumption.* Available online at http://www.ap.org/newmodel.pdf (accessed 20 January 2009).

Association of American Medical Colleges (AAMC). 2005. *Cultural Competence Education for Medical Students.* Available online at http://www.aamc.org/meded/tacct/culturalcomped.pdf (accessed 24 May 2007).

Auburn Council. 2007. *Auburn Council Cultural Plan, 2007–2017.* Sydney, Australia: Auburn Council.

Aveda. 2007. "A Dialogue for the Future: Aveda and Its Partners Discuss the Opportunities and Challenges of Indigenous Entrepreneurship." Press release, *Enhanced Online News,* 31 May. Available online at http://eon.businesswire.com/releases/aveda/indigenous/prweb 530248.htm (accessed 9 October 2007).

Baden-Powell, Major R.S.S. 1900. *The Downfall of Prempeh.* London: Methuen.

Barber, Benjamin. 2001. "Jihad vs. McWorld Revisited: Opening a Democratic Front in the Face of Terrorism." *Berlin Journal* (fall). Available online at http://www.benjaminbarber.com/revisited.html (accessed 20 January 2009).

Barry, Brian. 2000. *Culture and Equality.* Cambridge, Mass.: Polity Press.

Bartmann, Christoph. 2005. "Die Schutzimpfung" (The vaccine). *Süddeutsche Zeitung,* 22–23 October.

Baskerville, Rachel F. 2003. "Hofstede Never Studied Culture." *Accounting, Organizations, and Society* 28: 1–14.

Bayart, Jean-François. 2005. *The Illusion of Cultural Identity.* Chicago: University of Chicago Press.

BBC News. 2005a. "Bush Presses Putin on Democracy." 24 February.

———. 2005b. "Davis Attacks UK Multiculturalism." 3 August.

———. 2006a. "Police Demo Probe 'Will Be Swift.'" 6 February.

———. 2006b. "Australia Fury at Cleric Comments." 26 October.

———. 2006c. "The Islamic Veil across Europe." 17 November.

———. 2007a. "Schools Must Teach 'Britishness.'" 25 January.

———. 2007b. "Younger Muslims 'More Political.'" 29 January.

———. 2007c. "Crofters' Indigenous Rights Call." 25 March.

———. 2007d. "BBC and Bob Geldof to Map Mankind." 14 April.

———. 2007e. "Police Plea on Genital Mutilation." 11 July.

———. 2007f. "Egypt 'to Copyright Antiquities.'" 25 December.

Becker, S. A., E. Wunderer, and J. Schulz-Gambard. 1998. *Muslimische Patienten: Ein Leitfaden zur interkulturelle Verstandigung in Krankenhaus und Praxis* (Muslim patients: Guidelines for inter-cultural understanding in hospitals and private practice). Munich: Zuckschwerdt.

Beikler, Sabine. 2007. "Sürücü-Mord kommt wieder vor Gericht" (Sürücü murder in court again). *Tagesspiegel* (Berlin), 19 August. Available online at http://www.tagesspiegel.de/berlin/PolizeiJustiz-Fall-Sueruecue-Integration;art126,2361361 (accessed 20 January 2009).

Beinart, Peter. 2006. "To the Brink." *The New Republic*, 27 November.

Bell, Daniel T. 2006. *Beyond Liberal Democracy: Political Thinking for an East Asian Context.* Princeton, N.J.: Princeton University Press.

Benhabib, Seyla. 2002. *The Claims of Culture: Equality and Diversity in the Global Era.* Princeton, N.J.: Princeton University Press.

Bennett, Tony, ed. 2000. "Acting on the Social: Art, Culture, and Government." *American Behavioural Scientist* 43, no. 9: 1412–1428.

———. 2002. *Differing Diversities: Cultural Policy and Cultural Diversity.* Strasbourg, France: Council of Europe.

Berman, Ilan. 2001. "Slouching toward Eurasia?" *Perspective* 12, no. 1. Available online at http://www.bu.edu/iscip/vol12/berman.html (accessed 20 January 2009).

Berman, Marshall. 1983. *All That Is Solid Melts into Air: The Experience of Modernity.* New York: Simon & Schuster.

Besteman, Catherine, and Hugh Gusterson. 2005. *Why America's Top Pundits Are Wrong: Anthropologists Talk Back.* Berkeley: University of California Press.

———. 2008. "Response to Matti Bunzl: Public Anthropology, Pragmatism, and Pundits." *American Anthropologist* 110, no. 1: 61–63.

Bincsik, Mónika. 2006. "Az 'örök Buddha egyszerű tisztelője': Van Gogh japonizmusa" ("A 'simple devotee of the eternal Buddha': Van Gogh's *japonisme*"). In Geskó Judit, ed. *Van Gogh Budapesten* (Van Gogh in Budapest), 359–373. Budapest, Hungary: Museum of Fine Arts, Vince.

Bissell, Tom. 2006. "Euphorias of Perrier: The Case against Robert D. Kaplan." *Virginia Quarterly Review* 82, no. 3: 235–252.

———. 2007. "Those Wild and Crazy Estonians." *The New Republic*, 15 January. Available online at http://www.tnr.com/doc.mhtml?i=200 70115&s=bissell011507 (accessed 20 January 2009).

Blakeney, Michael. 1995. "Milpurrurru and Ors v Indofurn Pty Ltd and Ors—Protecting Expressions of Aboriginal Folklore under Copyright Law." *Murdoch University Electronic Journal of Law* 2, no. 1. Available online at http://www.murdoch.edu.au/elaw/issues/v2n1/ blakeney21.html (accessed 27 September 2007).

Blofeld, Sir John. 2004. *Independent Inquiry into the Death of David Bennett.* Cambridge: Norfolk, Suffolk, and Cambridgeshire Strategic Health Authority, 2004. Available online at http://www.irr.org.uk/pdf/ bennett_inquiry.pdf (accessed 20 January 2009).

Bode, Maarten. 2007. "Taking Traditional Knowledge to the Market." *IIAS News* (Leiden), no. 45: 23.

Bond, Michael Harris. 1986. *The Psychology of the Chinese People.* Hong Kong: Hong Kong University Press.

Bourdieu, Pierre. 1986. "The Forms of Capital." In John G. Richardson, ed. *Handbook for Theory and Research for the Sociology of Education,* 241–258. Westwood, Conn.: Greenwood Press.

Boutros-Ghali, Boutros. 1994. "Foreword." In Alexander Ewen, ed. *Voice of Indigenous Peoples,* 13. Santa Fe, N.Mex.: Native American Council of New York City.

Bowen, John R. 1996. "The Myth of Global Ethnic Conflict." *Journal of Democracy* 7, no. 4: 3–14.

Braithwaite, Ronald L., and Sandra E. Taylor. 1992. *Health Issues in the Black Community.* Hoboken, N.J.: Jossey-Bass.

Breidenbach, Joana, and Pál Nyíri. 2008. "The Altai Road: Visions of Development across the Russian-Chinese Border." *Development and Change* 39, no. 1: 123–145.

Bringa, Tone. 1995. *Being Muslim the Bosnian Way: Identity and Community in a Central Bosnian Village.* Princeton, N.J.: Princeton University Press.

———. 2005. "Haunted by the Imaginations of the Past: Robert Kaplan's *Balkan Ghosts.*" In Catherine Besteman and Hugh Gusterson, eds. *Why America's Top Pundits Are Wrong: Anthropologists Talk Back,* 60–64. Berkeley: University of California Press.

Broder, Henry M. 2006. "Dialog? Nein Danke!" (A dialogue? No thanks!). *Spiegel Online,* 25 April. Available online at http://www.spiegel.de/kultur/gesellschaft/0,1518,403133,00.html (accessed 13 March 2007).

Brown, Keith. 2005. "Samuel Huntington, Meet the Nuer: Kinship, Local Knowledge, and the Clash of Civilizations." In Catherine Besteman and Hugh Gusterson, eds. *Why America's Top Pundits Are Wrong: Anthropologists Talk Back,* 43–59. Berkeley: University of California Press.

Brown, Michael F. 1998. "Can Culture Be Copyrighted?" *Current Anthropology* 39, no. 2: 193–222.

———. 2004. "Owning Culture: Anthropology and Its Intellectual Properties." *Anthropology News* 45, no. 4. Available online at http://www.williams.edu/go/native/owningculture.htm (accessed 22 July 2008).

———. 2005. "Heritage Trouble: Recent Work on the Protection of Intangible Cultural Property." *International Journal of Cultural Property,* no. 12: 41–61.

Bulliet, Richard W. 2004. *The Case for Islamo-Christian Civilization.* New York: Columbia University Press.

Bunzl, Matti. 2008. "The Quest for Anthropological Relevance: Borgesian

Maps and Epistemological Pitfalls." *American Anthropologist* 110, no. 1: 53–60.

Buruma, Ian. 2007. "The Peculiar Death of European Multiculturalism." *Taipei Times*, 16 April, 9.

Butler, John E., Phillip H. Phan, Borje O. Saxberg, and Soo Hoon Lee. 2001. "Entrepreneurial Succession, Firm Growth, and Performance in the Asian Business Context." *Journal of Enterprising Culture* 9, no. 4: 407–436.

Callahan, William A. 2003. "Beyond Cosmopolitanism and Nationalism: Diasporic Chinese and Neo-Nationalism in China and Thailand." *International Organization*, no. 57: 481–517.

Campbell, David. 1999. "Contra Wight: The Errors of Premature Writing." *Review of International Studies* 25, no. 2: 321.

Canning, Simon. 2007. "Telstra Hit over Virtual Uluru." *The Australian*, 24 May. Available online at http://www.news.com.au/business/story/ 0,23636,21785853-462,00.html (accessed 20 January 2009).

Cantle, Ted. 2006. "Parallel Lives." *Index on Censorship*. 3 November. Available online at http://www.eurozine.com/articles/2006-11-03-cantle-eu.html (accessed 20 January 2009).

Caryl, Christian. 2007. "What about the Iraqis?" *New York Review of Books*, 11 January, 36–39. Available online at http://www.nybooks. com/articles/19793 (accessed 20 January 2009).

Casanova, José. 2006. "Aggiornamenti? Katholische und Muslimische Politik im Vergleich" (Aggiornamenti? Catholic and Muslim politics in comparison). In *Jahrbuch 2005–2006*, 200–217. Berlin: Wissenschaftskolleg.

Chakrabarty, Dipesh. 1988. "Conditions for Knowledge of Working-Class Conditions: Employers, Government, and the Jute Workers of Calcutta, 1890–1940." In Ranajit Guha and Gayatri Chakravorty Spivak, eds. *Selected Subaltern Studies*, 259–310. New York: Oxford University Press.

Chan, Anita, and Zhu Xiaoyang. 2003. "Disciplinary Labour Regimes in Chinese Factories." *Critical Asian Studies* 35, no. 4: 559–584.

Chen Wei. 2006. "Lüyoudi nongmin wenti yanjiu—yi Guangdong Danxiashan jingqu wei li / A Study on Peasants' Problems in Scenic Area: Case Study of Danxia Mountain in Guangdong Province." Presented at the Third China Tourism Forum, Hong Kong, 15–16 December.

Cheng Chaoze. 1995. *Zouchu shan'ao de Zhongguo* (China: Coming out of the valley). Shenzhen, China: Haitian Chubanshe.

Chitsike, Colletah. 2000. "Culture as a Barrier to Rural Women's Entrepreneurship." *Gender and Development* 8, no. 1: 71–77.

Chong, Nilda. 2002. *The Latino Patient: A Cultural Guide for Health Care Providers*. Yarmouth, Maine: Intercultural Press.

Chrétien, Jean-Pierre. 2003. *The Great Lakes of Africa: Two Thousand Years of History.* London: Zone Books.

Christen, Kimberly. 2007. "The Politics of Search: Archival Accountability in Aboriginal Australia." Paper presented at the Media in Transition Conference, Massachusetts Institute of Technology, Cambridge, 28 April.

Chua Beng Huat. 1995. *Communitarian Ideology and Democracy in Singapore.* London: Routledge.

Clifford, James. 1986. "Partial Truths." In James Clifford and George Marcus, eds. *Writing Culture: The Poetics and Politics of Ethnography,* 1–26. Berkeley: University of California Press.

Cohen, Lenard J. 1993. *Broken Bonds: The Disintegration of Yugoslavia.* Boulder, Colo.: Westview Press.

Cohen, Patricia. 2007. "In Books, a Clash of Europe and Islam." *New York Times,* 8 February. Available online at http://www.nytimes.com/2007/02/08/books/08circ.html (accessed 20 January 2009).

Cohen, Phil. 1998. "Totem and Taboos." *New Scientist,* 29 August, 5.

Cohn, Bernard. 1987. "The Census, Social Structure, and Objectification in South Asia." In *An Anthropologist among the Historians and Other Essays.* New Delhi: Oxford University Press.

Coll, Steve. 2005. *Ghost Wars: The Secret History of the CIA, Afghanistan, and Bin Laden from the Soviet Invasion to September 10, 2001.* London: Penguin.

College van Burgemeester & Wethouders. 2006. *Rotterdamse Burgerschapscode* (Rotterdam residents' code). Rotterdam, Netherlands: College van Burgemeester & Wethouders.

Conklin, Beth A. 1997. "Body Paint, Feathers, and VCRs: Aesthetics and Authenticity in Amazonian Activism." *American Ethnologist* 24, no. 4: 711–738.

Coombe, Rosemary. 1991. "Objects of Property and Subjects of Politics: Intellectual Property Rights and Democratic Debate." *Texas Law Review* 69: 1853–1880.

Costello, Tim, Brendan Smith, and Jeremy Brecher. 2007. "Labour Rights in China." *Post-Autistic Economics Review,* no. 41: 34–38.

Cowling, Maurice. 1993. "Joseph Needham and the History of Chinese Science." *New Criterion* 11, no. 6. Available online at http://www.newcriterion.com/archive/11/feb93/cowling.htm.

Cowlishaw, Gillian. 2008. "Ethnography and Suburban Mythology." Seminar at the Anthropology Department, Macquarie University, Sydney, Australia, 10 April.

Cox, Taylor, Jr. 1994. *Cultural Diversity in Organizations: Theory, Research, and Practice.* San Francisco: Berrett-Koehler.

Cuno, James. 2001. "U.S. Art Museums and Cultural Property." *Connecticut Journal of International Law* 16, no. 2: 189–196.

Currie, Duncan. 2005. "Asian Values. George W. Bush Hit a Rhetorical Home Run Last Week in Japan." *The Weekly Standard*, 23 November. Available online at http://www.weeklystandard.com/check.asp?id Article=6391&r=cimsf (accessed 20 January 2009).

Dahlén, Tommy. 1997. *Among the Interculturalists: An Emergent Profession and Its Packaging of Knowledge*. Stockholm Studies in Social Anthropology, no. 38. Stockholm.

DaimlerChrysler Corporation. 2006. *Diversity Enterprise-wide*. Available online at http://www.daimlerchrysler.com/Projects/c2c/channel/files/134734_DiversityOct2006.pdf (accessed 15 June 2007).

Dälken, Michaela, and Mohammad Heidari. 2004. *Fit und kompetent—für eine interkulturelle Zukunft! Konfliktlösungen im interkulturellen Kontext. Beispielen aus Verwaltungen und öffentlichen Betrieben* (Fit and competent—for an intercultural future! Conflict resolution in an intercultural context. Examples from government and public services). Düsseldorf: DGB Bildungswerk.

Dannenbeck, Clemens, and Hans Lösch. 2001. "Herkunft (er)zählt: Orientierungen im Dschungel ethnischer Differenzen" (Background counts: Orientations in the jungle of ethnic difference). *DED-Brief* (newsletter of the German Development Service), no. 3: 31–33.

Danner, Mark. 2006. "Iraq: Bush's Fantasy War." *New York Review of Books*, 21 December, 81–96.

Dávila, Arlene M. 2001. *Latinos, Inc.: The Marketing and Making of a People*. Berkeley: University of California Press.

De Atkine, Norvell B. 2002. "Preface." In Raphael Patai. *The Arab Mind*. Long Island, N.Y.: Hatherleigh Press. Available online at http://www.meforum.org/article/636 (accessed 25 January 2009).

Deger, Jennifer. 2007. "Incorporating Images: Photography and Contemporary Yolngu Mournings." Paper presented at Macquarie University, Sydney, Australia, 9 August.

Department of Canadian Heritage. 1988. Canadian Multiculturalism Act. Available online at http://www.canadianheritage.gc.ca/progs/multi/policy/act_e.cfm (accessed 22 April 2007).

Dombrowski, Kirk. 2002. "The Praxis of Indigenism and Alaska Native Timber Policies." *American Anthropologist* 104: 1062–1073.

Donovan, Bill. 1997. "Fake Healers Plague Navajo Nation." *High Country News* (Paonia, Colo.), 13 October. Available online at https://www.hcn.org/issues/116/3714 (accessed 25 January 2009).

Downey, Greg. 2007. Comment on Joana Breidenbach, in "Bob Geldorf [*sic*], the Saviour of the Cultures of the World?" *Culture Matters*, 28 May. Available online at http://culturematters.wordpress.com/2007/04/19/bob-geldorf-the-saviour-of-the-cultures-of-the-world/#comments (accessed 27 November 2007).

Drake, Michael S. 2003. "Representing 'Old Countries': The Strategic Representation of Culture as Heritage in the Asia-Europe Summit Meetings." In Stephanie Lawson, ed. *Europe and the Asia-Pacific: Culture, Identity, and Representations of Region*, 33–49. London: RoutledgeCurzon.

Dugger, Celia. 2006. "Cambodia Tries Nonprofit Path to Health Care." *New York Times*, 8 January. Available online at http://www.nytimes. com/2006/01/08/international/asia/08cambodia.html (accessed 25 January 2009).

Easterly, William. 2006a. *The White Man's Burden: Why the West's Efforts to Aid the Rest Have Done So Much Ill and So Little Good.* London: Penguin.

———. 2006b. "Why Doesn't Aid Work?" *Cato Unbound*, 3 April. Available online at http://www.cato-unbound.org/2006/04/03/ william-easterly/why-doesnt-aid-work/ (accessed 18 April 2007).

Ebner, Martin. 2001. "Im Exil vor den Taliban" (In exile from the Taliban). *Tageszeitung* (Berlin), 27 October. Available online at http:// www.taz.de/nc1archiv/archiv-start/?ressort (accessed 25 January 2009).

Eco, Umberto. 2001. "The Roots of Conflict." *The Guardian*, 13 October. Available online at http://www.guardian.co.uk/education/2001/oct/13/ socialsciences.highereducation (accessed 25 January 2009).

Edmonds, Alexander. 2005. *Health Service Delivery and Utilization in Timor-Leste: A Qualitative Study.* Report for the World Bank. Washington, D.C.

———. 2006. *Making Health Care Decisions in the Solomon Islands: A Qualitative Study.* Report for the World Bank. Washington, D.C.

———. Forthcoming. *In the Universe of Beauty: Sex, Race, and Plastic Surgery in Brazil.* Durham, N.C.: Duke University Press.

El Guindi, Fadwa. 1999. *Veil: Modesty, Privacy, Resistance.* Oxford: Berg.

Ellmeier, Andrea, and Béla Rásky, eds. 2006. *Differing Diversities: Eastern European Perspectives.* Strasbourg, France: Council of Europe.

Eriksen, Thomas Hylland. 1997. "The Nation as a Human Being—A Metaphor in Mid-Life Crisis? Notes on the Imminent Collapse of Norwegian National Identity." In Karen Fog Olwig and Kirsten Hastrup, eds. *Siting Culture*, 103–122. London: Routledge & Kegan Paul.

———. 2001. "Between Universalism and Relativism: A Critique of the UNESCO Concepts of Culture." In Jane K. Cowan, Marie-Bénédicte Dembour, and Richard A. Wilson, eds. *Culture and Rights: Anthropological Perspectives*, 127–148. Cambridge: Cambridge University Press, 2001.

———. 2006a. *Engaging Anthropology: The Case for a Public Presence.* Oxford: Berg.

———. 2006b. "Diversity versus Difference: Neo-liberalism in the Minority Debate." In Richard Rottenburg, Burkhard Schnepel, and Shingo Shimada, eds. *The Making and Unmaking of Difference*, 13–36. Bielefeld, Germany: Transaction.

———. 2006c. "An Old Warhorse Revisited." *Savage Minds,* 12 January. Available online at http://savageminds.org/2006/01/12/an-old-warhorse-revisited/ (accessed 16 September 2007).

Escobar, Arturo. 1995. *Encountering Development: The Making and Unmaking of the Third World.* Princeton, N.J.: Princeton University Press.

Esposito, John, and Dalia Mogahed. 2008. *Who Speaks for Islam?* Washington, D.C.: Gallup.

Esteva, Gustavo. 1996. "Development." In Wolfgang Sachs, ed. *The Development Dictionary,* 6–25. New York: Zed Books.

Etounga-Manguelle, Daniel. 2000. "Does Africa Need a Cultural Adjustment Program?" In Lawrence E. Harrison and Samuel P. Huntington, eds. *Culture Matters: How Values Shape Human Progress,* 65–79. New York: Basic Books.

European Network for Indigenous Australian Rights. 2003. "Aussies' Broken Rules." 12 January. Available online at http://www.eniar.org/news/didge2.html (accessed 5 October 2007).

Fadiman, Anne. 1997. *The Spirit Catches You and You Fall Down.* New York: Farrar, Straus and Giroux.

Fang Ning, Wang Xiaodong, and Song Qiang, eds. 1999. *Quanqiuhua yinmou xia de Zhongguo zhi lu* (China's Road in the Globalization Conspiracy). Beijing: Zhongguo Shehui Kexue Chubanshe.

Federal Commissioner for Migration, Refugees, and Integration. 2005. *A Manual for Germany.* Berlin: Federal Commissioner for Migration, Refugees, and Integration.

Ferguson, James. 1990. *The Anti-Politics Machine: "Development," Depoliticization, and Bureaucratic Power in Lesotho.* Cambridge: Cambridge University Press.

Fernea, Elizabeth Warnock. 1969. *Guests of the Sheik: An Ethnography of an Iraqi Village.* New York: Anchor Books.

Fichte, Johann Gottlieb. 1808. *Reden an die deutsche Nation* (Addresses to the German nation). Berlin: Realschulbuchhandlung.

Fickling, David. 2004. "Bestseller on Honour Killing 'Is a Fake.'" *The Guardian,* 26 July. Available online at http://www.guardian.co.uk/world/2004/jul/26/books.booksnews (accessed 25 January 2009).

Fish, Allison. 2006. "The Commodification and Exchange of Knowledge in the Case of Transnational Commercial Yoga." *International Journal of Cultural Property* 13: 189–206.

Fisher, Glen. 1998. *The Mindsets Factor in Ethnic Conflict: A Cross-Cultural Agenda.* Yarmouth, Maine: Intercultural Press.

Fitzgerald, Michael. 2006. "Intel's Hiring Spree." *Technology Review* (MIT), 14 February. Available online at http://www.technologyreview. com/InfoTech-Hardware/wtr_16340,294,p1.html?a=f (accessed 25 January 2009).

Fix, Michael. 2005. "Immigration, Education Reform, and Urban Schools." *Metropolis World Bulletin* 5: 9–11. Available online at http://www.international.metropolis.net/research-policy/World/ World%20Bulletin_vol5_e.pdf (accessed 15 June 2007).

Forster, E. M. 1961. *A Passage to India*. Harmondsworth, England: Penguin.

Forte, Maximilian C. 2006. "Amerindian@Caribbean: Internet Indigeneity in the Electronic Generation of Carib and Taino Identities." In Kyra Landzelius, ed. *Native on the Net: Indigenous and Diasporic Peoples in the Virtual Age*, 132–151. London: Routledge.

Fox, Jonathan. 2005. "Advocacy Research and the World Bank: Propositions for Discussion." In Marc Edelman and Angelique Haugerud, eds. *The Anthropology of Development and Globalization: From Classical Political Economy to Contemporary Neoliberalism*, 306–312. Malden, Mass.: Blackwell.

Friedman, Sara L. 2004. "Embodying Civility: Civilizing Processes and Symbolic Citizenship in Southeastern China." *Journal of Asian Studies* 63, no. 3: 687–718.

Fu Huiling, and D. W. Choy. 2004. "From Mediation to Adjudication: Settling Labor Disputes in China." *China Rights Forum*, no. 3: 17–20.

Fukuyama, Francis. 1992. *The End of History and the Last Man*. New York: The Free Press.

———. 2002. "Has History Started Again?" *Policy* 18, no. 2: 3–7.

———. 2004. "How Academia Failed the Nation: The Decline of Regional Studies." *SAISPHERE* (winter). Available online at http:// www.sais-jhu.edu/se/util/display_mod.cfm?MODULE=/se-server/ mod/modules/semod_printpage/mod_default.cfm&PageURL=/ pressroom/publications/saisphere/2004/fukuyama.htm&VersionObj ect=889287&Template=904567&PageStyleSheet=904570 (accessed 25 January 2009).

Gahama, Joseph. 1983. *Le Burundi sous administration belge*. Paris: CRA.

Galbraith, Peter L. 2006. "Mindless in Iraq." *New York Review of Books*, 10 August, 28–31.

Gallagher, Tom. 1997. "My Neighbour, My Enemy: The Manipulation of Ethnic Identity and the Origins and Conduct of War in Yugoslavia." In David Turton, ed. *War and Ethnicity: Global Connections and Local Violence*, 47–75. Rochester, N.Y.: Boydell Press.

Gallup, John Luke, and Jeffrey Sachs. 1998. "Geography and Economic Growth." Paper prepared for the Annual Bank Conference on